2016 Minutes of the General Assembly Cumberland Presbyterian Church

Office of the General Assembly

Cumberland Presbyterian Church

October 2016

8207 Traditional Place
Cordova (Memphis), Tennessee 38016

©2016 Office of the General Assembly, CPC

All Rights Reserved. No part of this book may be reproduced or transmitted in any form or by any means, electronic or mechanical, including photocopying, recording, or by any information storage or retrieval system, without permission in writing from the publisher. For information address Office of the General Assembly, Cumberland Presbyterian Center, 8207 Traditional Place, Cordova (Memphis), Tennessee, 38016-7414.

Published and distributed by The Discipleship Ministry Team, CPC
Memphis, Tennessee

The Discipleship Ministry Team of the Ministry Council of the Cumberland Presbyterian Church is the successor organization to the Board of Christian Education of the Cumberland Presbyterian Church.

Funded, in part, by your contributions to Our United Outreach.

First Edition 2016

ISBN-13: 978-1945929045
ISBN-10: 1945929049

OUR UNITED OUTREACH
Made Possible In Part By Your Tithe To Our United Outreach

Vision of Ministry

Biblically-based and Christ-centered
    born out of a specific sense of mission,
    the Cumberland Presbyterian Church strives to be true to its heritage:
    to be open to God's reforming spirit,
    to work cooperatively with the larger Body of Christ,
    and to nurture the connectional bonds that make us one.
The Cumberland Presbyterian Church seeks—to be the hands and feet of Christ in witness and service to the world and, above all, the Cumberland Presbyterian Church lives out the love of God to the glory of Jesus Christ.

TABLE OF CONTENTS

Vision of Ministry .... Title Page
Program 3
Commissioners 5
Youth Advisory Delegates 6
Committees and Abbreviations 6
Committee Meeting Rooms 6
Committee Assignments 7
Assembly Meetings and Officers 8
By Laws of General Assembly Corporation 11
Memorial Roll of Ministers 21
Living General Assembly Moderators 22
Membership of Boards and Agencies 23

Reports
    Moderator 31
    Stated Clerk 32
    Ministry Council Report One 38
    Ministry Council Report Two 45
    Board of Stewardship, Foundation and Benefits 58
    Board of the Historical Foundation 69
    Board of Trustees of Memphis Theological Seminary 76
    OUO Committee 90
    Commission on Chaplains and Military Personnel 92
    Permanent Judiciary Committee 94
    Nominating Committee 96
    Place of Meeting Committee 98
    Unified Committee on Theology and Social Concerns 100
    Unification Task Force 110
    Board of Trustees of Bethel University 116
    Board of Trustees of the Cumberland Presbyterian Children's Home 117
    Joint Committee on Amendments 125

Memorials 126

Agency Budgets 129

General Assembly Minutes 138

Audits 149

Appendices 293

Church Calendar 319

THE CUMBERLAND PRESBYTERIAN CHURCH

PROGRAM SCHEDULE

Assembly Meetings:	Sheraton Music City Hotel
General Assembly Office:	Cheekwood
Women's Ministry Office:	Bellmont
Retiring Moderator:	The Reverend Michele Gentry, Andes Presbytery
Host:	Nashville Presbytery (CPC) & Elk River Presbytery (CPCA)
Pastor Host:	The Reverend Don Tabor (CPC) and The Reverend Rosemary Herron (CPCA)
Worship Director:	The Reverend Fran Vickers, Presbytery of East Tennessee
Music Director:	The Reverend Paula Louder, Nashville Presbytery

SUNDAY, JUNE 19, 2016

Location	Time	Event	Location
Sheraton	3:00 p.m.	Orientation for Commissioners and Youth Advisory Delegates	Two Rivers
		Orientation for Committee Chairs and Co-Chairs	
		(Commissioner/YAD packets may be picked up before or after the orientation session.)	
		Registration for Women's Ministry Convention	Bellmont
Sheraton		Setup displays	Plantation Lobby
Sheraton	4:00 p.m.	Convention Choir Rehearsal	Ballroom A-B
Sheraton	7:30 p.m.	Joint Evangelism Conference Worship Service	Ballroom A-E

FIRST DAY - MONDAY, JUNE 20, 2016

Location	Time	Event	Location
Sheraton	7:30 a.m.	Women's Ministry Registration (open until 5:00 p.m.)	Bellmont
Sheraton	8:00 a.m.	Registration for Commissioners and Youth Advisory Delegates	Cheekwood
		(for those who did not register on Sunday)	
Sheraton	8:30 a.m.	Joint Opening GA Worship/Communion Service	Ballroom A-E
Sheraton	9:00 a.m.	Women's Ministry Registration (open until 5:00 p.m.)	Bellmont
	10:00 a.m.	Break	
Sheraton	10:30 a.m.	Joint Evangelism Conference Workshop	Ballroom A-D
	12:00 p.m.	CPCA National Sunday School Convention Luncheon	Ballroom E
Sheraton	2:00 p.m.	Joint Evangelism Conference Workshop	Ballroom A-D
	3:00 p.m.	Break	
	3:15 p.m.	Constitution of the CPC General Assembly	Ballroom F
		Adoption of the Agenda	
		Report of the Credentials Committee	
		Election of Moderator	
		Election of Vice-Moderator	
		Presentation by the Stated Clerk, Mike Sharpe	
		Communications	
		Corrections to Preliminary Minutes	
		Committee Appointments and Referrals to Committees	
		Welcome, Pastor Host, Local Officials	
		Introduction of Board and Agency Representatives	
Holiday Inn	4:30 p.m.	General Assembly Committees meet	*Consult room location listing*
Sheraton	4:30 p.m.	Women's Ministry Regional Council Meeting and Dinner	McGavock C
	5:30 p.m.	Dinner Break	

EVENING PROGRAM

Location	Time	Event	Location
Sheraton	7:30 p.m.	Joint Worship (CPC/CPCA) (led by Young Adult & Youth)	Ballroom A-E
Sheraton	8:30 p.m.	Joint Moderator's Reception (CPC/CPCA) honoring	Hotel Lobby
		the Moderator and Vice-Moderator of the General Assembly,	
		the Immediate Past Moderator, the President-Elect and	
		the President of the Cumberland Presbyterian Women's Ministry	
		and National Missionary Society Officers	
Sheraton	9:00 p.m.	Convention Choir Rehearsal (1 hr)	Ballroom A-B

MINUTES OF THE GENERAL ASSEMBLY 2016

SECOND DAY - TUESDAY, JUNE 21, 2016

Location	Time	Event	Location
Sheraton	7:30 a.m.	Convention Registration	Bellmont
		Convention Choir Rehearsal	Ballroom A-B
Holiday Inn	8:30 a.m.	GA Committee Meetings (devotional in Committees)	Consult room location listing
Sheraton	8:30 a.m.	Opening Worship - Women's Ministry Convention and National Missionary Society	Ballroom A-C
	10:00 a.m.	Break	
Sheraton	10:30 a.m.	Women's Ministry Convention	Ballroom A-C
Sheraton	12:30 p.m.	CPCA National Missionary Society Luncheon	Ballroom D-E
Sheraton	2:00 p.m.	Women's Ministry Convention Reconvenes	Ballroom A-C
Sheraton	6:00 p.m.	Bethel University Dinner	Ballroom E

EVENING PROGRAM

Location	Time	Event	Location
Sheraton	7:30 p.m.	Joint Celebration of Generations: Interacting Together	Ballroom D
Sheraton	8:30 p.m.	Joint Reception Honoring Women in Ministry	Ballroom A-B

THIRD DAY - WEDNESDAY, JUNE 22, 2016

Location	Time	Event	Location
Sheraton	7:00 a.m.	CPCH Breakfast	Ballroom E
Sheraton	8:30 a.m.	Joint Devotions led by Global Community	Ballroom A-C
	9:00 a.m.	Break	
Holiday Inn	9:30 a.m.	GA Committees Meet	Consult room location listing
Sheraton	9:30 a.m.	Women's Ministry Convention Reconvenes	Ballroom A-C
Sheraton	12:00 p.m.	Memphis Theological Seminary & the Program of Alternate Studies Luncheon	Ballroom E
Sheraton	2:00 p.m.	Women's Ministry Outreach Projects (2-5:00 p.m.)	TBA
		Joint Evangelism Conference Workshops (2-3:15pm)	Ballroom A-C
Holiday Inn/ Sheraton	5:00 p.m.	Conclusion of Committee Meetings	Consult room location listing

EVENING PROGRAM

Location	Time	Event	Location
Sheraton	7:30 p.m.	Evening Worship – A Celebration of New Ministries	Ballroom A-D

FOURTH DAY - THURSDAY, JUNE 23, 2016

Location	Time	Event	Location
Sheraton	8:30 a.m.	Devotional, Ms. Shelby Webb, YAD, Missouri Presbytery	Ballroom A-C
Sheraton	9:00 a.m.	General Assembly Business	Ballroom E-F
Sheraton	9:00 a.m.	Women's Ministry Convention Reconvenes	Ballroom A-C
	12:00 noon	Lunch Break	
Sheraton	12:00 p.m.	Cumberland Presbyterian Women's Luncheon	McGavock's Ballroom
Sheraton	2:00 p.m.	General Assembly Business	Ballroom E-F
	5:00 p.m.	Dinner Break Take Down Displays	

EVENING PROGRAM

Location	Time	Event	Location
Sheraton	7:30 p.m.	General Assembly Business Closing Worship: Reverend Perry Rice, Red River Presbytery	Ballroom E-F

(In the event that business is not concluded on Thursday, the closing worship will be at the conclusion of business on Friday morning.)

COMMISSIONERS
to the
ONE HUNDRED EIGHTY-SIXTH GENERAL ASSEMBLY

PRESBYTERY	MINISTER	COMMITTEE	ELDER	COMMITTEE
Andes (2)	Michele Gentry	C/HF		
Arkansas (2)	Thomas Campbell	TSC/UTF	Barry Bray	S/E
	Roberta Johnson	C/HF	Helen McGowan	TSC/UTF
Cauca Valley (3)	Johnny Montano	M/M		
Choctaw (1)	Randy Jacob	J	Lola Mae John	S/E
Columbia (2)	John Blair	CPCH/HE	Nita Pike	TSC/UTF
	Joe Wiggins	MC/C/D		
Covenant (3)	Brent Ballow	S/E	Karen Ordway	C/HF
	Larry Buchanan	C/HF	Elaine Overton	CPCH/HE
	David Fackler	M/M	Jennifer Potter	MC/C/D
Cumberland (3)	Wallace Renner	J	Boyd Day	TSC/UTF
	Sam Romines	CPCH/HE	David Maddox	M/M
	Joe Vaught	S/E	Carlos Phelps	J
Cumberland East Coast (1)	Douglas Park	MC/C/D		
	Seungno Kim	S/E		
Del Cristo (1)	Don Wilson	S/E	Scott Fanning	CPCH/HE
East Tennessee (3)	Ronnie Duncan	M/M	Nicole Crisp	C/HF
	Josephina Sanchez	TSC/UTF	Terry Murray	M/M
			Thomas Witmer	CPCH/HE
Grace (3)	Derek Jacks	TSC/UTF	Steve Arledge	S/E
			Charles Gould	MC/C/D
	Jan Overton	J	Mary Jo Ray	TSC/UTF
Hong Kong (2)	(NONE)			
Hope (1)	Jimmy Peyton	M/M	Randy Weathersby	J
Japan (1)	Nobuko Seki	M/M	Takeshi Yohena	M/M
Missouri (1)	Randy Crawshaw	CPCH/HE	Mary Lyn Hunter	M/M
Murfreesboro (4)	Vernon Burrow	M/M	Donald Dickerson	MC/C/D
	B J Hancock	MC/C/D	Charlene Tatum	S/E
	Kevin Medlin	CPCH/HE	Gary Walker	TSC/UTF
	Joyce Merritt	S/E	Courtney Weeks	J
Nashville (3)	Ray DeVries	TSC/UTF	Jim Crowell	CPCH/HE
	Paul Tucker	S/E	Billie Jean Neil	J
	Dwayne Tyus	J	Carol Warren	C/HF
North Central (2)	J C McDuffee	TSC/UTF	Victory Moore	J
	Kevin Small	MC/C/D	Jedd Tolen	C/HF
Red River (3)	Kristi Lombard	CPCH/HE	Denna Gordon	C/HF
	Perryn Rice	J	Robin Hughes	TSC/UTF
	Marian Sontowski	MC/C/D	Kathy McIntire	MC/C/D
Robert Donnell (1)	Cardelia Howell-Diamond	TSC/UTF	Dennis Bogart	CPCH/HE
Tenn./Georgia (2)	Jim Buttram	MC/C/D	George Holland	S/E
	Phillip Layne	C/HF	Christy Miller	J
	Kriss McGowan	M/M	Garry Stoneciper	MC/C/D
Trinity (2)	Mary Kathryn Kirkpatrick	MC/C/D	John Dougherty	C/HF
	Ray Santilliano	M/M		
West Tennessee (6)	Bryon Forester	C/HF	Joe Hames	S/E
	Linda Glenn	J	John Lewis	MC/C/D
	Melissa Goodloe	CPCH/HE	Ronnie Parks	J
	Jim Hamblin	S/E	Edith Umbarger	C/HF
	Anne Hames	TSC/UTF		

YOUTH ADVISORY DELEGATES
to the
ONE HUNDRED EIGHTY-SIXTH GENERAL ASSEMBLY

(Each Presbytery is eligible to send two Youth Advisory Delegates)

PRESBYTERY	DELEGATE	COMMITTEE
Arkansas	Zeke Lake	S/E
	Elizabeth Warren	CPCH/HE
Choctaw	Jose Garcia	J
Columbia	Ryan Day	M/M
	Jonathan Norton	MC/C/D
Covenant	(no youth)	
Cumberland	(no youth)	
del Cristo	(no youth)	
East Tennessee	Hannah Crisp	MC/C/D
	Sarah Cagle	CPCH/HE
Grace	Justin Barkley	MC/C/D
	David Fowler	M/M
Hope	Allison Hood	S/E
	James Hood	CPCH/HE
Japan	(no youth)	
Missouri	Shelby Webb	M/M
Murfreesboro	Kaylee Liehr	C/HF
	Izzy Wood	TSC/UTF
Nashville	Kimberly Pinson	M/M
North Central	Madeline Stence	J
	Charli Uhlrich	S/E
Red River	Cameron Kurtz	S/E
	Alyssa Mason	TSC/UTF
Robert Donnell	Emma Stewart	C/HF
Tennessee Georgia	Justyn Pretel	TSC/UTF
Trinity	Sophie Daniel	TSC/UTF
	Abby Herman	C/HF
West Tennessee	Eleanor Forester	CPCH/HE
	Rande Johnson	J

COMMITTEES ABBREVIATIONS AND MEETING ROOMS

Sheraton Music City

ABBREV.	COMMITTEE	MEETING ROOMS
C/HF	Chaplains/Historical Foundation	Oaklands
TSC/UTF	Theology & Social Concerns/Unification Task Force	Evergreen

Holiday Inn - 2nd floor

ABBREV.	COMMITTEE	MEETING ROOMS
CHCP/HE	Children's Home/Higher Education	Ocoee
J	Judiciary	Mississippi
MC/C/D	Ministry Council/Communications/Discipleship	Hickory
M/M	Missions/Ministry	Harpeth
S/E	Stewardship/Elected Officers	Cumberland

COMMITTEE ASSIGNMENTS

1. **CHAPLAINS/HISTORICAL FOUNDATION** *(Sheraton - Oaklands)*
   Chair: Rev. Michele Gentry   **Co-Chair:** Rev. Byron Forester
   Ministers: Larry Buchanan, Roberta Johnson, Phillip Lane
   Elders: Nicole Crisp, John Dougherty, Denna Gordon, Karen Ordway, Jedd Tolen, Edith Umbarger
   Youth Advisory Delegates: Abby Herman, Kaylee Liehr, Emma Stewart

2. **CHILDREN'S HOME/HIGHER EDUCATION** *(Holiday Inn - Ocoee)*
   Chair: Rev. Sam Romines   **Co-Chair:** Rev. Kristi Lombard
   Ministers: John Blair, Randy Crawshaw, Melissa Goodloe, Kevin Medlin
   Elders: Dennis Bogart, Jim Crowell, Scott Fanning, Elaine Overton, Thomas Witmer
   Youth Advisory Delegates: Sarah Cagle, Eleanor Forester, James Hood, Elizabeth Warren

3. **JUDICIARY** *(Holiday Inn - Mississippi)*
   Chair: Rev. Perryn Rice   **Co-Chair:** Rev. Jan Overton
   Ministers: Linda Glenn, Randy Jacob, Wallace Renner, Dwayne Tyus
   Elders: Christy Miller, Victory Moore, Billie Jean Neil, Ronnie Parks, Carlos Phelps, Randy Weathersby, Courtney Weeks
   Youth Advisory Delegates: Jose Garcia, Rande Johnson, Madeline Stence

4. **MINISTRY COUNCIL/COMMUNICATIONS/DISCIPLESHIP** *(Holiday Inn - Hickory)*
   Chair: Rev. Jim Buttram   **Co-Chair:** Rev. Mary Kathryn Kirkpatrick
   Ministers: B J Hancock, Douglas Park, Marian Santowski, Kevin Small, Joe Wiggins
   Elders: Donald Dickerson, Charles Gould, John Lewis, Kathy McIntire, Jennifer Potter, Garry Stoneciper
   Youth Advisory Delegates: Justin Barkley, Hannah Crisp, Jonathan Norton

5. **MISSIONS/MINISTRY** *(Holiday Inn - Harpeth)*
   Chair: Rev. Jimmy Peyton   **Co-Chair:** Elder Mary Lyn Hunter
   Ministers: Vernon Burrow, Ronnie Duncan, David Fackler, Kriss McGowan, Johnny Montano, Ray Santilliano, Nobuko Seki
   Elders: David Maddux, Terry Murray, Takeshi Yohena
   Youth Advisory Delegates: Ryan Day, Daniel Fowler, Shelby Webb

6. **STEWARDSHIP/ELECTED OFFICERS** *(Holiday Inn - Cumberland)*
   Chair: Rev. Don Wilson   **Co-Chair:** Rev. Joyce Merritt
   Ministers: Brent Ballow, Jim Hamblin, Paul Tucker, Joe Vaught
   Elders: Steve Arledge, Barry Bray, Joe Hames, George Holland, Lola John, Charlene Tatum
   Youth Advisory Delegates: Allison Hood, Cameron Kurtz, Zeke Lake, Charli Uhlrich

7. **THEOLOGY & SOCIAL CONCERNS/UNIFICATION TASK FORCE** *(Sheraton - Evergreen)*
   Chair: Rev. Thomas (Tom) Campbell   **Co-Chair:** Rev. Cardelia Howell-Diamond
   Ministers: Ray DeVries, Anne Hames, Derek Jacks, J C McDuffee, Josephina Sanchez
   Elders: Boyd Day, Robin Hughes, Helen McGowan, Nita Pike, Mary Jo Ray, Gary Walker
   Youth Advisory Delegates: Sophie Daniel, Alyssa Mason, Kimberly Pinson, Justyn Pretel, Izzy Wood

8. **CREDENTIALS:**
   Chair: Reverend Linda Glenn
   Members: Reverend Ray DeVries, Elder Robin Hughes
   Youth Advisory Delegate: Daniel Fowler

ASSEMBLY MEETINGS AND OFFICERS

Historical Review of the Stated Meetings and Officers of:

THE CUMBERLAND PRESBYTERY, 1810-1813

Date	Place	Moderator	Clerk	Members
1810, February	Sam McAdow's House, Dickson Co., TN	Samuel McAdow	Young Ewing	3
1810, March 20	Ridge Meeting-House, Sumner Co., TN.	Samuel McAdow	Young Ewing	14
1810, October 23	Lebanon Meeting-House	Finis Ewing	Young Ewing	16
1811, March 19	Big Spring, Wilson Co., TN	Robert Bell	Young Ewing	19
1811, October 9	Ridge Meeting-House	Thomas Calhoun	David Foster	23
1812, April 7	Suggs Creek Meeting-House	Hugh Kirkpatrick	James B. Porter	28
1812, November 3	Lebanon, KY	Finis Ewing	Hugh Kirkpatrick	22
1813, April 6	Beech Meeting-House, Sumner Co. TN	Robert Bell	James B. Porter	34

THE CUMBERLAND SYNOD, 1813-1828

Date	Place	Moderator	Clerk	Members
1813, October 5	Beech Meeting-House	William McGee	Finis Ewing	13
1814, April 5	Suggs Creek	David Foster	James B. Porter	27
1815, October 17	Beech Meeting-House	William Barnett	David Foster	15
1816, October 15	Free Meeting-House, TN	Thomas Calhoun	David Foster	22
1817, October 21	Mt. Moriah, KY	Robert Donnell	Hugh Kirkpatrick	27
1818, October 20	Big Spring, TN	Finis Ewing	Robert Bell	27
1819, October 19	Suggs Creek, TN	Samuel King	William Barnett	24
1820, October 17	Russellville, KY	Thomas Calhoun	William Moore	30
1821, Third Tues. in Oct.	Russellville, KY	Minutes not recorded		
1822, October 15	Beech Meeting-House	James B. Porter	David Foster	47
1823, October 21	Russellville, KY	John Barnett	Aaron Alexander	48
1824, October 19	Cane Creek, TN	Samuel King	William Moore	68
1825, October 18	Princeton, KY	William Barnett	Hiram McDaniel	76
1826, Third Tues. in Oct.	Russellville, KY	Minutes not recorded		
1827, November 20	Russellville, KY	James S. Guthrie	Laban Jones	63
1828, October 21	Franklin, TN	Hiram A. Hunter	Richard Beard	94

THE GENERAL ASSEMBLY, 1829-

Date	Place	Moderator	Clerk	Members
1829, May 19	Princeton, KY	Thomas Calhoun	F. R. Cossitt	26
1830, May 18	Princeton, KY	James B. Porter	F. R. Cossitt	36
1831, May 17	Princeton, KY	Alex Chapman	F. R. Cossitt	34
1832, May 15	Nashville, TN	F. R. Cossitt	F. R. Cossitt	36
1833, May 21	Nashville, TN	Samuel King	F. R. Cossitt	35
1834, May 20	Nashville, TN	Thomas Calhoun	James Smith	48
1835, May 19	Princeton, KY	Sam King	James Smith	42
1836, May 17	Nashville, TN	Reuben Burrow	James Smith	43
1837, May 16	Lebanon, TN	Robert Donnell	James Smith	49
1838, May 15	Princeton, KY	Hiram A. Hunter	James Smith	47
1840, May 19	Elkton, KY	Reuben Burrow	James Smith	55
1841, May 18	Owensboro, KY	William Ralston	C. G. McPherson	56
1842, May 17	Owensboro, KY	Milton Bird	C. G. McPherson	57
1843, May 16	Owensboro, KY	A. M. Bryan	C. G. McPherson	68
1845, May 20	Lebanon, TN	Richard Beard	C. G. McPherson	95
1846, May 19	Owensboro, KY	M. H. Bone	C. G. McPherson	86
1847, May 18	Lebanon, Ohio	Hiram A. Hunter	C. G. McPherson	71
1848, May 16	Memphis, TN	Milton Bird	C. G. McPherson	100
1849, May 16	Princeton, KY	John L. Smith	C. G. McPherson	75
1850, May 21	Clarksville, TN	Reuben Burrow	Milton Bird	102
1851, May 20	Pittsburgh, PA	Milton Bird	Milton Bird	71
1852, May 18	Nashville, TN	David Lowry	Milton Bird	107
1853, May 17	Princeton, KY	H. S. Porter	Milton Bird	108
1854, May 16	Memphis, TN	Isaac Shook	Milton Bird	112
1855, May 15	Lebanon, TN	M. H. Bone	Milton Bird	101
1856, May 15	Louisville, KY	Milton Bird	Milton Bird	99
1857, May 21	Lexington, MO	Carson P. Reed	Milton Bird	106
1858, May 20	Huntsville, AL	Felix Johnson	Milton Bird	124
1859, May 19	Evansville, IN	T. B. Wilson	Milton Bird	131
1860, May 17	Nashville, TN	S. G. Burney	Milton Bird	168
1861, May 16	St. Louis, MO	A. E. Cooper	Milton Bird	51
1862, May 15	Owensboro, KY	P. G. Rea	Milton Bird	58
1863, May 21	Alton, IL	Milton Bird	Milton Bird	73
1864, May 19	Lebanon, OH	Jesse Anderson	Milton Bird	65
1865, May 18	Evansville, IN	Hiram Douglas	Milton Bird	78
1866, May 17	Owensboro, KY	Richard Beard	Milton Bird	155
1867, May 16	Memphis, TN	J. B. Mitchell	Milton Bird	176
1868, May 21	Lincoln, IL	G. W. Mitchell	Milton Bird	184
1869, May 20	Murfreesboro, TN	S. T. Anderson	Milton Bird	173
1870, May 19	Warrensburg, MO	J. C. Provine	Milton Bird	167

THE CUMBERLAND PRESBYTERIAN CHURCH

Date	Place	Moderator	Clerk	Members
1871, May 18	Nashville, TN	J. B. Logan	Milton Bird	173
1872, May 16	Evansville, IN	C. H. Bell	Milton Bird	182
1873, May 15	Huntsville, AL	J. W. Poindexter	John Frizzell	165
1874, May 21	Springfield, MO	T. C. Blake	John Frizzell	185
1875, May 20	Jefferson, TX	W. S. Campbell	John Frizzell	169
1876, May 18	Bowling Green, KY	J. M. Gill	John Frizzell	184
1877, May 17	Lincoln, IL	A. B. Miller	John Frizzell	171
1878, May 16	Lebanon, TN	D. E. Bushnell	John Frizzell	205
1879, May 15	Memphis, TN	J. S. Grider	John Frizzell	143
1880, May 20	Evansville, IN	A. Templeton	John Frizzell	194
1881, May 19	Austin, TX	W. J. Darby	John Frizzell	187
1882, May 18	Huntsville, AL	S. H. Buchanan	John Frizzell	188
1883, May 17	Nashville, TN	A. J. McGlumphey	T. C. Blake	204
1884, May 15	McKeesport, PA	John Frizzell	T. C. Blake	148
1885, May 21	Bentonville, AR	G. T. Stainback	T. C. Blake	185
1886, May 20	Sedalia, MO	E. B. Crisman	T. C. Blake	193
1887, May 19	Covington, OH	Nathan Green	T. C. Blake	187
1888, May 17	Waco, TX	W. H. Black	T. C. Blake	217
1889, May 16	Kansas City, MO	J. M. Hubbert	T. C. Blake	217
1890, May 15	Union City, TN	E. G. McLean	T. C. Blake	220
1891, May 21	Owensboro, KY	E. F. Beard	T. C. Blake	213
1892, May 19	Memphis, TN	W. T. Danley	T. C. Blake	229
1893, May 18	Little Rock, AR	W. S. Ferguson	T. C. Blake	226
1894, May 17	Eugene, OR	F. R. Earle	T. C. Blake	167
1895, May 16	Meridian, MS	M. B. DeWitt	T. C. Blake	208
1896, May 21	Birmingham, AL	A. W. Hawkins	J. M. Hubbert	200
1897, May 20	Chicago, IL	H. S. Williams	J. M. Hubbert	224
1898, May 19	Marshall, MO	H. H. Norman	J. M. Hubbert	221
1899, May 18	Denver, CO	J. M. Halsell	J. M. Hubbert	181
1900, May 17	Chattanooga, TN	H. C. Bird	J. M. Hubbert	230
1901, May 16	West Point, MS	E. E. Morris	J. M. Hubbert	226
1902, May 15	Springfield, MO	S. M. Templeton	J. M. Hubbert	255
1903, May 21	Nashville, TN	R. M. Tinnon	J. M. Hubbert	247
1904, May 19	Dallas, TX	W. E. Settle	J. M. Hubbert	251
1905, May 18	Fresno, CA	J. B. Hail	J. M. Hubbert	249
1906, May 17	Decatur, IL	Ira Landrith	J. M. Hubbert	279
1906, May 24	Decatur, IL	J. L. Hudgins	T. H. Padgett	106
1907, May 17	Dickson, TN	A. N. Eshman	J. L. Goodknight	140
1908, May 21	Corsicana, TX	F. H. Prendergast	J. L. Goodknight	136
1909, May 20	Bentonville, AR	J. T. Barbee	J. L. Goodknight	142
1910, May 19	Dickson, TN	J. H. Fussell	J. L. Goodknight	144
1911, May 18	Evansville, IN	J. W. Duvall	J. L. Goodknight	109
1912, May 16	Warrensburg, MO	J. D. Lewis	J. L. Goodknight	119
1913, May 15	Bowling Green, KY	J. H. Milholland	J. L. Goodknight	112
1914, May 21	Wagoner, OK	F. A. Brown	J. L. Goodknight	105
1915, May 20	Memphis, TN	William Clark	D. W. Fooks	116
1916, May 18	Birmingham, AL	J. L. Price	D. W. Fooks	125
1917, May 17	Lincoln, IL	F. A. Seagle	D. W. Fooks	102
1918, May 16	Dallas, TX	C. H. Walton	D. W. Fooks	117
1919, May 15	Fayetteville, AR	J. H. Zwingle	D. W. Fooks	101
1920, May 15	McKenzie, TN	J. E. Cortner	D. W. Fooks	123
1921, May 19	Greenfield, MO	Judge John B. Tally	D. W. Fooks	108
1922, May 18	Greeneville, TN	Hugh S. McCord	D. W. Fooks	102
1923, May 17	Fairfield, IL	P. F. Johnson, D. D.	D. W. Fooks	105
1924, May 15	Austin, TX	D. M. McAnulty	D. W. Fooks	93
1925, May 21	Nashville, TN	W. E. Morrow	D. W. Fooks	114
1926, May 20	Columbus, MS	I. K. Floyd	D. W. Fooks	111
1927, May 19	Lakeland, FL	T. A. DeVore	D. W. Fooks	97
1928, May 21	Jackson, TN	J. L. Hudgins	D. W. Fooks	97
1929, May 16	Princeton, KY	H. C. Walton	D. W. Fooks	98
1930, May 15	Olney, TX	O. A. Barbee	D. W. Fooks	92
1931, May 21	Evansville, IN	J. L. Elliot	D. W. Fooks	98
1932, May 19	Chattanooga, TN	G. G. Halliburton	D. W. Fooks	104
1933, June 14	Memphis, TN	W. B. Cunningham	D. W. Fooks	94
1934, June 14	Springfield, MO	A. C. DeForest	D. W. Fooks	103
1935, June 13	McKenzie, TN	C. A. Davis	D. W. Fooks	104
1936, June 18	San Antonio, TX	E. K. Reagin	D. W. Fooks	100
1937, June 16	Knoxville, TN	George E. Coleman	D. W. Fooks	109
1938, June 16	Russellville, AR	D. D. Dowell	D. W. Fooks	117
1939, June 15	Marshall, MO	E. R. Ramer	D. W. Fooks	126
1940, June 13	Cookeville, TN	Keith T. Postlethwaite	D. W. Fooks	116
1941, June 19	Denton, TX	L. L. Thomas	D. W. Fooks	120
1942, June 18	McKenzie, TN	George W. Burroughs	D. W. Fooks	108
1943, June 17	Paducah, KY	A. A. Collins	D. W. Fooks	94
1944, June 15	Bowling Green, KY	I. M. Vaughn	D. W. Fooks	94
1945, May 31	Lewisburg, TN	S. T. Byars	Wayne Wiman	103
1946, June 13	Birmingham, AL	C. R. Matlock	Wayne Wiman	105
1947, June 12	Knoxville, TN	Morris Pepper	Wayne Wiman	108

Date	Place	Moderator	Clerk	Members
1948, June 17	Nashville, TN	Paul F. Brown	Wayne Wiman	105
1949, June 16	Muskogee, OK	Blake Warren	Wayne Wiman	109
1950, June 15	Los Angeles, CA	L. P. Turnbow	Wayne Wiman	98
1951, June 14	Longview, TX	John E. Gardner	Wayne Wiman	105
1952, June 12	Memphis, TN	Emery A. Newman	Wayne Wiman	120
1953, June 18	Gadsden, AL	Charles L. Lehning, Jr.	Wayne Wiman	107
1954, June 17	Dyersburg, TN	John S. Smith	Wayne Wiman	124
1955, June 16	Lubbock, TX	Ernest C. Cross	Shaw Scates	118
1956, June 21	Cookeville, TN	Hubert Morrow	Shaw Scates	118
1957, June 21	Evansville, IN	William T. Ingram, Jr.	Shaw Scates	119
1958, June 18	Birmingham, AL	Wayne Wiman	Shaw Scates	116
1959, June 17	Springfield, MO	Virgil T. Weeks	Shaw Scates	120
1960, June 15	Nashville, TN	Arleigh G. Matlock	Shaw Scates	130
1961, June 21	Florence, AL	Ollie W. McClung	Shaw Scates	126
1962, June 20	Little Rock, AR	Eugene L. Warren	Shaw Scates	126
1963, June 19	Austin, TX	Franklin Chesnut	Shaw Scates	117
1964, June 17	Chattanooga, TN	Vaughn Fults	Shaw Scates	123
1965, June 16	San Francisco, CA	Thomas Forester	Shaw Scates	114
1966, June 15	Memphis, TN	John W. Sparks	Shaw Scates	124
1967, June 21	Paducah, KY	Raymon Burroughs	Shaw Scates	123
1968, June 19	Oklahoma City, OK	Loyce S. Estes	Shaw Scates	115
1969, June 18	San Antonio, TX	J. David Hester	Shaw Scates	116
1970, June 17	Knoxville, TN	L. C. Waddle	Shaw Scates	116
1971, June 16	Jackson, TN	E. Thach Shauf	Shaw Scates	116
1972, June 19	Kansas City, MO	Claude D. Gilbert	Shaw Scates	110
1973, June 18	Ft. Worth, TX	Thomas H. Campbell	Shaw Scates	101
1974, June 17	Bowling Green, KY	David A. Brown	Shaw Scates	116
1975, June 16	McKenzie, TN	Roy E. Blakeburn	Shaw Scates	120
1976, June 21	Tulsa, OK	Hubert W. Covington	T. V. Warnick	115
1977, June 30	Tampa, FL	Fred W. Bryson	T. V. Warnick	122
1978, June 19	McKenzie, TN	Jose Fajardo	T. V. Warnick	120
1979, June 18	Albuquerque, NM	James C. Gilbert	T. V. Warnick	126
1980, June 16	Evansville, IN	Robert L. Hull	T. V. Warnick	126
1981, June 15	Denton, TX	W. Jean Richardson	T. V. Warnick	126
1982, June 21	Owensboro, KY	W. A. Rawlins	T. V. Warnick	124
1983, June 20	Birmingham, AL	Robert G. Forester	T. V. Warnick	127
1984, June 11	Chattanooga, TN	C. Ray Dobbins	T. V. Warnick	125
1985, June 17	Lexington, KY	Virgil H. Todd	Roy E. Blakeburn	125
1986, June 23	Odessa, TX	James W. Knight	Roy E. Blakeburn	125
1987, June 15	Louisville, KY	Wilbur S. Wood	Roy E. Blakeburn	125
1988, June 6	Tulsa, OK	Beverly St. John	Robert Prosser	119
1989, June 12	Knoxville, TN	William Rustenhaven, Jr.	Robert Prosser	96
1990, June 25	Ft. Worth, TX	Thomas D. Campbell	Robert Prosser	88
1991, June 24	Paducah, KY	Floyd T. Hensley, Jr.	Robert Prosser	106
1992, June 22	Jackson, TN	John David Hall	Robert Prosser	102
1993, June 21	Little Rock, AR	Robert M. Shelton	Robert Prosser	100
1994, June 20	Albuquerque, NM	Donald C. Alexander	Robert Prosser	100
1995, June 19	Nashville, TN	Clinton O. Buck	Robert Prosser	102
1996, June 17	Huntsville, AL	Merlyn A. Alexander	Robert Prosser	95
1997, April 11	Nashville, TN	Merlyn A. Alexander	Robert Prosser	80
1997, June 16	Louisville, KY	W. Lewis Wynn	Robert Prosser	95
1998, June 15	Chattanooga, TN	Masaharu Asayama	Robert Prosser	97
1999, June 21	Memphis, TN	Gwendolyn Roddye	Marjorie Shannon	96
2000, June 19	Bowling Green, KY	Bob G. Roberts	Robert D. Rush	96
2001, June 18	Odessa, TX	Randolph Jacob	Robert D. Rush	88
2002, June 17	Paducah, KY	Bert L. Owen	Robert D. Rush	95
2003, June 23	Knoxville, TN	Charles McCaskey	Robert D. Rush	96
2004, June 21	Irving, TX	Edward G. Sims	Robert D. Rush	87
2005, June 27	Franklin, TN	Linda H. Glenn	Robert D. Rush	91
2006, June 18	Birmingham, AL	Donald Hubbard	Robert D. Rush	87
2007, June 18	Hot Springs, AR	Frank Ward	Robert D. Rush	84
2007, December 7	Nashville, TN	Frank Ward	Robert D. Rush	62
2008, June 7	Japan	Jonathan Clark	Robert D. Rush	82
2009, June 15	Memphis, TN	Sam Suddarth	Robert D. Rush	86
2010, June 13	Dickson, TN	Boyce Wallace	Robert D. Rush	88
2011, June 20	Springfield, MO	Don M. Tabor	Michael Sharpe	82
2012, June 18	Florence, AL	Robert D. Rush	Michael Sharpe	90
2013, June 17	Murfreesboro, TN	Forest Prosser	Michael Sharpe	93
2014, June 16	Chattanooga, TN	Lisa Anderson	Michael Sharpe	86
2015, June 20	Colombia, South America	Michele Gentry	Michael Sharpe	91

BYLAWS

Bylaws of the Cumberland Presbyterian Church General Assembly Corporation
A Non-profit Religious Corporation Organized and Existing
Under the Laws of the State of Tennessee

ARTICLE 1-RELIGIOUS CORPORATION

1.01 Purpose. The Cumberland Presbyterian Church is a spiritual body comprised of a portion of the universal body of believers confessing Jesus Christ as Lord and Savior. As an ecclesiastical body, the Cumberland Presbyterian Church is a connectional Church which includes all of the judicatories of the Church. The highest judicatory of this ecclesiastical body is the General Assembly of the Cumberland Presbyterian Church (referred to in these Bylaws as "the Church"). This corporation has been formed to serve and support the Church by holding real and personal property of the Church, employing staff to serve the Church, and performing other secular and legal functions.

1.02 Ecclesiastical Authority Not Limited by Corporate Powers. The enumeration in state statutes or these Bylaws of specific powers which may be exercised by the Commissioners, Board of Directors, or the officers of the corporation when acting in their corporate capacity shall not limit their authority when acting in their ecclesiastical capacity for the Church.

1.03 Church Authorities. The doctrine of the Cumberland Presbyterian Church, expressed in the Confession of Faith, Constitution, Rules of Discipline, and Rules of Order of the Cumberland Presbyterian Church, shall have precedence over any inconsistent provision of these Bylaws.

ARTICLE 2-TERMINOLOGY

2.01 Delegates. The corporation's delegates shall be called "Commissioners."
2.02 General Assembly. A meeting of the Commissioners shall be called a "General Assembly."
2.03 President. The corporation's president shall be called the "Stated Clerk."
2.04 Ecumenical Representative. A person who is not a member of a Cumberland Presbyterian Chuch or presbytery but who supports the mission of a denominational entity and is elected to a term of service on that entity shall be called an "Ecumenical Representative."

ARTICLE 3-OFFICES

3.01 Location. The principal office of the corporation in the State of Tennessee shall be located in Shelby County, Tennessee. The corporation may have such other offices, either within or outside the State of Tennessee, as the General Assembly or the Board of Directors may direct from time to time.

ARTICLE 4–COMMISSIONERS

4.01 Commissioners. The Commissioners shall have the powers and authority described in the corporation's charter and these Bylaws. Included among them are the power to:

- a. Elect the elected members of the Board of Directors.
- b. Approve any amendment to the corporation's charter except an amendment to delete the names of the original directors; to change the name of the registered agent, or to change the address of the registered office;
- c. Elect and remove the Moderator, Stated Clerk, and the Engrossing Clerk.
- d. Fill vacancies on the corporation's various boards, agencies and committees, and on the boards of any subsidiaries;
- e. Approve the merger or dissolution of the corporation, or the sale of substantially all of the corporation's assets; and
- f. Transact such other business of the corporation as may properly come before any meeting of the Commissioners.

4.02 Selection of Commissioners: Number and Qualifications. Commissioners shall be selected by the presbyteries. A presbytery shall be entitled to send one minister and one elder for each 1,000, or fraction thereof, active members (including ordained clergy) in the presbytery. Each elder selected as a Commissioner must be serving as a member of a session at the time of the General Assembly at which he or she will serve. A Commissioner shall continue to serve until no longer qualified or until his or her successor is selected and qualified. The clerk of each presbytery shall certify the presbytery's duly elected commissioners, youth advisory delegates, and alternates to the Stated Clerk in a manner provided by the Stated Clerk.

4.03 Youth Advisory Delegates. Each presbytery may select not more than two youth advisory delegates who should be from 15 through 19 years of age. Advisory delegates may serve as members with full rights on General Assembly committees, but shall not vote as Commissioners.

4.04 Annual Meeting and Notice. The Commissioners shall meet annually at a date and time established by the General Assembly. The meeting shall be continued from day to day until adjournment. Written notice of the meeting shall be mailed to the stated clerks of all presbyteries and published in the Cumberland Presbyterian at least sixty (60) days prior to the proposed meeting.

4.05 Special Meetings and Notice. The Moderator, or in case of the Moderator's absence, death, or inability to act, the Stated Clerk, may with the written concurrence or at the written request of twenty Commissioners, ten of whom shall be ministers and ten elders, representing at least five presbyteries, call a special meeting of the Commissioners. If warranted by a change of circumstances, a called special meeting may be cancelled by the Moderator, or in case of the Moderator's absence, death, or inability to act, the Stated Clerk, with the written concurrence of at least ten of the Commissioners who requested or concurred in the call of the special meeting. Written notice of any special meeting shall be mailed to the stated clerks of all presbyteries, to all Commissioners, and to their alternates at least sixty (60) days prior to the meeting. The notice shall specify the particular business of the special meeting, and no other business shall be transacted.

4.06 Place of Meeting. The General Assembly may designate any place within or outside the state of Tennessee as the place for an annual meeting. If the Commissioners fail to designate a place for an annual meeting, or if an emergency requires the place to be changed, the Board of Directors may designate a place for the annual meeting. The Moderator or the Stated Clerk, as the case may be, when calling a special meeting shall designate the time and place of the meeting in the notice of the meeting.

4.07 Quorum. Any twenty or more Commissioners, of whom at least ten are ministers and ten elders, entitled to vote shall constitute a quorum at any General Assembly. When a quorum is once present to organize a meeting, business may continue to be conducted and votes taken despite the subsequent withdrawal of any Commissioner. A meeting may be adjourned despite the absence of a quorum.

4.08 Voting. Every Commissioner shall be entitled to one vote, which must be cast by the Commissioner in person; no proxies are permitted. All corporate actions shall be taken by majority vote except as otherwise provided by the corporation's parliamentary authority. Voting for members of the Board of Directors shall be non-cumulative.

ARTICLE 5-BOARD OF DIRECTORS

5.01 Authority. The Board of Directors shall manage the business and affairs of the corporation except for any power or authority which is reserved to the Commissioners or delegated to any other agency of the corporation. The Board of Directors is authorized to amend the corporation's charter only to delete the names of the original directors; to change the name of the registered agent; or to change the address of the registered office.

5.02 Composition of the Board of Directors. The Board of Directors shall consist of seven (7) members, who shall be the directors of the corporation. Six (6) members shall be elected by the Commissioners and the Stated Clerk shall serve by virtue of office. All members, whether elected or ex officio, shall have all of the privileges of office.

5.03 Qualification for Election. Each person elected to the Board of Directors shall be a natural person who is a person in good standing of a presbytery or local Cumberland Presbyterian Church. No two directors shall be from the same presbytery, provided, however, that a director who moves from one presbytery to another may continue to serve until the expiration of his or her term of office.

5.04 Election and Tenure. The elected members of the Board of Directors shall serve terms of three (3) years each. The terms shall be staggered so that two (2) directors shall be elected each year. Each person elected shall serve until his or her successor has been elected and qualified.

5.05 Action of Board in Emergency or By Default. If, for any reason, the General Assembly fails to fill a vacancy on the Board of Directors at the next General Assembly, then the Board of Directors may fill the vacancy by majority vote of the members then in office.

5.06 Meetings. The Board of Directors shall meet annually or more often at such time and place as it may set. Special meetings may be called by or at the request of the Stated Clerk or any three directors at any place, either within or outside the state of Tennessee.

5.07 Notice. Notice of any meeting shall be given at least five (5) days before the date of the meeting, except that notice by mail shall be given at least ten (10) days before the date of the meeting. Notice may be communicated in person; by telephone, fax, or electronic mail; or by first class mail or courier. Except as specifically provided by these Bylaws, neither the business to be transacted at nor the purpose of any special or regular meeting of the Board of Directors need be specified in the notice of the meeting.

5.08 Notice of Special Actions. Any meeting of the Board of Directors at which one or more of the following actions shall be considered must be preceded by seven (7) days written notice to each member that the matter will be voted upon, unless notice has been waived. Actions requiring such notice are: amendment or restatement of the corporate charter; approval of a plan of merger for the corporation; sale of all or substantially all of the corporation's assets; and dissolution of the corporation.

5.09 Officers of the Board of Directors. The Board of Directors may have such officers of the board as it may deem appropriate.

5.10 Quorum and Voting. A majority of the members shall constitute a quorum for the transaction of business at any meeting of the Board of Directors. When a quorum is once present to organize a meeting, it is not broken by the subsequent withdrawal of any of those present. A meeting may be adjourned despite the lack of a quorum. The vote of a majority of the members present at a meeting at which a quorum is present shall be the act of the Board of Directors unless a greater vote is specifically required by the Charter or the Bylaws.

5.11 Conference Meetings. Any or all the members of the Board of Directors or any committee designated by it may meet by means of conference telephone or similar communications equipment which permits all persons participating in the meeting to hear each other simultaneously. A member who participates in a meeting by such means is deemed to be present in person at the meeting.

5.12 Action by Written Consent. Whenever the members of the Board of Directors are required or permitted to take any action by vote, such action may be taken without a meeting on written consent, setting forth the action so taken and signed by all of the members entitled to vote,

5.13 Emergency Actions. If the Board of Directors determines by a vote of three-fourths of all its members that an emergency exists of such magnitude as to threaten the work of the whole Church, or of all boards and other agencies of the Church, and that the emergency requires action before the next meeting of the General Assembly, then the Board of Directors shall exercise the powers of the Commissioners in such emergency.

5.14 Compensation. Members of the Board of Directors shall receive no compensation in their capacity as members of the Board of Directors. Members may be paid their expenses, if any, of attendance at each meeting of the Board of Directors.

5.15 Removal of Directors. An elected member of the Board of Directors may be removed by the Commissioners for misfeasance or if he or she is no longer qualified to be elected to the Board of Directors.

ARTICLE 6-WAIVER OF NOTICE

6.01 Written Waiver. Any notice required to be given to any member of the Board of Directors or a Commissioner under these Bylaws, the Charter, or the laws of Tennessee may be waived. The waiver shall be in writing, signed (either before or after the event requiring notice) by the person entitled to the notice, and delivered to the corporation.

6.02 Waiver by Attendance. The attendance of a member of the Board of Directors or a Commissioner at any meeting shall constitute a waiver of notice of the meeting, unless the person attends a meeting for the express purpose of objecting to the transaction of any business because the meeting was not properly called or convened.

ARTICLE 7-MODERATOR AND VICE-MODERATOR

7.01 Nomination and Election. At the beginning of each annual meeting the General Assembly shall elect a Commissioner to serve as Moderator until the next annual meeting. Nominations for Moderator shall come from the floor. One nominating speech, not to exceed ten minutes, shall be permitted on behalf of each nominee. If there is more than one nominee, the election shall be conducted by written ballot. A committee appointed and supervised by the Stated Clerk shall receive the ballots, count them, and certify the election. If no nominee receives a majority of the votes cast, a run-off election shall be conducted. Only those leading nominees who together received a majority of the votes cast on the preceding ballot shall be included in the run-off election.

7.02 Nature of Office. The Moderator of the General Assembly is the ecclesiastical head of the Cumberland Presbyterian Church during the tenure of the office and a spiritual representative of the Cumberland Presbyterian Church wherever God leads. The Moderator receives a precious gift and great opportunity for service in the Church: the freedom to go anywhere and to listen to the mind, heart and spirit of the denomination and to speak with and to the Church. The office of Moderator has great honor and respect, and the person elected to the Office is a priest, prophet, and pastor of the Church at large. The Moderator prays with and for the work of the Spirit of God in the life of the denomination at every opportunity. The Moderator participates in the life and work of the Church as far as possible, and pays particular attention to ecumenical relations, especially with the Cumberland Presbyterian Church in America. Judicatories, congregations, and others are urged to invite the Moderator, and the Moderator is encouraged to attend meetings of Church entities and judicatories to observe the life and work of the Church at every level.

7.03 Duties and Privileges of Office.
    a. The Moderator shall preside at all meetings of the General Assembly.
    b. The Moderator shall appoint, with the consent of the General Assembly, such special committees as are needed;
    c. The Moderator shall serve as chairperson of the General Assembly Program Committee and as a member of the Place of Meeting Committee;
    d. The Moderator shall perform such other duties as may be assigned by the General Assembly.
    e. The Moderator shall serve as an advisory member of the Ministry Council during tenure in office and for the year following tenure.
    f. The Moderator shall observe the places and times God is calling the Church to service, assess the need for a Denominational response to God's call, and report items that concern the General Assembly.
    g. The Moderator shall wear the official cross and stoles of office during the term of office.

7.04 Expenses of Office. Any allowance budgeted by the General Assembly to offset the expenses of the Moderator shall be administered by the Stated Clerk. Persons issuing an invitation to the Moderator are encouraged to agree in advance on arrangements for the payment of travel expenses. Upon the Moderator's retirement from office, a gavel and a replica of the Moderator's cross shall be presented to the Moderator.

7.05 Vice-Moderator. The General Assembly shall elect a Vice-Moderator in like manner. The Vice-Moderator shall perform such duties as may be assigned by the Moderator of the General Assembly and perform the duties of the Moderator in the event of the Moderator's disability or absence from office for any reason.

7.06 Removal. The Moderator or Vice-Moderator may be removed by the General Assembly whenever in its judgment the removal would serve the best interests of the corporation.

ARTICLE 8-STATED CLERK

8.01 President. The Stated Clerk is the principal executive officer of the corporation and shall also have the titles of "president" and "treasurer".

8.02 Nomination and Election. The Nominating Committee may nominate the serving Stated Clerk for re-election. If the Nominating Committee declines to nominate the serving Stated Clerk for re-election, or if the Stated Clerk has vacated the office, resigned, or declined to be re-nominated, then the Corporate Board shall conduct a search for and nominate a candidate to the General Assembly. In either event, further nominations may be made by the Commissioners. The Commissioners shall elect the Stated Clerk by majority vote.

8.03 Term of Office. The Stated Clerk shall be elected to a term of four (4) years. The regular term of office begins on January 1 and ends on December 31. There is no limit on the number of terms which may be served by an individual Stated Clerk.

8.04 Duties. The Stated Clerk shall be concerned with the spiritual life of the Church and with maintaining and strengthening a united witness for the Church. The Stated Clerk shall also generally supervise and control the business affairs of the corporation and see that all orders and resolutions of the General Assembly are carried into effect. In fulfillment of these duties, the Stated Clerk shall:
    01. Have responsibility to provide for the orderly governance of the Church in accordance with the Constitution, Rules of Order and Rules of Discipline.
    02. Maintain records of the corporation and respond to requests for official records of General Assembly actions and interpretations of its actions.

03. Represent the Church when an official of the General Assembly is needed.
04. Represent the Cumberland Presbyterian Church in establishing and maintaining relations with other Churches, particulary those of the Presbyterian and Reformed tradition, and in addressing common concerns.
05. Sign all documents on behalf of the corporation or the Cumberland Presbyterian Church.
06. Represent the corporation or the Church in litigation or other legal matters affecting the Cumberland Presbyterian Church, including the selection and employment of legal counsel.
07. Make suitable arrangements for General Assembly meetings, including researching possible meeting sites, contracting for facilities, and arranging space for committee meetings and sessions of the General Assembly;
08. Provide for printing and other communication needs of the General Assembly while in session.
09. Call meetings of the Place of Meeting Committee and the Program Committee.
10. Prepare and distribute an information form to be completed by Commissioners for the Moderator's use in making committee appointments.
11. Advise the Moderator in the appointment of committees.
12. In consultation with the Moderator, refer all matters to come before the next General Assembly; and provide copies of all such referrals to the Commissioners and advisory delegates before the General Assembly convenes.
13. Prepare and distribute preliminary minutes and an agenda for General Assembly meetings which shall provide time for the consideration of any appropriate business, including memorials from a judicatory or denominational entity delivered to the Stated Clerk in writing by April 30.
14. Supervise the recording and publication of minutes and a summary of actions taken by each General Assembly.
15. Make copies of General Assembly minutes available to ordained ministers, licentiates, candidates, commissioners, clerks of sessions, members of denominational entities, schools of the Church, synod, and presbytery clerks, to the Stated Clerk's exchanges and other interested persons in order to encourage lower judicatories and persons in the Church to implement the actions of the General Assembly.
16. File the minutes of each General Assembly with the Historical Foundation as a permanent record.
17. Maintain and update annually the Digest of the General Assembly actions.
18. Represent the Church at large on the Ministry Council.
19. Provide support services for the Moderator and all denominational entities.
20. Receive and make any appropriate response to communications to the Cumberland Presbyterian Church or General Assembly.
21. Maintain a name and address file on congregations, session clerks, pastors, and other leadership of congregations with statistical information about congregations, presbyteries, and synods.
22. Solicit, receive, publish, and disseminate annual reports from churches.
23. Review reports by denominational entities and assist them in complying with correct reporting and budgeting procedures and in avoiding duplication of work.
24. Hold, report annually, and distribute as authorized by the General Assembly or the Ministry Council the Contingency Fund and all other General Assembly Funds not entrusted to the care of a denominational entity.
25. Call the Judiciary Committee into session or by other means secure the advice of the committee on appropriate matters.
26. Communicate with presbyteries and synods on behalf of the General Assembly and attend their meetings from time to time.
27. Provide training for presbytery and synod clerks and orientations for General Assembly commissioners.
28. Generally perform duties as are prescribed in the Constitution or directed by the General Assembly.

8.05 Removal. The Stated Clerk may be removed by the General Assembly whenever in its judgment the removal would serve the best interests of the corporation.

ARTICLE 9-OTHER OFFICERS

9.01 Secretary. The chief executive officer of the Ministry Council shall, by virtue of office, be the secretary of the corporation, and shall in general perform all duties incident to the office of secretary.

9.02 Engrossing Clerk. The Engrossing Clerk shall be elected by the General Assembly to a term of four (4) years. The regular term of office begins on January 1 and ends on December 31. There is no limit on the number of terms which may be served by an individual Engrossing Clerk. The Engrossing Clerk shall serve as Stated Clerk pro tempore during the meeting of the General Assembly in the event the Stated Clerk is absent or unable to serve. The Engrossing Clerk shall perform such other duties as may from time to time be prescribed by the Board of Directors or the General Assembly.

9.03 Additional Officers. The corporation may have such additional officers as it may from time to time find necessary or appropriate.

ARTICLE 10-ORGANIZATION AND RELATIONSHIPS

10.01 Generally. The following are denominational entities related to the Cumberland Presbyterian Church:

01. Subsidiary corporations: Board of Stewardship, Foundation and Benefits of the Cumberland Presbyterian Church; Memphis Theological Seminary of the Cumberland Presbyterian Church; Ministry Council of the Cumberland Presbyterian Church.
02. Related corporations: Bethel University; Cumberland Presbyterian Children's Home; Historical Foundation of the Cumberland Presbyterian Church and the Cumberland Presbyterian Church in America.
03. Commissions: Chaplains and Military Personnel.
04. Committees: Committee on Nominations; Joint Committee on Amendments; Judiciary; Our United Outreach; Place of Meeting Committee; Program Committee; Unified Committee on Theology and Social Concerns.

10.02 Election and Tenure. The following qualifications and rules relate to service on any denominational entity.

01. Unless elected as an Ecumenical Representative, no person shall be qualified to serve except a member in good standing in a presbytery or local congregation of the Cumberland Presbyterian Church.
02. No person who is employed in an executive capacity including Chief Executive, Vice-President, Team Leader, Director, or equivalent in the Cumberland Presbyterian Church is eligible to serve on a denominational entity. No employee of a denominational entity is eligible for service on the same denominational entity.
03. Each person shall be elected for a term of three years unless elected to fill the remainder of an unexpired term. However, if a person elected to serve on a denominational entity where residence in a particular synod is a qualification for election shall move to another synod while in office, the term to which he or she was elected shall terminate at the close of the next meeting of the General Assembly. When nominating persons to boards and agencies, priority consideration be given to persons whose individual life and/or church involvement demonstrates a commitment to support Our United Outreach.
04. Members of the Committee on Nominations may not be elected to a consecutive term. All other persons may serve up to three consecutive terms for a total not to exceed nine years in office.
05. A Cumberland Presbyterian who has served on any entity is not eligible to serve on the same entity (except for an authorized consecutive term) until at least two (2) years have elapsed since the conclusion of the previous service.
06. A Cumberland Presbyterian who is serving on any entity is not eligible to serve on another entity until at least one (1) year has elapsed since the conclusion of the previous service.
07. An Ecumenical Representative who is serving or has served on any entity is not eligible to serve on any other entity (except for an authorized consecutive term on the same entity) until at least one (1) year has elapsed since the conclusion of the previous service.

10.03 Resignation or Removal.

01. Any person serving on a denominational entity who is no longer qualified or eligible

to serve shall be deemed to have resigned.
02. Any person serving on an incorporated denominational entity may resign by delivering written notice of resignation to the secretary or an executive officer of the denominational entity, who shall promptly report the resignation to the Stated Clerk. Any person serving on an unincorporated denominational entity may resign by delivering written notice of resignation to the Stated Clerk. A resignation is effective when delivered unless some other effective date is specified in the written resignation.
03. No member who continues to meet the standard requirements for election or appointment to any denominational entity shall be removed from office except for misfeasance. Removal of a person elected by the General Assembly shall be by vote of the General Assembly.

10.04 Board of Stewardship, Foundation and Benefits. The corporation shall elect the eleven (11) directors of the Board of Stewardship as provided in its charter.

10.05 Cumberland Presbyterian Children's Home. The corporation shall elect the fifteen (15) directors of Children's Home as provided in its corporate articles. The corporation shall elect the directors in such a manner that, immediately following any election, there shall be at least six (6) directors who are members of ecumenical partners of the Children's Home.

10.06 Historical Foundation. The corporation shall elect six (6) of the twelve (12) directors of the Historical Foundation as provided in its charter. The corporation shall elect the directors of the Historical Foundation in such a manner that, immediately following any election, there shall be at least one (1) member from each synod and no person shall be elected if the election would cause two directors from the same presbytery to be serving simultaneously. The remaining six (6) directors shall be elected by the Cumberland Presbyterian Church in America.

10.07 Memphis Theological Seminary. The corporation shall elect the twenty-four (24) directors of Memphis Theological Seminary as provided in its charter. The corporation shall elect the directors in such a manner that, immediately following any election, there shall be at least eleven (11) directors who are members of ecumenical partners of the Seminary.

10.08 Ministry Council.
01. The corporation shall elect the fifteen (15) directors of the Ministry Council as provided in its charter.
02. The corporation shall elect the directors of the Ministry Council in such a manner that immediately following any election, there shall be three (3) directors from each synod; at least six (6) but no more than nine (9) directors who are ordained clergy; and no more than nine (9) directors of the same gender.
03. The Stated Clerk, Moderator, and Immediate Past Moderator shall be designated as Advisory Members to the board of directors of the Ministry Council. In addition, the corporation shall elect three (3) Youth Advisory Members who shall be between the ages of 15 – 17 be elected for 1-year terms, with eligibility for re-election for one additional term.

10.09 Commission on Chaplains and Military Personnel. The commission shall consist of three (3) members elected by the corporation.

ARTICLE 11-COMMITTEES

11.01 General. The corporation shall have the committees provided for in these Bylaws and such other standing or special committees as the General Assembly may create from time to time. Except as otherwise provided in these Bylaws, the Moderator, in consultation with the Stated Clerk, shall appoint all committees.

11.02 Committees of Commissioners and Youth Advisory Delegates. Prior to each General Assembly, the Moderator, in consultation with the Stated Clerk, shall organize the Commissioners and Youth Advisory Delegates into the following committees: Chaplains/Missions/Pastoral Development, Children's Home/Historical Foundation, Higher Education, Judiciary, Ministry Council/Communications/Discipleship, Stewardship/Elected Officers, and Theology and Social Concerns. Each committee shall consider such matters expected to come before the General Assembly as are referred to it by the Stated Clerk. Any denominational organization, the work of which is affected by a matter before a committee, shall be entitled to address the committee.

11.03 Committee on Nominations.

01. The committee shall consist of ten (10) persons elected by the corporation in such a manner that, immediately following any election, the committee shall have at least one minister and one lay person from each synod. It is preferred but not required that no two members shall be from the same presbytery.
02. Approximately one third of the members of the committee shall be elected each year by the General Assembly and shall serve one term not to exceed three years.
03. The committee shall meet not earlier than February 15 each year and shall nominate to the General Assembly qualified persons to fill all vacancies to be filled by vote of the General Assembly, including vacancies on the Committee on Nominations, unless another method of nomination is provided in these Bylaws. The report of the committee shall list the names of nominees, the presbytery if a minister, and the presbytery and the local congregation if a lay person. The Committee on Nominations shall be intentional in nominating persons who represent the global nature of the Church.
04. Presbyteries and synods and their moderators and stated clerks are requested to assist the Committee on Nominations by recommending persons for any position by providing the name and qualifications of the potential nominees to the Stated Clerk no later than February 1 on a form to be provided by the Stated Clerk. Nominations from the floor shall also be in order.
05. No person shall be nominated for election by the General Assembly unless the nominee has within the past year given his or her consent to the nomination.

11.04 Joint Committee on Amendments. The Judiciary Committee shall appoint as many as five of its members to act in committee with an equal number of members of the Judiciary Committee of the Cumberland Presbyterian Church in America. Upon the request of the General Assembly of the Cumberland Presbyterian Church or the General Assembly of the Cumberland Presbyterian Church in America, this Joint Committee shall prepare for the consideration of both general assemblies proposed amendments to the Confession of Faith, Catechism, Constitution, Rules of Discipline, Directory for Worship, and Rules of Order.

11.05 Judiciary Committee.
01. The committee shall consist of nine (9) persons elected by the corporation in such a manner that, immediately following any election, the committee shall have at least four members (4) who are ordained ministers and at least three (3) members who are licensed attorneys-at-law. The Stated Clerk shall be staff liaison to the committee, attending its meetings and providing resources and counsel.
02. The committee shall meet at least annually upon the call of its chairperson or the Stated Clerk.
03. The committee shall provide advice and counsel to the Stated Clerk. Upon the written request of any judicatory or denominational entity made to the chairperson or Stated Clerk, the committee shall render an advisory opinion on matters of church law or procedure. The chairperson shall secure the views of all members of the committee and write the advisory opinion based on the majority view of the members. The committee shall not render legal opinions on matters of civil law nor otherwise engage in the practice of law.
04. At least one member of the committee shall attend each meeting of the General Assembly to advise with its officers and Commissioners on matters of church law or procedure. At the Moderator's request a member of the committee shall be available to advise the Moderator during the business sessions of the General Assembly.
05. The committee shall be a commission within the meaning of section 2.5 of the Rules of Discipline to hear and determine appeals from synods.

11.06 Our United Outreach Committee.
01. The committee shall consist of five (5) persons elected by the corporation in such a manner that, immediately following any election, the committee shall have one person from each synod. Seven (7) additional members will include a member of the Ministry Council, a member of the Corporate Board, a member of the Board of Stewardship, Foundation and Benefits, a member of the Board of Trustees of the Historical Foundation, and a Cumberland Presbyterian member of the Boards of Trustees of Bethel University, the Cumberland Presbyterian Children's Home, and Memphis Theological Seminary. The executives of the above named denominational entities

shall serve as non-voting, Resource/Advocacy members.
02. The Office of the General Assembly will be responsible for the expenses of the representative of each synod. The represented denominational entities will be responsible for the expenses of their representatives and executives.

11.07 Place of Meeting. The committee shall consist of the Moderator, the Stated Clerk and a representative of the Cumberland Presbyterian Women's Ministries.

11.08 Program Committee. The committee shall consist of the Moderator, Stated Clerk, Director of Ministries, Assistant to the Stated Clerk who serves as secretary, the pastor of the host church, four elected representatives designated by the Ministry Council from among its ministry teams, and one representative designated by each of the following: Bethel University, Board of Stewardship, Foundation, and Benefits, Cumberland Presbyterian Children's Home, Historical Foundation, Memphis Theological Seminary, and the Cumberland Presbyterian Women's Ministry. The committee will begin planning for two years prior to the meeting of a particular General Assembly.

11.09 Unified Committee on Theology and Social Concerns. The committee shall consist of eight (8) members elected by the corporation, the Stated Clerk, and the President of Memphis Theological Seminary. At least one member of the committee other than the Seminary's president shall be a Cumberland Presbyterian member of the faculty of Memphis Theological Seminary.

ARTICLE 12-INDEMNIFICATION

12.01 Indemnification. The corporation shall indemnify any director, officer or employee who is, or is threatened to be, made a party to a completed, pending, or threatened action or proceeding from any liability arising from the director's, officer's or employee's official capacity with the corporation. This indemnification shall extend to the personal representation of a deceased person if the person would be entitled to indemnification under these Bylaws if living.

12.02 Costs and Expenses Covered by Indemnification. Indemnification provided under these Bylaws shall extend to the payment of a judgment, settlement, penalty, or fine, as well as attorney's fees, court costs, and other reasonable and necessary expenses incurred by the director or officer with respect to the action or proceeding.

12.03 Limitation on Indemnification. No indemnification shall be made to or on behalf of any person if a judgment or other final adjudication adverse to that person establishes his or her liability:
01. for any breach of the duty of loyalty to the corporation;
02. for acts or omissions not in good faith or which involve intentional misconduct or a knowing violation of law; or
03. for any distribution of the assets of the corporation which is unlawful under Tennessee law.

ARTICLE 13-TRUSTEE FOR THE CORPORATION

13.01 Trustee. The Board of Stewardship, Foundation and Benefits of the Cumberland Presbyterian Church, a nonprofit corporation existing under the laws of the state of Tennessee, holds certain real property and other assets of the Church as trustee for the use and benefit of the Church. The Board of Stewardship may continue to hold such real property and other assets, but after the adoption of these Bylaws, it shall hold those assets as trustee for the use and benefit of the Cumberland Presbyterian Church General Assembly Corporation.

13.02 Other Assets. Other, additional property may from time to time be conveyed to the Board of Stewardship to be held by it as trustee for the corporation. All assets held by the Board of Stewardship as trustee for the corporation shall be held at the pleasure and direction of the General Assembly.

ARTICLE 14-PARLIAMENTARY AUTHORITY

14.01 Designation. The parliamentary authority of the corporation in all meetings shall be the latest revised edition of the Rules of Order as set out in the Confession of Faith and Government of the Cumberland Presbyterian Church. In matters not provided for in the Rules of Order, the parliamentary authority shall be Robert's Rules of Order, latest revised edition.

14.02 Standing Rules. The following shall be Standing Rules for meetings of the General Assembly and may be suspended as provided in the parliamentary authority. (see Rules of Order 8.34c)

Standing Rules

1. Unless otherwise determined by the General Assembly or by the Stated Clerk in the event of an emergency, the annual General Assembly shall meet on the third or fourth Monday of June at two o'clock in the afternoon to organize, elect a moderator and transact business, and shall close on Thursday or Friday of the same week.

2. Reports of all standing and special committees shall be considered in the order established by the Moderator in consultation with the Stated Clerk. Committee reports may be presented orally or in writing provided to all Commissioners and youth advisory delegates. Those presenting committee reports shall have the opportunity to make remarks and give explanation, such presentations not to exceed ten minutes unless time is extended by two-thirds vote taken without debate. All committee recommendations shall be submitted in writing.

3. All materials from denominational entities for consideration or action by a General Assembly shall be submitted to the Stated Clerk at least thirty (30) days before the meeting of General Assembly.

4. Resolutions and memorials proposed for adoption by individual commissioners rather than denominational entities or judicatories of the Cumberland Presbyterian Church shall be introduced no later than the close of business on the second day of a meeting of General Assembly, and, when introduced, shall be referred by the Moderator, in counsel with the Stated Clerk, to the appropriate committee or committees for report and recommendations to the Assembly.

ARTICLE 15-REPORTS AND AUDITS

15.01 Congregational Reports. Annually by December 1, the Stated Clerk shall send to session clerks statistical forms for reporting congregational data. Session clerks shall mail the completed forms to presbytery clerks by February 1. The presbytery clerk shall mail the composite statistical report for all congregations of a presbytery to the Stated Clerk by February 10.

15.02 Institutional Reports. In order to be considered for inclusion in the General Assembly budget, all denominational entities shall deliver to the Stated Clerk an annual report including a concise description of the organization's work during the previous year and a line item budget for the forthcoming year. Financial reports should be condensed as much as possible while conveying all essential information on the organization's operations. All denominational entities except academic institutions on a fiscal year are requested to maintain their books on a calendar year.

15.03 Reporting Schedule. An electronic copy and two written copies of the annual report signed by two officers of the organization shall be delivered to the Stated Clerk by March 15 each year. Organizations requesting funds from Our United Outreach shall submit multi-year program budgets to the Our United Outreach Committee.

15.04 Audits. Organizations and operations included in the General Assembly budget shall be audited annually by a certified public accountant. Copies of the auditor's report, including any recommendations for changes in the procedures relating to internal financial controls, shall be delivered to the Stated Clerk. Organizations with total receipts of $100,000 or less are not required to have an audit but shall submit their books and financial statements to the Stated Clerk annually.

15.05 Bonds. Each organization or person whose financial records are required to be audited shall have a fidelity bond in an amount adequate to protect all funds held by the organization or person.

ARTICLE 16-AMENDMENTS

16.01 Manner of Amendment. Except as provided below, these Bylaws may be amended or repealed only by the affirmative vote of two-thirds of the votes cast in a duly constituted meeting of the General Assembly. No portion of the Bylaws may be amended or repealed by the Board of Directors. Fair and reasonable notice of any proposed amendment shall be provided as required by state law.

16.02 Extraordinary Actions. In order to be effective the following actions must be approved by (1) the affirmative vote of two consecutive General Assemblies, or (2) a ninety percent (90%) vote of a single General Assembly.

01. Terminating the existence of a denominational entity named in Bylaw 10.01
02. Creating a new denominational entity other than a temporary committee or task force.
03. Decreasing the Our United Outreach budget allocation to a denominational entity by more than 40% of the amount distributed to it during the previous calendar year; or
04. Taking any other actions which would cause a drastic change in the mission or structure of the Cumberland Presbyterian Church.

MEMORIAL ROLL OF MINISTERS

IN MEMORY OF
MINISTERS LOST BY DEATH

NAME	PRESBYTERY	AGE	DATE
Blakeburn, Roy E.	East Tennessee	87	04/14/16
Hatcher, Carlton	Cumberland	86	01/01/16
Malone, Michael	Murfreesboro	49	05/28/16
Moss, Larry	Covenant	74	11/26/15
Ortiz, Jaime	Andes	83	03/26/16
Phelps, Earl	West Tennessee	87	04/20/16
Smith, Billy T.	Nashville		06/16/16
Talley, James E.	Cumberland	89	03/15/16

LIVING GENERAL ASSEMBLY MODERATORS

2014—REV. LISA ANDERSON, 1790 Faxon Avenue, Memphis, TN 38112
2013—REV. FOREST PROSSER, 1157 Mountain Creek Road, Chattanooga, TN 37405
2012—REV. ROBERT D. RUSH, 17822 Deep Brook Drive, Spring, TX 77379
2011—REV. DON M. TABOR, 9611 Mitchell Place, Brentwood, TN 37027
2010—REV. BOYCE WALLACE, Cra 101 No 15-93, Cali, Colombia, South America
2009—ELDER SAM SUDDARTH, 206 Ha Le Koa Court, Smyrna, TN 37167
2008—REV. JONATHAN CLARK, 88 Woodcrest Drive, Winchester, TN 37398
2007—REV. FRANK WARD, 8207 Traditional Place, Cordova, TN 38016
2006—REV. DONALD HUBBARD, 2128 Campbell Station Road, Knoxville, TN 37932
2005—REV. LINDA H. GLENN, 49 Mason Road, Threeway, TN 38343
2004—REV. EDWARD G. SIMS, 2161 N. Meadows Drive, Clarksville, TN 37043
2003—REV. CHARLES MCCASKEY, 679 Canter Lane, Cookeville, TN 38501
2001—REV. RANDOLPH JACOB, 610 W. Adams Street, Broken Bow, OK 74728
1999—ELDER GWENDOLYN G. RODDYE, 3728 Wittenham Drive, Knoxville, TN 37921
1998—REV. MASAHARU ASAYAMA, 3-15-9 Higashi, Kunitachi-shi, Tokyo, JAPAN
1996—REV. MERLYN A. ALEXANDER, 80 N. Hampton Lane, Jackson, TN 38305
1995—REV. CLINTON O. BUCK, 4986 Warwick, Memphis, TN 38117
1993—REV. ROBERT M. SHELTON, 7128 Lakehurst Avenue, Dallas, TX 75230
1992—REV. JOHN DAVID HALL, 109 Oddo Lane SE, Huntsville, AL 35802
1990—REV. THOMAS D. CAMPBELL, PO Box 315, Calico Rock, AR 72519
1989—REV. WILLIAM RUSTENHAVEN, Jr., 703 W. Burleson, Marshall, TX 75670
1988—ELDER BEVERLY ST. JOHN, 5436 Edmondson Pike Apt 75A, Nashville, TN 37211
1981—REV. W. JEAN RICHARDSON, 7533 Lancashire, Powell, TN 37849

IN MEMORY OF:

Moderator of the 145th General Assembly

REV. ROY E BLAKEBURN

Died April 14, 2016

Moderator of the 152nd General Assembly

REV. WILLIAM A. RAWLINS

Died December 22, 2015

GENERAL ASSEMBLY OFFICERS

MODERATOR
THE REVEREND DWAYNE TYUS
426 W Old Hickory Boulevard
Madison, TN 37115
dwayne.tyus@gmail.com
(615)720-2564

VICE MODERATOR
THE REVEREND NOBUKO SEKI
4-12-42-403 Shimorenjyaku
Mitaka-shi Tokyo
181-0013 JAPAN
nobukoseki866@gmail.com
(042)248-5379

STATED CLERK AND TREASURER
THE REVEREND MICHAEL SHARPE
8207 Traditional Place
Cordova, TN 38016
(901)276-4572
FAX (901)272-3913
msharpe@cumberland.org

ENGROSSING CLERK
THE REVEREND VERNON SANSOM
7810 Shiloh Road
Midlothian, TX 76065
(972)825-6887
vernon@sansom.us

THE BOARD OF DIRECTORS OF THE GENERAL ASSEMBLY CORPORATION

(Members whose terms expire in 2017)
(1)REV. JOHN BUTLER, 501 Cherokee Drive, Campbellsville, KY 42718
   jbutler@iccable.com
(1)MS. BETTY JACOB, PO Box 158, Broken Bow, OK 74728
   chocpres@pine-net.com

(Members whose terms expire in 2018)
(1)MS. CALOTTA EDSELL, 7044 Woodsong Cove, Germantown, TN 38138
   cedsell@hotmail.com
(1)REV. NORLAN SCRUDDER, 29688 S 534 Road, Park Hill, OK 74451
   ndscrudder@gmail.com

(Members whose terms expire in 2019)
(2)MR. TIM GARRETT, 150 Third Avenue South, Suite 2800, Nashville, TN 37201
   tgarrett@bassberry.com
(2)REV. BOBBY COLEMAN, 704 E Webb Street, Mountain View, AR 72560
   bobby.coleman@gmail.com

*Ecumenical Partners   +Cumberland Presbyterian Church in America

MINISTRY COUNCIL

(Members whose terms expire in 2017)
(2)REV. DONNY ACTON, 1413 Oakridge Drive, Birmingham, AL 35242
(3)REV. MICHELE GENTRY DE CORREAL, Urb San Jorge casa 28, Km 8 via a La Tebaida Armenia, Quinido, COLOMBIA, SOUTH AMERICA
(2)REV. LANNY JOHNSON, 120 S Mill Street, Morrison, TN 37357
(1)MR. ADAM MCREYNOLDS, PO Box 162, Bethany, IL 61914
(2)REV. TOM SANDERS, 4201 W Kent Street, Broken Arrow, OK 74012

(Members whose terms expire in 2018)
(2)MR. KENNETH BEAN, 1035 Stonewall Street N, McKenzie, TN 38201
(1)REV. PHILLIP LAYNE, 10699 Griffith Highway, Whitwell, TN 37397
(1)REV. PAULA LOUDER, 98 Gallant Court, Clarksville, TN 37043
(2)REV. RON MCMILLAN, 675 Kimberly Drive, Atoka, TN 38004
(1)MS. VICTORY MOORE, 17388 Chandlerville Road, Virginia, IL 62691
(1)MS. PATRICIA SMITH, PO Box 86, Smiths Grove, KY 42171 (deceased)

(Members whose terms expire in 2019)
(1)MS. KAREN AVERY, 9420 Layton Court NE, Albuquerque, NM 87111
(3)REV. TROY GREEN, 105 Cobb Hollow Lane, Petersburg, TN 37144
(1)MS. TSURUKO SATOH, 8710 Hickory Falls Lane, Pewee Valley, KY 40056
(1)REV. MIKE WILKINSON, 1504 Clear Brook Drive, Knoxville, TN 37922

YOUTH ADVISORY MEMBERS
(1)MR. CAMERON ALDERSON, 122 E Cherry Street, Chandler, IN 47610
(2)MR. CALEB DAVIS, 502 S Alley Street, Jefferson, TX 75657
(2)MS. EMILY MAHONEY, 31 Barbara Circle, McMinnville, TN 37110
(1)MS. CHARLI UHLRICH, 250 County Road 1950 N, Bethany, IL 61914

ADVISORY MEMBERS
REV. MICHAEL SHARPE, 8207 Traditional Place, Cordova, TN 38016
REV. DWAYNE TYUS, 901 W Old Hickory Boulevard, Madison, TN 37115

COMMUNICATIONS MINISTRY TEAM

(Members whose terms expire in 2017)
(3)MS. B. DENISE ADAMS, 126 Ray, Monticello, AR 71655
(2)MS. DUSTY LUTHY, 400 S Friendship Road Apt G, Paducah, KY 42003

(Members whose terms expire in 2018)
(3)REV. MICHAEL CLARK, 80 Bryan Drive, Winchester, TN 37398
(3)REV. JAMES D. MCGUIRE, 220-2 Southwind Circle, Greeneville, TN 37743

(Members whose terms expire in 2019)
(2)REV. NICHOLAS CHAMBERS, 11300 Road 101, Union, MS 39365
(2)REV. STEVEN SHELTON, 7886 Farmhill Cove, Bartlett, TN 38135

*Ecumenical Partners   +Cumberland Presbyterian Church in America

DISCIPLESHIP MINISTRY TEAM

(Members whose terms expire in 2017)
(2)MS. LE ILA DIXON, 4406 John Reagan Street, Marshall, TX 75672
(2)REV. DREW GRAY, 8220 Timberland Drive, West Paducah, KY 42086
(3)MS. SAMANTHA HASSELL, 510 N Main Street, Sturgis, KY 42459
(Members whose terms expire in 2018)
(3)MS. JOANNA WILKINSON, 1174 Tanglewood Street, Memphis, TN 38114
(2)MS. RACHEL COOK, 210 Bynum Street, Scottsboro, AL 35768
(2)REV. CHRISTIAN SMITH, 475 State Street, Cookeville, TN 38501
(Members whose terms expire in 2019)
(2)REV. NANCY MCSPADDEN, 120 Roberta Drive, Memphis, TN 38112
(2)REV. JOSEFINA SANCHEZ, 7 Hancock Street, Melrose, MA 02176

MISSIONS MINISTRY TEAM

(Members whose terms expire in 2017)
(2)REV. JAMES BUTTRAM, 103 Golfcrest Lane, Oak Ridge, TN 37830 (resigned)
(3)REV. JIMMY BYRD, 176 E Valley Road, Whitwell, TN 37397
(1)MS. DONNA CHRISTIE, 3221 Whitehall Road, Birmingham, AL 35209
(3)REV. RICARDO FRANCO, 7 Hancock Street, Melrose, MA 02176
(1)MRS. MS. KAREN TOLEN, 6859 A East County Road 000N, Trilla, IL 62469
(Members whose terms expire in 2018)
(3)REV. JIM BARRY, 1405 Anna Street, Hixson, TN 37343
(2)MR. TIM CRAIG, 8958 Carriage Creek Road, Arlington, TN 38002
(2)REV. CARDELIA HOWELL-DIAMOND, 1580 Jeff Road NW, Huntsville, AL 35806
(3)MS. SHERRY POTEET, P.O. Box 313, Gilmer, TX 75644
(2)MS. MELINDA REAMS, 10 W Azalea Lane, Russellville, AR 72802
(Members whose terms expire in 2019)
(3)REV. MAKIHIKO ARASE, 3-355-4 Kamikitadai Higashiyamato-Shi, Tokyo, 207-0023 JAPAN
(2)REV. VICTOR HASSELL, 510 N Main Street, Sturgis, KY 42459
(2)MR. DOMINIC LAU, 3820 Anza Street, San Francisco, CA
(2)MS. BRITTANY MEEKS, 2664 Morning Sun Road, Cordova, TN 38016
(2)REV. CHRIS WARREN, 906 Prince Lane, Murfreesboro, TN 37129

PASTORAL DEVELOPMENT MINISTRY TEAM

(Members whose terms expire in 2017)
(2)REV. AMBER CLARK, 80 Bryan Drive, Winchester, TN 37398
(2)REV. DREW HAYES, 6322 Labor Lane, Louisville, KY 40291
(Members whose terms expire in 2018)
(2)REV. DUAWN MEARNS, 107 Westoak Place, Hot Springs, AR 71913
(3)REV. LINDA SNELLING, 15791 State Highway W, Ada, OK 74820
(Members whose terms expire in 2019)
(2)REV. SANDRA SHEPHERD, 525 Summit Oaks Court, Nashville, TN 37221
(2)REV. PATRICK WILKERSON, 7719 S Whispering Oak Circle, Powell, TN 37849

*Ecumenical Partners   +Cumberland Presbyterian Church in America

GENERAL ASSEMBLY BOARD OF:

I. TRUSTEES OF BETHEL UNIVERSITY

(Members whose terms expire in 2016)
(1)MR. JEFF AMREIN, 11711 Paramont Way, Prospect, KY 40059
(3)DR. LARRY A. BLAKEBURN, 790 Emory Valley Road Apt 714, Oak Ridge, TN 37830
(2)*JUDGE BEN CANTRELL, 415 Church Street #2513, Nashville, TN 37219
(2)+DR. ARMY DANIEL, 3125 Searcy Drive, Huntsville, AL 35810
(3)MR. LAWRENCE (LADD) DANIEL, 13023 Taylorcrest, Houston, TX 77079
(1)MR. BILL DOBBINS 5716 Quest Ridge Road, Franklin, TN 37064
(2)DR. ROBERT LOW, c/o New Prime, Inc., 2740 W Mayfair Avenue, Springfield, MO 65803
(3)MR. BEN T. SURBER, 1145 Hico Road, McKenzie, TN 38201

(Members whose terms expire in 2017)
(2)*MS. LISA COLE, PO Box 198615, Nashville, TN 37219
(2)MR. CHESTER (CHET) DICKSON, 24 W Rivercrest Drive, Houston, TX 77042
(1)REV. NANCY MCSPADDEN, 120 Roberta Drive, Memphis, TN 38112
(3)MR. BOBBY OWEN, 1625 Cabot Drive, Franklin, TN 37064
(2)DR. ED PERKINS, 721 Paris Street, McKenzie, TN 38201
(1)MR. KENNETH (KEN) D. QUINTON, 2912 Waller Omer Road, Sturgis, KY 42459
(3)REV. ROBERT (ROB) TRUITT, 1238 Old East Side Road, Burns, TN 37029
(1)REV. ROBERT (BOB) WATKINS, 10950 West Union Hills Drive #1356, Sun City, AZ 85373

(Members whose terms expire in 2018)
(3)MR. CHARLIE GARRETT, 107 Willow Green Drive, Jackson, TN 38305
(2)+REV. ELTON C. HALL, SR., 305 Tiffton Circle, Hewitt, TX 76643
(2)MS. DEWANNA LATIMER, 1077 Jr. Jones Road, Humboldt, TN 38343
(1)MR. LYNDLE MCCURLEY, 198 Rock Creek Drive, Mountain Home, AR 72653
(1)*DR. E. RAY MORRIS, PO Box 924528, Norcross, GA 30010
(1)MR. STEVE PERRYMAN, 535 Ranch Road, Rogersville, MO 65742

Trustee Emeritus – Dr. Vera Low, 3653 Prestwick Court, Springfield, MO 65809 (deceased)

II. TRUSTEES OF CUMBERLAND PRESBYTERIAN CHILDREN'S HOME

(Members whose terms expire in 2016)
(2)*MR. RICHARD DEAN, 2140 Cove Circle North, Gadsden, AL 35903
(1)MRS. KAY GOODMAN, 1042 Bobcat Road, Sanger, TX 76266
(2)REV. MELISSA KNIGHT, 9799 Savoy Way, Live Oak, CA 95953
(2)MS. PATRICIA LONG, 525 E Oak Street, Aledo, TX 76008

(Members whose terms expire in 2017)
(1)MS. CAROLINE BOOTH, 2200 Westview Trail, Denton, TX 76207
(3)MS. MAMIE HALL, 305 Tiffton Circle, Hewitt, TX 76643
(1)MR. CHARLES HARRIS, 3293 Birch Avenue, Grapevine, TX 76051
(1)MR. KNIGHT MILLER, 1035 Garden Creek Circle, Louisville, KY 40223
(1)MR. JOHN O'CARROLL, 1701 Live Oak Lane, Southlake, TX 76092
(3)REV. DON TABOR, 9611 Mitchell Place, Brentwood, TN 37027

(Members whose terms expire in 2018)
(1)REV. DUANE DOUGHERTY, 212 County Road 4705, Troup, TX 75789
(1)MRS. CAROLYN HARMON, 4435 Newport Highway, Greeneville, TN 37743
(1)DR. ROBIN HENSON, 8220 Westwind Lane, North Richland Hills, TX 76182
(1)REV. JOYCE MERRITT, 3929 Snail Shell Cove, Rockvale, TN 37153

*Ecumenical Partners   +Cumberland Presbyterian Church in America

III. TRUSTEES OF HISTORICAL FOUNDATION

(Members whose terms expire in 2017)
(3)+MS. EDNA BARNETT, 7 Breezewood Cove, Jackson, TN 38305
(2)MR. MICHAEL FARE, 401 E Deanna Lane, Nixa, MO 65714
(2)*MS. DOROTHY HAYDEN, 3103 Carolina Avenue, Bessemer, AL 35020
(1)+MS. PAT WARD, 2620 Rabbit Lane, Madison, AL 35756
(3)+REV. RICK WHITE, 124 Towne West, Lorena, TX 76655
(Members whose terms expire in 2018)
(1)REV. LISA OLIVER, 110 Allen Drive, Hendersonville, TN 37075
(3)DR. SIDNEY L. SWINDLE, 4407 Swann Avenue, Tampa, FL 33609
(Members whose terms expire in 2019)
(1)MS. ROBIN HUGHES, 1205 Olde Bridge Road, Edmond, OK 73034
(3)REV. MARY KATHRYN KIRKPATRICK, 401 1/2 Henley-Perry Drive, Marshall, TX 75670
(1)MS. ASHLEY LINDSEY, 2090 Claypool Boyce Road, Alvaton, KY 42122

IV. TRUSTEES OF MEMPHIS THEOLOGICAL SEMINARY OF THE CUMBERLAND PRESBYTERIAN CHURCH

(Members whose terms expire in 2017)
(1)*REV. NANCY COLE, 3346 Arcadia Drive, Tuscaloosa, AL 35404
(1)REV. ANNE HAMES, 118 Paris Street, McKenzie, TN 38201
(2)*REV. ROBERT MARBLE, 515 Shamrock Drive, Little Rock, AR 72205
(2)REV. JENNIFER NEWELL, 2322 Marco Circle, Chattanooga, TN 37421
(1)REV. SUSAN PARKER, 655 York Drive, Rogersville, AR 35652
(1)REV. STEWART SALYER, 2211 Foxfire Road, Clarksville, TN 37043
(3)+DR. JOE WARD, 2620 Rabbit Lane, Madison, AL 35758
(3)*MS. RUBY WHARTON, 1183 E Parkway South, Memphis, TN 38114
(Members whose terms expire in 2018)
(3)REV. KEVIN BRANTLEY, 729 Old Hodgenville Road, Greensburg, KY 42743
(1)REV. KEVIN HENSON, 1101 Bear Creek Parkway, Ste 3210, Keller, TX 76248
(1)REV. LINDA HOWELL, PO Box 80050, Keller, TX 76244
(3)MR. MARK MADDOX, 225 Oak Drive, Dresden, TN 38225
(2)MS. SONDRA RODDY, 2583 Hedgerow Lane, Clarksville, TN 37043
(3)MR. TAKAYOSHI SHIRAI, 25 Minami Kibogaoka Asahi-ku, Yokohama, Kanagawa-ken 241-0824 JAPAN
(2)*REV. MELVIN CHARLES SMITH, 1263 Haynes Street, Memphis, TN 38114
(2)*MS. LATISHA TOWNS, The Med, 877 Jefferson Avenue, Memphis, TN 38103
(Members whose terms expire in 2019)
(3)MR. MICHAEL R. ALLEN, 149 Windwood Circle, Alabaster, AL 35007
(2)*MR. JOHNNIE COOMBS, PO Box 127, Blue Mountain, MS 38610
(3)MS. DIANE DICKSON, 24 West Rivercrest, Houston, TX 77042
(1)*MS. JANE ASHLEY FOLK, 4405 Dunwick Lane, Fort Worth, TX 76109
(2)*DR. RICK KIRCHOFF, 2044 Thorncroft Drive, Germantown, TN 38138
(3)*DR. INETTA RODGERS, 1824 S Parkway E, Memphis, TN 38114
(1)*DR. DEBORAH SMITH, 584 E McLemore Avenue, Memphis, TN 38106
(1)MS. MARIANNA (MOLLY) WILLIAMS, 947 Troy Avenue, Dyersburg, TN 28024

V. STEWARDSHIP, FOUNDATION AND BENEFITS

(Members whose terms expire in 2017)
(1)REV. RANDY DAVIDSON, PO Box 880, Ada, OK 74821
(3)MR. CHARLES DAY, 9312 Owensboro Road, Falls of Rough, KY 40119
(3)MS. SYLVIA HALL, 930 Sherry Circle, Hixson, TN 37343
(3)MR. JACKIE SATTERFIELD, 2303 County Road 730, Cullman, AL 35055

*Ecumenical Partners   +Cumberland Presbyterian Church in America

(Members whose terms expire in 2018)
(3)MR. ANDREW B. FRAZIER, JR., 107 Doris Street, Camden, TN 38320
(1)MR. JAMES SHANNON, 2307 Littlemore Drive, Cordova, TN 38016
(2)MR. MICHAEL ST. JOHN, 324 Carriage Place, Lebanon, MO 65536
(Members whose terms expire in 2019)
(2)REV. CHARLES (BUDDY) POPE, 2391 Fairfield Pike, Shelbyville, TN 37160
(3)MS. SUE RICE, 1301 Brooker Road, Brandon, FL 33511
(3)MS. DEBBIE SHELTON, 1255 MG England Road, Manchester, TN 37355
(1)MS. ANDREA SMITH, 1715 Water Cure Road, Winchester, TN 37398

GENERAL ASSEMBLY COMMISSIONS:

I. MILITARY CHAPLAINS AND PERSONNEL

(2) Term Expires in 2017–REV. MARY MCCASKEY BENEDICT, 892 Pen Oak Drive, Cookeville,
   TN 38501
(1) Term Expires in 2018–REV. TONY JANNER, 104 Northwood Drive, McKenzie
   TN 38201
(2) Term Expires in 2019–REV. CASSANDRA THOMAS, 1920 Dancy Street, Fayetteville,
   NC 28301

These three persons and the Stated Clerk represent the denomination as members of the Presbyterian Council for Chaplains and Military Personnel, 4125 Nebraska Avenue NW, Washington, DC 20016

GENERAL ASSEMBLY COMMITTEES

I. JUDICIARY

(Members whose terms expire in 2017)
(1)REV. HARRY CHAPMAN, 4908 El Picador Court SE, Rio Rancho, NM 87124
   wrightrev2gmail.com
(2)REV. ROBERT D. RUSH, 12935 Quail Park Drive, Cypress, TX 77429
   rushrd74@comcast.net
(3)MR. WENDELL THOMAS, JR., 1200 Paradise Drive, Powell, TN 37849
   volbaby@comcast.net
(Members whose terms expire in 2018)
(2)REV. ANNETTA CAMP, 2263 Mill Creek Road, Halls, TN 38040
   anetta@cumberlandchurch.com
(3)MS. KIMBERLY SILVUS, 1128 Madison Street, Clarksville, TN 37040
   kgsilvus@gmail.com
(1)MR. BILL TALLY, 907 Tipperary Drive, Scottsboro, AL 35768
   wtally@scottsboro.org
(Members whose terms expire in 2019)
(3)REV. ANDY MCCLUNG, 919 Dickinson Street, Memphis, TN 38107
   scubarev@att.net
(1)MS. RACHEL MOSES, 1138 Blaine Avenue, Cookeville, TN 38501
   coachrach@aol.com
(1)REV. JAN OVERTON, 3320 Pipe Line Road, Birmingham, AL 35243
   jan@crestlinechurch.org

*Ecumenical Partners   +Cumberland Presbyterian Church in America

II. JOINT COMMITTEE ON AMENDMENTS

The committee consists of five members of the Judiciary Committee of the Cumberland Presbyterian Church in America and the Cumberland Presbyterian Church.

III. NOMINATING

(Members whose terms expire in 2017)
(1)REV. TOBY DAVIS, 502 S Alley Street, Jefferson, TX 75657
 pastortobydavis@gmail.com
(1)MS. ELLIE SCRUDDER, 29688 S 535 Road, Park Hill, OK 74451
 escrudder@gmail.com
(1)REV. KEVIN SMALL, 6492 E 400th Road, Martinsville, IL 62442
 revkev61@gmail.com

(Members whose terms expire in 2018)
(1)REV. THOMAS CAMPBELL, PO Box 343, Calico Rock, AR 72519
 tdcampbellar@gmail.com
(1)MS. HEATHER MORGAN, 1468 Williams Cove Road, Winchester, TN 37398
 htmorgan87@gmail.com

(Members whose terms expire in 2019)
(1)MRS. FRANCES DAWSON, PO Box 904, Scottsboro, AL 35768
 rdpfcd@scottsboro.org
(1)MS. FAYE DELASHMIT, 2705 Garrett Drive, Bowling Green, KY 42104
 steve.delashmit@twc.com
(1)REV. DEREK JACKS, 341 Shadeswood Drive, Hoover, AL 35226
 pastorderek@homewoodcpc.com
(1)REV. STEPHEN LOUDER, 98 Gallant Court, Clarksville, TN 37043
 pastorsteve@clarksvillecpc.com
(1)MS. JANIE STAMPS, 4008 Logan Lane, Fort Smith, AR 72903
 bjstamps@msn.com

IV. OUR UNITED OUTREACH COMMITTEE

(Members whose terms expire in 2017)
(3)MS. SHARON RESCH, PO Box 383, Dongola, IL 62926
(3)REV. WILLIAM RUSTENHAVEN III, PO Box 1303, Marshall, TX 75671

(Members whose terms expire in 2018)
(2)MR. RANDY WEATHERSBY, 6130 US Highway 278 E, Cullman, AL 35055
(2)MS. ROBIN WILLS, 4607 E Richmond Shop Road, Lebanon, TN 37090

(Members whose terms expire in 2019)
(1)REV. BRUCE HAMILTON, 1037 Binns Drive, Monticello, AR 71655

V. PLACE OF MEETING

THE STATED CLERK OF THE GENERAL ASSEMBLY
THE MODERATOR OF THE GENERAL ASSEMBLY
A REPRESENTATIVE OF WOMEN'S MINISTRIES OF THE MISSIONS MINISTRY TEAM

*Ecumenical Partners   +Cumberland Presbyterian Church in America

VI. UNIFIED COMMITTEE ON THEOLOGY AND SOCIAL CONCERNS

(Members whose terms expire in 2017)

(1)+MS. SHARON COMBS, PO Box 122, Sturgis, KY 42459
   (270)860-4175
(1)+REV. EDMOND COX, 249 Mimosa Circle, Maryville, TN 37801
   (865)789-6161
(2)+DR. NANCY FUQUA, 1963 County Road 406, Towncreek, AL 35672
   fuq23@bellsouth.net; (256)566-1226
(2)REV. RANDY JACOB, PO Box 158, Broken Bow, OK 74728
   chocpres@pine-net.com; (580)584-3770; (580)236-2469 cell
(1)+REV. LARUTH JEFFERSON, 25757 Primose Lane, Southfield, MI 48033
   (248)945-0349
(1)+DR. PHILLIP REDRICK, 228 Church Street NW, Huntsville, AL 35801
   (256)882-6333
(1)+REV. ROBERT E THOMAS, 1017 N Englewood, Tyler, TX 75702
   (903)592-0238

(Members whose terms expire in 2018)

(2)REV. GEORGE ESTES, 7910 Cloverbrook Lane, Germantown, TN 38138
   geoestes@gmail.com; (901)755-6673
(2)REV. SHELIA O'MARA, 533 Loughton Lane, Arnold, MD 21012
   chaplainshelia@aol.com; (410)757-5713; (443)370-7218 cell
(2)MR. DAVID PHILLIPS-BURK, 3325 Bailey Creek Cove N, Collierville, TN 38017
   dlphillipsburk@aol.com; (256)520-1380

(Members whose terms expire in 2019)

(3)+MRS. JIMMIE DODD, c/o Hopewell CPCA, 4100 Millsfield Highway, Dyersburg, TN 38024
   dodd125@gmail.com
(3)REV. BYRON FORESTER, 2376 Eastwood Place, Memphis, TN 38112
   bforester@bellsouth.net; (901)246-1242
(1)REV. MARCUS HAYES, 2901 Sandage Avenue, Apt 304, Fort Worth, TX 76109
   marcus.hayes@att.net
(2)REV. JOHN A. SMITH, 916 Allen Road, Nashville, TN 37214
   john.a.smith.81@gmail.com; (615)545-6486
(3)+ELDER JOY WALLACE, 6940 Marvin D Love Freeway, Dallas, TX 75237
   jwallace@wlgllc.net

President of Memphis Theological Seminary - Ex-officio Member
   REV. JAY EARHEART-BROWN, 866 N McLean Boulevard, Memphis, TN 38107
   jebrown@memphisseminary.edu; (901)278-0367

OTHER DENOMINATIONAL PERSONNEL

REPRESENTATIVES TO:

American Bible Society: REV. MICHAEL SHARPE, 8207 Traditional Place, Cordova, TN 38016

Caribbean and North American Area Council, World Communion of Reformed Churches: STATED CLERK MICHAEL SHARPE, 8207 Traditional Place, Cordova, TN 38016

(Member whose terms expire in 2017)

(2)MS. LAURIE SHARPE, 3423 Summerdale Drive, Bartlett, TN 38133

THE REPORT OF THE MODERATOR

As so many Moderators before me, I feel this report must start by expressing my heartfelt gratitude to the 185th General Assembly for the honor of electing me to serve as Moderator. Although distance and conditions of travel from South America necessarily limited somewhat my presence in presbyteries, I hope I have lived up to the expectations confided in me. I sincerely want to express gratitude to Mike Sharpe who, as Stated Clerk, was invaluable in helping me along the way, as well as to Kip Rush who so ably fulfilled his role as Vice-moderator.

Although travel was somewhat limited, I feel the new possibilities of connecting through social media opened up avenues of communication to overcome geographical circumstances.

Throughout this year, as I met with presbyteries and councils in the United States and Latin America, as I participated in Board meetings and met with individuals and local congregations, I have been:
- enthusiastic about the growth of Memphis Theological Seminary and Bethel College, and their commitment to continued excellence;
- excited about the new mission possibilities opening up in several new countries, and by the response of persons who have perceived and answered a call to serve a missionaries;
- encouraged by presbyteries that motivate their churches to actively participate in our denominational programs through Our United Outreach;
- uplifted as I observed presbyteries shepherd the churches and mentor probationers under their care;
- heartened by presbyteries that stand firm to uphold our doctrinal heritage, refusing to take shortcuts in ministry;
- affirmed in my belief that the Cumberland Presbyterian Church is faithful to its call to extend the Good News of Salvation in Jesus Christ;
- entirely blessed by the opportunity to serve Christ through the Cumberland Presbyterian Church. Thank you for this opportunity.

Having had the unique opportunity to serve our denomination on the Ministry Council before my election as Moderator, this year was an opportunity to observe the ways in which the Council is responding to the needs of the church at large. However, I realize Ministry Council can only work to the capacity of those who actively participate in its processes. Therefore, I would like to offer the following suggestion to presbyteries and local churches instead of a recommendation to General Assembly:

SUGGESTION 1: That both presbyteries and local churches actively recruit and encourage qualified leaders to prayerfully consider opportunities to serve as members of the Ministry Council and the Ministry Teams, submitting their information and recommendation forms in a timely manner to the Nominations Committee.

Be assured I will continue to keep this denomination, its presbyteries, churches and agencies in my prayers.

Respectfully submitted,
Michele Gentry, Moderator,
Moderator of the 185th General Assembly

THE REPORT OF THE STATED CLERK

I. THE OFFICE OF THE STATED CLERK

The Constitution, the Rules of Discipline, the Rules of Order, and the General Assembly Bylaws (found in the front of the General Assembly Minutes) list the many responsibilities for the person who holds the position of Stated Clerk, the primary task is to maintain and strengthen a united witness for the Church. The Stated Clerk shall also generally supervise and control the business affairs of the Corporation, and see that all directives of the General Assembly are implemented.

The Office of the General Assembly also provides budgeting, accounting, and support services for commissions, committees, agencies and task forces without executive assistance.

Additional services and activities provided through the office of the Stated Clerk this past year include:
- Providing assistance to the Unification Task Force
- Developing and maintaining a web presence for the following General Assembly Committees/Commissions without staff: Nominating Committee, Unified Committee on Theology and Social Concerns, Commission on Military Chaplains and Personnel, Our United Outreach Committee and the Unification Task Force.
- Creation of spring and fall Denominational Updates, a compilation of talking points obtained from each board and agency that may be shared by visiting denominational staff and the moderator when making visits to presbyteries and in other settings. The updates are also shared with presbytery clerks.
- Development of a Travel Chart, to assist with the coordination of travel plans by denominational staff to meetings of presbyteries. The travel chart is also shared with presbytery clerks.
- Provided orientation/training to several of the General Assembly boards, agencies and presbyteries on the use of video conferencing technology for their meetings.
- Hosted the annual conference for Presbytery and Synod Clerks.

A significant portion of the Stated Clerk's time has been spent responding to various judicial and legal questions affecting local churches and presbyteries. The Clerk is appreciative for advice provided to this office from both the Permanent Judiciary Committee and from Mr. Jamie Jordan who serves as legal counsel for the Office of the General Assembly.

The Stated Clerk is grateful to the Church for calling him to serve in this position and appreciates the support of the Church for the Office and for the person who holds this position.

II. STAFF

Ms. Elizabeth Vaughn continues to serve as the Assistant to the Stated Clerk, a position that requires her to maintain accurate records of ministers, probationers, congregations, record income and expenses and to authorize payment of all items in the Office of the General Assembly budget. The Church is fortunate to have a person with such knowledge, efficiency and dedication to work. The Stated Clerk and the Assistant to the Stated Clerk are currently the only employees of the Office of the General Assembly.

Reverend Vernon Sansom was elected by the 182nd General Assembly to fill the position of Engrossing Clerk, and began his term of service January 1, 2013. Reverend Sansom is to be commended for the accuracy in recording the minutes of the General Assembly. Vernon also leads the orientation session for those who serve as the chairperson and co-chairperson for each General Assembly appointed Committee and provides valuable assistance in the preparation of committee reports at each meeting of the General Assembly.

III. ECUMENICAL RELATIONSHIPS

The Cumberland Presbyterian Church has always been involved in ecumenical relationships. Through co-operative ministries, chaplains for the military and veteran's hospitals are endorsed, migrant workers and persons in Appalachia are served, and missionaries are sent into a variety of countries. Through ecumenical partnerships disaster relief funds are distributed. Through working co-operatively church school and camping materials are developed. The Cumberland Presbyterian witness is more effective through participation with other Christians in these and various other ministries.

A. CUMBERLAND PRESBYTERIAN CHURCH IN AMERICA

The Cumberland Presbyterian Church in America and the Cumberland Presbyterian Church have one heritage, one Confession of Faith and share in several co-operative relationships and ministries such as the Historical Foundation, the United Board of Christian Discipleship, youth ministry, and the Unified Committee on Theology and Social Concerns. The Cumberland Presbyterian Church in America and the Cumberland Presbyterian Church also participate with other Reformed bodies in ministry. Although working through partnerships, the witness of the Cumberland Presbyterian Church in America and the Cumberland Presbyterian Church would be greatly enhanced through a union of the two denominations.

B. WORLD COMMUNION OF REFORMED CHURCHES

Both The Cumberland Presbyterian Church and the Cumberland Presbyterian Church in a America are members of World Communion of Reformed Churches (WCRC). The WCRC was formed in 2010 by a merger of the World Alliance of Reformed Churches and the Reformed Ecumenical Council. The WCRC represents approximately eighty million members of two hundred thirty denominations from one hundred seven countries, including Reformed, Congregationalists, Presbyterian and United Churches. Resources and updates from the World Communion of Reformed Churches are available on their website: (www.wcrc.ch).

Reverend Christopher Ferguson has been installed as the new general secretary of the WCRC and will office in Hanover, Germany where the headquarters for WCRC is now located. Setri Nyomi, former general secretary, concluded his second and final term (14 years) last summer, was not eligible to serve anther term.

The WCRC meets every seven years. The next meeting of the general Council will be held in Erfurt, Germany, June 2017 and will coincide with the 500th Anniversary of the Reformation. The theme for the 26th general Council is *Living God, Renew and Transform Us* (based on Romans 12:2 and Luke 4:16-19).

IV. REVIEW OF THE COVENANT RELATIONSHIPS

The Covenant Relationship currently in place with both Bethel University and the Cumberland Children's Home requires a review of the relationship at least every five years. In order to reaffirm the relationship and to make any desirable changes, it will be necessary for persons designated by the Board of Trustees of Bethel and the Children's Home to work with persons appointed by the Stated Clerk and Moderator and to report to the 187th General Assembly through the Office of the Stated Clerk.

V. EVALUATION COMMITTEE

The 181st General Assembly formed an committee with the task of evaluating the following entities following the implementation of current denominational structure: Ministry Council, The Board of Stewardship, Foundation and Benefits, the General Assembly Corporate Board. The Committee made its final report to General Assembly in 2013. By action of the 183rd General Assembly, the next evaluation was scheduled to begin this fall (2016) and would also include Memphis Theological Seminary and the Historical Foundation in addition to the enities included in the previous evaluation.

In light of the scheduled review of the Covenant Relationships with both Bethel University and the Cumberland Presbyterian Children's Home this next year, the Office of the General Assembly requests that the Evaluation Committee that was slated to begin it's work in 2016, be delayed for one year.

RECOMMENDATION 1: That the appointment of the Evaluation Committee be postponed until 2017.

VI. THE CORPORATE BOARD

In the called meeting in December 2007, the General Assembly elected a new board of directors for the General Assembly Incorporation. With the merging of program boards into the Ministry Council, trust funds would become more vulnerable in the event the corporation was sued. The General Assembly Bylaws, Article 5 outlines the responsibilities for the Corporate Board.

The corporate board met twice this past year. At the suggestion of the Center Interagency Team and encouragement of the Board of Stewardship, the Board purchased two adjacent lots that were a part of the initial planned office development that comprise the Denominational Center Campus in Memphis. The assessed value for each lot was $71,500. The actual purchase price for both lots was just $60,000. The purchase was made primarily to protect the current value of the Center Property and help serve as a buffer zone between the increased commercial development that borders the property.

The Center Interagency Team (CIT) comprised of the Center's Principle Executive Officers, continues to be responsible for oversight of the day-to-day maintenance and property needs at the Denominational Center. Current CIT members include: Mike Sharpe (Office of the General Assembly), Robert Heflin (Board of Stewardship, Foundation and Benefits), Susan Gore (Historical Foundation), and Edith Old (Ministry Council). The Shared Services budget covers the cost for maintaining the Center offices and property (see page 137).

VII. LEGAL ISSUES

A suit has been brought by two women claiming that improper acts of a sexual nature occurred while they were teenagers attending the Milburn Chapel Church. The suit was brought against individuals from the church as well as the presbytery, synod, and general assembly. The General Assembly has $1,000,000 of insurance coverage and is being defended by trial counsel retained by the insurance company and by the General Assembly's own general counsel. As Stated Clerk, I have been advised by the General Assembly's attorneys not to discuss the facts of the case. The case is in the early stages at this point, but I am keeping the General Assembly's Permanent Committee on the Judiciary advised and will make future reports to GA as necessary.

VIII. MINUTES OF THE GENERAL ASSEMBLY

The Office of the General Assembly continues to make the minutes of the General Assembly available on a CD, and mailing them to persons requesting them. The resource center also prints and sells a few printed copies of the General Assembly Minutes each year. For information contact Matthew Gore, mhg@cumberland.org. It is permissible to download and print a copy of the minutes from the website (www.cumberland.org/gao).

IX. ENDORSEMENT FOR MODERATOR

The Reverend Dwayne Tyus, Nashville Presbytery, has been endorsed by his presbytery as Moderator of the 186th General Assembly.

X. STATISTICAL INFORMATION

The annual congregational report forms are sent to the session clerk on December 1, and due in the office of the Stated Clerk of the Presbytery on February 1, and all reports are to be in the Office of the General Assembly by February 10.

In 2015 a hundred and seventy-nine congregations failed to report, thus statistics are not accurate. The statistics for a non-reporting congregation may be several years old, but it is the latest information available. The General Assembly Office continues to shorten and simplify the reporting process. Efforts also continue to further simplify online reporting for those able to utilize the technology. Hard copies of the report forms will still be made available for those congregations who do not have access to the internet.

The 178th and 179th General Assembly directed "that each presbytery request that its Board of Missions or similar agency, as they minister to the needs of the churches within their presbyteries, remind the churches that it is important that they submit annual reports which are part of our history and offer assistance when needed in preparation of these reports." If a congregation fails to receive a report, a duplicate form can be requested from the Office of the General Assembly or one may be printed from the web site (www.cumberland.org/gao), and going to the section on congregational reports.

Compiled statistical information is available in the annual Yearbook available online (www.cumberland.org/gao) or in print format, available through Cumberland Resource Distribution – resources@cumberland.org (901-276-4581)

VIII. CHURCH CALENDAR 2016-2017

The 182nd General Assembly, directed the Office of the General Assembly to be responsible for reporting the "Church Calendar" to the General Assembly for adoption in 2013 and all future years. Listed below are the dates received from the Boards and Agencies of the denomination.

RECOMMENDATION 2: That the 186th General Assembly approve the following dates for the 2016-2017 Church Calendar:

CHURCH CALENDAR 2016-2017

July-2016
9	Program of Alternate Studies Graduation
9-23	PAS Summer Extension School, Bethel, McKenzie, TN
19-23	Presbyterian Youth Triennium, Purdue University, Lafayette, IN

August-2016
6	BU Commencement
20	MTS Fall Semester Begins
21	Seminary/PAS Sunday
22	BU Fall Semester Begins
28-Sept 25	Christian Education Season
30	BU Spring Convocation

September-2016
3	MTS Opening convocation
11	Senior Adult Sunday
18	Christian Service Recognition Sunday
18	International Day of Prayer and Action for Human Habitat

October-2016
	Clergy Appreciation Month
2	Worldwide Communion Sunday
9	Pastor Appreciation Sunday
23	Native American Sunday

November-2016
	Any Sunday Loaves and Fishes Program
1	All Saints Day
4	World Community Day (Church Women United)
6	Stewardship Sunday
6-9	The Forum
13	Day of Prayer for People with Aids and Other Life-Threatening Illnesses
13	Bible Sunday
20	Christ the King Sunday
27-Dec 25	Advent in Church and Home

December-2016
	Any Sunday Gift to the King Offering
10	BU Commencement
24	Christmas Eve
25	Christmas Day

January-2017
6	Epiphany
9	BU Spring Semester Begins
9-10	Stated Clerks' Conference
11	Human Trafficking Awareness Day
13-16	Faith in 3D
15	Deadline for receipt of 2016 Our United Outreach Contributions
18-20	Ministers Conference, St Columba Conference Center, Bartlett, Tennessee

February-2017
           Black History Month
1   Annual congregational reports due in General Assembly office
4   Denomination Day
5   Historical Foundation Offering
5   Our United Outreach Sunday
5   Souper Bowl Sunday
12   Youth Sunday
24-25   30-Hour Famine

March-2017
           Women's History Month (USA)
1   Ash Wednesday, the beginning of Lent
1–April 16 Lent to Easter
19   Children's Home Sunday
26-April 1 National Farm Workers Awareness Week

April-2017
2-8   Family Week
9   One Great Hour of Sharing
9   Palm/Passion Sunday
13   Maundy Thursday
14   Good Friday
16   Easter
28-29   30-Hour Famine

May-2017
5   Friendship Day (Church Women United)
6   BU Commencement
13   MTS Closing Convocation & Graduation
28   Memorial Day Offering for Military Chaplains & Personnel for USA churches

June-2017
4   Pentecost
4   Stott-Wallace Missionary Fund Offering/World Mission Sunday
19-23   General Assembly
20-22   CPWM Convention
25-30   Cumberland Presbyterian Youth Conference, Bethel University, McKenzie, Tennessee

July-2017
8   Children's Fest
8   Program of Alternate Studies Graduation
8-22   PAS Summer Extension School, Bethel, McKenzie, Tennessee

August-2017
1-Sept 30   Christian Education Season
5   BU Commencement
19   MTS Fall Semester Begins
20   Seminary/PAS Sunday
21   BU Fall Semester Begins
29   BU Spring Convocation
30   MTS Opening convocation

September-2017
10   Senior Adult Sunday
17   Christian Service Recognition Sunday
17   International Day of Prayer and Action for Human Habitat

October-2017

	Clergy Appreciation Month
1	Worldwide Communion Sunday
15	Pastor Appreciation Sunday
22	Native American Sunday

November-2017

	Any Sunday Loaves and Fishes Program
1	All Saints Day
3	World Community Day (Church Women United)
5	Stewardship Sunday
8-11	The Forum
12	Day of Prayer for People with Aids and Other Life-Threatening Illnesses
12	Bible Sunday
26	Christ the King Sunday

December-2017

	Any Sunday Gift to the King Offering
3-25	Advent in Church and Home
9	BU Commencement
24	Christmas Eve
25	Christmas Day

XI. CONTINGENCY FUND

The Stated Clerk is to hold, distribute and report annually the General Assembly Contingency Fund (see Bylaws 8.04, #24). Below is a summary of 2015 Contingency Fund Activity.

Summary of 2015 Activity

Balance Forward 1/1/2015 $ 16,475.95

Income in 2015:
  Our United Outreach/Contributions $16,859.52
  Interest   1,366.33
  Total Income: **$18,225.85**

There were no expenditures in 2015:

Total Fund Balance as of 12/31/15   *$34,701.80

***Restricted Funds:**

$ 4,100.00   The current balance designated by the 178th General Assembly to print the Catechism in the various languages represented in the church.

1,011.51   Pastoral Development Ministry Team/General Assembly Ordination Task Force

Total Amount of *Restricted Funds: $ 5,111.51 (12/31/15)

Total Amount of Unrestricted Amount: $29,590.29 (12/31/15)

Total Fund Balance: $34,701.80 (12/31/15)

Respectfully submitted,
Michael Sharpe, Stated Clerk

THE REPORT ONE OF THE MINISTRY COUNCIL

To the 186th General Assembly of the Cumberland Presbyterian Church in session in Nashville, Tennessee, June 20-24, 2016.

I. MINISTRY COUNCIL

A. INTRODUCTION

The Ministry Council serves as the primary long- and short-range program planning agency of the Church, striving to ensure that all segments work on a unified mission and human and material resources are distributed and utilized to carry out ministries of the Church in an effective manner. The Ministry Council is accountable to the General Assembly.

Due to the scope of the work related to denominational ministries under the Ministry Council (MC) umbrella, our report has historically been lengthy, necessitating division of the report among multiple General Assembly committees. At the urging of the Stated Clerk to limit the report to "recommendations for action and new ministries" and with the desire to provide crucial information in a concise manner, we made significant changes to the format of our report this year. This shorter report focuses on **new ministries** and **recommendations for action** and includes minimal information about ongoing ministries. Supplemental information related to ongoing ministries will be provided to Commissioners and others at General Assembly. This supplemental information is stored in the denomination's archives and at *http://cpcmc.org/mc/ga16-supplement/*. Visitors to our booth at General Assembly may view the Ministry Council website to learn how and where to locate information about all Ministry Council ministries and resources.

Even with a significantly abbreviated report to the General Assembly, it is nonetheless crucial that committees dealing with sections of the report and the entire General Assembly understand that the Ministry Council is one body, made up of interconnected groups: the Ministry Council Board of Directors and four Ministry Teams. While each group has specifically designated responsibilities, the ministries of the Church are accomplished through cooperative effort. To better communicate how the Ministry Council and Ministry Teams function as a unit, we asked that committees that will address sections of the report meet jointly first, allowing time for Ministry Council's representative to General Assembly, Chairperson Reverend Troy Green and four Ministry Team Leaders to present a brief overview of the collaborative work of the Ministry Council.

1. Ministry Council (MC) and Ministry Team (MT) Elected Membership and Terms

Terms of Reverend Jill Carr, Elizabeth Horsley, Gwen Roddye, and Reverend Sam Romines expire in 2016; all have completed three terms and are ineligible for re-election. These four were among the original members of the Ministry Council. The Council expresses its deep appreciation for their dedicated service during the formative/transitional years of the Ministry Council's work. In addition, the Council mourns the loss of Pat Smith, elected in 2015, who was only beginning her work as a Ministry Council member. Terms of Youth Advisory members Carolina Gillis and Emily Mahoney expire in 2016 and they are ineligible for re-election. We express our appreciation to both for their service.

The **Ministry Teams** plan and implement the program ministries of the Church and are made up of Staff and elected Team members. Ministry Teams report to the Ministry Council. **Staff** are employees of the Ministry Council. **Elected Ministry Team members** are elected by the Ministry Council. A complete list of elected members is available on the Ministry Council website. *http://cpcmc.org/mcstaff-nonstaff/*. The Ministry Council website provides information related to training and the covenant agreements by which Ministry Council and Ministry Team members commit to abide.

Ministry Team Staff:
- **Communications Ministry Team (CMT):** Senior Art Director Sowgand Sheikholeslami and CMT Leader Mark J. Davis.
- **Discipleship Ministry Team (DMT):** Coordinator of Children and Family Ministry Jodi Hearn Rush (Nashville, Tennessee office); Coordinator of Youth and Young Adult Ministry Reverend Nathan Wheeler; Coordinator of Adult and Third-Age Ministry Cindy Martin; Coordinator of Resource Development and Distribution Matt Gore; Shipping Clerk Greg Miller; and DMT Leader Reverend Elinor S. Brown.

- **Missions Ministry Team (MMT)**: Coordinator for Women's Ministry and Congregational Ministry Reverend Doctor Pam Phillips-Burk; Director Global Missions Reverend Lynn Thomas (Birmingham, Alabama office); Manager, Finance and Administration Jinger Ellis; Evangelism and New Church Development Reverend T. J. Malinoski; Cross-Culture Immigrant USA Ministry Reverend Johan Daza; Julie Min, part-time Bilingual English-Korean Administrative Assistant; and MMT Leader Reverend Dr. Milton Ortiz.
- **Pastoral Development Ministry Team (PDMT)**: PDMT Leader Reverend Chuck Brown.

2. Global Ministries Leadership Team (GMLT)

GMLT is made up of the Ministry Team Leaders and Director of Ministries. GMLT works together to apply the Ministry Council's vision/mission to many varied programs and resources, coordinating ministries in a unified, collaborative manner.

3. Administration

Director of Ministries, Edith B. Old, provides administrative, financial and human resources to the Teams. The Director is under direct employment of and is responsible to the Ministry Council. The Director gives executive leadership to the Ministry Council in accomplishing duties defined in its Bylaws and supervises the Global Ministries Leadership Team. The Assistant to the Executive Director position is currently vacant due to budget constraints.

B. GENERAL INFORMATION

1. Meetings

Ministry Council has met twice in regular session since the 185th General Assembly. Summaries of Action for all Ministry Council meetings are at *http://cpcmc.org/mc/soa/*. The current formula for meetings: last full weekend in January; 3rd weekend of April unless it coincides with Easter; and last full weekend in August. **Future Meetings - August 26 (Fri)** in the Memphis area – Orientation for **newly-elected Ministry Council/ Ministry Team Members. August 27-28 (Sat-Sun)** in the Memphis area – Ministry Council and Ministry Teams (all members) meet concurrently.

RECOMMENDATION 1: That the 186th General Assembly amend the Ministry Council Bylaws, ARTICLE III, BOARD OF DIRECTORS, AUTHORITY, AND MEETINGS, Section E., Meetings "The board of directors shall meet at least three times annually upon the call of the president or secretary . . ." to "The board of directors shall meet a least twice a year upon the call of the president or secretary . . ." beginning in 2017. (MC Bylaws online at http://cpcmc.org/mc/bylaws/)

2. Denominational Leadership Pool

We express appreciation to the Nominating Committee of the General Assembly, challenged to match leaders to boards in keeping with required quotas and the even more vital challenge of trying to match leaders with specific spiritual gifts to areas of need. We believe God calls people across the denomination to servant leadership; the limited number of applicants on file does not reflect the abundance of qualified leaders within the church. For boards and agencies to work effectively, the Nominating Committee needs the greatest possible number of qualified leaders to consider. This year, a record five new members (a full 1/3 of the voting membership) will be elected to the Council.

RECOMMENDATION 2: That the 186th General Assembly urge each congregation and presbytery to proactively recruit and encourage qualified leaders to prayerfully consider opportunities to serve as elected board members at the denominational level, to include the Ministry Council and all other denominational entities.

II. MINISTRIES

A. ONGOING MINISTRIES

Ongoing ministries are detailed in the supplement given to all Commissioners to this General Assembly and may be downloaded at *http://cpcmc.org/mc/ga16-supplement/*. The one ongoing ministry for which the Ministry Council requests action is the **Certificate in Cumberland Presbyterian (CP) Studies**:

In June 2014 and January 2015, PDMT partnered with Memphis Theological Seminary (MTS) to offer Advanced CP Studies. A Spanish interpreter was present to assist 8 Spanish-speaking students. Since the initial class, the steering committee revamped the program, which will now be a Certificate in CP Studies. The complete program will be offered in January 2017 and January 2018. A Korean interpreter will assist Korean-speaking students. It is the steering committee's intention to solicit at least one participant from each presbytery. To that end, the Ministry Council makes the following recommendation:

RECOMMENDATION 3: That the 186th General Assembly urge each presbytery to budget funds in both 2017 and 2018 to send one participant to the Certificate in CP Studies program.

B. NEW MINISTRIES

1. In addition to activities for youth, children and families at General Assembly, this year there will be **activities for Young Adults at General Assembly:** Young Adults will have several opportunities during the week at GA to get together and fellowship with one another. Third Age adults will also have that opportunity and to talk about what adults need from the church.

2. Kaleo (pronounced Ka-Le-Ho): Collaborative effort among Pastoral Development Ministry Team, Discipleship Ministry Team and Memphis Theological Seminary. This event will be for young people who have heard the call of God and are discerning their calling. A grant proposal was submitted for funding for this event. If the grant is not available, plans are to launch the event in June 2017 with alternate funding.

3. CPYC Brand: Joanna Wilkinson, graphic artist and a Discipleship Ministry Team elected member, designed a new CPYC branding logo. The image is a triquetra, trefoil knot or trinity knot (3-cornered knot.) Three colors of interwoven trinity knots represent three key words (friends, fellowship and faith); when pulled, you have a friendship knot. We hope it will carry on for years as a symbol of what CPYC is and needs to be.

4. New Church Developments (NCDs): Mission Ministry Team is committed to starting new churches as an effective means of evangelism, providing encouragement, guidance, regular contact, administrative and financial support and supervision. Mission Ministry Team assists 19 NCDs in the US (9 Cross-Culture) and 3 overseas.

New Exploration Initiatives (NEI) explore a geographical area where there is no Cumberland Presbyterian presence, secure leadership, and gather a group for study, fellowship and worship. As the NEI grows, Mission Ministry Team approaches the respective presbytery to partner on an New Church Development. This new focus is designed to free the presbytery from initial fears of starting something new and from the financial burden of determining if an New Church Development is feasible that often discourage presbyteries and its agencies from pursuing new endeavors. Two NEIs are in process in the United States. **New Church Starters Recruitment and Training**: The offices of Evangelism and New Church Development and Cross-Culture Immigrant Ministries USA Program diligently provide guidance and support to current New Church Development leaders within the USA. To address the need for education, fellowship and recruitment, Missions Ministry Team is planning a Church Starters Conference to provide education and fellowship opportunities for current leaders and offer encouragement and assistance to those who may hear God's call to be a church starter.

RECOMMENDATION 4: That the 186th General Assembly urge each presbytery to budget funds in 2017 for current and potential new church development leaders to attend a Church Starters Conference hosted by the MMT in fall 2017.

5. Church Assimilation: The Cumberland Presbyterian Church is open to receiving churches from other ecclesiastical bodies. The Constitution of the Cumberland Presbyterian Church in section 10.0 includes guidelines for receiving churches under provisional status. While under the supervision of a presbytery, a church can have official representation at the presbyterial level. Missions Ministry Team is aware of at least nine presbyteries that have reported working with both English- and non-English speaking congregations under provisional status in the USA. Church assimilation through the provisional status is one method to assist denominational growth of the Cumberland Presbyterian Church.

RECOMMENDATION 5: That, in an effort to broaden Cumberland Presbyterian ministry within the United States, the 186th General Assembly encourage presbyteries to invite and welcome churches interested in assimilation into the Cumberland Presbyterian Church and to seek guidance from Missions Ministry Team for information and counsel.

6. Evangelism Training: Evangelism training is promoted, planned and conducted to encourage, inspire and inform churches and their leaders for the purpose of sharing the good news of Jesus Christ. Numerical growth for the local church is a secondary outcome of its primary design for evangelistic purposes and efforts. On request, evangelism training and workshops are held for the local church, groups of churches and presbyteries. There is great need for presbyteries to strengthen all churches within its bounds for both evangelistic development and growth.

RECOMMENDATION 6: That the 186th General Assembly recommend that presbyteries encourage local churches within their bounds to invite Missions Ministry Team to hold evangelism training for the local church and groups of churches for the purpose of encouraging and equipping church leaders and members in sharing the good news of Jesus Christ with others and providing empowering methods and means that people can apply in their context.

7. Global Social Action: A new Hot Lunch Program was started in **Guatemala** using the Loaves and Fishes offering to fund a 3-year program that will feed, provide healthcare, tutoring and Bible classes to a select group of 15 children.

8. Newly-Endorsed Cumberland Presbyterian (CP) Missionaries: John and Joy Park were deployed to the Philippines in January 2016. John will work with new church development and leadership development in Iloilo, Philippines. **Jacob and Lindsey Sims** applied to be endorsed CP missionaries and work in Brazil as church planters. It is our hope they will be in Brazil by early 2017. **Patrick and Jessica Wilkerson** applied to be endorsed CP missionaries and work in Latin America. The place of their service is still being explored. They hope to be on the mission field later in 2017 or early 2018. **There are currently 17 missionaries working for the CP Church and an additional 4 CP missionaries working with interdenominational mission organizations.** To learn more visit *http://cpcmc.org/mmt/missionaries/*.

9. New Mission Fields: Missions Ministry Team approved **Haiti** as a new mission field. Hope Presbytery is hosting the work that consists of six provisional churches and six candidates for the ministry. Missions Ministry Team approved the formation of a council of churches to help coordinate the work in Haiti. Missions Ministry Team will work with Progam of Alternate Studies to find ways to train candidates in Haiti. Missions Ministry Team approved **Australia** as a new mission field. Missions Ministry Team organized a council of churches in Australia that consists of six Korean provisional churches and five provisional pastors. Missions Ministry Team has promoted Progam of Alternate Studies classes in Australia to help the new pastors and churches. The Koza Cumberland Presbyterian Church established a satellite ministry 50 years ago to meet the needs of Japanese Cumberland Presbyterian immigrants living in **Brazil**. The church that was established eventually became part of Japan Presbytery. As the years passed, the church became more and more Brazilian in attendance and language. In early 2016, Japan Presbytery asked Missions Ministry Team to assume responsibility for the work in Brazil and to recognize it as a new mission field of the Cumberland Presbyterian Church. It is no longer a Japanese immigrant ministry; it is a Brazilian congregation with Portuguese as the primary language. Missions Ministry Team is working with the Cumberland Presbyterian Church in Brazil, helping develop Brazilian leadership and looking at new ways to plant more Cumberland Presbyterian churches to reach the people in Brazil.

10. Young CPW New Initiative: Two events were held in February 2015 to consider a new approach to women's ministry with a specific focus upon needs and involvement of young women – post-high school to age 35. The overwhelmingly positive response led to calling a consultant for this new initiative: Abby Prevost, a candidate for the ministry from Grace Presbytery, who serves as youth director at Flat Lick Cumberland Presbyterian Church in Hopkinsville, Kentucky, while attending Memphis Theological Seminary. A retreat was held in west Tennessee in February 2016 with 24 young women present. A similar retreat is planned for October 2016 in east Tennessee. The goal is to hold two regional retreats a year in order to build community and establish a sustained ministry.

RECOMMENDATION 7: That the 186th General Assembly recommend that each presbytery appoint a young woman to represent their presbytery at one of these events and serve as a point of contact between the Young Women Planning Team and the presbytery.

11. Work with Presbyterial Boards of Missions: In an effort to partner closely with presbyterial Boards of Missions in their work, Missions Ministry Team is planning a two-day event in spring 2017 near Memphis, Tennessee. The **Listening to the Spirit–Serving with Conviction** event will invite participants to envision new ways to offer support and guidance to small or struggling churches and to churches searching for pastoral leadership, as well as permit Boards of Missions to explore ways to assist churches in becoming more engaged in missions in their communities and around the world.

RECOMMENDATION 8: That the 186th General Assembly recommend that each presbytery include a line item in their 2017 budget to send two or more representatives from their Board of Missions to the event. Cost per person is approximately $100.

12. Choctaw Ministries: Dating back to 1819, ministry with the Choctaws served as the first mission of the Cumberland Presbyterian Church. Choctaw Presbytery is the only remaining indigenous Native American governing body among all mainline traditions. The presbytery consists of seven churches and four ordained ministers in southeastern Oklahoma. Ministry in this area is challenging with 22-27% of its population below the poverty level according to census bureau statistics. There is a renewed emphasis in ministry with Choctaw Cumberland Presbyterians. The office of Evangelism and New Church Development met with Choctaw Presbytery three times in 2016 to develop short- and long-range planning based upon Choctaw-identified needs including church building repair and maintenance, leadership for and within the presbytery, programming aimed specifically for Choctaw youth and young adults, and new church developments within the geographic reach of the presbytery.

RECOMMENDATION 9: That the 186th General Assembly encourage churches, presbyteries and synods to be in prayer and become actively involved in the mission to and with Choctaw Cumberland Presbyterians to address immediate needs and future planning.

13. Japanese Christian Church: Cumberland Presbytery, Japan Presbytery and Missions Ministry Team worked with the New Church Development to form **the first Japanese Cumberland Presbyterian Church in the United States** (organized September 2015) and the first Japanese church in Louisville, Kentucky. We praise God for the beginning and future of the Japanese Christian Church as an organized Cumberland Presbyterian Church.

14. Interculturality Internship Opportunities: *"Interculturality"* is building relationships between/among two or more cultures to find mutuality in the midst of diversity and differences. The majority of cross-culture churches need particular English-speaking ministries. These might focus on adults, young adults, youth, or children who are bilingual (for some, English is their first language). There are currently more than 50 different cross-culture ministries among churches, New Church Developments, New Exploration Initiatives and presbyteries, (Choctaw Presbytery and East Coast Korean Presbytery), offering potential intercultural fields for internships. English-speaking seminary/Program of Alternate Studies students, planters, or laypersons interested in approaching a culture other than their own may apply for a short-term intercultural internship. Missions Ministry Team will post opportunities and send invitations to apply. Contact Johan Daza at *JDaza@cumberland.org* or T.J. Malinoski at *TMalinoski@cumberland.org*.

RECOMMENDATION 10: That the 186th General Assembly encourage Boards of Mission (or their equivalent) in United States presbyteries to fund intercultural internship opportunities among probationers, ordained ministers or lay persons within those presbyteries who might be interested in participating in one of the cross-culture ministries in the United States.

15. Digital Publications – Beginning fall 2016, The Cumberland PRESBYTERIAN magazine will offer a digital subscription (*http://cpcmc.org/cpmag-subscribe/*). Communications Ministry Team is also moving toward transforming *The Missionary Messenger into a digital publication. Both publications would be in both print and digital formats for the foreseeable future.*

16. A Program Planning Calendar (PPC) is now included in every subscription to The Cumberland Presbyterian magazine. The PPC will ship with the July or August 2016 issue. A limited number of copies of the PPC will be available for one-off purchase.

17. Audio/Visual Services: Communications Ministry Team now offers Audio/Visual documentation services. A successful live audio feed of portions of the 185th General Assembly held in Cali, Colombia, made it accessible to Cumberland Presbyterians unable to attend the event. The 2016 Ministers Conference, held at the Brenthaven Cumberland Presbyterian Church in Brentwood, Tennessee, was videotaped. The three lecture videos were made available on the Ministry Council website during March 2016; a DVD set of both the lectures and two of the three sermons is available for purchase at $25.00 per set (includes s/h). We anticipate extending this service to include meetings, seminars, conferences, and other Cumberland Presbyterian gatherings, to benefit those who cannot physically attend. Contact *cmt@cumberland.org* for more information.

18. Ministry Council website, Facebook, Twitter: The Ministry Council launched a redesigned website in January 2016. Built on the popular open-source blogging platform Wordpress, the site offers much greater flexibility in adding new features. At launch, it included a revamped "Find a Church" feature; fully hyper-linked copy of the Confession of Faith (*http://cpcmc.org/cof/*), Constitution, and Order of Worship, with hyper-linked scripture references; a dynamic and downloadable Program Planning Calendar (*http://cpcmc.org/events/month/*); and automatic links to social media outlets. Visit (*http://cpcmc.org*) for resources, news and information, event registration, blogs, announcements, and links of interest to Cumberland Presbyterians. Visit the Ministry Council, Discipleship Ministry Team, and Missions Ministry Team on Facebook. Follow @MinistryCouncil on Twitter.

III. FUNDING

A. OUR UNITED OUTREACH (OUO)

Diminished returns on investments and shortfalls in OUO adversely affected the Ministry Council budget. In the process, several important points were articulated:

*Ministry Council, Ministry Teams and Team Leaders make every effort to stay within our means, which results in continually having to make cuts and revise plans due to underfunding.

*Ministry Council/Ministry Team staff feel called to our ministries and have voluntarily foregone salary increases and travel reimbursements; unlike some other denominational entities, the Ministry Council no longer underwrites dependent health insurance benefits.

*More than ever before, Ministry Teams share in planning, facilitating, and funding, and without that cooperative effort, more positions and ministries would have to be cut. Missions Ministry Team and Discipleship Ministry Team frequently cover expenses of the other teams when revenue is short resulting in serious adverse cash flow; these two teams have modest flexibility to do this since they have ILPs (investment loan accounts) from which transfers can be made. This too affects cash flow, pulling from undesignated/invested funds. This is not a long-term solution as these funds are not limitless.

January is an especially difficult month: for the second year in a row NO Our United Outreach distribution was made during the month, a result of carrying over the previous year's Our United Outreach contributions into mid-January (a 2016 bank holiday pushed the closing date for 2015 to January 20, 2016.) Every year, Missions Ministry Team and Discipleship Ministry Team transfer funds from ILPs to cover Ministry Council expenses, including the January meeting of Ministry Council/Ministry Teams. Ministry Council continues reduce meeting costs, but many other expenses cannot be reduced.

RECOMMENDATION 11: As many churches do not consider giving to Our United Outreach as a tithe as it was envisioned, and that a number of churches do not contribute anything to Our United Outreach, that General Assembly prayerfully consider and recommend opportunities to significantly revitalize Our United Outreach. Opportunities might include but not be limited to setting the deadline for Our United Outreach contributions "to be postmarked by December 31".

B. ENDOWMENTS

Endowments help significantly to fund ministries. Donations to the following would allow them to begin to support ministry. Contact esb@cumberland.org to donate.

Need: $ 469.88	Christian Education Programs	Endowment No. 806330	Giving For Good	Level to reach: $3,000
Need: $ 911.35	Christian Education Programs	Endowment No. 806140	Jean Garrett	Level to reach: $5,000
Need: $2,567.30	Children's Ministry	Endowment No. 806370	Jake Tyler Children's Ministry	Level to reach: $5,000
Need: $449	General Support -Missions	Endowment No. 804150	Jose & Fanny Fajardo	Level to reach: $10,000
Need: $1,055	Missionary Magazine	Endowment No. 803400	Marguerite D. Richards	Level to reach: $10,000
Need: $1,565	General Support -Missions	Endowment No. 804200	Freda Mitchell Gilbert	Level to reach: $10,000
Need: $1,720	General Support -Missions	Endowment No. 804300	Rubye Johnson May	Level to reach: $10,000
Need: $ 5,190.52	Awards/Encouragement – CPC/CPCA Students at MTS	Endowment No. 810010	R & R Baugh	Level to reach: $10,000
Need: $ 8,466.01	Scholarships for Conference (Oklahoma, Red River Pres. & far away)	Endowment No. 810020	L Brown (Beth Brown)	Level to reach: $10,000

A complete list of all Ministry Council/Ministry Team endowments, including those highlighted above appears within the Board of Stewardship section of the preliminary Minutes.

IV. MINISTRY COUNCIL CONCLUSION

This is an exciting time to be engaged in ministry in the Cumberland Presbyterian Church. We are embracing a truly global identity and new technology that puts the whole world at our doorstep. We see a new generation of Cumberland Presbyterians serving in leadership roles throughout the church. We pray for a day when the Ministry Council and Ministry Teams can focus on the excitement of spreading the Word throughout the world without the constant pressure of limited human and financial resources influencing every decision. We would welcome an opportunity to do ministry in a culture of abundance, when Cumberland Presbyterians everywhere commit to sharing in the work of the church by supporting Our United Outreach and when leaders rise up from all across the denomination to further the work of the church around the world.

The Ministry Council elected members and staff remain committed to serving God through the Cumberland Presbyterian Church and ask that the Church remain in prayer for our work. We are thankful for the guidance of the Holy Spirit as we work to enhance and implement ministries that draw people to Christ.

Respectfully Submitted,
The Ministry Council of the CPC
Reverend Sam Romines, President
Reverend Lanny Johnson, First Vice President
Reverend Jill Carr, Second Vice President
Adam McReynolds, Secretary
Edith B. Old, Director of Ministries/Treasurer

THE REPORT NUMBER TWO OF THE MINISTRY COUNCIL

To the 186th General Assembly of the Cumberland Presbyterian Church in session in Nashville, Tennessee, June 20-24, 2016.

I. INTRODUCTION

The Ministry Council Corporation Annual Meeting of the Board of Directors was April 15 and 16, 2016, after the March 15 deadline for board/agency reports to be submitted to General Assembly. Summaries of Action of all Ministry Council meetings are at *http://cpcmc.org/mc/soa/*.

II. RECOMMENDATIONS

A. LEADERSHIP REFERRAL SERVICES

Since 1949, when the denomination began assisting ministers and congregations in the search process, the Missions Ministry Team and its predecessor have had responsibility for this important work in our denomination. From the time the Commission on the Ministry (now Pastoral Development Ministry Team) hired its first full-time employee, the person in that role has worked with Missions Ministry Team to assist with ministers who needed special assistance in the discernment process of following God's Call.

Since 2007, when the Ministry Council was formed, we have worked diligently to unite the work of the various teams into a more cohesive whole. With the launch of the new web-based Leadership Referral Services (LRS), there has been some improvement in efficiency, but there has been a growing concern that there needs to be continuing human interaction in the process. While the Missions Ministry Team has a long history of working with congregations through the search process, there has been a growing sense that there is a need for increasing the services to our clergy who may be discerning a need to pursue a new phase in their Call. Because the Pastoral Development Ministry Team has the responsibility of working with ordained clergy and probationers in our denomination, and in an attempt to better meet the needs of our clergy and our congregations as they navigate the search process, the Ministry Council is recommending the following change in the LRS system.

Pastoral Development Ministry Team Leader Reverend Chuck Brown will assume primary responsibility for LRS and will work closely with ministers through the search process. In the event that a congregation could be aided by the specialized help of the Missions Ministry Team, a member of that staff will be called on to provide assistance to the congregation from a Missions perspective.

RECOMMENDATION 1: That the 186thGeneral Assembly approve shifting primary responsibility for the Leadership Referral Services (LRS) from the Missions Ministry Team to the Pastoral Development Ministry Team effective August 1, 2016.

B. GUIDELINES FOR CONGREGATIONS CONSIDERING MERGER

Recognizing the trend of numerical decline of church membership coupled with the increased action of presbyteries closing individual churches, the office of Evangelism and New Church Development has designed a manual for churches and presbyteries for use when merging two or more congregations. Merging congregations into one new church may be seen as an opportunity for new ministry and an alternative to closing churches. The brief manual provides general steps for considering merger with another congregation, including motivations and benefits for merging. A process has been developed with implementation for a plan of union of two or more congregations with the purpose of becoming a new church. (See Appendix)

RECOMMENDATION 2: That the 186th General Assembly adopt the manual entitled Guidelines for Congregations Considering Merger to assist churches and presbyteries interested in merging Cumberland Presbyterian churches to strengthen their worship, study and witness to the gospel.

C. GLOBAL INSTITUTIONS

The Cumberland Presbyterian Church is a global denomination with churches, presbyteries, councils, and institutions in countries around the world. Each year the General Assembly hears reports from institutions with historical connections to the Cumberland Presbyterian Church. These stateside institutions report directly to the Cumberland Presbyterian Church via General Assembly as to their progress, needs, and accomplishments. Bethel University, Historical Foundation, Memphis Theological Seminary and the Children's Home are the only institutions that currently send representatives and reports to General Assembly. However, there are other large and important Cumberland Presbyterian institutions outside the USA that do not have the opportunity to tell the General Assembly their stories of successful ministry in the name of the Cumberland Presbyterian Church. We have schools in South America and Asia that are directly owned and operated by their presbyteries. These schools and institutions openly promote themselves as part of the Cumberland Presbyterian Church and in fact the leadership of these institutions is selected by a Cumberland Presbyterian presbytery.

The fact is our presbyteries outside the USA supervise the schools and institutions within their presbytery and these presbyteries are part of the General Assembly. These institutions do have a direct relationship to General Assembly and decisions made by General Assembly directly impact these institutions. It is of value to all Cumberland Presbyterians that all Cumberland Presbyterian institutions have access to the General Assembly. The reality is the Cumberland Presbyterian Church is much larger than the four institutions we have historically recognized. In some cases the General Assembly was directly involved in the formation of these institutions through its mission agency. The Cumberland Presbyterian institutions outside the USA should have the right to present reports or send representatives to General Assembly to report to the appropriate General Assembly Committee. All Cumberland Presbyterians would benefit from information shared at General Assembly from all of our institutions. As in the USA, these schools and institutions provide valuable leadership and resources that benefit the Church. By being connected to General Assembly they can be a helpful influence and source of information to Cumberland Presbyterians in those countries where they exist. The expense and distance may make it difficult for institutions outside the USA to send representatives each year to General Assembly, but they could send written reports to General Assembly.

RECOMMENDATION 3: That the 186thGeneral Assembly give institutions that have a direct relationship (legal and/or expected to report) to a presbytery outside the USA the privilege of sending reports and/or representatives to General Assembly and that these institution's reports and/or representatives be assigned to a Committee of General Assembly.

III. MINISTRY COUNCIL CONCLUSION

We encourage all Commissioners to the 186th General Assembly and guests to "get recharged" at the Ministry Council booth in the exhibit area. The booth will offer a charging station for visitors to charge their phones and tablets while viewing live demonstrations of the Ministry Council's new website and the new Stott-Wallace video. The booth will also offer a wide variety of print materials to take back and share with congregations, groups and presbyteries. Ministry Council and Ministry Team (MT) staff and elected members serve as able booth hosts, eager to listen to ideas and concerns and to answer questions. We invite Commissioners and guests to actively seek out opportunities for ministry and to communicate ministry needs and challenges to the Ministry Council/Ministry Teams.

The 52 Ministry Council/Ministry Team elected members and 17 staff members remain committed to serving as conduits of information to and from the Council. Ministry Council/Ministry Team elected members and staff remain committed to serving God through the Cumberland Presbyterian Church and ask that the Church remain in prayer for our collaborative work. We are thankful for the guidance of the Holy Spirit as we work to enhance and implement ministries that draw people to Christ.

Respectfully Submitted,
The Ministry Council of the Cumberland Presbyterian Church
Rev. Sam Romines, President
Rev. Lanny Johnson, First Vice President
Rev. Jill Carr, Second Vice President
Adam McReynolds, Secretary
Edith B. Old, Director of Ministries/Treasurer

Cumberland Presbyterian Church
Missions Ministry Team

GUIDELINES FOR CHURCHES CONSIDERING MERGER
(Amalgamation)

T. J. Malinoski, Evangelism and New Church Development

Table of Contents
Introduction
- I. Considering Merger with Another Church
    - A. Self Assessment/Discernment Process
    - B. Motivations for Merger
- II. The Steps, Process and Implementation
    - A. A Theological Basis for Becoming a New Church
    - B. Initiating the Process
    - C. Discovering Compatibility
    - D. Roles and Responsibilities of Judicatories, Committees and Agencies
        - i. Roles and Responsibilities of Presbytery
        - ii. Roles and Responsibilities of Individual Sessions
        - iii. Roles and Responsibilities of Steering Committee
        - iv. Roles and Responsibilities of Joint Session
        - v. Roles and Responsibilities of the Missions Ministry Team
- III. The Plan of Union

    Agreement for Organizing Merged Churches
    Article I - Name
    Article II - Incorporation
    Article III - Session
    Article IV - Administrative Infrastructure
    Article V - Program Infrastructure
    Article VI - Ministerial Leadership
    Article VII - Church Staff
    Article VIII - Location
    Article IX – Ratification
- IV. Frequently Asked Questions

Appendix – Organization of a Particular Church, Admission of a New Church and Contact Information

INTRODUCTION

The Constitution of the Cumberland Presbyterian Church identifies a church as *a congregation of professing Christians, together with their baptized children, who have entered into a covenant agreement with each other to meet together regularly to worship God and study the word of God, to join together in a common witness to the gospel, and to engage in good works to which Christians are called; and who have adopted a certain form of government* (2.01). There are growing opportunities within the Cumberland Presbyterian Church where a church discovers that a group of professing Christians may enhance and strengthen their worship, study, witness to the gospel, and efforts of good works by merging with another Cumberland Presbyterian congregation.

The Missions Ministry Team recognizes that churches may be interested in merging with another Cumberland Presbyterian congregation. Terms such as *merger* and *union* are common words used to describe the process. The term *amalgamation* meaning the action, process or result of combining or uniting better describes the process of two or more churches coming together to make one. However, most will be more familiar with the terminology of *merger* and *union* therefore these terms will be used throughout the document. These guidelines have been developed as advisory steps to assist in a discernment process, exploratory meetings, roles and responsibilities of various agencies and groups, a plan of union and implementation.

I. CONSIDERING MERGER WITH ANOTHER CHURCH

A. SELF-ASSESSMENT/DISCERNMENT PROCESS

Determining if merger is right for your church requires self-assessment and discernment. The difficult task of assessing where your church is as you consider merger should not be overlooked. The needs of the physical structure and maintenance of the church facility can be daunting and difficult to ascertain. Flaking paint in the sanctuary, classrooms converted for storage or no longer used, dated appliances and furniture are examples to look for in your facilities. Areas of programming infrastructure may include discerning for a lack of children's ministry, outreach limited to homebound members or occasional events, plateau or loss of church membership, diminished budget assets, and lack of lay leadership at both the church and presbyterial levels. Below are a few general steps to consider in a discernment process for considering merger with another church:

- Reflect honestly on the current ministries in your church.

- List the things that you value about the way conditions currently are.

- List the things that you are concerned about for your church.

- Imagine the possibilities of what two or more churches could do together.

- Reflect on the church history of securing and retaining ministerial leadership.

- Compile a list of membership gains from the past ten years.

- Identify the financial status of the church's assets.

- Discuss where your church is going – goals, plans, visions, ideas.

- Discuss where you see your church in five years, ten years, fifteen years.

B. MOTIVATIONS FOR MERGER

Determining if merger is right for your church requires vision for the future. Motivations for a merger can be fear for survival, loss of membership, loss of income, difficulties in retaining ministerial leadership, aging facilities, and changes in the surrounding community. Motivations for a merger with another church may also have its advantages. Combined numbers in worship creates energy and communicates to others that there is a strong commitment to the worship of God. Merging churches will enhance children's groups and programs, assisting members through life transitions. In the area of personnel, a combined budget will allow for adequate staffing to resource areas of ministry, and a larger commitment to missions and outreach.

Considering Possible Merger – Concerns and Benefits
Examples –

Concerns:
- Plateau or loss of membership.
- Adequacy of current facilities versus new facility.
- Combining staff, church sessions and Sunday School classes.
- Name change.

Benefits:
- Growth potential – existing and new membership.
- Combined resources – members and finances.
- Enhanced worship experience.
- More opportunities for children, youth, and young adult activities.
- Adequately assisting individuals through various life transitions.
- Increased mission opportunities – local, regional, international.
- New excitement about existing and new ministries.
- Creating a stronger Christian presence in the local community.
- Creating a new church.
- Maximizing the use of church facility.

II. THE STEPS, PROCESS AND IMPLEMENTATION

A. A THEOLOGICAL BASIS FOR BECOMING A NEW CHURCH

For everything there is a season, and a time for every matter under heaven: a time to be born, and a time to die; a time to plant, and a time to pluck up what is planted; a time to kill, and a time to heal; a time to break down, and a time to build up; a time to weep, and a time to laugh; a time to mourn, and a time to dance; a time to throw away stones, and a time to gather stones together; a time to embrace, and a time to refrain from embracing; a time to seek, and a time to lose; a time to keep, and a time to throw away; a time to tear, and a time to sew; a time to keep silence, and a time to speak; a time to love, and a time to hate; a time for war, and a time for peace.   Ecclesiastes 3:1-8 NRSV

So if anyone is in Christ, there is a new creation; everything old has passed away; see everything has become new!   2 Corinthians 5:17 NRSV

The merger of two or more churches is, in essence, creating a new church. This church may be the blending of membership and resources into one. From a polity standpoint, a new church is being formed. There is a theological basis for merger as the writer of Ecclesiastes portrays life having transitions and seasons. The life of the church also has seasons of being planted, building, and even dying. We celebrate and mourn the life transitions of the church in the midst of change and also in the reflection of a church's lifespan and ministry. The merger of churches is to be seen and experienced as finding new life and becoming a new creation in Christ. Where two or more churches merge to become one, those churches have participated in God's gracious way of allowing old things to pass away making all things new.

B.   INITIATING THE PROCESS

The process may be initiated by the presbyterial Board of Missions or the Session of a particular church. Members of the church, the ministerial leadership of the church, or the Missions Ministry Team may approach a presbyterial Board of Missions or a Session to begin the conversation. However, the process can begin officially only through the two aforementioned judicatories. Any church considering a merger with another church will report the interest to the presbyterial Board of Missions and seek presbytery assistance.

C.   DISCOVERING COMPATIBILTY

Discovering the compatibility of churches is crucial for a merger. Each church has its own uniqueness: personality, approach to ministry, understanding God's Word, and expression of celebrating their relationship with God through worship. Churches considering merger must determine if they are theologically comparable, if the style of worship is similar, if their expectations of the minister are alike, and how programming within the churches is accomplished. This discovery can be tried through joint worship experiences, sharing facilities, combined programming, such as Vacation Bible School and sharing fellowship opportunities.

D.   ROLES AND RESPONSIBILITIES OF JUDICATORIES, COMMITTEES AND AGENCIES

<u>Roles and Responsibilities of Presbytery</u>

The presbytery will:

1. Appoint the presbyterial Board of Missions or a task force in the exploration of possible merger and make recommendations that a merger is both desirable and feasible.

2. Facilitate, through the presbyterial Board of Missions or appointed task force, the individual Sessions, steering committee and joint session in the exploration of and/or merger process.

3. Report regularly, through the presbyterial Board of Missions or appointed task force, to inform presbytery of progress.

4. The presbyterial Board of Missions or appointed task force will provide continued oversight and guidance of the merger process.

5. Recommend a plan of union through the presbyterial Board of Missions or appointed task force for consideration and approval.

<u>Roles and Responsibilities of Individual Sessions</u>

The Session will:

1. Consider the possibility of merger with other Cumberland Presbyterian congregation(s). Note: This consideration would imagine the possibilities of what two or more churches can do together.

2. Contact presbyterial Board of Missions (or its judiciary equivalent) for guidance, suggestions and input on merger. Note: The Session can also contact the Missions Ministry Team of the Cumberland Presbyterian Church for guidance.

3. Vote to pursue a conversation with other churches through a steering committee. Note: The steering committee will be composed of three active elders, one at larger member and the moderator of Session from each particular church.

4. Receive regular updates and reports from members of the steering committee.

5. Vote on the plan of union presented by the steering committee.

6. Inform the church, both verbally and by providing copies of the plan of union document and any additional documentation of the merger process, the concerns and benefits and ask for input.

7. Establish criteria/requirements of active membership for those who will vote on merger. Example: Active membership is one who has attended church at least one time per quarter, those who have made a financial contribution to the church and home-bound members can vote (non-binding) on the plan of union.

8. Compile list of active members and send the plan of union to the membership.

9. Seek the opinion of those in the church who are not members and encourage them to express their opinion concerning merger.

10. Encourage concerned individuals to express opinions in writing to the Session about the plan of union.

11. Choose a moderator and set a date for a congregational meeting for a non-binding vote on merger. Note: The moderator is to state the purpose of the meeting, share information on the plan of union, accept questions and statements about the plan of union.

12. Record the votes from the congregational meeting.

13. Vote on the plan of union after congregational vote is taken. Note: This vote can be taken during the Joint Session meeting.

Roles and Responsibilities of Steering Committee

The Steering Committee will:
1. Develop, review, and amend plan of union for the churches with the assistance of the presbytery.

2. Members of steering committee will report out regularly to the respective Session of their church.

3. Present the plan of union to the Sessions of the churches interested in merger.

4. Present the plan of union to the presbyterial Board of Missions or task force.

5. Organize a date for joint worship experiences alternating congregational worship spaces.

6. Organize fellowship activities for the churches to participate in.

Roles and Responsibilities of Joint Session

The Joint Session will:
1. Provide congregational voting results on merger.

2. Vote on the plan of union.

3. Dissolve steering committee.

4. Present the plan of union and the vote of merger to the presbyterial Board of Missions or the equivalent judicatory body.

Roles and Responsibilities of the Missions Ministry Team

The Missions Ministry Team will:

The Missions Ministry Team may be called upon to assist the presbytery, the Session, the steering committee or the joint session in an advisory role. Note: This call can assist in the self-assessment/discernment process of the local churches exploring the possibility of merger, input on community demographics, guidance in the merger process and implementation of the plan of union.

III. THE PLAN OF UNION

Agreement For Organizing Merged Churches

The following are articles of agreement to create a new church by uniting _____ and _____ Cumberland Presbyterian Churches. The purpose of this union is to provide for a strengthened Cumberland Presbyterian witness of professing Christians, together with their baptized children, who are entering into a covenant with each other to meet regularly to worship God, to study the word of God, to join together in a common witness to the gospel and to engage in the good works to which Christians are called as specified in the Constitution of the Cumberland Presbyterian Church. This union is for worship, study, witness and service in _____ area, the surrounding communities, and through the broader ministry of _____ Presbytery, the General Assembly of the Cumberland Presbyterian Church and in the world.

Article I
Name

The name of the church shall be determined by a congregational non-binding vote at a later date to help inform the Session in the determination of name for the newly formed church.

Article II
Incorporation

The merged churches shall cause a corporation to be formed under the appropriate laws of the state or region of _____ including but not limited to the 501c3 status. That corporation shall affirm that it is the goal and purpose of the church (to be named later) to present a united and unifying witness to the community on behalf of the Cumberland Presbyterian Church for worship, study, witness and service. The merged church shall be the successor in interest of the prior churches.

Article III
Session

The session shall consist of at least six (6) elders and the minister. The session will be divided into three (3) classes as follows:

1. Each current session will select three (3) members from their church to nominate on the new session.

2. One (1) member from each prior church will be elected to a one-year term.

3. One (1) member from each prior church will be elected to a two-year term.

4. One (1) member from each prior church will be elected to a three-year term.

5. For the first three (3) years, there shall be an equal number elected from each prior church.

Article IV
Administrative Infrastructure

The administrative structure shall include the following groups appointed by the Session and accountable to the Session.

A.   Finance and Administration

   1. Propose and oversee budget.

   2. Produce financial reports.

3. Arrange for audits.

4. Appoint persons to collect and record tithes and offerings and make appropriate reports.

5. Appoint persons to make, record and report expenditures.

6. Carry out other duties and functions as appropriate and/or assigned by the Session.

B. Personnel

1. Determine hiring policies.

2. Establish job descriptions and compensation packages.

3. Provide for periodic job description reviews and evaluations of staff; excluding minister of word and sacrament.

4. Carry out other duties and functions as appropriate and/or assigned by the Session.

C. Property

1. Oversee care of all property owned.

2. Determine appropriate use of facilities by outside groups/agencies.

3. Recommend policies for building and property use.

4. Carry out other duties and functions as appropriate and/or assigned by the Session.

Article V

Program Infrastructure

The program structure shall include the following ministries of the church to enable the congregation to accomplish its mission. These bodies/committees shall operate within the oversight of the Session, work within budget provisions and shall report to the Session through its session liaison(s).

A. Worship and Music

1. Provide for regular worship services.

2. Provide for the sacraments of baptism and communion.

3. Set policies and fees for weddings.

4. Set policies for funerals.

5. Plan services for festival days and other special services.

B. Christian Education

1. Provide spiritual growth.

2. Approve curriculum and make recommendations as needed.

3. Identify, call and select teachers.

4. Provide for teacher training.

5. Provide varied learning opportunities.

C. Missions

1. Have a strong emphasis on local, regional, national and international missions.

2. Emphasize evangelism among the church's members.

3. Keep church informed on mission opportunities.

4. Communicate the vision of mission beyond the church walls.

D. Stewardship

1. Communicate importance of stewardship of both time and financial resources.

2. Present the budget to the church.

3. Oversee stewardship drives/campaigns.

E. Member Care

1. Provide support for individuals within the church and their families.

2. Provide support for nonmember families who identify with the church.

3. Ensure adoption and assimilation of new people into the life of the church.

4. Provide special care for people in times of crisis and need.

5. Maintain accuracy of the church's membership rolls.

F. Fellowship and Recreation

1. Provide opportunities for congregational fellowship.

2. Provide opportunities for involvement with other churches.

Article VI
Ministerial Leadership
The ministerial leadership of the merged church will be provided by an ordained Cumberland Presbyterian minister.

Article VII
Church Staff
Before merger of the churches, the steering committee will determine the staffing and employment needs.

Article VIII
Location
The steering committee with the assistance of the presbytery, will determine the church's primary center for worship and ministries. The development and/or sale of properties will be subject to the consideration as the merged congregation's needs and may change as those needs become more evident. In the event of property sale or the cessation of using one of the church's property, efforts will be made, if feasible, to incorporate symbols from that location into the renovation or development of another property.

Article IX
Ratification
The two or more Cumberland Presbyterian churches will hold separate meetings to discuss and answer questions pertaining to this plan of union. Each church will then have the opportunity to vote "yes" or "no" concerning merger. The votes will be non-binding. Each Session will then make a final vote concerning merger. If merger is approved, the Sessions will then set a date for merger to become finalized. Final approval of any plan of union and renovation or disposition of property is the responsibility of the presbytery.

IV. FREQUENTLY ASKED QUESTIONS

During the exploration and transition of merging churches, questions will occur during the process. While not all questions can be anticipated below are some that are frequently asked.

How long does a merger process take?
The development of the plan of union will help determine timelines. From the initiation of the process of merger to the fulfillment of the plan of union, churches should prepare anticipate a process of approximately three to five years.

May our church get out of the merger process?
A church has the right to withdraw from the merger process until the presbytery votes favorably on the plan of union.

What if the church that is interested in a merger is from another ecclesiastical body or is an independent church?
If a church interested in a merger with a Cumberland Presbyterian church, the presbytery follows the Constitution 10.1-10.3. If the church is from another ecclesiastical body and wants to retain its connections with its current judicatory as a federated or union church, the presbytery follows the Constitution as described in 10.4.

What happens if a timeframe/deadline is missed during the implementation of the plan of union?
Timelines are to be set within the plan of union. Each merger is unique and therefore timelines will vary. Presbytery will determine a course of action if a timeline is missed during the implementation of the plan of union.

What happens to our church's endowments and bequests?
Depending on government laws, endowments and bequests will be acquired in the formation of the new particular church as described in the plan of union. The advice of an attorney may be required to ensure that all endowments are properly transferred to the new church.

Who is responsible for the sale and/or transfer of property?
The presbytery has the responsibility for the sale of property based upon 3.31-3.35 and 5.6 of the Constitution. Bylaws and articles of incorporation would make provisions for the transfer of property.

What should we do with session minutes and other archival records of the previous churches?
Session minutes, archival records, and items from the previous churches should be identified and transferred to the Historical Foundation of the Cumberland Presbyterian Church. If such minutes and records are to be retained by the newly formed particular church, copies of said records should be made, identified and transferred to the Historical Foundation of the Cumberland Presbyterian Church.

Who is to moderate the joint session?
The moderator of the joint session will be appointed by the presbytery.

What if the plan of union involves the dissolving of staff and ministerial positions?
Arrangements should be made for the transition of staff and ministerial positions to include termination allowances, unused vacation, sick leave, continuing education leave and a final date of employment.

What about the community organizations that currently use church facilities?
Community organizations using the facilities of the closing churches need to be informed of the plan of union and a timeframe will be set if the facility/property is to be sold.

APPENDIX
ORGANIZATION OF A PARTICULAR CHURCH

The Constitution Of The Cumberland Presbyterian Church 2.40 – 2.42

2.40 Organization of a Particular Church

2.41 A particular church can be organized only by the authority of the presbytery. In considering the formation of a new church, the presbytery shall be involved in the planning. Upon approval of presbytery for the organization of the church any minister who is a member of presbytery may preside at the organization and perform all the duties required, except where a commission for that purpose shall have been appointed by presbytery. The new church shall not be located within three miles of an existing church of the Cumberland Presbyterian Church/Cumberland Presbyterian Church in America without the approval of presbytery.

2.42 The steps in organizing a particular church are as follows:

a. Letters of transfer, or testimonials of current church membership, shall be presented by those who are members of a church. Others may be admitted to membership on reaffirmation of faith or on confession of faith in Christ, the church covenant, baptism (or confirmation of baptism) and examination as necessary.

b. These persons shall then be required to enter into covenant, by answering affirmatively the following question: *Do you, in reliance upon God for strength, solemnly promise and covenant with God and each other that you will walk together as an organized church according to the government of the Cumberland Presbyterian Church / Cumberland Presbyterian Church in America; that you will support the gospel as God has prospered you; that you will maintain this church, not only with your gifts, but also with your support of its work by your efforts and prayers; that you will seek in its fellowship to glorify the name and further the cause of our Lord Jesus Christ; and that you will work to maintain the purity and harmony of the whole body?*

c. After this, the presiding minister shall say: *I now declare that you are constituted a church according to the word of God and the government of the Cumberland Presbyterian Church/ Cumberland Presbyterian Church in America. In the name of the Father, and of the Son, and of the Holy Spirit. Amen.*

d. The members of the church shall proceed, with the presiding minister in charge, to determine the number of elders to be elected to constitute the session and the type of tenure to which they shall be elected and to elect elders. The ordination and installation of the elders may follow immediately or at a later date. At the option of the members, deacons may be elected, ordained, and installed at this time, at a subsequent congregational meeting, or not at all.

e. The presiding minister, or the commission appointed by the presbytery, shall be responsible for reporting on the organizational service, including a recommendation that the newly organized church be enrolled as a constituent member, at the next regular meeting of the presbytery. The report should include the date of organization, location, names of those acting on behalf of presbytery to organize the church, number of charter members and the list of officers elected.

ADMISSION OF NEW CHURCHES

Appendix 3 Of The Constitution Of The Cumberland Presbyterian Church

When a new church is organized, the session shall apply for the new church's admission into the presbytery in whose bounds it is located. The following form may be used:

TO THE PRESBYTERY OF _____

The undersigned respectfully declare that on the _____ day of _____, AD _____, a new church was organized at _____ by the Reverend _____ (or a commission of presbytery), which adopted the principles of the government of the Cumberland Presbyterian Church/Cumberland Presbyterian Church in America, and has a membership of _____. The following persons were elected as elders:_____, _____, _____. The following persons were elected as deacons:_____, _____, _____.

We apply to be received under your care, and promise as the session to comply with all the duties and obligations enjoined upon particular churches and their officers by the government of the Cumberland Presbyterian Church/ Cumberland Presbyterian Church in America.

_____

_____

_____

Date_____ Elders

CONTACT INFORMATION

Historical Foundation Of The Cumberland Presbyterian Church
Phone (901)276-8602

Susan Knight Gore, Archivist
skg@cumberland.org

General Assembly Office
Phone (901)276-4572

Mike Sharpe, Stated Clerk
msharpe@cumberland.org

Missions Ministry Team
Phone (901)276-4572

T. J. Malinoski, Director of Evangelism and New Church Development
TMalinoski@cumberland.org

THE REPORT OF THE
BOARD OF STEWARDSHIP,
FOUNDATION, AND BENEFITS

I. GENERAL INFORMATION

A. BOARD MEETINGS AND ORGANIZATION

The Board of Stewardship, Foundation and Benefits under the direction of its officers, President Charlie Floyd, Vice-president Mike St. John, Secretary Debbie Shelton, and Treasurer Robert Heflin, met two times in regular session.

B. BOARD MEMBERS WHOSE TERMS EXPIRE

Members whose terms expire at the 2016 General Assembly, with their years of service, are as follows: Charlie Floyd, nine years; Sue Rice, six years; Debbie Shelton, six years; and Reverend Buddy Pope, three years. Charlie Floyd is not eligible for another term. We want to thank Charlie for his service and dedication to the Board of Stewardship, Foundation and Benefits. Sue Rice, Debbie Shelton and Reverend Buddy Pope are eligible and have agreed to serve another three-year term.

C. BOARD REPRESENTATIVE TO THE 186TH GENERAL ASSEMBLY

The board's representative to the 186th General Assembly is Randy Davidson.

D. STAFF

Kathryn Gilbert Craig serves as Administrative Assistant, Mark Duck serves as Coordinator of Benefits, and Robert Heflin serves as Executive Secretary. Carolyn Harmon serves as the Planned Giving Coordinator for the Presbytery of East Tennessee. The Board appreciates the work Carolyn Harmon does in educating congregations of the legacy ministry that can be accomplished as individuals make planned gifts to their local congregations.

E. 2017 BUDGET

The 2017 line-item budget has been filed with the Office of the General Assembly.

F. 2015 AUDIT

Certified copies of the 2015 audit reports from Fouts and Morgan will be filed with the Office of the General Assembly in compliance with General Regulations E.5. and E.6. The 2015 audit will be printed in the audit section of the 2016 minutes.

II. FINANCIAL FOUNDATION DEVELOPMENT AND MANAGEMENT

A. PURPOSE

One area of the work of the board is in financial foundation development and management. The purpose of this program is as follows:
To secure a firm financial undergirding for the ongoing ministry of congregations and the agencies of presbyteries, synods, and the General Assembly as they bear witness to the saving love of God, the grace of our Lord Jesus Christ, and the fellowship and communion of the Holy Spirit.

B. 2015 IN REVIEW

The year 2015 proved to be a difficult year for investments. Both foreign and domestic markets continued to be volatile. The drop in oil prices and other uncertainties influenced investor anxiety. The markets were influenced by the emotions of investors.

The Russell 3000, one benchmark for domestic stocks, ended 2015, up 0.5%. A second benchmark, the S&P 500, was up 1.4%. The MSCI EAFE (Europe, Austrailasia and Far East), one benchmark for international stocks, was down 0.4% and MSCI Emerging Markets were down 14.6% in 2015.

Throughout 2015 the markets were up and down, much like a roller coaster. This caused stress for many investors, making it more imperative that we focus on investing for the long term.

We need to continue to be cautious about looking too far down the road. Sentiment and emotion rule the short term. We are confident that our investment manager, Gerber/Taylor can continue to help us navigate the sometimes turbulent ups and downs of the market. Since October 1981, Gerber/Taylor has done a wonderful job for the Cumberland Presbyterian Church.

C. BOARD OF STEWARDSHIP

The Board of Stewardship is ever mindful of expenses incurred and try to be good stewards of what has been entrusted to the Board. We are grateful for the faithful support from congregations and individuals through their contributions to Our United Outreach.

PaperSave

In an effort to be better stewards, the Board of Stewardship has implemented a paperless document management system. In excess of ten thousand pages of over 850 endowment files, over 300 retirement files, over 280 Investment Loan Program account files and about 50 loan files have been scanned. Future reports and documents will become a part of the paperless system. The staff enjoys the paperless system as it provides quicker response and better service to those who call with questions.

D. MANAGEMENT OF FUNDS

In January 2013, we combined the Growth/Income Endowment Fund and the Total Return Endowment Fund with a focus on not only interest and dividends but also growth in realized and unrealized gains/losses.

At the end of 2015 the Endowment Fund portfolio was under the co-management of Gerber/Taylor Management, RREEF America II, Clarion and Eagle MLP. The funds of the Retirement Program were co-managed by Gerber/Taylor Management, RREEF America II and Eagle MLP.

The church loan portion of the endowment portion of the endowment portfolio and the investments of the Cumberland Presbyterian Church Investment Loan Program, Inc. were under the management of board staff with the help of Hilliard Lyons.

III. ENDOWMENT PROGRAM

Since 1836, the board and its corporate predecessors have sought to be faithful trustees of the funds given into their hands to provide a permanent financial foundation for the work of congregations, presbyteries, synods, and General Assembly agencies. The work of the Endowment Program is the oldest responsibility of the board and fulfills a portion of that task to which all Cumberland Presbyterians are called: "Christian stewardship acknowledges that all of life and creation is a trust from God, to be used for God's glory and service."—*Confession of Faith for Cumberland Presbyterians 6:10.*

A. COMMUNICATION

The Endowment Program report will be distributed to all endowment program participants, general assembly board members, churches, and individual contributors.

Agencies, other participants, and interested parties received quarterly detailed reports on the postings to all their endowments. With the addition of names supplied by the agencies during the year, the number of persons receiving these reports continues to expand. In addition, special reports were made as requested.

B. ASSETS, INVESTMENT MIX, AND PERFORMANCE

1. Assets and Investment Mix

The assets of the Endowment Fund totaled $55,931,668 for 2015 at market value. The following table provides a breakdown of the investment mix:

Investment Mix
Securities & Investments

15.6%	US Equity	$8,725,340
11.6%	Real Assets	$6,488,074
14.6%	Fixed Income	$8,166,024
20.0%	Hedged Equity	$11,186,334
15.6%	Multi-Strategy	$8,725,340
2.6%	Opportunistic	$1,454,223
12.2%	International Stocks	$6,823,663
7.4%	Emerging Markets	$4,138,943
0.4%	Private Equity	$223,727
100.0%	**Total**	**$55,931,668**

2. Performance of the Endowment Fund

The Endowment Fund generated $187,391 in investment earnings during 2015. Net contributions and withdrawals were a negative $568,824. The change in market value was a loss of $756,215.

With the combining of the Growth/Income Fund and the Total Return Fund in January 2013, we also began paying out 5% (annualized) to the congregations, presbyteries and agencies. Previously agencies had difficulty in preparing budgets because of the unknown amount they would receive from endowment income. Now, they realize they will receive 5% in endowment income over a twelve-month period. With this information, they have a better idea how much endowment income they can expect. Earnings paid and payable to congregations, presbyteries and agencies totaled $1,901,308 for 2015.

3. Total Rate of Return for the Endowment Fund

The following table gives the annualized rates of return as contained in the report from Gerber/Taylor Associates for year end 2015:

	One Year Period 01/01/15 12/31/15	Five Year Period 01/01/11 12/31/15	Since Inception 09/30/81 12/31/15
Endowment Fund	-0.4%	6.4%	9.9%

C. ESTABLISHING AN ENDOWMENT AS A LEGACY

The Board of Stewardship, Foundation and Benefits manages over 800 endowments established for the benefit of congregations, presbyteries, synods, agencies and other special ministries of the Cumberland Presbyterian denomination. Many of these endowments were established by individuals as a legacy to continue to benefit long after they are no longer with us. Some of the endowments were established by congregations, presbyteries and synods to help further their specific ministries. Some of the endowments were started with very little. Through the years these endowments have grown and the beneficiaries are reaping the gifts of the endowment income and using it in ministry in their local area or worldwide. Please consider establishing an endowment.

D. ENDOWMENT PROGRAM LOANS

Historical Review

Through investing up to 40% of the assets of the Endowment Program in the witness of the Church, the message of good news concerning Christ is strengthened both in the United States and overseas. A survey of old files in the Historical Foundation and in the vault of the Board of Stewardship reveals the important role played by this aspect of the investment policy. Over the past sixty-five years from 1944 to 2009, 841 loans were made to congregations, presbyteries, and synods. From 2010 through 2015 an additional 17 loans have been made. Through these loans, $42,714,405 has been provided in financing for expansion of facilities and extension of witness.

A look at the different periods during which loans have been made provides a picture of growing endowments (and of post World War II inflation!).

Period	Loans	Total Loaned	Average
1944-49	35	$ 145,755	$ 4,164
1950-59	171	$ 1,360,441	$ 7,955
1960-69	208	$ 3,056,891	$ 14,697
1970-79	166	$ 3,609,084	$ 21,741
1980-89	101	$ 4,349,120	$ 43,061
1990-99	102	$ 14,440,837	$ 141,577
2000-09	58	$ 10,571,723	$ 182,271
2010-15	17	$ 5,180,554	$ 304,738

While looking at the table, it should be noted that the Cumberland Presbyterian Church Investment Loan Program began January 1, 2001. Since its creation most of the larger loans are made through the Investment Loan Program.

Down through the years, donors to endowments have found satisfaction in the knowledge that the prudent investment of their gifts strengthened not only the work of the particular churches, institutions, and causes which they designated to receive the income but also the broader witness of the Church.

E. OTHER CHURCH LOANS

In addition to loans from the Investment Loan Program and the Endowment Program there is another source available to the board for loans to churches.

Small Church Loan Fund

This fund, formerly known as the Revolving Church Loan Fund, was created through an endowment established by Lavenia Cole and gifts to the "Into the Nineties" Capital Gifts Campaign. All interest earned by the loans is added to the fund to increase the amount available for loans. There were seven loans from the Small Church Loan Program at the end of 2015 totaling $150,103.

The rate of interest for the Small Church Loans made during 2015 was based on the loan rate established by the Cumberland Presbyterian Church Investment Loan Program at the beginning of each quarter. These loans are generally small loans of $35,000 or less, amortized over five years.

F. REGIONAL PLANNED GIVING COORDINATORS

History

In 1993, the 163rd General Assembly commended the Board of Stewardship for "its vision in developing a program of planned giving in local congregations" and urged congregations "to be open to this new program and to take advantage of the assistance being offered" by the Board.

Further, it adopted recommendations to:

Approve a church-wide annual emphasis on planned gifts as a complementary part of the observation of the Family Week focus provided by the Board of Christian Education during May of each year; and

Urge each congregation to recognize the importance of promoting planned gifts as a part of its overall nurture of Christian stewardship among its members.

In response to the 1993 action, staff of the Board of Stewardship have made presentations to more than 150 congregations on the need to develop congregational endowments and encourage planned giving by church members.

At one time there were four Regional Planned Giving Coordinators. At the moment Carolyn Harmon is the only Regional Planned Giving Coordinators. She is an elder in the Cedar Hill Church, Greeneville, Tennessee, serving the Presbytery of East Tennessee. The other coordinators can no longer serve due to health conditions or other reasons. Though Carolyn is employed by the Presbytery of East Tennessee she has made presentations beyond her presbytery.

She can educate congregations and individuals regarding stewardship opportunities in planned giving. Often times the results of her work is not easily measured. It may be several years before her work bears fruit. Presentations can plant seeds which may bear fruit immediately or years down the road. What is of utmost importance is that the seeds are being planted.

The Board of Stewardship works to continue efforts of educating local congregations about the opportunities available through planned giving. It is through planned giving that current Cumberland Presbyterians can provide for effective ministry long after they are gone.

It is our prayer that God will bless the work of encouraging Cumberland Presbyterians to give generously to enhance the future ministry of all our churches.

IV. CUMBERLAND PRESBYTERIAN CHURCH INVESTMENT LOAN PROGRAM, INC.

In 1976, the board began a program to provide an opportunity for flexible investment of current temporary cash assets of congregations and agencies of the church. The primary purpose of the program is to provide income to participants as a foundation for ministry. On January 1, 2001, the assets of the original program, Cash Funds Management, were transferred to the new Cumberland Presbyterian Church Investment Loan Program, Inc.

For the year ending 2015, the assets for the Investment Loan Program were $16,853,197. There were 288 individual, congregation and agency accounts. At year end, deposits on account totaled $15,052,679. The total loans were $7,171,584 at year end.

For 2015, the corporation complied with the regulatory requirements in the states of Tennessee and Kentucky and was able to offer investment opportunities to individual Cumberland Presbyterians in the states of Tennessee, Kentucky, Texas, Missouri and New Mexico.

The board of directors is composed of the following: Mike St. John, president; Charlie Floyd, vice-president and Debbie Shelton, secretary, and Jackie Satterfield. Robert Heflin serves as Treasurer and Executive Secretary. During the past year, the board met twice in regular session.

In order to simplify administration and focus on the strengths of the Investment Loan Program, the board took action to limit the offering of notes and depository accounts to "ready access accounts." All note holders (individuals) and depository account holders (churches and church agencies) with funds invested in these "on demand" accounts participated in the $517,661 which the program paid in interest. For 2015 the interest rate paid to account holders was 3.5%. The interest rate paid to account holders can fluctuate from one quarter to the next. In recent years there has been renewed interest for congregations to open new accounts because the interest paid is higher than current CD rates.

The table below provides a breakdown of the investment mix.

Investment Loan Program
Securities & Investments

21.68%	Cash Equivalents	$2,087,630
11.05%	Preferred Stocks	$1,064,306
66.87%	Taxable Fixed Income	$6,440,032
0.40%	Multi Asset	$38,841
100.00%		**$9,630,809**

At the end of 2015 there were 23 loans to congregations made through the Investment Loan Program. The loan balance was $8,617,980. Every accountholder is investing in the future ministry of the Cumberland Presbyterian Church as well as receiving interest on that investment.

V. EMPLOYEE BENEFITS ADMINISTRATION AND RESEARCH

A. PURPOSE

The second of two broad areas of the work of the board is in employee benefits administration and research. The purpose of this program is as follows:

To support the lay and ordained employees of the church as they venture to be faithful under the call of Christ and the Church to the daily demands of providing leadership to congregations and Church agencies whom are the incarnation of the Body of Christ, the family of God at work in the world.

Employee benefits are reported in detail under headings IX. Retirement Program, X. Ministerial Aid Program, and XI. Insurance Program.

B. VISION

The board has a vision of uniform benefits for all Cumberland Presbyterian clergy, including group health insurance, group long-term disability coverage, and participation in the General Assembly's retirement plan. Ministers would then know what to expect when they are called to another church. No longer would some ministers have to do without what is considered in the secular world to be basic employee benefits. No longer would ministers and their families have to settle for being relegated to second class status. The reality is, as several General Assemblies have recognized, that this is possible if we work together in much the same manner that we send out missionaries and do a lot of other ministry. Good employee benefit plans are in place and they would be healthier and stronger if used and supported by all employees of the Cumberland Presbyterian Church.

VI. RETIREMENT PROGRAM

Since 1952, the board has provided a retirement program open to all church employees of the Cumberland Presbyterian Church. The program gives opportunity for churches and their employees to provide a source of retirement income based on voluntary contributions. In 1987, a new Cumberland Presbyterian Retirement Plan No. 2 was established as a qualified 403(b) defined contribution plan and in 1990 the General Assembly amended the plan to include the churches and employees of the Second Cumberland Presbyterian Church, now known as the Cumberland Presbyterian Church in America.

A. PLAN AMENDMENTS

As new needs arise or deficiencies in the original plan document for Cumberland Presbyterian Retirement Plan No. 2 became apparent, the General Assembly has the authority under Article IX Section 9.01 of the Plan to amend the same. In 2012 a revised plan document was approved by the General Assembly.

B. YEAR END REPORT

On December 31, 2015, there were 315 active participants in the Retirement Plan. There were 12 receiving direct monthly payments as a result of their elections. In addition to these participants, there were 13 persons who were receiving annuity payments purchased through the Plan and for whom the Plan issues 1099-R's.

During 2015, $1,461,432 was dispersed to or for participants, an increase of 34% over 2014's $1,091,879. Contributions totaled $663,084 and were down 11 % over 2014's $713,181. Realized and unrealized losses on investments totaled $310,078 compared to a gain in 2014 of $1,153,146. The rate of return credited to the accounts for the year was -0.8% compared to 5.7% for 2014. (Comparative annual rates of return for: previous three years—+6.1%, previous five years—+5.9%, and from the beginning of professional management in March, 1982—+9.4%.)

Effective January 1, 2011, Gerber/Taylor Management was retained to manage our stock portfolio. We have continued our relationship with Met West, a bond manager, and RREEF, a private real estate investment trust manager. Matt Robbins and Stacy Miller of Gerber/Taylor continue to be very helpful with keeping the board updated on market conditions and investment strategies.

VII. MINISTERIAL AID PROGRAM

A. MINISTERIAL AID

1. Full Benefit Recipients

As of March 2016 there are 3 Cumberland Presbyterian Church recipients of the full benefit of $510 per month (increased from $300 on July 1, 2010). The monthly total of these payments is $1,530.00; annually, $18,360.00 is paid. Beginning May 1, 2015, the method of distributing funds to overseas presbyteries was revised with the help of the Missions ministry team. Ministerial aid will now be offered in overseas presbyteries on an individual basis. Presently there are 5 recipients in Cauca Valley Presbytery and 4 recipients in Andes Presbytery that are receiving aid in the amount of $300 a month, for a total of $2,700 a month or $32,400 annually.

In October 2005, the board decided to distribute 75% of the previous year's surplus to the remaining recipients. This distribution was made in December 2015 with 2 state side recipients receiving $4,000.00 each and one recipients receiving $1,000 for a total distribution of $9,000.00. The Board of Stewardship has approved a cap of a maximum of $4,000 in lieu of large distributions that may have a negative effect on other benefits received, such as SSI, or state assistance.

2. Basic Requirements. The new basic requirements and amount for stateside recipients for the Ministerial Aid program were approved at the General Assembly of the Cumberland Presbyterian Church in June 2010. The poverty levels have been updated to the latest available figures. They are as follows:

Full Benefit of $510 a month for State Side Recipients

1. Minimum age is full retirement age set forth by the Social Security Administration.
2. Minimum years of service to the church - 15.
3. Can qualify for aid if a participant in the Cumberland Presbyterian Retirement Plan if income is below poverty level as established by the US Census Bureau.
4. Physical and/or mental disability (doctor's statement required) at any age, however, a minimum of ten years of service is required if less than 60 years of age.
5. Individuals' income cannot exceed federal poverty guidelines set forth for the year by the US Census Bureau. Poverty level is $11,880 a year or $990 a month for 2016.
6. Couples income cannot exceed federal poverty guidelines set forth for the year by the US Census Bureau. Poverty level is $16,020 a year or $1,335 a month for 2016.
(The GA Board of Stewardship is authorized to look at each case in light of unusual financial hardship; thus, application may be made even if income levels exceed the ceiling.)
7. Presbytery obtains information and approves (approval can be given by the committee or board charged by presbytery with this responsibility); certification of approval is sent to the General Assembly Board of Stewardship.
8. Surviving spouse is eligible if above items 2, 3 and 4 have been met.

**Note: Recipient is responsible to verify if receiving Ministerial Aid would affect his or her SSI, Social Security or other benefits.

Cumberland Presbyterian Church applicants must submit to the board a listing of assets and liabilities so the net worth can be determined. The board urges presbyteries to maintain contact with persons under the Ministerial Aid Program who live within their bounds. Should there be serious unmet needs, the presbytery is urged to contact the board so that it may determine how the Ministerial Aid program can be of assistance in meeting those needs.

3. Cumberland Presbyterian Church in America. The CPCA currently has 3 participants who receive monthly payments. As of June 1, 2015, the aid amount increased from $109 a month to $510 a month and the CPCA contributes 50% of the yearly aid and the CP Ministerial Aid Endowments 50%. The CPCA normally pays its share in June or July following their General Assembly.

4. Ministers in Overseas Presbyteries. As of May 1, 2015, with the help of the Missions Ministry Team, aid is available to those in overseas presbyteries who qualify on an individual basis. The Cumberland Presbyterian Church is present in 13 different countries and each country presents its unique legislation of how they manage pension plans according to laws and standards for salaries. The Mission Ministry Team will be the liaison between the Board of Stewardship and the Presbyteries outside of the United States aiding the Board in identifying the needs overseas and interpreting pension laws and standards for salaries. At present, aid is being sent to the Cauca Valley Presbytery and Andes Presbytery in Colombia, South America.

B. SPECIAL FINANCIAL NEEDS AID

At the Spring 2014 Board of Stewardship meeting, the Board approved the use of funds from the Ministerial Aid Cash Fund ILP to be used in special situations where illness has caused a financial hardship for those that are not eligible for Ministerial Aid. There were no funds disbursed in 2015.

VIII. INSURANCE PROGRAMS

The insurance programs of the board have been assigned by the General Assembly beginning in the middle of the previous century. Dental and Vision Insurance is the newest, begun in December 2008. Property and casualty insurance is the oldest, begun in 1951. While all of the insurance programs are important, group life and health insurance, begun in 1961, touches many lives in a personal way and often at times of deep anxiety. In all, about 214 men, women, and children depend on this program to meet their health care needs.

A. PROPERTY & CASUALTY INSURANCE

The Board of Stewardship, Foundation and Benefits secures property and casualty insurance coverage against accidental loss for the General Assembly Corporation, Board of Stewardship, Discipleship Ministry Team, Missions Ministry Team, Ministry Council, Communications Ministry Team, Pastoral Development Ministry Team, Memphis Theological Seminary, and Historical Foundation.

Our broker is Lipscomb & Pitts of Memphis, Tennessee. For 2016, Travelers Insurance carries our Property & Casualty policy and $2,500,000 in earth quake coverage. Mt. Hawley Insurance Company provides an additional $6,673,379 in earthquake coverage and Lloyds of London provides $10,000,000 in earthquake coverage. Philadelphia carries our Directors & Officers coverage and Hanover carries our General Liability, Crime, Automobile, and Umbrella policies. Workers Compensation coverage as of 10/23/2014 is with Bridgefield Casualty.

B. GROUP LONG TERM DISABILITY INSURANCE

The presbyteries of Arkansas, Columbia, Covenant, Cumberland, del Cristo, East Tennessee, Missouri, Murfreesboro, Nashville, North Central, Red River, Robert Donnell, Trinity, West Tennessee and The Center have now established non-contributory long term disability programs insured currently through Cigna. This leaves only four stateside presbyteries (Choctaw, Hope, Grace and Tennessee Georgia) without a program. The quarterly rate applied to participant's salaries is .345 per $100 of salary.

There are three primary reasons for ministers to want the coverage and for presbyteries to want to provide the protection. The group rate is significantly lower than individual policy rates and does not require a large cash outlay to cover all full-time ministers in a presbytery; housing allowance and/ or the fair rental value of a manse is included in the definition of salary for ministers; and, there is no medical qualification requirement in order to enroll. These advantages over individual policies make this coverage very attractive, especially to those who have previously purchased their own policies. In addition, a provision was negotiated with Cigna by the Board's consultant, whereby ministers, upon leaving a participating presbytery to serve in a non-participating presbytery, may continue the coverage if he or she so desires. The new employing church is then billed for the quarterly premium. There are now 8 ministers and two employees who are receiving or have received benefits from this insurance program. There are 185 participants as of January 1, 2016.

C. GROUP TRAVEL ACCIDENT INSURANCE

This policy provides twenty-four hour coverage on "named employees" for accidental death, dismemberment, or loss of sight while on business travel. The maximum benefit is $50,000 and there is also a $1,000 medical benefit. The annual premium is $900. We renew this policy every 3 years. Thirty-one named positions are covered under this policy.

D. GROUP HEALTH & LIFE INSURANCE

The board has used a fully-insured, managed care approach to provide group health insurance for Cumberland Presbyterian clergy and lay employees since March 1, 1999. Blue Cross/Blue Shield of Tennessee has been our insurance carrier since January 1, 2010. As of January 1, 2016, due to a potential 50% + increase in premiums with Blue Cross/Blue Shield of Tennessee, the group plan was split into 4 separate community rated groups with new carriers.

With the help from the Premium Stabilization Fund, premiums for the groups decreased 10% to 25% and out of pocket maximums increased from $1,000 or $1,500 depending on plan and level chosen. Lipscomb & Pitts, a Memphis based insurance company, is our insurance broker, and Craig Wright, our agent.

1. Loss Ratio.

A comparison of paid medical premiums and claims is made in order to calculate a loss ratio. The following table contains monthly and cumulative figures for the calendar year of 2015. For 2015, 134% of the medical premiums paid to Blue Cross were used to pay claims and stop-loss premiums. This compares to a loss ratio of 111% for 2014, 94% for 2013, 83% in 2012, and 91% in 2011.

MEDICAL EXPERIENCE REPORT

MONTH	MONTHLY MEDICAL PREMIUM	PAID CLAIMS	LOSS RATIO	CUMULATIVE MEDICAL PREMIUM	PAID CLAIMS	LOSS RATIO
Jan. 15	$160,423	$223,968	140%	$160,423	$223,968	140%
Feb. 15	$164,846	$193,196	117%	$325,269	$417,164	128%
Mar. 15	$161,131	$181,174	112%	$486,400	$598,338	123%
Apr. 15	$150,063	$188,299	125%	$636,463	$786,637	124%
May 15	$154,406	$218,761	142%	$790,869	$1,005,398	127%
Jun. 15	$151,303	$228,703	151%	$942,172	$1,234,101	131%
Jul. 15	$144,562	$187,952	130%	$1,086,734	$1,422,053	131%
Aug. 15	$147,344	$166,447	113%	$1,234,078	$1,588,500	129%
Sept.15	$137,001	$212,940	155%	$1,371,079	$1,801,440	131%
Oct. 15	$148,025	$192,640	130%	$1,519,104	$1,994,080	131%
Nov. 15	$144,098	$210,242	146%	$1,663,202	$2,204,322	133%
Dec. 15	$150,123	$231,774	154%	$1,813,325	$2,436,096	134%

2. Premiums.

Efforts to maintain affordable premiums and comprehensive coverage are the biggest challenges we face. Premiums for 2016 are listed below and reflect the assistance from the Premium Stabilization fund. The goal for 2016 is to utilize approximately $200,000 from the Premiums Stabilization Fund to help reduce the premiums participants pay for health insurance.

Health Insurance Premiums for 2016		
	Option 1	Option 2
Employee Only	$624	$500
Employee & Spouse	$1,237	$988
Employee & Child(ren)	$1,142	$912
Family	$1,775	$1,420

The Health Plans are on a calendar year as far as deductible and pricing is concerned. It is our objective to have the renewal pricing by no later than September 1 so presbyteries and agencies can have the figures for their fall meetings and better plan their budgets for the coming year. Periodically we seek bids from other carriers in an effort to keep premiums competitive. When this is done, we may not have the new premium information by September 1.

Open enrollment period is the month of December. It is during this time that an employee can enroll or change their health insurance coverage unless there are special circumstances.

3. Participation.

As of February 1, 2016, 132 employees and 82 dependents for a total of 214 people depend on the Cumberland Presbyterian Church Health Insurance Program. A breakdown of family units by size at February 1, 2016 is listed below.

FAMILY UNITS BY SIZE

	Number of Units	Total
Emp. Only	87	87
Spouse Only	0	0
E & 1	3	6
E & 2	3	9
E & 3	0	0
E & S	22	44
Families of 3	3	9
Families of 4	12	48
Families of 5	1	5
Families of 6	1	6
Families of 7	0	0
Total	132	214

The following table shows the enrollment figures from January 2015 to December 2015. As one can see the numbers fluctuate from month to month.

MONTHLY GROUP INSURANCE ENROLLMENT

	EMPLOYEE COVERAGE	DEPENDENT COVERAGE	TOTAL
January	100	50	150
February	97	54	151
March	94	53	147
April	90	52	142
May	91	51	142
June	88	51	139
July	86	50	136
August	86	48	134
September	88	44	132
October	89	46	135
November	90	45	135
December	92	46	138

4. Premium Stabilization Reserve (Formerly Emergency Reserve)

The Premium Stabilization Reserve is invested in the Endowment Fund and had a balance of $1,974,117 as of December 31, 2015. The Emergency Health Insurance Reserve was established in compliance with the 1992 General Assembly directive to be used in "emergency" situations to match presbyterial emergency fund disbursements. The 1998 General Assembly approved the Board's recommendation to allow the Board to use the Emergency Reserve to maintain the stability of the group health and life insurance plan. This allows these funds to be used for purposes outside of the original scope of the reserve. For 2015 the Board of Stewardship reduced the premiums charged by Blue Cross by $50 for Employee coverage and $80 for Dependent coverage. In 2015, the Board of Stewardship used $101,640 to help offset some of the cost of the health insurance premiums and have estimated that approximately $200,000 will be used in 2016 to help in reducing premiums for the health insurance participants.

GENERAL ASSEMBLY REFERRALS

The 185th General Assembly asked that the Board of Stewardship and the Unified Committee on Theology and Social Concerns have joint responsibility to properly answer the 184th General Assembly's inquiry:

"That the Board of Stewardship and the Committee on Theology and Social Concerns have joint responsibility to properly answer the 184th General Assembly's inquiry pertaining to what is currently covered by the health insurance benefits and to clarify anything that might be in conflict with the Confession of Faith and previous General Assembly statements regarding the sanctity of life. The jointly tasked responsibilities along with findings will be reported to the 186th General Assembly."

Mark Duck, representing the Board of Stewardship, met with the Unified Committee on Theology and Social Concerns to identify areas to be explored with the denominational Health insurance provider and has found that the current health insurance policy appears to be in compliance with the Confession of Faith and previous statements regarding the sanctity of life. There has been a recent change in insurance providers and so far no conflicts have been noted. Any conflicts found will be referred to the committee for review.

5. Dental and Vision Insurance

On December 1, 2008, we began offering Dental and Vision insurance, on a voluntary basis, for anyone working at least 30 hours or more for any Cumberland Presbyterian Church, its agencies, boards, and institutions. Peter Whitely is the agent of record. At present there are 69 participating employees.

6. Jessie W. Hipsher Health Insurance Endowment

The Jesse W. Hipsher Health Insurance Endowment was created as the first step in the board's goal to raise $10,000,000 in endowments for the support of the Cumberland Presbyterian Health and Life Insurance Program. The endowment was established on March 6, 2004. At its establishment $11,450 had been raised. The balance of the endowment as of December 31, 2015 was $41,580.01.

7. Health Education / E-Mail Newsletter

To further educate participants in matters concerning healthcare, participants receive a monthly e-newsletter entitled, TopHealth, published by Oakstone Publishing. The monthly e-newsletter is full of health related tips that can be easily implemented by readers. The two page newsletter can be read within a matter of minutes. Dr. Ann tips on healthy eating are also included with the e-newsletter monthly. Also initiated in 2008 is the E-Mail newsletter that is designed as an information tool to help the participants of the Health and Retirement programs stay on top of happenings within the Board of Stewardship.

8. Wellness Program

On-line resources for maintaining good health, on-line seminars on various health issues, and course for things such as stress and resiliency, nutritional help, how to cope with illness and many more are available through the web sites of our insurance providers.

Respectfully submitted,
Randy Davidson, Board Member
Robert Heflin, Executive Secretary.

THE REPORT OF THE HISTORICAL FOUNDATION

I. GENERAL INFORMATION

A. OFFICERS OF THE BOARD

The officers of the board are as follows: Reverend Rick White, president; Pam Davis, vice-president; and Sidney Milton, secretary. Susan Knight Gore is the director and treasurer of the Historical Library and Archives.

B. BOARD REPRESENTATIVES TO THE CPC & CPCA GENERAL ASSEMBLIES

The board's representative to the 186th General Assembly of the Cumberland Presbyterian Church is Reverend Lisa Oliver. The alternate is Michael Fare.

The board's representative to the 141st General Assembly of the Cumberland Presbyterian Church in America is Reverend Rick White. The alternate is Edna Barnett.

C. MEMBERSHIP AND MEETINGS OF THE BOARD

The board is currently composed of the following members: from the Cumberland Presbyterian Church in America—Edna Barnett, Vanessa Barnhill, Dorothy Hayden, Pat Ward, and Rick White, from the Cumberland Presbyterian Church—Pam Davis, Michael Fare, Mary Kathryn Kirkpatrick, Sidney Milton, Lisa Oliver, and Sidney Swindle.

The Board of Trustees met, September 18, 2015, and February 26, 2016.

D. MEMBERS WHOSE TERMS EXPIRE

The second term of Mary Kathryn Kirkpatrick expires with the 2016 meeting of the Cumberland Presbyterian General Assembly, and she is eligible for reelection. The third terms of Pam Davis and Sidney Milton expire with the 2016 meeting of the Cumberland Presbyterian Church General Assembly, and they are not eligible for reelection.

The third term of Vanessa Barnhill expires with the 2016 meeting of the Cumberland Presbyterian Church in America General Assembly, and she is not eligible for reelection.

E. STAFF

Susan Knight Gore serves as the Archivist of the Historical Foundation. Missy Rose is the archival assistant for the Foundation.

II. ASSEMBLY REPORTING

As a matter of official structure, relative to the CPC, there is a Board of Trustees composed of members from both the CPC and CPCA, and relative to the CPCA, there is a committee composed of members from the CPCA.

III. PROGRAMS AND ACTIVITIES

A. HISTORY INTERPRETATION AND PROMOTIONAL ACTIVITIES

1. The 1810 Circle

In order to enlist the financial support of interested members of our churches in the work of the Foundation, the 1810 Circle was created. Membership is based on a financial contribution of $25 or more per year. Income through such gifts enables the Foundation to meet expenditures and is vital to the continued work of the Foundation.

We appreciate the support given to the Foundation by all members of the 1810 Circle and encourage other members of the Cumberland Presbyterian Church and the Cumberland Presbyterian Church in America to join this donor group.

RECOMMENDATION 1: That the General Assembly make congregations and presbyteries aware of the 1810 Circle and encourage new members to support this endeavor annually.

2. Patrons
Persons who contribute $100 or more to one of the endowments of the Historical Foundation become patron members and receive a certificate. Patron memberships may also be given in honor or in memory of an individual.

3. Heritage Churches
Congregations contributing a minimum of $1,000 to an endowment of the Historical Foundation become Heritage Churches and receive a framed certificate. There are six categories of recognition and churches can move from one level to another.

Heritage Church $1,000 - $4,999
Silver Heritage Church $5,000 to $9,999
Golden Heritage Church $10,000 to $24,999
Platinum Heritage Church $25,000 to $49,999
Diamond Heritage Church $50,000 to $99,000
Jubilee Heritage Church $100,000 and up

4. Presbyterial Heritage Committees/Presbyterial Historians
To promote interest in the work of the Foundation and to nurture work in history on the presbyterial level, the Historical Foundation seeks to work cooperatively with the Presbyterial Heritage Committees/Presbyterial Historians of both general assemblies. The brochure, *Suggestions for Heritage Committees and Presbyterial Historians,* is available from the Foundation. The board expresses its appreciation to the presbyteries that have Heritage Committees/Presbyterial Historians.

5. Denomination Day Offering
The 2016 Denomination Day Offering was designated to fund the conversion of fragile and deteriorating analogue media to digital formats in order that it might better be preserved.

The Foundation expresses appreciation to congregations and others groups who received special offerings for the work of the Historical Foundation on Denomination Day. This special offering provides an opportunity for congregations to directly contribute to the support of the Historical Foundation as well as the Foundation supplying educational materials to each congregation.

RECOMMENDATION 2: That congregations be encouraged to have a special offering on the Sunday designated as Denomination Day to help support the special project designated for that year.

B. PUBLICATIONS

1. Promotional Materials
The Historical Foundation provides promotional materials describing its purpose and work, the various means of financially supporting this work, and listings of available publications and prints for sale through the Foundation. These materials are available on the Foundation's website.

2. Publication Series
The Foundation has a number of titles and prints available for purchase. Income from the sale of these items goes into the Historical Foundation Trust, a permanent endowment supporting the Foundation's work. Titles available are:

1883 Confession of Faith.
1895 Cumberland Cook Book.
Cumberland Presbyterianism and Arminianism Compared/Contrasted on Selected Doctrines by Joe Ben Irby.
Faith Once Delivered; Some Indispensable Doctrines of the Christian Faith by Joe Ben Irby.
Family of Faith: Cumberland Presbyterians in Harrison County [Texas], 1848-1998 by Rose Mary Magrill.
History of East Side Cumberland Presbyterian Church, Memphis, Tennessee, Memphis Tennessee: 1926-1986, by the Historical Committee.

History of the Cumberland Presbyterian Church by B. W. McDonnold.
Jerusalem Cumberland Presbyterian Church: A Documentary and Pictorial History by Anne Elizabeth Swain Odom.
Legacy of Grace: Louisiana and Texas Cumberland Presbyterian People & Places of Trinity Presbytery by Rose Mary Magrill.
Life and Thought of Finis Ewing by Joe Ben Irby.
Life and Thought of Milton Bird by Joe Ben Irby.
Life and Thought of Reuben Burrow by Joe Ben Irby.
Life and Thought of Robert Verrell Foster by Joe Ben Irby.
Life and Thought of Stanford Guthrie Burney by Joe Ben Irby.
Life and Times of Finis Ewing by F. R. Cossitt.
Soundings by Morris Pepper.
Theological Snippets by Joe Ben Irby.
This They Believed by Joe Ben Irby.
What Cumberland Presbyterians Believe by E. K. Reagin.
Women Shall Preach: Celebrating 125 Yeas of Ordained Women in Ministry in the Cumberland Presbyterian Church.
Prints of the *Samuel McAdow Home* and the *First Meeting of Cumberland Presbytery*.
These items are available for sale from Cumberland Presbyterian Resources.

RECOMMENDATION 3: That the General Assembly make presbyteries, congregations, and individuals aware that the Historical Foundation is interested and has funds to publish books on topics concerning the Cumberland Presbyterian Church and Cumberland Presbyterian Church in America.

3. Denomination Day Resources

All the Past is but the Beginning of Beginning (Denomination Day resource) is available on the Foundation's web site under the Resources section: http://www.cumberland.org/hfcpc/resource/. It includes eight dramas intended to present the birth of the Cumberland Presbyterian Church and the Cumberland Presbyterian Church in America. A hard copy may be requested from the Foundation office.

4. Online Promotion

Recognizing the increasing value of emerging social media, the Historical Foundation employs a Facebook group, "Historical Foundation of the CPC & CPCA," to engage an expanding audience of Cumberland Presbyterians in denominational history and heritage. By showcasing collection acquisitions, the Foundation expands the knowledge of those materials sought for preservation as well as the nature of archival development.

C. HISTORICAL FOUNDATION AWARDS

1. Award in Cumberland Presbyterian History

The Foundation encourages the writing and publication of papers on all aspects of the history of the Cumberland Presbyterian Church in America and the Cumberland Presbyterian Church. One means of promoting such writing is the Historical Foundation Award in Cumberland Presbyterian History. A $300 prize is awarded to the author entering the best paper on any CPC or CPCA history subject which meets in form and content the requirements set by the Board of Trustees and judged by the board appointed awards committee. All manuscripts submitted to the competition become property of the Foundation and are added to the Historical Library and Archives.

The contest follows the calendar year, and entries for the 2016 competition are encouraged. All entries will be accepted through December 2016 for this year's contest. Any entries received following the deadline of December 31st will be automatically entered in the 2017 competition.

Guidelines and entry forms for submitting manuscripts to the competition are available from the Foundation office as well as on the internet, http://www.cumberland.org/hfcpc/Awards.htm. The Historical Foundation appreciates the participation of past and future CPCA and CP historians in this program.

2. Awards of Recognition

Awards of recognition are certificates given to organizations or individuals in recognition of historic events or contributions to the preservation of our heritage as Cumberland Presbyterians. Appropriate applications for the award are: particular churches celebrating anniversaries of their organization; any judicatory or agency celebrating publication of a written history; celebrations of history or historic event in a creative or unusual manner; individuals who have provided continued service for 50 years or more as members of a local congregation or presbytery; individuals who have served for 40 years or more in a continuing leadership role (including pastors) within a local church. Individuals, churches, or presbyterial heritage committees may make application for the issuing of an award by contacting the Foundation office. Application forms are supplied by the Foundation office as well as the internet, http://www.cumberland.org/hfcpc/Awards.htm.

D. RELATIONSHIPS

Presbyterian Historical Society of the Southwest

The Presbyterian Historical Society of the Southwest is an agency of The Synod of the Sun, Presbyterian Church (USA) and Cumberland Presbyterian Churches in Arkansas, Louisiana, Oklahoma and Texas. Members of the Cumberland Presbyterian Church who serve on the board of this organization are Reverend Norlan Scrudder and Dr. Rose Mary Magrill.

IV. HISTORICAL LIBRARY AND ARCHIVES

A. RESEARCH SERVICE

The Foundation's main research commitment is to the agencies, local congregations, and members of the Cumberland Presbyterian Churches. Since the Historical Library and Archives of the Historical Foundation serves as the official repository for the Cumberland Presbyterian General Assemblies, this is our focus. Although the separation of research into two types designated by their mode of access has been rapid and dramatic, both the traditional and "cyber" mode contribute to and enhance the other.

1. Traditional/Physical Access

Hands on access to primary source material remains the vital heart of historic and theological research. Rather than being diminished by increased electronic resources, traditional research has broadened due to heightened awareness of primary sources in an expanding information age. The Foundation receives research requests by personal visitors, mail, e-mail, and telephone. As time permits, requests are researched. Responses are sent to the requestor, as well as pertinent information on ministers, congregations, presbyteries and synods being placed on our website for future researchers.

2. Electronic Access

The Foundation's website continues to expand in order to provide greater access to the materials in the Historical Library and Archives. As well as being a research tool, the internet provides an invaluable and inexpensive means of promotion for the physical collections of the Historical Library and Archives, the activities of the Historical Foundation, and for the greater community of faith called Cumberland Presbyterians. Information at the site includes: general information about the Foundation, entire texts of important historical documents, historical information on particular congregations, ministers, presbyteries, and synods. The gateway URL to the Foundation's website is http://www.cumberland.org/hfcpc/.

B. ACQUISITIONS

The Historical Library and Archives regularly receives items published by the two denominations, *Minutes of the General Assembly of the Cumberland Presbyterian Church, Preliminary Minutes of the General Assembly of the Cumberland Presbyterian Church, Yearbook of the General Assembly of the Cumberland Presbyterian Church, The Cumberland Presbyterian, Missionary Messenger, Minutes of the General Assembly of the Cumberland Presbyterian Church in America, Preliminary Minutes of the General Assembly of the Cumberland Presbyterian Church in America,* and *The Cumberland Flag.* Synods and presbyteries deposit four copies of their printed minutes in the Historical Library and Archives. In addition, books, pamphlets, theses, dissertations, records and publications of general assembly, boards, agencies, institutions, and task forces; records and publications of synods and presbyteries, session records and other materials of particular churches, biographical material of Cumberland Presbyterian and Cumberland Presbyterian Church in America ministers, photographs, audiovisual materials, and museum items were among the accessions received. The 2015 Accession List closed with 238 accession groups.

Some of the highlights added to the collection in 2015 include:

Audiovisual Items
Jerusalem Cumberland Presbyterian Church. Murfreesboro, Tennessee. Worship Services. DVD. 2010-2014.
Fajardo, Jose D. (1913-2015). DVD of funeral service. February 24, 2015.

Books
Campbell, John P. *Plea for Christian Union.* Nashville, Tenn.: Published for the author, 1860.
Correal, Primitivo. *Los Recuerdos Tienen la Palabra.* Primera Edicion. Armenia, Quindio, South America: Editorial San Jose, 2007.
Gillham, Wm. B. *The Aeolian Lyrist: New Collection of Psalm and Hymn Tunes, Adapted to the Various Metres in General Use; With a Few Anthems and Set Pieces.* In Three Parts. By Rev. Wm. B. Gillham, Pastor of the First C. P. Church in Columbia, Tenn. Cincinnati: Published by Applegate & Co. Louisville, Ky.: By the Cumberland Presbyterian Board of Publication, and Sold by Booksellers Generally Throughout the South and West, 1853.
Hubbard, Don. *The Effects of the Civil War on the Cumberland Presbyterian Churches of the Presbytery of East Tennessee.* The Heritage Committee of the Presbytery of East Tennessee of the Cumberland Presbyterian Church, 2014.
Wallace, Boyce. *Cumberland Presbyterian Missionaries in Colombia 1925-2015. A Gathering of Former Missionaries and Relatives in Cali on June 21, 2015.*

Periodicals
Ladies' Pearl. Vol. VII, No. 6 (March 1874).
My Baby and its Church. Volume VI (April, 1952) No. 10 and Volume XII (Mune 1957) Number 6.
The Cumberland Presbyterian, 1875-1896.
The Cumberland Presbyterian Banner, March 27, 1908-April 9, 1909.

Institutions
Bethel College. McKenzie, Tennessee. *The Corporal.* 1925 and 1926.
Missouri Valley College. Marshall, Missouri. *Sabiduria.* 1939.

Minister's Records
Robert Glynn Forester (1922-1997), Azel Freeman (1818-1886), James Cayce Gilbert (1925-2012), James David Hester (1931-2014), Joe Lane Hudgins (1857-1939), Samuel Lucky Noel (1876-1959), Homer R. Robinson (1901-1990), Virgil Holcomb Todd (1921-2014).

Museum Items
Allsboro CPC. Commemorative plate, 1874-1957.
Beaver Creek CPC. Commemorative plate.
Bells Chapel CPC. Commemorative plate and quilt.
Garfield CPC (Garfield, Washington) Glass paperweight.
Richland Presbytery. Moderator's gavel, 1934-1962.

Other Congregational Records
Christ CPC (Lutz, Florida). Cumberland Presbyterian Women's Ministry. Faith Circle Minutes 2005-2014.
Clarks's Grove CPC (Maryville, Tennessee). Church directories, 1973, 1990, and 1998.
Dyer CPC (Dyer, Tennessee). Cookbook. *Heavenly Delights*, 1997.
Holly Grove CPC (Princeton, Alabama). Sunday School Records. 1921-1931, 1934-1936, 1938-1939, 1946, 1956-1964, 1967-1997, 1999-2000.
First CPC (Birmingham, Alabama) Orders of Worship, 1961-1962.

Photographs
McMinnville Presbytery. Zwingle Retreat Summer Camp, 1939.
Oklahoma Synod. Photo album.
Mt. Sterling CPCA (Sturgis, Kentucky)

Postcards
Greeneville CPC (Greeneville, Tennessee)
James Millikin University (Decatur, Illinois)
Mineral Wells CPC (Mineral Wells, Texas)
Missouri Synod. Pertle Springs Missouri. August 1909 and 1910.
West Point CPC (West Point, Mississippi)

Presbyterial Records
Brazos River Presbytery. (CPCA). Minutes of the District Sunday School Convention, 1925-2000.
Ohio Valley Presbyterial Missionary Society (CPCA). Music Clinic Minutes, 1979-1985.

Sermons
> Forester, Jesse Clem (1915-1983). Sermons. 2 boxes.
> McGregor, David Vincent, Jr. (1927-2014). Sermons. 8 boxes.

Session Records
> Holly Grove CPC (Princeton, Alabama). 1965-1997.
> Mangum CPC (Mangum, Oklahoma). 1990-2015.
> Mount Hebron CPC (Goreville, Illinois) 1989-2012.
> Mount Joy CPC (Parsons, Tennessee) 1881-1947
> New Providence CPC (Clarksville, Tennessee) 1963-1985, 1987-2005.
> Paris CPC (Paris, Arkansas) 1987-2009.
> Shiloh CPC (Palmyra, Tennessee) 1972-2012.
> St. Andrew CPC (El Dorado, Arkansas) 1958-2001.

Synodical Records
> Texas Synod. (CPCA). Minutes 1974-1998.

RECOMMENDATION 4: That the General Assembly encourage all congregations to preserve their session records by depositing them in the Historical Foundation.

RECOMMENDATION 5: That the General Assembly instruct each synod and presbytery to deposit their minutes in a timely fashion with the Historical Foundation.

The Historical Foundation can provide on-site assistance to both presbyteries and individual congregations. On the presbyterial level, we can assist the appropriate agency to evaluate materials left when a church has ceased to be viable and has been closed. This can eliminate speculation on the presbytery's part as to what is, or is not, material to be preserved. For congregations we can provide a similar service helping them to determine what can and should be archived.

RECOMMENDATION 6: That the General Assembly instruct presbyteries to locate the session records when closing a church and then deposit them in the Historical Foundation.

V. BIRTHPLACE SHRINE

The Birthplace Shrine located at Montgomery Bell State Park near Dickson, Tennessee was dedicated June 18, 1960. This site consists of the Memorial Chapel and a replica of the Reverend Samuel McAdow's log house. Since 1994, the Foundation has been responsible for the preservation of the Birthplace Shrine. Four endowments provide funds for maintenance and repairs: the Grace Johnson Beasley Birthplace Shrine Fund, the Birthplace Shrine Fund, the Henry Evan Harper Endowment for Cumberland Presbyterian History, and the P.F. Johnson Memorial Endowment. Gifts to these endowments provide for the continued preservation of the Birthplace Shrine. Interested donors are encouraged to contact the Foundation office. Another means of support are the fees collected from couples who use the chapel for their wedding ceremony. These funds are added to the Birthplace Shrine Fund and earnings are used for maintenance and special projects. The Board encourages individuals and groups to visit the Birthplace Shrine as an act of remembering our heritage and envisioning our future as Cumberland Presbyterians.

Groups and individuals are encouraged to contact the Foundation to set up work days and special projects. The Foundation thanks the Heritage Committee of Nashville Presbytery and the Charlotte Cumberland Presbyterian Church for their continuing volunteer upkeep of the property.

VII. FINANCIAL CONCERNS AND 2017 BUDGET

A. BUDGETS

The 2017 line-item budget of the Historical Foundation has been filed with the CPC General Assembly Office.

B. ENDOWMENTS

> Anne Elizabeth Knight Adams Heritage Fund
> Rosie Magrill Alexander Trust

Paul H. and Ann M. Allen Heritage Fund
Grace Johnson Beasley Birthplace Shrine Fund
Birthplace Shrine Fund
James L. and Louise M. Bridges Heritage Fund
Mark and Elinor Swindle Brown Heritage Fund
Sydney and Elinor Brown Heritage Fund
Centennial Heritage Endowment
Walter Chesnut Heritage Fund
Lavenia Campbell Cole Heritage Fund
Cumberland Presbyterian Church in America Heritage Fund
Cumberland Presbyterian Women Archival Supplies Endowment
Bettye Jean Loggins McCaffrey Ellis Heritage Fund
Samuel Russell & Mary Grace (Barefoot) Estes Endowment
Family of Faith Endowment
Gettis and Delia Snyder Gilbert Heritage Fund
James C. and Freda M. Gilbert Heritage Fund
James C. and Freda M. Gilbert Trust
Mamie A. Gilbert Trust
Henry Evan Harper Endowment for Cumberland Presbyterian History
Ronald Wilson and Virginia Tosh Harper Endowment
Historical Foundation Trust
Donald and Jane Hubbard Heritage Fund
Cliff and Jill Hudson Heritage Fund
Robert and Kathy Hull Endowment
Into the Nineties Endowment
Joe Ben Irby Heritage Fund
P. F. Johnson Memorial Endowment
Irene A. Kiefer Endowment
Chow King Leong Endowment
Dennis Lawrence & Elmira Castleberry Magrill Trust
J. Richard Magrill Heritage Fund
Joe Richard and Mary Belle Magrill Trust
Gwendolyn McCaffrey McReynolds Heritage Fund
Jimmie Joe McKinley Heritage Fund
Edith Louise Mitchell Heritage Fund
Lloyd Freeman Mitchell Heritage Fund
Snowdy Clifton and Lillian Walkup Mitchell Heritage Fund
Rev. Charles and Paulette Morrow Endowment
Virginia Sue Williamson Morrow Heritage Fund
Anne Elizabeth Swain Odom Heritage Fund
Martha Sue Parr Heritage Fund
Florence Pennewill Heritage Fund
Morris and Ruth Pepper Endowment
Publishing House Endowment
Mable Magrill Rundell Trust
Samuel Callaway Rundell Heritage Fund
Paul and Mary Jo Schnorbus Heritage Fund
Roy and Mary Seawright Shelton Heritage Fund
Shiloh CPC Ellis County Texas Endowment
Hinkley and Vista Smartt Heritage Fund
John William Sparks Heritage Fund
Irvin Scott and Annie Mary Draper Swain Heritage Fund
F. P. Waits Historical Trust

Respectfully submitted,
ick White, President
Susan Knight Gore, Archivist

THE REPORT OF THE BOARD OF TRUSTEES OF MEMPHIS THEOLOGICAL SEMINARY

Introduction

Memphis Theological Seminary is the only seminary of the Cumberland Presbyterian Church. Our history is traced back through the Cumberland Presbyterian Theological Seminary in McKenzie to the organization of the graduate School of Theology at Cumberland University and the Theological Department at Bethel College, both of which began in 1852. Those two schools of theology continued the legacy begun in the work of founder Finis Ewing, who educated candidates for the ministry in his home, and many other ministers, who trained young candidates in homes, churches, and on the trail. For one hundred fifty seven years, Cumberland Presbyterians have been providing formal theological education for the church's ministers. For almost two hundred years, the Cumberland Presbyterian Church has valued the importance of an educated ministry.

With the denomination's decision to move its seminary to Memphis in 1964, Memphis Theological Seminary of the Cumberland Presbyterian Church began to serve a larger and more diverse student body. Though students from other denominations were admitted during the McKenzie years, the move to a major metropolitan area opened the opportunity to attract more students from more denominations. Today, Memphis Theological Seminary has one of the most diverse student populations, in terms of denomination and race, of any seminary in the United States. This theological and denominational diversity provides a rich environment for educating pastors, chaplains, Christian educators, and other leaders for the church of Jesus Christ. The sign on our campus that faces Union Avenue reads: "Memphis Theological Seminary: an Ecumenical Mission of the Cumberland Presbyterian Church." Every Cumberland Presbyterian can be proud of the mission our seminary fulfills of educating our own church leaders, and leaders from more than 25 other denominations.

We, the trustees and administration of Memphis Theological Seminary are privileged to be a part of this legacy, born out of and guided by the ecumenical and evangelical spirit of the Cumberland Presbyterian Church. We look forward to what God has in store for our ministry in the future. With gratitude for God's grace, guidance and provision in the past year, we make the following report to the 186th General Assembly of the Cumberland Presbyterian Church, meeting June 20-24 in Nashville, Tennessee.

I. BOARD OF TRUSTEES

A. OFFICERS

The following officers were elected by the Board of Trustees to serve during the past academic year: Moderator – Mr. Tim Orr (Cumberland Presbyterian elder, Newbern, Tennessee); Vice-moderator – Reverend Jennifer Newell (Presbyterian Church minister, Tennessee-Georgia Presbytery); Secretary – Mrs. Sondra Roddy (Cumberland Presbyterian elder, Clarksville, Tennessee); Treasurer – Mrs. Cassandra Price-Perry (Vice President of Operations and CFO, MTS).

B. BOARD REPRESENTATIVE

Reverend Susan Parker, Hope Presbytery, was elected to serve as the Board's representative to this meeting of the General Assembly. Mrs. Sondra Roddy was elected alternate.

C. MEETINGS

The Board of Trustees has met twice since the last meeting of General Assembly: October 1-2, 2015 and February 11-12, 2016. The Board is scheduled to meet one more time before the meeting of General Assembly, on May 13, 2016. In addition to full Board meetings, standing committees meet on a regular schedule between Board meetings, usually by conference call.

Members of our Board of Trustees devote significant time and resources to their work on behalf of the seminary. By rule of the General Assembly, thirteen of the twenty-four members are Cumberland Presbyterians. The other eleven members of the Board represent six different denominations.

D. EXPIRATION OF TERMS

The terms of eight of twenty-four members of the Board of Trustees expire each year. Five of the eight whose terms expire this year are eligible to succeed themselves and have agreed to serve another three year term: Mr. Michael R. Allen (Cumberland Presbyterian, Alabaster, Alabama); Mr. Johnny Coombs (United Methodist, Blue Mountain, Mississippi); Mrs. Diane Dickson (Cumberland Presbyterian, Houston, Texas); Reverend Doctor Rick Kirchoff (United Methodist, Germantown, Tennessee), and Reverend Doctor Inetta Rodgers (Baptist, Memphis, Tennessee). All have served faithfully and contributed greatly to the life of the seminary. We are grateful for their willingness to continue serving if re-elected.

Two of our trustee submitted their resignations in May of 2015 because of health concerns: Ms. Pat Meeks (Cumberland Presbyterian, Cordova, Tennessee); and Reverend Doctor Robert M. Shelton (Cumberland Presbyterian, Dallas, Texas). In addition, three trustees will complete their eligibility at this meeting of General Assembly: Mr. Dan Hatzenbuehler (Episcopal, Memphis, Tennessee); Mr. Tim Orr (Cumberland Presbyterian, Newbern, Tennessee); and Mrs. K. C. Warren (Presbyterian, USA, Memphis, Tennessee).

RECOMMENDATION 1: That the General Assembly express its gratitude to the five trustees named above for their faithful service to Memphis Theological Seminary and the Cumberland Presbyterian Church.

E. WORK OF THE BOARD

The trustees continue to develop their administrative procedures and practices to provide the best possible governance to the life of the seminary. For the past nine years we have had 100% participation by trustees in giving to the Annual Fund, and in participating actively in the work of MTS.

The Board has prioritized strategic planning and the development of alternate revenue streams for the coming year.

F. "MINISTRY FOR THE REAL WORLD"

The 183rd General Assembly approved a recommendation from our Board granting us permission to engage in a major capital campaign for Memphis Theological Seminary. After two years in the quiet phase, the Board authorized a comprehensive campaign, titled, "Ministry for the Real World," which was launched publicly in October of 2015. The Board authorized a goal of $25 million to be raised through 2020, with approximately $10 million committed to operations, $10 million to capital improvements, including the construction of a new chapel, and $5 million for endowment.

As of the writing of this report, we have secured approximately $10 million in gifts and pledges toward the goal. What follows is the case statement for the campaign.

MINISTRY FOR THE REAL WORLD
Scholarship, Piety and Justice
MEMPHIS THEOLOGICAL SEMINARY
March 24, 2014

MINISTRY FOR THE REAL WORLD
TWO CENTURIES OF MAKING A DIFFERENCE.

"Academic scholarship is a major hallmark of Memphis Theological Seminary. The school feeds both the minds and spirits of its students. Rigorous scholastic study and intellectual discussion of the Bible from different points of view are encouraged." The goal is to foster informed critical thinkers. It is not to promote the agenda of Memphis Theological Seminary. When students graduate, they have the knowledge and practical tools to be effective ministers. They live their lives according to the teachings and values of the Bible. Graduates are well prepared to positively impact individuals, congregations and society." – Mrs. Ruby Wharton, Esq., Trustee

In 1821, a pastor's dedication to theological education and inclusiveness gave rise to the first theological school west of the Mississippi. Thirty years later, out of the same Spirit, a theological department was established at Bethel College (now Bethel University) in McKenzie, Tennessee, an institution of the Cumberland Presbyterian Church.

Over one hundred years later, in 1964, in order to reach more ministers for the Gospel, the seminary was moved to Memphis and renamed Memphis Theological Seminary. It was intentionally opened as an ecumenical seminary that welcomes men and women of all faiths, cultures and ages. The philosophy and values of the seminary are as meaningful today as they were two centuries ago. The school focuses on scholarship, piety and justice. Inherent in these three words are powerful concepts that differentiate MTS from other seminaries.

- Scholarship implies disciplined, traditional study, but it also involves becoming a discerning critical thinker. Graduates are compelling spiritual servant leaders and thoughtful ministers. They are able to explain Biblical passages within both their historical context and their relevancy in today's world—and in such a way that lives are transformed.

- Piety involves our heart-felt devotion to God. True piety leads to compassion, selflessness, universal love and respect for all of God's creation. As Dr. Martin Luther King, Jr. described so eloquently when he wrote, "Our goal is to create a beloved community, and this will require a qualitative change in our souls as well as a quantitative change in our lives."

- Justice does not refer to civil law. It is much more. Without the practice of justice as described in the Bible, love, liberty and even life cannot flourish. Love alone does not ensure equality. Biblical justice involves care for the poor and powerless and leads to inclusiveness, understanding and compassion. It is respecting all people, even those who are very different from you. It is actively participating in righting wrongs whenever and however they present themselves.

Our student population is very diverse and reflects the real world. There are no age, gender, economic, cultural, theological or racial barriers here. Our graduates will be ministering to many different populations and denominations. Their experience at MTS helps them understand how to work toward a beloved community.

Some of the most respected and influential ministers in the Mid-South are graduates of Memphis Theological Seminary. They are acknowledged for their depth of Biblical and religious knowledge and their ecumenism. They are respected for their ability to influence both religious and secular communities.

Wherever our graduates serve, they impact the lives of those they touch. They are formed to be ministers in the real world.

Our graduates touch thousands of lives in their chosen ministry. They become pastors, youth ministers, educators and chaplains in hospitals, prisons and the military.

For over fifty years, the seminary has occupied the magnificent turn-of-the-century Newburger Mansion in midtown Memphis. We have worked hard to maintain the original beauty of this grand home. Warmth and intimacy are created by cascading stairways, arched doorways, and handcrafted woodwork. It is the beautiful face we show to the public. In more recent years, we have added two adjoining mansions in response to a growing student body and the faculty and staff hired to serve them.

The three homes have served us well, but with enrollment reaching 325 students, we have outgrown them. Because of the reputation and impact of our graduates, our enrollment continues to grow. We believe we can reach an enrollment of 450 students in the not-too-distant future. Together students will represent over 30 denominations, several states and a few countries.

The Newburger Mansion's prized Ballroom is our makeshift chapel. Unfortunately it can only seat one-fifth of our student body. We are grateful to have resided in the homes on beautiful East Parkway during our time of growth. We will always maintain them. They will continue to serve us well as library space, offices and intimate gathering spaces for small discussion groups. But it is urgent that we expand our campus and construct a chapel and an academic building. We have acquired property adjacent to our campus for both structures. Now we must build. Our future depends on it.

PREPARING FOR ANOTHER TWO HUNDRED YEARS OF MINISTRY FOR THE REAL WORLD

The Board and administration of Memphis Theological Seminary have thought long and hard about the future of the seminary. We have prayed for God to guide us in our decision making. In order to ensure our future, we must undertake three important and much-needed projects without delay.

1. A new chapel is a top priority. We have made do with a small converted ballroom for too long.

2. We need a building to house our new, groundbreaking Methodist House of Studies. Methodists represent the single largest contingent of students at MTS. With faculty offices and meeting space, the Methodist House of Studies will relieve pressure on MTS's limited academic facilities.

3. Significantly increasing our endowment and underwriting an important faculty chair will enable MTS to prosper and grow. It will help us become financially stable and ready to withstand any potential financial crises for the next two hundred years. Like most seminaries, we are tuition dependent. At last report our endowment was $9.2 million. This does not generate sufficient interest income to meet the growing demands of our expanding student body. It is crucial that we double the endowment immediately. It will allow us to meet the increasing need for scholarships and financial aid. And it will be a cushion to protect MTS from unforeseen emergencies.

While MTS serves a variety of denominations, its' roots extend back to the Cumberland Presbyterian tradition. By fully endowing the Baird-Buck Chair in Cumberland Presbyterian Studies, we will ensure that our Cumberland Presbyterian students are fully prepared to serve the congregation to which they are sent.

Successfully completing these projects will enable MTS to aggressively pursue its mission well into the twenty-first century: To educate men and women for ordained and lay Christian ministry in the church and the world by shaping and inspiring lives devoted to scholarship, piety and justice.

Project One: Construct a new free-standing chapel

We are blessed to have already received two wonderfully generous gifts designated for our new chapel. The first is an extraordinary cash donation of $1 million. This significant gift is a vote of confidence in Memphis Theological Seminary. It recognizes the difference our graduates make in the world.

The second is one of the oldest and finest pipe organs in the South. It was donated to us by the Union Avenue United Methodist Church. It is an acknowledgement of the role we play in preparing strong spiritual leaders. The pipe organ was manufactured in 1924 by the M.P. Moller Organ Company. In today's dollars, it is estimated to be worth $550,000—a valuable and prestigious gift. Moller pipe organs are also installed in the chapels at Camp David and Lincoln Center.

Both gifts are true blessings and will enable MTS to construct a chapel that

- Reflects our identity, purpose and excellence.
- Is large and adaptable enough for different denominations within the seminary to conduct worship services reflective of their cultures and expressions of faith.
- Provides a place of worship that will accommodate our entire student body.
- Replicates in a small way the churches in which graduates will preach. This will give students the experience of speaking from a real pulpit rather than a small podium.
- Has the proper acoustics to showcase the beautiful Moller pipe organ.
- Will allow us to offer certificates or degrees in church music and organ music.

Project Two: Construct a home for the Methodist House of Studies

There has long been a perceived gap between "the academy" and "the church." We at MTS have become convinced that such a binary way of thinking is deeply flawed. The relationship between seminary and church ought to be marked by an organic, mutually beneficial partnership. Within that partnership, it is the seminary's calling to be in service to the church—preparing women and men for pastoral leadership and resourcing the current ministry needs of pastors and congregations.

We at MTS believe that there is a point of intersection between the mission of the seminary and the mission of the church. Our commitment is to focus our resources and attention at that point of intersection. We are planning a major new initiative in the life of MTS—the Methodist House of Studies. Under the direction of faculty member Dr. Andrew C. Thompson, the Methodist House of Studies will serve as a "community within a community" where our Methodist students can take advantage of the best in Wesleyan theological formation within MTS' richly ecumenical context. The House of Studies will also serve as a vehicle for connecting the resources of MTS with the needs of the wider church. This link will offer pastors and congregations new avenues and contexts for mission and ministry.

The proposed building will house professors' offices and provide meeting space for this groundbreaking program. Given our facilities limitations, the additional space will contribute to the success of this important program.

The ecumenical partnership between Memphis Theological Seminary and the United Methodist Church goes back for decades. And from a strong foundation we believe a vital future can be cultivated and grown. At this crucial juncture in the life of both seminary and church, we are excited to anticipate advancing the relationship between the two with the creation of a home at MTS for the Methodist House of Studies.

Project Three: Significantly increase our endowment and endow the Baird-Buck Chair in Cumberland Presbyterian Studies

Without a larger endowment, we cannot fully execute our mission. Cassandra Price-Perry, Vice President of Operations/CFO, explains this very well.

"I am here to use my financial skills to help students respond to their call by God to ministry. Because of our small endowment, the number and size of our scholarships and financial aid packages are limited. We are not able to enroll as many highly qualified and motivated students as we would like because they can't afford the cost of attendance—books, fees, travel, food and other miscellaneous expenses."

Our tuition is certainly not exorbitant, but nor is it cheap. Many students find it difficult to fund the entire three years required to receive a degree.

Sadly, this compromises our commitment to being an ecumenical school that welcomes everyone who meets our academic requirements. We have cut our operating expenses to the bone during the economic downturn. Still, we can only offer financial assistance to just a portion of the students who apply. Only with philanthropy will it be possible to provide financial assistance to the many motivated and qualified students who are called to serve.

Founded by the Cumberland Presbyterian Church, Memphis Theological Seminary has proclaimed the inclusiveness of the Gospel message for more than 150 years. A fully endowed Baird-Buck Chair in Cumberland Presbyterian Studies will ensure that the vibrant tradition which has guided MTS for eight generations will inspire seminarians for many years to come.

MAKING A REAL DIFFERENCE: MINISTRY FOR THE REAL WORLD

The graduates of Memphis Theological Seminary proclaim and embody God's message of redemption, justice and peace in service to others. Our graduates guide people in their faith and help them understand why they believe. This is powerful. They ignite people's hearts in love for Jesus Christ and support them in walking in His way. They model Christ-like behavior, and in doing so they transform the lives of those they touch—in church, in the grocery store, on a bus or in prisons. They shatter prejudice. They stand in the face of desperation and offer hope. They provide for those with nothing, and they teach others to do the same. The world is a better place because of their real world ministry—a ministry that is persuasive, practical and purposeful.

"Today, mainline religions are grappling with retaining membership. Our emphasis is on academics, practical application and an inclusive approach to theology. This prepares our graduates to be relevant and meaningful ordained and lay ministers in the real world today. This is the only way they can serve and embody God's mission of redemption, justice and peace in service to the New Creation of Jesus Christ. "My father attended this seminary, so it was only natural that I followed in his footsteps. Now that I am president, I am blessed to be leading the initiative to bring our facilities into the twenty-first century. We cannot wait. Our campus must reflect the extraordinary academic excellence within its walls." – Dr. Daniel J. Earheart-Brown, President

Angel, must I give again, I ask in dismay. And must I keep giving and giving and giving it away? Oh no, said the angel, his glance pierced me through. Just keep giving 'til the Lord stops giving to you.

THIS MINISTRY FOR THE REAL WORLD CAMPAIGN IS NOT REALLY ABOUT NEW BUILDINGS

It is about the people.
It is about the highly qualified professors who work inside them. It is about the committed and passionate students who are following God's call to ministry. Sometimes they leave successful careers. Their families make significant economic and lifestyle changes. They do this to serve God, humanity and all of creation. Their lives are transformed. And as a result, our lives are changed. And the world is a better place because of them. Adequate classrooms and a student center will support students on their rigorous academic and spiritual journey. They deserve a real chapel in which to pray, preach, meditate and

seek God's further counsel. A chapel filled with the music of a real pipe organ. And joyous voices joined in praise. Finally, Memphis Theological Seminary deserves facilities that truly reflect the excellence of its high academic standards. Its commitment to forming extraordinary ministers for the real world must be celebrated with quality facilities.

You have the power make a real and powerful difference. Your support ensures the success of our campaign. It also secures the future of Memphis Theological Seminary. With your support we will be able to continue to graduate outstanding ministers for the real world. Prayerfully consider your role in supporting our important undertaking. And as you do, please consider the wisdom of this poem. It reflects the insights of a very generous philanthropist.

YOUR SUPPORT HAS A POWERFUL RETURN

A donation to Memphis Theological Seminary means that your investment will be leveraged in extraordinary ways.

A message from Tim Orr, Chair of the Board Trustees, Memphis Theological Seminary

Dear Friends,

As you consider your participation in the Ministry for the Real World Campaign, you can rest assured that your investment will be leveraged in extraordinary ways. The check I write to Memphis Theological Seminary is multiplied many times over. I am not just writing a check for the seminary. My donation impacts global society.

Here is what I mean. People come here because they are called to ministry. MTS forms them into leaders—Christian leaders with Christian values. Their lives are changed forever. But it doesn't stop there. Everyone touched by one of our graduates is changed also. MTS prepares ministers to be relevant and compelling in the real world. In a world that is spiritually bankrupt, they are effective in their congregation and in all of society. Their lives are transformed, and they are given the tools and skills to transform the spirit of our global society— and they do. I ask you, 'what investment has this powerful a return?'

I hope you will join me at this turning point in the life of Memphis Theological Seminary. Your prayers and generosity will ensure that MTS continues to prepare men and women for transformation ministry to the real world.

Faithfully,
Tim Orr

RECOMMENDATION 2: That the General Assembly encourage individuals, churches, and groups across the Cumberland Presbyterian Church to consider investing in the development of future leaders through the "Ministry for the Real World" campaign.

II. ADMINISTRATION

A. PRESIDENT

Daniel J. (Jay) Earheart Brown, Ph.D., became the seventh President of Memphis Theological Seminary August 1, 2005. Jay had served on the faculty of MTS since August, 1997, having previously served as a pastor in Nashville, Tennessee, and Lexington, Kentucky. He is a life-long Cumberland Presbyterian and son of a Cumberland Presbyterian minister. He is a graduate of Bethel College (B.A.), Memphis Theological Seminary (M.Div.), and Union Theological Seminary in Richmond, Virginia (Ph.D.). He will complete his eleventh year in this position at the end of the current academic year.

B. VICE PRESIDENT OF ACADEMIC AFFAIRS/DEAN

Reverend R. Stan Wood, D.Min., was appointed to serve as Interim Vice President of Academic Affairs and Dean in May, 2010. Doctor Wood had previously served MTS as Clara Scott Associate Professor of Ministry and Director of the Doctor of Ministry Program. He is an ordained minister in the Cumberland Presbyterian Church in America and currently serves as Pastor of the Mt. Tabor CPCA in Jackson, Tennessee. Doctor Wood has announced his retirement effective at the end of next academic year July 31, 2017. The Board will begin a search in the fall of 2016 for our next VP of Academic Affairs and Dean. We covet your prayers for us in this important search.

D. VICE PRESIDENT OF ADVANCEMENT

In October 2014, Doctor Keith Gaskin began work as Vice President of Advancement, coming to MTS after over twenty years of experience in development work for higher education, including service at Mississippi State University and the University of Alabama. He is a layman in the Presbyterian Church. Keith holds a Ph.D. in higher education leadership from Mississippi State University.

Doctor Gaskin has brought to his work at MTS a proven track record of higher education fundraising, a commitment to the mission of MTS, and the ability to manage and build on the efforts of those who have gone before him. He has worked well with faculty and staff to encourage participation across the seminary in the work of development.

E. VICE PRESIDENT OF OPERATIONS/CFO

Mrs. Cassandra Price-Perry began work with MTS in August 2010 as Vice President of Operations and Chief Financial Officer. She is a Certified Public Accountant with over 20 years of experience in business and accounting. Cassandra is an active laywoman in her Roman Catholic Church in Southaven, Mississippi. She has received high praise from our auditors and our Board for her work over the past almost six years.

III. INSTRUCTION

A. DEGREE PROGRAMS

Memphis Theological Seminary offers four degree programs and three certificate programs, including the certificate offered through the Program of Alternate Studies. The Master of Divinity is the basic degree program for persons preparing for ordained ministry in many denominations. It continues to be our largest degree program, with over 70% of students enrolled. The M.Div. requires 87 semester hours and takes three years of full-time study to complete.

The Master of Arts (Religion) degree is an academic degree for persons seeking to pursue further graduate studies. The M.A.R. requires 48 semester hours and takes two years of full-time study to complete. The faculty launched a major revision to the MAR in the fall of 2015 to clarify its role as an academic degree.

The Doctor of Ministry degree is a professional degree designed for pastors and other ministers who have at least three years of full-time work in ministry after their M.Div. and who want to engage in further theological reflection on the practice of ministry. The D.Min. is designed around five two-week residencies, in January and July, and the implementation of and report on a major project in ministry. It usually takes 3-5 years to complete.

In the spring of 2013, we awarded our first new degree in several years: the Master of Arts in Youth Ministry (MAYM). Through our partnership with the Center for Youth Ministry Training in Brentwood, Tennessee, and the new certificate program in youth ministry through the Cumberland Presbyterian Church, we have over 40 students enrolled in this degree program. MTS currently has the second largest master's program in youth ministry in the United States.

In the spring of 2016, we were approved by our accrediting bodies (The Southern Association of Colleges and Schools, and the Association of Theological Schools in the United States and Canada) to offer a new degree, the Master of Arts in Christian Ministry (MACM). This degree program will begin in the fall of this year with concentrations offered in Christian Education, Urban Ministry, and Social Justice Ministry. The MACM is a 42 hour degree for persons interested in pursuing specialized ministries. We plan to offer additional concentrations in the future (possibly rural ministry, counseling, etc.)

At Commencement in May of 2015, Memphis Theological Seminary awarded the Master of Arts in Youth Ministry degree to eleven graduates. Eight persons were awarded the Master of Arts (Religion) degree. Forty-eight persons were awarded the Master of Divinity degree, and six were awarded the Doctor of Ministry degree. Of these seventy-three graduates, twelve were Cumberland Presbyterians.

Cumberland Presbyterian Master of Arts in Youth Ministry graduate was:
Samantha Hassell, Covenant Presbytery

Cumberland Presbyterian Master of Divinity graduates were:
- Cliff Barna, West Tennessee Presbytery
- Jill Carr, Missouri Presbytery
- Joshua Harper, Murfreesboro Presbytery
- Shirley Ostrander, West Tennessee Presbytery
- Rian Puckett, West Tennessee Presbytery
- Noah Quinton, Covenant Presbytery
- Paul Tucker, Murfreesboro Presbytery
- Glenn Warren, Nashville Presbytery
- Dennis Weaver, Covenant Presbytery

Cumberland Presbyterian Doctor of Ministry graduates were:
- Linda Glenn, West Tennessee Presbytery
- Gloria Villa Diaz, Trinity Presbytery

B. CERTIFICATE PROGRAMS

In addition to the five degree programs, MTS offers the following certificates:
- Program of Alternate Studies of the Cumberland Presbyterian Church
- Drug and Alcohol Addiction Counseling Graduate Certificate
- James Netters Certificate in Ministry
- Certificate in Wesleyan Studies

C. FACULTY

For the current academic year, Memphis Theological Seminary has thirteen full-time teaching faculty and two administrative faculty members who teach part-time. In addition, the seminary curriculum is greatly enhanced by the work of twenty-five to thirty adjunct professors, most of whom are active in pastoral or other ministries.

Members of the MTS faculty continue to publish books and articles both for the academy and the church. Many faculty members preach in area churches on a regular basis, deliver lectures for local churches and judicatories, deliver papers at academic conferences, and write articles for a wide range of readers.

Two new tenure track faculty members joined the MTS community for the current academic year. Doctor Courtney Pace (Ph.D. from Baylor University) is Assistant Professor of Church History. Doctor Janel Kragt Bakker (Ph.D. from American University) serves as Assistant Professor of Mission, Evangelism and Culture.

Under the leadership of VP/Dean Wood, the faculty is working toward implementation of our new M.Div. curriculum for the fall of 2016. Under the new curriculum, there will be greater emphasis on integration of learning for pastoral leadership. It will also continue to strengthen our focus on the practice of ministry as imaginative leadership drawing from the resources of scripture and tradition in particular cultural contexts.

D. ENROLLMENT

Total enrollment in Memphis Theological Seminary for the fall term of 2015 was 365, including all degree and certificate programs. We continued to see a slight drop in enrollment in our largest degree program, the Master of Divinity. This dip in our enrollment in the fall led to budget adjustments during the year, and an increased effort to recruit new students. We invested in a new recruiter to focus on our African American constituency. Our largest number of students come from the United Methodist Church, with 25% of total enrollment. Cumberland Presbyterians are the second largest denomination represented in the student body with just under 15% of all students.

We continue to work to recruit Cumberland Presbyterian students, and to lift up the call of God to ordained ministry in the church. We call on all Cumberland Presbyterians to pray that God will continue to call men and women to the office of ministry, and that they will be well prepared through our educational institutions to lead growing and vibrant congregations in the ministry of Jesus Christ to the world.

RECOMMENDATION 3: That the General Assembly urge all probationers to consider Memphis Theological Seminary and the Program of Alternate Studies as their first options for meeting educational requirements for ordained ministry.

D. PROGRAM OF ALTERNATE STUDIES

Beginning in 1984, at the behest of the General Assembly, the Program of Alternate Studies has faithfully filled a vital niche, preparing for ministry those who are hindered from the traditional route of theological education. This has been a source of vitality for the denomination and provided much-needed leadership for hundreds of congregations. Since its inception a total of 193 women and men have graduated from this program. Currently there are 55 active students preparing for ordained ministry through this route or fulfilling the constitutional requirement for Cumberland Presbyterian Studies. This has, once again, been a most fulfilling year of ministry. As the only approved alternate route for educational preparation of clergy in the Cumberland Presbyterian Church we remain always on the cutting edge of new frontiers. In the midst of ever-shifting realities we are approaching the task with open minds and attempting to be sensitive to the context and the Spirit.

PAS ROLE IN UNIFICATION EFFORTS

We are encouraged that, in the talks regarding unification between the CPC and the CPCA, PAS has been mentioned as a key potential player. We have expanded the Advisory Council, adding Reverend Doctor Gloria Lynne Herring. This now includes two persons from the CPCA. We are eager to explore how we can play a positive role. We need to be talking and imagining together NOW how we can be most useful. We believe that delaying consideration of the issues that relate to ministerial preparation will result in a major impediment to the desired unification. We would respectfully request that the GA encourage those involved in planning to include us in the conversation as soon as practical. We are sending a similar request to the GA of the CPCA.

ONLINE COURSES

We have completed the experimental phase for all four Cumberland Presbyterian Studies courses and each has been developed for teaching in an online format. Our approach is asynchronous (students log-on according to their schedule) and dialogical (students respond to questions and interact within a framework on a closed discussion board). A variety of resources are used including print and digital material, original lectures (video and written), videotaped classroom and panel discussions, as well as other websites. It is our intent, at present, to offer all these courses online annually. To familiarize the presbyteries with the online experience, and to foster further collaboration in the process, we have invited the chair (or someone designated) of each Probationer Care Committee to audit, without charge, to one of the four courses during the next year. Please help us spread the word. They may contact the PAS office 901-334-5854 or email kpatten@memphisseminary.edu for instructions.

The PAS Advisory Council authorized the development of other courses within our curriculum incrementally over the next several years with this stipulation: that no more than 50% of a student's courses may be taken online, assuring that substantial course work will be in traditional classroom settings. This includes the students who only need CP Studies courses. Two of the four must be taken at SES. The thinking is that, along with the content, there is a strong benefit to being immersed in the Cumberland Presbyterian ethos.

PAS-COLOMBIA

We have been developing an education program for this context for about four years now. This branch of our program has come into its own and the process is working for the presbyteries of Colombia. They are creatively offering five courses per year, allowing students to complete their studies in six years. A total of 16 are currently enrolled. Our office continues to develop courses for translation into Spanish. We commend retiring Moderator, Reverend Michele Gentry, and her able Advisory Council, for PAS Colombia. We express thanks to the Stated Clerk for allowing us to highlight our budding work by making presentations at the General Assembly in Cali last summer.

SUMMER EXTENSION SCHOOL

The dates for this year's SES are July 9-23 on the campus of Bethel University. Graduation will be the first day, July 9th. Reverend Elinor Brown, Discipleship Ministry Team Leader, will be our commencement speaker. We anticipate three graduates.

We urge clergy and lay-leaders to take advantage of the wonderful opportunity for development and continuing education by auditing one or more of the terrific courses we will offer. We are, again, partnering with the PDMT to provide a clergy retreat during Block III, July 19-23.

During that same block we will be offering Church, Culture & Mission. This outstanding course, taken by M.Div. students along with PAS students, will be led by Doctor H. Stanley Wood. Doctor Wood is a recognized expert in the fields of evangelism, new church development, and congregational leadership. He has developed a denomination-wide national strategy for church planting and a coaching program for church planters, as well as designing and leading many national New Church Development conferences. He currently directs "The Sower's Field," a non-profit corporation dedicated to church planting and development. We are thrilled to have him bring that expertise to the Cumberland Presbyterian Church.

POSSIBLE NEW ARENA

The PAS Advisory Council has voted to explore partnership with "The Sower's Field" in creating a certification program for potential new church development leaders. In the era of church decline, a real need is to develop new congregations with the ability to reach and disciple new people in the North American context. The key in establishing these communities of faith is leadership. In the Cumberland Presbyterian Church (and many others) there is no pool of women and men who have desire, gifts, and training for this endeavor. Doctor Wood is a recognized authority in this field and has worked with various seminaries to develop a program to identify and resource church planters. We are in conversation with him. The idea would be to have an ongoing cohort where missional leaders (PAS and seminary students, current pastors, and lay-leaders) are nurtured and given tools to continue to discern and develop the gifts for this unique calling. As a result we would create a pool of persons for presbyteries and denominational staff to be able to access when planning for new church development. The idea is in infancy and may unfold in unforeseen ways, but it holds promise.

GLOBAL/CROSS-CULTURAL PARTNERSHIP

There are diverse needs for ministry preparation in a variety of contexts. We are collaborating with Missions Ministry Team in global outreach to help supply critical education necessary for assimilation of potential Cumberland Presbyterian pastors in South America, Asia, and Haiti. We are working with the Missions Ministry Team to provide integrity to our ordination process through ministerial preparation. We are also returning, this summer, to the practice of offering a Spanish-language cohort during SES in collaboration with our Cross-Cultural Ministries Leader.

Respectfully,
Michael Qualls, Director

E. NEW ACADEMIC INITIATIVES

In Fall 2010, we began offering courses toward a certificate in drug and alcohol addiction counseling. This new program, which has been led by Cumberland Presbyterian minister and counselor Doctor Johnie Welch, promises to meet an important need in our society and in our region. Due to health concerns, Doctor Welch was unable to continue in this role after the 2012 academic year. Currently, Reverend Terry Kinnaman, a Cumberland Presbyterian minister from Columbia Presbytery and licensed counselor working for the State of Tennessee, is coordinating this program in a part-time capacity.

In the spring of 2012, we began a new certificate program targeted for African American ministers in the Memphis area who do not have the educational background to enroll as degree students at MTS. The James Netters Certificate Program, we believe that there is a need for such certificate level education for many in our area and hope to expand this work in the future.

In the spring of 2016 we received word from our accreditors that we have been approved for a new degree program, the Master of Arts in Christian Ministry. This degree is designed for persons who are called to ministries other than ordained pastoral ministry. The new two-year degree will begin enrolling students in the fall of 2016. Students will choose between concentrations in Christian Education, Urban Ministry, and Social Justice. Additional concentrations to be added may include Children and Family Ministries, Rural Ministry, and other specialized ministries.

Our Master of Arts in Youth Ministry degree is, we think, the second largest graduate degree program in youth ministry in the United States. We continue to cooperate with the Center for Youth Ministry Training in Brentwood, Tennessee to offer a graduate residency in youth ministry.

In the fall of 2016 we will begin implementation of a major revision to our Master of Divinity curriculum. The revised curriculum will provide more opportunity for team teaching and cross-disciplinary work focused on integration of theology and practice for ministry.

F. ACCREDITATION

Memphis Theological Seminary holds dual accreditation by the Association of Theological Schools in the United States and Canada (ATS), and the Southern Association of Colleges and Schools (SACS). Every ten years, member schools go through an extensive process of re-accreditation review.

Our last accreditation visit occurred in 2008, at which time we were fully affirmed for the next ten years by both accrediting bodies.

IV. FACILITIES

A. LEADERSHIP

Since the fall of 2015, our facilities and safety department has been ably led by Mr. Greg Spencer and a dedicated staff of facilities technicians. Mr. Spencer has more than twenty years of experience in construction and facilities management. He served in this role for two years previously, and after a brief stint in facilities management in corporate environment, Greg returned to our MTS leadership. We are grateful for his service.

B. DEBT ON PROPERTY

In 2015 we were able to secure a commercial loan to repay our debt to the Board of Stewardship for the purchase of properties adjacent to our campus. That long term debt now stands at less than $1.5 million, less than a third of our annual budget amount. This low debt allows us to operate as efficiently as possible.

C. COMMUTER HOUSING

MTS began to convert its student housing from individual rentals to commuter housing in the 1998. Currently, MTS provides commuter housing, with very reasonable nightly rates, for about fifty students each week of the regular term. The need for such commuter housing has continued to grow, as has income from such rentals. Our ability to serve students from about a 250 mile radius around Memphis, through block scheduling of classes and provision of affordable commuter housing, has had a significant impact on the growth of the student body over the past ten years.

D. CAMPUS WORK GROUPS

We have been blessed in recent years by adult and youth work groups who have come to MTS during the summer months to help repair and maintain our campus housing. Groups have come from Trilla, Illinois; Greeneville, Tennessee; Florence, Alabama; Bowling Green, Kentucky; and Collierville, Tennessee, and the youth from West Tennessee Presbytery to volunteer their time in a variety of areas. We encourage work groups who would be willing to help the seminary in this way to contact Mr. Greg Spencer in the Facilities Office of the seminary.

E. SAFETY

The Office of Safety of MTS continues to explore ways to enhance the safety of our students in the context of our urban campus. Through the use of lighting, security officers, secure locks, and well articulated safety plans, the seminary seeks to provide a safe environment for students and visitors to our campus.

During past six years, MTS has contracted with a local security company to provide regular patrols around our neighborhood. This additional safety measure has been well received by our students and by our neighbors. We continue to seek ways to provide a safe environment for our campus community.

V. ADVANCEMENT AND FINANCE

A. BUDGET

Our Board of Trustees will approve a budget for the 2013-2014 academic year at its May meeting. Copies of that budget will be provided at the meeting of General Assembly.

After two years of significant budget reductions in the worst of the recession, we have begun to restore some of the cuts as income has improved the past two years. We continue to be very conservative in our budget planning as we work to recover from the effects of the recession. We were able to give modest raises to our employees last year. Our employees deserve much credit for hanging in with us through some tough economic times.

B. SCHOLARSHIPS AND GRANTS

We continue to cultivate relationships with foundations whose mission closely aligns with ours. The following grants for scholarships and other projects have been received in recent years:

1. The Henry Luce Foundation (2012-2014)

To support At the River: Theology & Arts Program at MTS, the Henry Luce Foundation granted $150,000 payable over 3 years, double their initial investment in 2009-2011. The Luce Foundation is located in New York City and funds programs like these on a large scale across the country. In 2014, we conclude this round of funding, but with a new Theology & Arts director and program focus, we anticipate a new opportunity for Luce Foundation funding.

2. The Wilson Family Foundation

The Wilson family, founders of the Holiday Inn hotel chain and great philanthropists in Memphis, has renewed their funding of the Wilson Scholarships at $15,000 for 2013-14.

3. The H.W. Durham Foundation

In 2013, the Memphis-based H.W. Durham Foundation renewed its gift of $5,000 to provide 5 $1,000 scholarships for students who are 55+ years of age. These Durham Scholars will represent much of our student body who are second-career students.

4. The First Tennessee Foundation

This Foundation provides a gift of $10,000 to partner with MTS in the course "Money, Markets & Ministry," taught by Dr. Jay Earheart-Brown. We are in our fourth year of this level of support.

5. The Lilly Endowment (2013-2018)

With a three-year grant totaling $249,371, followed by a second grant of $140,000 MTS is creating a unique program to increase financial literacy and decrease debt among our student population, and long term, the congregations they serve.

C. ENDOWMENTS

1. The Baird-Buck Chair of Cumberland Presbyterian Studies

Doctor Clinton Buck, Professor Emeritus of Christian Education at MTS, knowing the need for more focused teaching in CP heritage, has converted an existing endowment that was originally begun with the hopes of endowing a chair in Christian Education. Subsequent to Doctor Buck's decision, the late Mrs. Thalia Baird, widow of former President and Professor Doctor Colvin Baird, converted an endowment they had designated for general operations. Together with The Reverend J.T. Buck Scholarship Endowment Fund established in 1979 to provide scholarship assistance for Cumberland Presbyterian students at Memphis Theological Seminary, the new endowment was established with an initial principal balance of approximately $112,000. To-date, the fund has grown to more than $350,201, thanks to generous contributions from many Cumberland Presbyterians. The purpose of this endowment is to strengthen the Cumberland Presbyterian Church by establishing an endowed professorship with a primary focus of teaching Cumberland Presbyterian history, theology, church administration and the practice of ministry that is particular to the Cumberland Presbyterian Church. The goal is to raise $1.5 million to fully fund this endowed chair.

2. Rev. Hillman and Lorene Moore Endowed Scholarship Fund

Hillman Moore established this endowment fund on October 10, 2013, to be funded with a future gift of a bequest from his estate. It will be used to provide scholarship funds for training Cumberland Presbyterian students at Memphis Theological Seminary.

3. Wes and Susan Brantley Endowment

On October 15, 2013, the Brantley family of Ada, Oklahoma, was deeply saddened by the death of Susan Brantley, wife of former MTS trustee Wes Brantley, and mother of current trustee Kevin Brantley. In her memory, Wes has established the Wes and Susan Brantley Endowment to support general operating expenses of the seminary.

4. Brooksville Cumberland Presbyterian Church Scholarship Endowment

After 129 years of ministry in the Brooksville, Mississippi, area, the Session of the Brooksville CP Church decided to close the church due to lack of growth in the changing rural town. The closing service of praise and thanksgiving was held on January 13, 2013, led by Reverend Jearl Hunley (M.Div. '67), who served the church for 12 years. Many family, friends and former members came back for this occasion.

In March, Grace Presbytery held its spring meeting and voted to use one-half of the proceeds of the sale of the church building to establish a memorial scholarship that will provide tuition support for CP students in the years to come. First preference will be given to MTS students from Grace Presbytery.

5. The Davis/Winston Scholarship for National Baptist Students

In the waning days of the spring semester 2013, one CP and one United Methodist student listened as three fellow students talked about the struggles they have in paying their seminary tuition. For these two students, all or most of their tuition is paid by their denomination. For the others, all National Baptists, humble servants with sweet spirits, the story is completely different.

Moved by the Holy Spirit through their student colleagues, they sought a way to establish a scholarship to help future National Baptist students. In recognition of the blessing received when seminary education is paid in full or in part by scholarship and/or denominational assistance, and in honor of exemplary and invigorating teaching by professors Doctor Christopher B. Davis and Doctor Eric Winston, they established a scholarship to support National Baptist students at MTS.

6. Dr. Alfred DeWayne Hill Scholarship Endowment Fund

Mrs. Doris Thomas Hill remembers that her late husband was always grateful for the financial assistance he received to attend seminary. "In his memory and because of our need to continue Doctor Hill's practice of sowing into the lives of students, especially faith leaders, I am pleased to establish the Dr. Alfred DeWayne Hill Scholarship Endowment Fund" to support scholarships for African American students.

7. Rev. David and Leota Watson Scholarship Endowment Fund

A new endowment has been established to honor the ministry of the late Reverend David Watson. His widow, Mrs. Leota Watson, has chosen to direct the endowment earnings to support scholarships for Cumberland Presbyterian students attending MTS. Those who knew and loved Reverend Watson and appreciate his and Leota's ministry are invited to send a gift to fully establish the Rev. David and Leota Watson Scholarship Endowment Fund. Every gift matters. Perhaps in the Fall semester 2014, a David Watson Scholar will be announced.

8. Rev. Walter (Pete) Palmer Endowment for the Program of Alternate Studies

This endowment was funded from a significant bequest from Reverend Palmer. The endowment will provide program support for the PAS summer extension school and scholarship aid for needy students.

9. Other Endowment funds

Many Cumberland Presbyterians and others continue to support endowments that have been established through the years to fund our work. Currently, the total MTS endowment, managed by the Board of Stewardship of the Cumberland Presbyterian Church, is just over $10 million. The Advancement Office and President are available at any time to discuss endowment gifts with potential donors.

D. ESTATE GIFTS

MTS received estate gifts during the past year from the following faithful servants of Jesus Christ:
- Rev. Dr. Virgil Todd (alumnus, former Professor of Old Testament)
- Rev. Dr. J. David Hester (alumnus, former President and Professor of Evangelism)
- Rev. Walter (Pete) Palmer (alumnus)

In addition, we have received word that MTS will be receiving a bequest from the estate of former trustee Pat Meeks, who died in April of this year.

We continue to have conversations with friends and donors about the importance of remembering MTS (and their local churches, and other ministries they care deeply about) in their estate plans. We publish a list of those who have informed our office that they have included MTS in their will. That group is known as the Heritage Society. The Heritage Society is listed in every issue of The Lamp, our magazine for alumni and friends.

F. SEMINARY/PAS SUNDAY

We have many churches in our denomination, and in other denominations we serve who recognize Seminary Sunday in their local churches. This provides time for education of members about the work of MTS and the Program of Alternate Studies and provides an opportunity for members to make a special one-time gift to support the work of the seminary. Please contact the seminary for more information on how you can recognize Seminary Sunday in your local church, and to request a speaker for the occasion.

RECOMMENDATION 4: That the third Sunday in August, (August 21, 2016 and August 20, 2017) be included in the General Assembly Calendar as Seminary/PAS Sunday, and that the General Assembly encourage all churches to share information about MTS and PAS and receive a special offering on that day, or a more convenient day of the session's choosing.

G. ANNUAL FUND

Memphis Theological Seminary could not operate without the faithful contribution of its alumni and friends. Annual Fund contributions help us keep the cost of tuition down, so that students do not leave seminary with a large burden of debt to have to pay during their early years in ministry. Annual Fund contributions have grown steadily over the past fifteen years, as income from Our United Outreach has declined.

In some respects, the income we receive from OUO puts us in a better position than many theological seminaries, whose income from denominational sources has declined significantly over the past twenty years. Our income from OUO has remained relatively steady and over that time period. However, as a percentage of our total income, OUO has fallen from almost 20% to about 3% of our operating budget. We are grateful for the commitment of Cumberland Presbyterians to the ministry of MTS, and all our common ministries, expressed so tangibly through giving to Our United Outreach.

At the same time, we do not expect income from denominational contributions to increase significantly in the future. This means that we are required to put more time and energy into fund raising than ever before. We are grateful for the many alumni who have made a financial contribution to our ministry this year. We are also grateful for all the faithful laypersons who have given to the Annual Fund because they know the importance of an educated ministry to the life and health of our denomination.

H. AUDIT REPORT

The auditing firm of Zoccola Kaplan, P.C. has audited the books of Memphis Theological Seminary for the 2014-2015. The audit was unqualified, and noted several significant improvements in the financial position of MTS. Copies of that report have been filed with the office of the Stated Clerk.

Respectfully submitted,
Tim Orr, Moderator of the Board of Trustees
Daniel J. Earheart-Brown, President
Memphis Theological Seminary

THE REPORT OF THE
OUR UNITED OUTREACH COMMITTEE

The 2009 General Assembly established a denominational Our United Outreach Committee to be made up of 12 voting representatives, one from each Synod and the rest from the church programs and institutions. Executives from the church programs and institutions participate on the Committee as advisory members. This Committee meets annually unless there is a needed called meeting.

A goal of the Our United Outreach Committee is to encourage ALL churches to contribute to Our United Outreach. Approximately 30 percent of the churches do not give anything with a high percentage of other churches not giving at the 10 percent level. This past year, 2015, the budgeted goal for Our United Outreach was $2,900,000 – 89% giving was achieved. While this was an admirable achievement, the Committee seeks to involve ALL churches with Our United Outreach giving and at a greater level of giving.

I. OUR UNITED OUTREACH FUNDS ALLOCATION

The Our United Outreach Committee met March 4, 2016, to allocate the Our United Outreach funds for the 2017 year. The Our United Outreach allocation basis for 2017 is $2,800,000.

The 2013 General Assembly had one funding request from the Unification Task Force which was for $20,000 a year starting in 2014 but was increased to $30,000 for 2016 and increased to $35,000 for 2017.

A line item of $25,000 for Legal Fees has been re-instated for 2017. These requests, along with the Development Coordinator's salary/benefits, have been approved as guaranteed amounts and are deducted from the goal amount prior to allocation purposes.

RECOMMENDATION 1: That General Assembly adopt the following Our United Outreach allocations for 2017:

The allocation is to be as follows:	$2,800,000.00	
Development Coordinator		92,044.00
Legal Fees		25,000.00
Unification Task Force		35,000.00
	Sub-total	152,044.00
(Amount to be allocated)	$2,647,956.00	
Ministry Council	$1,323,978.00	50%
Bethel University	132,398.00	5%
Children's Home	79,439.00	3%
Stewardship	159,877.00	6%
General Assembly Office	211,836.00	8%
Memphis Theological Seminary/	185,357.00	7%
Program of Alternate Studies		
Historical Foundation	79,439.00	3%
Shared Services	436,913.00	16.5%
Contingency	13,240.00	5%
(Next four items total 1%)		
Comm. on Chaplains	10,247.00	.387%
Judiciary Committee	9,665.00	.365%
Theology/Social Concerns	3,601.00	.136%
Nominating Committee	2,966.00	.112%
	$ 2,67,956.00	
Our United Outreach Goal	$2,800,000.00	

From the agencies listed above, all should be self-explanatory except maybe Shared Services. Maintenance, utilities, mowing, trash pick-up, pest extermination, and custodial are all examples of Shared Services for agencies sharing the Cumberland Presbyterian Center.

II. NEW MODEL TO INCREASE PROMOTION OF OUR UNITED OUTREACH ACROSS THE DENOMINATION

During the second half of 2015 and the first quarter of 2016 the Our United Outreach Committee considered, voted unanimously to approve, and began implementation of Cliff Hudson's plan to modify our efforts toward a Regional Representative model. It is our hope and desire that this newly expanded model will cover more territory, be conducive to the creation of more relationships between pastors, sessions, and congregations, and increase awareness further across the church.

In this plan, Director Hudson will remain as general overseer of our efforts, but on a part-time basis. He will continue to be the primary contact person for Tennessee-Georgia, Robert Donnell, Murfreesboro, Columbia, and Nashville presbyteries and will share the load with Carolyn Harmon in East Tennessee presbytery.

Elder Calotta Edsel will be primarily responsible for West Tennessee and Arkansas presbyteries. Reverend Jeff McMichael will be primarily responsible for Covenant, Cumberland, and North Central presbyteries.

Reverend Susan Parker will be primarily responsible for Grace and Hope presbyteries. We are excited about the possibilities for greater "reach" into the larger church and expect a high level of planning, co-ordination, and collaboration between the regional representatives

We will continue to recruit in other areas of the church not yet covered.

III. OUR UNITED OUTREACH PARTICIPATION

All boards and agencies of the Cumberland Presbyterian denomination are made up of individuals who possess the leadership abilities to plan, implement, and fulfill the ministry calling of the church. The denominational nominating committee always strives to find the best candidates for vacancies on denominational boards and agencies. In an effort to strengthen the importance of supporting Our United Outreach and affirm those congregations that regularly contribute, we propose the following recommendation.

RECOMMENDATION 2: That the following statement be added to the By-Laws of the General Assembly, Article 10.02 Election and Tenure: 03. No person shall be elected to any board whose church does not support Our United Outreach; however, an individual may directly give financial support to Our United Outreach and be eligible to serve on boards and agencies and that the remaining numbers under that Article be re-numbered accordingly.

The Our United Outreach Committee members are enthusiastic in their approach to the development of total participation in this program of the church.

Respectfully submitted,
Ron Gardner, Chairperson
Reverend Lanny Johnson, Vice-Chairperson
Sharon Resch – Secretary
and the Our United Outreach Committee

THE REPORT OF THE COMMISSION ON MILITARY CHAPLAINS AND PERSONNEL

The Commission on Military Chaplains and personnel represents the Cumberland Presbyterian Church on the Presbyterian Council for Chaplains and Military Personnel (PCCMP). The commission does its work through the Council which has its headquarters in Washington D.C. and represents also the Cumberland Presbyterian Church in America, Presbyterian Church (USA) and the Korean Presbyterian Church Abroad. The Cumberland Presbyterians who are members of the Commission for the Cumberland Presbyterian Church for the PCCMP include Reverend Cassandra Thomas, Reverend Tony Janner, Reverend Mary McCaskey Benedict and Stated Clerk the Reverend Michael Sharpe.

I. REPRESENTATION

The The term of the Reverend Cassandra O. Thomas expires in 2016. For 2015, one of the four PCCMP Executive Board positions is filled by CPC member: the Reverend Cassandra O. Thomas as Secretary. The Reverend Mary McCaskey Benedict remains the Chairperson of the Personnel Committee. The Revered Tony Janner joined the Council filling the unexpired term of Lowell Roddy. The chair of the PCCMP is now Bill Nisbet (PCUSA) and the vice-chair is Sung-Joo Park (PCUSA).

II. RESPONSIBILITY OF THE PCCMP

1. Provide ecclesiastical endorsement for chaplains of the United States Armed Forces who are serving on active duty or in the Reserves/National Guard. The PCCMP also endorses chaplains for the Department of Veterans Affairs. In addition, the PCCMP endorses PCUSA teaching elders into chaplaincy positions with the Civil Air Patrol and the Federal Bureau of Prisons.
2. Provide pastoral support for chaplains and their families.
3. Provide a unified and influential voice for member denominations to the National Council on Ministry to the Armed Forces in matters relating to the ministry and welfare of PCCMP-endorsed clergy.
4. Provide representation to denominational agencies and ecumenical bodies with respect to matters relating to United States military personnel, veterans and their families.
5. Promote closer communications between chaplains and denominational judicatories.
6. Carry out other duties as may be requested by the member denominations.

III. ANNUAL PCCMP MEETING

The annual meeting of the PCCMP takes place in the fall, with representatives of the member denominations in attendance. In 2015, the Council met in Memphis at the Cumberland Presbyterian Church Headquarters. In 2016, the Council will meet in Louisville. During this meeting, the Council discusses and takes action as necessary on business that comes to its attention during the year. The 2015 meeting was conducted under the leadership of the PCCMP's director, the Reverend Dr. Lawrence P. Greenslit, a 27-year Navy veteran who is a teaching elder in the PCUSA. The previous director, the Reverend Ed Brogan, retired in May 2014. Sometimes, candidates for ecclesiastical endorsement will come before the Interview Committee at this meeting. Generally, candidates are required to submit an application, school transcripts, proof that their presbytery approves their seeking this call, and letters of reference. After the documents are gathered, candidates are interviewed personally to determine if they should be endorsed for active duty or service with the Reserve/National Guard and/or Veteran's Administration (VA). A recommendation for each candidate is then submitted to the Council. If they are approved by the Council, they make an application to the various branches of service. The PCCMP maintains sound working relations with the Chief of Chaplains for each branch of the ministry and the VA. In addition, work is being done to provide support to Civil Air Patrol chaplains of the PCCMP Presbyterian members and for the PCUSA, oversight to those seeking to be chaplains for the Federal Department of Justice. Of note for clergy interested in applying to be chaplains in the Navy, a new policy requires two years of post-ordination pastoral experience as part of their package submission.

IV. SUPPORT FOR THE COUNCIL

The The Council receives financial support from the four denominations listed above and often receives individual, judicatory and church support. We are facing some difficult times in securing finances in the very near future. We will seek to be faithful stewards in caring for our chaplains and their families.

The Cumberland Presbyterian Churches support this ministry by taking an annual Memorial Day Offering. We would encourage all churches to consider an offering at that time, or another time to support our involvement in the PCCMP. Congregations may conduct a special offering at a time it deems convenient: some of the suggested days are the Four Chaplains Sunday, which is traditionally held on the first Sunday in February, the Sunday closest to Independence Cay or Veteran's Day. In these ways Cumberland Presbyterians are able to show support for all men and women who serve or have served in the United States Armed Services, Reserves, National Guard, VA and CAP as well as their families. These offerings should be sent to the General Assembly Stated Clerk who forwards them to the Council for its outreach, mission and maintenance efforts. The Commission expresses deep appreciation to all congregations that collected offerings for the PCCMP during the past year.

V. CUMBERLAND PRESBYTERIAN CHAPLAINS

We are proud to say that our denomination has a total of 17 men or women currently involved in various forms of chaplaincy around the world,

	Active Duty	Reserves	Other
Army	3	2	
Air Force	1	1	
Navy	1	1	
VA	4		
National Guard		1	
Chaplain Candidates			3

Please remember to pray for those serving in this important ministry and their families. You can find the names of those serving in the General Assembly Yearbook of the Cumberland Presbyterian Church.

Additional information may be found by checking the Cumberland Presbyterian Church website: www.cumberland.org/ccmp or the PCCMP website: www.pccmp.org.

Respectively Submitted,
Reverend Mary McCaskey Benedict
Reverend Tony Janner
Reverend Cassandra Thomas

THE REPORT OF THE
PERMANENT JUDICIARY COMMITTEE

The Judiciary Committee met February 26, 2016, in Huntsville, Alabama. Present were Annetta Camp, Harry Chapman, Andy McClung, Robert Rush, Kimberly Silvus, Bill Tally, Wendell Thomas, and Felicia Walkup. Also attending were Jaime Jordan, legal counsel, and Mike Sharpe, Stated Clerk of General Assembly. Sherry Ladd was excused.

I. ORGANIZATION OF THE COMMITTEE

Kimberly Silvus was elected chairperson andAndy McClung was elected secretary.

II. MEMORIALS

The committee reviewed two memorials from Covenant Presbytery and found both to be in proper order to come before the 186th General Assembly.

III. REFERRAL

The 184th General Assemblyinstructed this committee to "work in concert with the Missions Ministry Team" to develop a constitutional amendment which would make legal the MMT's assumption of the responsibilities of a presbytery in developing new churches outside of the U.S. The directive's use of the phrase "the Missions Ministry Team (or its successor)" inspired us to think beyond current organizational structure and allow for future changes. Therefore, this committee developed and approved the following proposed constitutional amendment to be sent to the Joint Committee on Amendments:

"The General Assembly, in order to promote the mission work of the Church and the development of new churches outside the United States, may authorize its mission entity, a judicatory, or a commission to act in the place of a presbytery with respect to persons, ministers, and churches lying outside the bounds of the United States and outside the bounds of any existing presbytery. In such a case, the body so designated shall have with respect to the persons, ministers, and churches under its care the same jurisdiction, authority, and responsibilities which are otherwise granted to a presbytery, and the General Assembly rather than a synod shall provide for the oversight and responsibility of the body's ecclesiastical actions."

RECOMMENDATION 1: That contingent upon ratification of the proposed constitutional amendment, the General Assembly designate the Missions Ministry Team as the mission entity authorized to function as a presbytery in accordance with the proposed constitutional amendment.

As each presbytery engages in ministry, it enjoys the oversight of a synod. This committee believes it is important to replicate that relationship in instances in which any other entity legally functions as a presbytery and therefore makes the following recommendation:

RECOMMENDATION 2: That the General Assembly Bylaw 11.05, which refers to the Judiciary Committee, be amended by inserting "11.05.06. The committee shall have oversight of and responsibility for ecclesiastical decisions made by a body acting in the place of a presbytery with respect to mission work and mission fields. The oversight and responsibility exercised by the committee shall be the same as that exercised by a synod with respect to a presbytery under its care. The committee shall have oversight of and responsibility for ecclesiastical decisions made by a body acting in the place of a presbytery with respect to mission work and mission fields. The oversight and responsibility exercised by the committee shall be the same as that exercised by a synod with respect to a presbytery under its care. When the committee is performing this role, the Stated Clerk may appoint up to two temporary members from the applicable mission field to serve for the limited purpose of oversight and review.

IV. JOINT COMMITTEE ON AMENDMENTS

This committee appointed Robert Rush, Kimberly Silvus, Wendell Thomas, and Felicia Walkup to represent the Cumberland Presbyterian Church on the Joint Committee on Amendments, meeting April 7-8 in Nashville, Tennessee.

V. SAFE SANCTUARY

The 184th General Assembly (2014) encouraged all congregations to adopt and practice a Safe Sanctuary plan.

RECOMMENDATION 3: That the stated clerk's office of each presbytery, rather than the Office of the General Assembly, be designated as the repository for the Safe Sanctuary plans for churches within that presbytery.

VI. REVIEW OF SYNOD MINUTES

The committee reviewed the minutes of Synod of the Southeast and Synod of the Midwest and found both to be in order.

VII. GENERAL ASSEMBLY REPRESENTATIVES

Robert Rush will serve as this committee's representative to the 186th General Assembly and Andy McClung will serve as the alternate.

Respectfully submitted,
The Judiciary Committee

THE REPORT OF THE NOMINATING COMMITTEE

The Nominating Committee consists of a minister and a lay person from each synod, preferably from different presbyteries. Members may serve a three year term, but cannot succeed themselves. Cumberland Presbyterian members of any board or committee can be re-elected to the same board after a two year absence. Ecumenical representatives may be re-elected to the same board after a one year absence. With the exception of the Nominating Committee any person elected to serve on a denominational entity may serve three consecutive terms. Filling an unexpired term counts as one term, thus members of any entity do not always serve nine years before completing eligibility on a board/agency.

The members of the various Ministry Teams are no longer elected by the General Assembly, but are to be appointed by the Ministry Council.

*Ecumenical Representative   +Cumberland Presbyterian Church in America

The Committee submits the following list of nominees:

I. STATED CLERK

Reverend Michael Sharpe, Red River Presbytery, Mission Synod, for a four-year term.

II. ENGROSSING CLERK

Reverend Vernon Sansom, Red River Presbytery, Mission Synod, for a four-year term.

III. BOARD OF DIRECTORS, GENERAL ASSEMBLY CORPORATION

Reverend Bobby Coleman, Arkansas Presbytery, Synod of Great Rivers, for a three-year term.
Mr. Tim Garrett, Brenthaven Congregation, Nashville Presbytery, Tennessee Synod, for a three-year term.

IV. MINISTRY COUNCIL

Ms. Victory Moore, Shiloh Congregation, North Central Presbytery, Synod of the Midwest,
    for a two-year term.
Ms. Vicky Hoover Ainley, McKenzie First Congregation, West Tennessee Presbytery, Synod of Great Rivers,
    for a three-year term.
Ms. Tsuruko Satoh, Louisville Japanese Congregation, Cumberland Presbytery, Synod of the Midwest,
    for a three-year term.
Reverend Troy Green, Columbia Presbytery, Tennessee Synod, for a three-year term.
Ms. Karen Avery, Heights Congregation, Presbytery del Cristo, Mission Synod,
    for a three-year term.
Reverend Mike Wilkinson, Knoxville First Congregation, Presbytery of East Tennessee, Synod of the Southeast,
    for a three-year term.
Ms. Charli Uhlrich, Youth Advisory Member, Bethany Congregation, North Central Presbytery,
    Synod of the Midwest, for a one-year term.
Mr. Cameron Alderson, Youth Advisory Member, Chandler Congregation, Covenant Presbytery,
    Synod of the Midwest, for a one-year term.
Mr. Caleb Davis, Youth Advisory Member, Trinity Presbytery, Mission Synod, for a one-year term.

V. HISTORICAL FOUNDATION

Ms. Robin Hughes, Eastlake Congregation, Red River Presbytery, Mission Synod, for a three-year term.
Reverend Mary Kathryn Kirkpatrick, Trinity Presbytery, Mission Synod, for a three-year term.
Ms. Ashley Lindsey, Bowling Green Congregation, Cumberland Presbytery, Synod of the Midwest, for a
    three-year term.

VI. MEMPHIS THEOLOGICAL SEMINARY

Reverend Stewart Salyer, Bethel Congregation, Nashville Presbytery, Tennessee Synod,
    for a one-year term.
Reverend Anne Hames, West Tennessee Presbytery, Synod of Great Rivers, for a one-year term.
Mr. Michael Allen, Alabaster First Congregation, Robert Donnell Presbytery, Synod of the Southeast,
    for a three-year term.
*Mr. Johnnie Coombs, an ecumenical partner, for a three-year term.
Ms. Diane Dickson, Houston First Congregation, Trinity Presbytery, Mission Synod, for a three-year term.
*Dr. Deborah Smith, an ecumenical partner, for a three-year term.
*Dr. Rick Kirchoff, an ecumenical partner, for a three-year term.
Ms. Marianna (Molly) Williams, Newbern Congregation, West Tennessee Presbytery, Synod of Great Rivers,
    for a three-year term.
*Dr. Inetta Rodgers, an ecumenical partner, for a three-year term.
*Ms. Jane Ashley Folk, an ecumenical partner, for a three-year term.

VII. BOARD OF STEWARDSHIP, FOUNDATION AND BENEFITS

Ms. Andrea Smith, Winchester Congregation, Murphreesboro Presbytery, Tennessee Synod,
    for a three-year term.
Reverend Charles (Buddy) Pope, Columbia Presbytery, Tennessee Synod, for a three-year term.
Ms. Sue Rice, Hope Congregation, Grace Presbytery, Synod of the Southeast, for a three-year term.
Ms. Debbie Shelton, Manchester Congregation, Murfreesboro Presbytery, Tennessee Synod,
    for a three-year term.

VIII. COMMISSION ON CHAPLAINS AND MILITARY PERSONNEL

Reverend Cassandra Thomas, Red River Presbytery, Mission Synod, for a three-year term.

IX. JUDICIARY

Ms. Rachel Moses, Cookeville Congregation, Murfreesboro Presbytery, Tennessee Synod,
    for a three-year term.
Reverend Andy McClung, West Tennessee Presbytery, Synod of Great Rivers, for a three-year term.
Reverend Jan Overton, Grace Presbytery, Synod of the Southeast, for a three-year term.

X. NOMINATING

Reverend Derek Jacks, Homewood Congregation, Grace Presbytery, Synod of the Southeast,
    for a three-year term.
Ms. Faye Delashmit, Bowling Green Congregation, Cumberland Presbytery, Midwest Synod,
    for a three-year term.
Reverend Stephen Louder, Clarksville Congregation, Nashville Presbytery, Tennessee Synod,
    for a three-year term.
Ms. Janie Stamps, Fort Smith Congregation, Arkansas Presbytery, Synod of Great Rivers,
    for a three-year term.
Ms. Frances Dawson, Christ Church Congregation, Robert Donnell Presbytery, Synod of the Southeast,
    for a one-year term.

XI. OUR UNITED OUTREACH COMMITTEE

Reverend Bruce Hamilton, Rose Hill Congregation, Arkansas Presbytery, Synod of Great Rivers,
    for a three-year term.

XII. UNIFIED COMMITTEE ON THEOLOGY AND SOCIAL CONCERNS

Reverend Marcus Hayes, Liberty Congregation, Murfreesboro Presbytery, Tennessee Synod,
    for a three-year term.
Reverend Byron Forester, West Tennessee Presbytery, Synod of Great Rivers, for a three-year term.
Reverend John A Smith, Nashville Presbytery, Tennessee Synod, for a three-year term.

THE REPORT OF THE
PLACE OF MEETING COMMITTEE

The Place of Meeting Committee consists of the Moderator, a representative of the Cumberland Presbyterian Women's Ministry, and the Stated Clerk who serves as the chairperson. The representative of the Cumberland Presbyterian Women's Ministry is the Convention Coordinator.

The 165th General Assembly, "authorized the committee to select meeting places up to five years in the future and that preference be given that keeps, insofar as possible, the General Assembly and the Convention of Cumberland Presbyterian Women's Ministry, and guest rooms in one facility. It is recognized that these places are hard to find and may cost some additional monies. The place of meeting committee will use its best judgment." The 173rd General Assembly approved exploring the use of college campuses and very large conference centers in addition to hotels/convention centers. When the Office of the General Assembly receives an invitation from a congregation or a presbytery, the Stated Clerk makes a site visit. If adequate facilities are discovered, a follow up visit is made by the Stated Clerk, the Assistant to the Stated Clerk, and the Convention Coordinator of the Cumberland Presbyterian Women's Ministry.

Unless the General Assembly sets aside Bylaw 14.02 Standing Rules 1 to allow for a different meeting time, the annual meeting is the third or the fourth week of June.

Commissioners, delegates to Conventions, and visitors are encouraged to stay at the General Assembly/Convention hotel, to assure meeting the contracted room block. Hotel contracts also include a commitment on food and beverages, thus it is important for boards/agencies to continue to sponsor special meal functions. The luncheons/dinners provide opportunities for the sponsoring agencies/boards to keep the church informed about their respective programs, thus enhancing support.

I. INFORMATION ABOUT FUTURE GENERAL ASSEMBLIES

If a congregation or a presbytery is interested in hosting the General Assembly/Convention, the Office of the General Assembly will provide information on hosting responsibilities. Hosting the General Assembly/Convention is a service to the Church, allowing the Church to celebrate the good ministries occurring within a particular presbytery, and provides persons within a presbytery the opportunity to participate more fully in the annual meeting. Continued discussions with the leadership of the Cumberland Presbyterian Church in America regarding joint meetings of the General Assemblies in 2018 and 2019 may also impact future meeting locations.

In the event that no invitation is received in a particular year or a situation arises requiring a change of venue for a particular year, the Corporate Board will be responsible for selecting a place of meeting.

II. SCHEDULE OF FUTURE GENERAL ASSEMBLIES

187th   Tampa, FL area   June 19-23, 2017
(to be hosted by the Florida Churches of Grace Presbytery)

188th   Norman, OK (near Oklahoma City)   June 18-22, 2018
(to be jointly hosted by Choctaw Presbytery and the
Oklahoma Churches of Red River Presbytery)

III. SCHEDULE OF MEETINGS BY PRESBYTERIES

The following schedule shows the annual meetings and the year that the General Assembly last met in the bounds of a particular presbytery.

Andes & Cauca Valley	2015	East Tennessee	2003
Chattanooga	2014	Covenant	2002
Murfreesboro	2013	del Cristo	2001
Hope & Robert Donnell	2012	Cumberland	2000
Missouri	2011	Tennessee-Georgia	1998
Nashville	2010	Robert Donnell	1996
West Tennessee	2009	Nashville	1995
Japan	2008	North Central	1980
Arkansas	2007	Trinity	1969
Grace	2006	Hope	1961
Columbia	2005	Murfreesboro	1956
Red River	2004		

Respectfully submitted,
Michael G. Sharpe
Pam Phillips Burk
Michele Gentry

THE REPORT OF THE UNIFIED COMMITTEE ON THEOLOGY AND SOCIAL CONCERNS

I. MEETING AND OFFICERS

The Unified Committee on Theology and Social Concerns met at the Cumberland Presbyterian Church center on October 9-10, 2015 and by teleconference February 19, 2016. The following officers were elected during the fall meeting: Reverend Shelia O'Mara (CPC) and Reverend Edmund Cox (CPCA) Co-Chairs; and Reverend Nancy Fuqua (CPCA), Secretary.

II. EXPIRATION OF TERMS

The Committee notes that the terms of service for Ms. Lezlie Daniel, Reverend Jimmie Dodd, Reverend Byron Forester, Reverend John Smith and Ms. Joy Wallace all expire in 2016. Each member, except Lezlie Daniel, is eligible to be reelected.

III. GENERAL ASSEMBLY REPRESENTATIVES

The Committee elected Reverend John Smith to serve as the representative to the meeting of the Cumberland Presbyterian Church General Assembly in Nashville, Tennessee.

IV. GENERAL ASSEMBLY REFERRALS

The 185th General Assembly directed the Unified Committee on Theology and Social Concerns "find a means to make all theological and social statements from General Assembly easily accessible for anyone to read." The committee discussed several options and will comply with General Assembly direction. This will take some time to make statements available as only the last ten years of General Assembly minutes are digitized. Minutes older than ten years will need to be scanned and searched for approved statements.

The 185th General Assembly requested "that the Board of Stewardship and the Unified Committee on Theology and Social Concerns have joint responsibility to properly answer the 184th GA's inquiry pertaining to what is currently covered by health insurance benefits and clarify anything that might conflict with the Confession of Faith and previous actions of the General Assembly statements regarding sanctity of life." The committee has consulted with the Board of Stewardship and Cumberland Presbyterian Church Stated Clerk. There has been a recent change in insurance providers and so far no conflicts have been noted. Any conflicts found will be referred to the committee for review.

V. STUDY PAPERS

The Committee presents the following papers for consideration by the General Assemblies: "Homelessness as a Justice Issue-A Theological Response: (Reverends Byron Forester and Shelia O'Mara) and "A Confessional Response to Discrimination" (Reverend John Smith).

RECOMMENDATION 1: That the General Assemblies accept the papers, "Homelessness as a Justice Issue-A Theological Response" and "A Confessional Response to Discrimination" as study papers and that they be used to initiate thought and discussion within the Cumberland Presbyterian Church and the Cumberland Presbyterian Church in America.

RECOMMENDATION 2: That the Office of the General Assembly of both denominations make these papers available to churches through the stated clerks of the presbyteries.

The Committee revised its Guide to the Process of Writing Papers which is available on the website (www.cumberland.org/uctsc).

VI. WORKS IN PROGRESS

The Committee is currently discussing theological reflections on the following concerns for future papers to be submitted at the October 2016 committee meeting: Gun control/racial profiling; elder abuse; and hermeneutics-understanding interpretation of Scripture.

VII. UNIFICATION EFFORTS

The Committee affirms and supports the work of the Unification Task Force and any recommendation it may have for delaying the timeline for unification and the need to revise the proposed plan for unification.

RECOMMENDATION 3: That a Sunday be set aside as Unification Sunday and that all churches have a service geared toward unification.

VIII. CHURCH CALENDAR

The Committee supports the ongoing focus by the Women's Ministry of the Cumberland Presbyterian Church on Domestic Violence and would like to see an addition to the church calendar to give a denomination wide focus on the topic.
Nation wide October is National Domestic Violence Awareness Month.

RECOMMENDATION 4: That National Domestic Violence Awareness Month be added to the church calendar for the month of October.

Respectfully Submitted,
Unified Committee on Theology and Social Concerns

HOMELESSNESS AS A JUSTICE ISSUE-A THEOLOGICAL RESPONSE

Foxes have holes, and birds of the air have nests, but the Son of Man has nowhere to lay his head. Luke 9:58

Three days a week they come to Manna House, located near downtown Memphis. They come in ragged clothes, worn out shoes, the few belongings they have stuffed into backpacks. They come by themselves or in clusters of two or three. They come by foot or by bicycle. They come for a shower, a change of clothes, a bag containing socks and hygiene items. And coffee. Lots of coffee. They come to get off the streets for a while, to relax on the couches and stuffed chairs, or in the shady backyard to play checkers, chess, or Scrabble. Manna House is a place of hospitality for folks who are poor, unsheltered, and who need somewhere to stay for a few hours without anyone telling them to "move on."

Another way Manna House offers hospitality to guests is through listening acceptance. Every person who comes has a story to share. The stories are about how they spent the night, an illness, about some hurt they are carrying around, or about a concern for another guest. Quite often the stories are about how they came to a place in their lives where they no longer have a permanent place to live.

Each story about how people land in a situation where they no longer have a shelter that they can call home is a bit different but many have common roots. For some it was the loss of a job, then the savings were used up and then there was no money to pay the rent. Many are unable to work due to physical limitations, quite often as a result from an injury at the place of employment. Many deal with addictions, mental health issues, or personality disorders that are untreated and leave them unable to concentrate or to be around other people in close quarters for more than a short time. Some have returned from wars and have been wounded, experience Post Traumatic Stress Syndrome, or are otherwise scarred so that functioning in a so-called "normal" society has become extremely difficult. The stories that are told in the most halting and hushed tones are the ones told of emotional, physical, and sexual abuse as a child.

It's impossible to accurately count the number of homeless people in America because they are so hard to locate. A report, "The State of Homelessness in America 2015" published by the National Alliance to End Homelessness counts over 578,000 adults as being without shelter. This report, however, does not count children. The National Center on Family Homelessness documents more than 2.5 million children who are living in what the U. S. Department of Education defines "the lack of a fixed, regular and adequate nighttime residence." The Department documents that more than 1.2 million of these are students who sleep in cars, parks, and motels. An estimated 900,000 are in situations called "doubling up". They reside with relatives or friends.

Children who grow up in foster care are much more likely to experience homelessness later in life. As they reach age 18 many are moved out of the system with few life skills that enable them to survive without the support of a family to encourage them. They are more likely than children reared in traditional families to engage in substance abuse, drop out of school, become incarcerated, and thus find themselves on the streets with few employment prospects and no place to go, and little trust in social systems to which they can turn. (National Alliance to End Homelessness)

According to a 2014 series of articles in the *USA Today* entitled *The Cost of Not Caring*, an estimated one-fifth of the people who live on the streets are suffering from some form of mental illness. Schizophrenia, bi-polar disorder, or severe depression can all be managed with the right medication and counseling, but when the medicine runs out and there is no support or care given, then these disorders are left untreated and the struggles progress. Those who are without medicine or have no caregiver can quickly wind up living on the streets. They are often prone to public psychotic outbursts. The police, who have minimum training in dealing with the mentally ill, are called and the offender is usually jailed. Eventually, sometimes weeks or months, the charges are dropped and the person is released to go back on the streets and the cycle repeats itself.

The National Coalition on the Homeless estimates that as many as fifty per cent of people who are homeless have substance abuse problems. Addictions can be both a cause and a result of being homeless. Those who are addicted to drugs or alcohol can quickly spiral downward, losing employment, the support of families and friends, and then housing. There is often a connection between mental illness and substance abuse. These people are sometimes not eligible for public housing because of failed drug tests. Access to rehabilitation centers frequently is not an option because of the very nature of addiction. People who are addicted are very successful at convincing themselves that they are not addicted. If one does enter a recovery program the lack of a permanent place to live decreases the likelihood of the success of the treatment.

Another group with an elevated risk of homelessness are those who have been discharged from prison with no place to go (endhomelessness.org/file/4365_file_The_Demographics_of_Homelessness).

Sometimes there are situations that occur while the person was incarcerated that have led to the breakup of the person's family: divorce, illness, and any factor that causes families to become alienated. So a person is released from jail or prison and no longer has a home or a permanent address. Jobs are hard to come by for someone who as a criminal record, especially if there is not an address to list on a job application.

For LGBT (Lesbian, Gay, Bisexual, Transgender) people the challenges of living on the street are greatly increased. They have endured the pain of being rejected by their families. LGBTs must face the social stigma of being whom they are which adds to the emotional and mental challenges of life on the streets. Not only is finding employment difficult, they very often are rejected by shelters that neither accept nor respect them as people. They are at a heightened risk of being victims of violence, theft, substance abuse, rape, and engaging in survival sex (prostitution). (nationalhomeless.org/issues/lgbt)

The Annual Homeless Assessment Report to Congress and the 2015 State of Homelessness in America both state that on any given night there are 50,000 veterans who have no place to call home. Service members who have served their country in a time of war come back to America to find that while their country supported the troops while they were in the military, there is a dearth of support when they are discharged. Contributing factors are a lack of income due to limited education and a lack of transferable skills, combat related physical and mental health issues and disabilities, substance abuse, and weak social networks due to problems adjusting to civilian life. The National Coalition for Homeless Veterans reports that the number of female veterans has increased by 242 per cent between the years 2005 to 2014. Forty per cent of female veterans who are getting assistance have children.

Divorce as a cause for homelessness is another factor that is difficult to document because it is so interrelated to all the other factors. The loss of a combined income, of a support system along with legal fees, health issues, and lack of a job all send people into a way of living that they had not planned on. (endhomelessness.org)

Despite our conventional perception that people who live on the streets are there because of bad choices or sinful living, homelessness can also occur when there is no family dysfunction, no divorce, no substance abuse, or cataclysmic event. There can be a series of unanticipated expenses that lead to loss of a home. Bills cannot be paid. Overdue notices arrive. Credit is denied or unattainable and eviction eventually results.

"The poor have it hard and the hardest thing they have is us." Daniel Berrigan

Once the permanent address disappears the journey back to self-sustainability is difficult and the barriers often become insurmountable. The practice of payday lending heaps debt on people with no viable option for repayment. The monthly notes quickly become more than what borrowers spend on food. Grocery shopping itself becomes difficult, as folks do not have the means to buy in bulk. Without the use of an automobile transportation becomes an added expense. Cabs and bus fares eliminate trips to the supermarket so shopping at the high priced convenience stores consume more of the income. Public transit to a welfare office can turn that visit into an all day wait which means having to take time off from a job in which they can easily be replaced.

In the United States laws are being passed that criminalize poverty. New York City has recently passed an ordinance that forbids sleeping on subway trains (*The New York Post*, Feb. 3, 2016)."Despite the fact that communities all over the country lack adequate affordable housing and shelter space, cities are continuing to penalize people forced to live on our streets and in our public spaces. Criminalization measures often prohibit activities such as sleeping/camping, eating, sitting, and/or begging in public spaces and include criminal penalties for violations of these laws. Some cities have enacted restrictions that punish groups and individuals for serving food to homeless people. Many of these measures appear to be designed to move homeless persons out of sight, or even out of a given city." *How America Punishes Its Poor* (TalkPoverty.org. by Rebecca Vallas).

Just before the 2016 Super Bowl the city of San Francisco forced people who had been living on the streets in an area that would host several events leading up to the game to leave. Those people were taken to shelters that were already overcrowded. The events for which they were removed were events that were free to the public, but evidently, not to the sector of the public who are unhoused (*Christian Science Monitor*, February 4, 2016).

Then God said, "Let us make humankind in our image, according to our likeness", Genesis 1:26

In all the demographic groups and all the factors that contribute to people being without homes there are several threads that intertwine but the most common reason is a breakdown of relationships: relationships between families, friends, support networks, government. The most damaging, saddest, and for Christians, the most telling broken relationship is the one between unsheltered people and the church. Over the decades as the rate of homelessness has increased, mainstream denominations have largely ignored what should be a major concern of Christianity: ministering to those in need.

In the first chapter of Genesis we are told that persons are created in the very image of God and are given the responsibility to be stewards of creation. Being created in God's image assures that each person is valuable and full of dignity. Given that we are all that important to God we must treat all persons with the same respect.

Let justice roll down like waters, and righteousness like an ever-flowing stream. Amos 5:24

God creates and sustains the creation and part of that sustainability is the calling God issues for justice. *"For I the Lord love justice* (Is. 61:4) *"For the Lord loves justice* (Psalm 37:28). *The Lord, "who executes justice for the orphan and the widow, and who loves the strangers, providing them with food and clothing."* (Deut. 10:18).

God's concern for oppressed people is addressed throughout the scriptures. Exodus 3:7-8 speaks of how God hates oppression and will act in history to relieve suffering. In Amos 2:7 God tells of how mistreating the poor and afflicted profanes God's name. Similarly, we are told that when we address the problems of the poor, we are helping God (Proverbs 19:17) and when we do not we show contempt for God (Proverbs 14:31).

The justice of God of which Amos writes is unequivocally addressed to the relationship of those who are oppressed by those who rule over them. *"Thus says the Lord God: "Enough, O Princes of Israel! Put away violence and oppression, and do what is just and right. Cease your evictions of my people, say the Lord God"* (Ezekiel 45:9).

According to the prophets not only does God call for all people to be treated justly, God will move against peoples and nations that refuse to do so. Amos and Isaiah warned that God would be so outraged because of unfair economic practices and idolatry that Israel and Judah would be destroyed and taken into captivity (Amos 2:7, 5:11, Is 10:1-4). People and societies that build wealth by oppressing the poor are not living compatibly with the will of God.

Perhaps the strongest and plainest instruction humans are given regarding how other humans are to be treated comes from Micah 6:8. *"What does the Lord require of you but to do justice, and to love kindness, and walk humbly with your God?"*

Doing justice does not mean merely helping the poor cope with their problems, but removing the injustice that oppressed them. To "love kindness" is to show compassion for all of God's children and people who live on the bottom rungs of society; the homeless and hungry are the most deserving of our kindness. To walk humbly with our God calls for us to journey with God into the places where God goes no matter if those places are among people who are on the margins of society and not generally accepted by society. We are called to humbly follow God's commands for us to minister to those who are, as Pete Gathje, co-director of Manna House writes *"on the margins of the marginalized."* (Manna House blog). Isaiah 9 and 11 speak of the promise of a Messiah who will bring righteousness and justice for all.

Just as you did it to one of the least of these, who are members of my family, you did it to me. Matthew 25:40

For Christians the plight of the poor and homeless becomes a justice issue. Our theological response to this injustice must be to offer love. (I Corinthians 13). The love we are called to share is manifested in hospitality and work to relieve the oppression of the poor.

Christian hospitality is centered in the life and presence of Jesus Christ. Jesus, in Matthew 5:17 said to the crowds gathered on the mountain that he had come to fulfill what the prophets foretold. Throughout the gospels Jesus moves from one group to another teaching that building the kingdom means reaching out to those who society has labeled as the outcasts. He heals the sick, cures the lame, feeds the hungry, and dines with sinners. In Luke 10:25-37 instruction is given on how we are to respond to those who have been cast aside. Echoing the prophets, Matthew 11:20-24 speaks to the woes that will befall unrepentant cities

Jesus goes to great detail in laying out what needs to be done in order to inherit the kingdom (Matthew 25:31-46). He identifies what non-actions will eliminate people from the kingdom and then proclaims that committing those very acts are the requirements for enjoying life in the kingdom.

What good is it, my brothers and sisters, if you say you have faith, but do not works? James 2:14

In 2010 the Iona Fellowship, a Cumberland Presbyterian community of faith in midtown Memphis, Tennessee, established a "Burrito Ministry". Working out of the First United Methodist Church in downtown, a group of volunteers gathers every Tuesday to cook and assemble 160 burritos. After a prayer of gratitude for being called to serve, the group moves outside to an area beside the church where guests have assembled. Each guest is greeted with unqualified love and acceptance. Each one receives a bag with two burritos, a bottle of water, and some cookies. Donated clothing is handed out and during the cold weather months. Blankets, hats, scarves, gloves, shoes, and hand warmers are made available. The only action required of the guests is that they show up. The Burrito Ministry began on October 5, 2010 and has never missed a Tuesday. According to co-director Reverend Barry Anderson, through February of 2016 the Burrito Ministry has handed out over 42,000 burritos to those whom Jesus calls his brothers and sisters.

An outgrowth of the Burrito Ministry has been the Nashville Burrito Ministry, begun in 2013. A varying number of churches participate several of which are Cumberland Presbyterian.

The Urban Bicycle Food Ministry of Memphis (UBFM) also has its roots in the Burrito Ministry. Developed by a Cumberland Presbyterian minister, Reverend Tommy Clark, in 2012, the goal of UBFM is "to fulfill the gospel on two wheels". Twice a week this group gathers to make burritos and then heads out on bicycles to meet the hungry where they are, and to engage people more intimately.

Room in the Inn Ministry began in a single church in Nashville in 1986 in response to the plight of unsheltered people shivering through cold winter nights. The concept is simple: offer a warm, safe place to spend the night, a bed, a hot meal, a shower, a change of clothes, a light breakfast, and friendly conversation. The guiding principle for Room in the Inn is the principle of respect for all people. There are now close to 200 churches in the Nashville area, including several Cumberland Presbyterian churches that are involved in this ministry to homeless people.

In 2011 Colonial Cumberland Presbyterian Church brought the Room in the Inn concept to Memphis. What began in one church has now spread to 23 churches in the Memphis area, including five Cumberland Presbyterian churches that welcome strangers in for food, warmth, and shelter. Guests are picked up at a designated area and taken to a church. Each church hosts 10-12 guests. This means that on every night of the week during the cold weather months (November 1 through March 31) shelter and a warm bed is provided for folks who live on the street. Not every church who participated in RITI has adequate facilities to host a group, so they travel to Colonial or other churches and serve as hosts for that night; providing the meal and fellowship. Any of these ministries can easily be developed in any town with proper planning and training.

Another common perception of homelessness is that it is unique to large cities. Certainly unsheltered people are more visible in the cities but homelessness is also pervasive in rural areas. An estimated 9 per cent of unsheltered people live in small towns. The causes for not having adequate shelter in rural areas is the same as that the cities: lack of affordable housing and inadequate income being the chief reasons, but all the factors that contribute to having no permanent address are at work in the small towns as well. Compounding the problem in rural areas is the lack of any support services. People will relocate to the cities where services are more accessible.

Having a smaller number of those to minister to does not prevent small town or rural congregations from providing ministries to people in need. Most counties have some sort of food bank (Community Food Banks) to which many churches contribute. An avenue that churches in closer proximity to urban areas use to help is to partner with ministries already in action. The West Union Cumberland Presbyterian Church now offers its building as a Room in the Inn ministry allowing the unsheltered people in an urban area to have *"that country church"* experience. The Hopewell Cumberland Presbyterian Church in Benton County, Mississippi has a "blanket party" every November right before Thanksgiving. Layers of fleece are purchased then stitched and knotted together to form a blanket that is big enough for an adult to wrap up in and be protected from the cold wind. The blankets are taken to Memphis where they are distributed to the guests at the Burrito Ministry or at Room in the Inn.

In Newbern, Tennessee the Cumberland Presbyterian Church busies itself stocking a clothes closet which provides clothing to people whose clothes are too tattered, too dirty, the wrong size, and too uncomfortable to continue wearing. The church provides a stock of healthy food staples for people whose pay is too low to purchase enough food to last till the next payday. The food pantry is open three Thursdays per month. Because of funding, the sharing is limited to one distribution per family per month. In this way the congregation is allowed to spend time that allows for conversation. Conversation allows for relationships and relationships build trust. As the trust builds guests begin to speak of others they know who are in need but who may be physically unable to come or who may have special needs and do not know how to sign up for assistance.

For Pastor Steve Rogers offering clothing and food has unveiled other needs. Rogers has learned that there are unsheltered people, including children in Newbern but they are not generally known about. They are able to "double up", living with other family members or friends. The church is continuing to search for creative ways to minister to poor and unsheltered people in area where resources for that problem are severely lacking.

Project Vida, located in El Paso, Texas is a joint partnership between the Cumberland Presbyterian Church and PCUSA denominations and is supported by Presbytery del Cristo (Cumberland Presbyterian Church). Located in the center of El Paso in one of the nation's most impoverished neighborhoods, the programs have been based on dialogue with the community to proactively address needs to include homelessness, housing, health clinics/education/wellness and education.

The gospel of Jesus Christ is good news for the poor. The scriptures of the Bible continually call us out for being complicit with those who possess all the power and wealth and abandoning the people that God loves and cares about the most. As Christians who believe in the words of the Bible we are called to address the injustice and oppression in our society. We do this by participating in our ministries to those who live in need. We also do this by petitioning our governments; local, state, and national, to discontinue policies that place heavy burdens on the poor among us. We can address our elected leaders and the leaders of our communities and most of all, the leaders of our churches and call for them to engage the homeless on a more personal basis, to be in relationship with them, to listen to them, to hear their stories. When we come to truly know those who are oppressed, then we can begin to understand God's outrage at injustice.

STUDY QUESTIONS

1. What good works am I (or my church) doing to care for the homeless and the poor?
2. What are some things I can do to get involved?
    a. Determine community needs.
    b. Involve others who are also concerned.
    c. Join homeless coalitions.
    d. Donate time, food, clothing or money,
    e. Contact local elected officials.
3. My church is small and we don't have a lot of money. How can we do something and make a difference?
4. Share examples of what you, your church or community is doing to address homelessness and care for the poor. Send your examples to any member of the Unified Committee for Theology and Social Concerns. Member names and contact info can be found on the USTSC webpage.

A CONFESSIONAL APPROACH TO DISCRIMINATION

The introduction to the 1984 Confession of Faith states, *"There is a direct relationship between the church's confession of faith and her life and witness as a people in covenant with God and each other. The faith of the church orders and shapes the life of the people of God . . ."* As part of the Presbyterian and Reformed family the Cumberland Presbyterian Church is a church based on a Confession of Faith. The Confession of Faith for Cumberland Presbyterians is not to take the place of Scripture but to give direction and guidance to our community. It exists to provide a framework upon which we, as a covenant community, can affirm our faith and have a basis upon which to bear witness to all of creation of the grace of God as it is displayed in the person of Jesus.

FOUNDATIONAL PRINCIPLES

The Cumberland Presbyterian Church formed itself around the idea that all people were free to respond to the call of the Holy Spirit and come into covenant relationship with their creator. The Cumberland Synod, meeting in 1813 set forth four points of dissention from the Westminster standards. The first point was, *"There are no eternal reprobates."* By stating this dissention the founding fathers of our denomination made the bold claim that all people stood equally before God and were free to enter into relationship with God.

As we have journeyed from that original confession, our denomination has grown as a covenant community. We have wrestled with issues such as slavery and the ordination of women. The journey has not always been smooth and at times portions of the Church did not see eye to eye however up till this point the Cumberland Presbyterian Church has always come out on the side upholding the belief that there is dignity in every living creature and adjusted our practices accordingly.

Our society at the present moment once again offers our denomination a chance to affirm our faith in the light of our Confession of Faith and the scripture. We see the effects of racism and discrimination. Many of our brothers and sisters in the Cumberland Presbyterian Church in America have felt the effects of being profiled and suffered injustices at the hands of those in power. We also see states passing laws allowing discrimination based upon religious beliefs. We see the effects of these laws in the news on a regular basis. As a denomination who seeks to define itself based upon God's unconditional love for all of humanity, the time is now for us to stand and confess our faith and stand against the domination system which seeks to oppress and exploit.

In this paper I propose three affirmations upon which to combat discrimination in any form. These affirmations are drawn from the 1984 Confession of Faith and the supporting scriptures. These affirmations build upon one another just as our Confession of Faith builds upon itself to tell the story of scripture. These affirmations seek to provide a position for the Church as she seeks to be a voice of witness to the love of Jesus for all people and to faithfully fulfill her calling to care for her neighbor.

THE DIGNITY OF ALL PERSONS

First and foremost the Cumberland Presbyterian Church Confession of Faith affirms the dignity of all persons as created being of God. Section 1.10 states, *"God is the creator of all that is known and unknown. All creation discloses God's glory, power, wisdom, beauty goodness, and love."* Cumberland Presbyterians believe that all that is made comes from God and that this creation is good. Throughout the first chapter of Genesis one sees the declaration that as God looked over creation it was declared good. This goodness which is inherent in all of creation on the basis that all things were made from God must be affirmed as a basis upon which we build relationships with others.

Section 1.11 states, *"Among all forms of life, only human beings are created in God's own image. In the sight of God, male and female are created equal and complementary. To reflect the divine image is to worship, love, and serve God."* Cumberland Presbyterians recognize that the human family has abused the freedom which was given to us as part of creation (Sections 2.01 and 2.02). We recognize that, *"In rejecting their dependence on God and in willful disobedience, the first human parents disrupted community with God, for which they had been created. They became inclined toward sin in all aspects of their being."* (Section 2.03) We also confess in section 2.04 that *"this condition becomes the source of all sinful attitudes and actions."* Cumberland Presbyterians understand and affirm the existence of sin but we do not affirm that this sin takes away a person's humanity. Sin may de-face the image of God but it does not erase it. The church's call is to help people to understand that in Christ this broken relationship has been reconciled and that there is healing for the broken image of God in all of us. However we, as the covenant community, can only effectively accomplish this mission if we recognize that God's image exists in all people regardless of who they are or what their station in life is. The image of God is inherent in persons due to their status as created beings of God.

As Cumberland Presbyterians affirm the dignity of all persons then we will begin to see that the discrimination of any person for any reason is not only wrong but is a sin against the God in whose image that person was created. Understanding and affirming the image of God in all persons also helps to understand our belief in the all-encompassing care that God provides to creation.

THE EXTENT OF GOD'S PROVIDENTIAL CARE

In recognizing that all persons are created in the image of God we also understand, as section 1.12 states, that *"the natural world is God's. Its resources, beauty, and order are given in trust to all peoples, to care for, to conserve, to enjoy, to use for the welfare of all, and thereby to glorify God."* God's creation was given to humanity for the use of humanity. Creation is not meant to be hoarded or accumulated for the use and benefit of only a few but the resources we have are to be used for the benefit of all. We must always advocate for the fair and equal distribution of resources for the benefit of those who do not have access to them.

This understanding of the proper use of creation and resources is mirrored in God's own providential care to creation. Section 1.13 states, *"God exercises providential care over all creatures, peoples, nations, and things. The manner in which this care is provided is revealed in the scriptures."* Matthew 5:45 which is used as a supporting scripture reference for section 1.13 states, *"For God makes the sun rise on the evil and on the good, and sends rain on the just and on the unjust."* God's providence does not extend to a small few but to all of creation just as the benefits of the resources of creation also are to be used for the welfare of all.

This providence is for the purpose of setting creation free from its bondage to sin and death, and seeing it renewed in Jesus Christ (Section 1.15). Section 1.16 states, *"God never leaves or forsakes his people. All who trust God find this truth confirmed in awareness of his love, which includes judgment upon sin, and which leads to repentance and to greater dependence upon divine grace. All who do not trust God are, nevertheless, under that same providence, even when they ignore or reject it. It is designed to lead them also to repentance and to trust in divine grace."* This is an important confession for the church. This statement recognizes that God is present to all of creation and for the very same purpose. All of creation receives the benefit of God's continual and constant presence guiding and drawing all persons to trust in divine grace. This benefit is afforded to those who trust God and those who don't. God's providence is given due to God's unconditional grace and God's love for all of creation.

As we begin to affirm that God's providence extends to all people we begin to recognize our role in ensuring that resources are afforded to all persons and we do our best to advocate that this is done equally and justly. We begin to recognize that God is present even to those who do not recognize it and if God is present to them then so must we be. As we affirm God's all-encompassing providence then we also recognize any attempt to discriminate or withhold resources from another person is a sin. We are to care and serve all persons equally as created beings of God as each and every one is cared for by their creator.

THE NATURE OF THE CHURCH'S MISSION

We understand our mission as the church is *"...to witness to all persons who have not received Christ as Lord and Savior"* (Section 5.28). This however means much more than conversions and professions of faith. *"The church is called into being and exists to reach out to those who have not experienced God's grace in Christ and to nourish them with all the means of grace."* (Section 5.29). Having affirmed both the dignity of each individual and the extent to which God cares for all of creation, it is assumed that the nature of our mission, as the church, is to reach beyond the boundaries of our congregation and care for all of creation. What does this witness and nourishment look like in a society dealing with issues such as rampant discrimination and legalized marginalization?

Our confessional standards provide us direction in what this means in response to these challenges that we see in our present society. Section 6.30 states, *"The covenant community, governed by the Lord Christ, opposes, resists, and seeks to change all circumstances of oppression—political, economic, cultural, racial—by which persons are denied the essential dignity God intends for them in the work of creation."* This statement of faith is the natural and logical outgrowth of the basic affirmation from our Confession as stated above. If all people are created in the image of God and if all people receive the benefit of God's providential care then as God's people we are to bear witness to these truths through our own actions as the covenant community.

Our work within society is spelled out even further in section 6.31. It states, *"The covenant community affirms the lordship of Christ who sought out the poor, the oppressed, the sick and the helpless. In her corporate life and through her individual members, the church is an advocate for all victims of violence and all those who the law or society treats as less than persons for whom Christ died."* We as the church recognize the mission of Christ to those that society had deemed unworthy. Therefore since we are Christ's body, we are called to continue that work. The confession calls us as the church to advocate for those marginalized and abused members of society. We as the church are their voice. We are the ones who come alongside of them just as Christ came along side us. We are Christ to them and, as their advocates, serve a prophetic role to our society.

Our confession, however, does not stop there. Section 6.31 continues by stating, *"Such advocacy involves not only opposition to all unjust laws and forms of injustice but even more support for those attitudes and actions which embody the way of Christ, which is to overcome evil with good."* Our calling goes beyond merely opposing systems of injustice. We are called to support those attitudes which seek to witness to the way of Jesus. We are called to support vehicles of change. We must be involved in our community seeking ways to do good. This is a call to action. It is a call to not just be vocal but to be active. It is a call to actually do something as the church on behalf of those in society who are unable to do something on their own. Our mission as the church is not to just issue altar calls but to oppose any and all forms of injustice and seek to build a society based on the just and equitable treatment of all God's creation. This is a society that is based upon the basic assumptions that everyone has dignity due to their status as creatures of God and that everyone is under the parental care of God.

We have been known as a church who avoids political situations. We maintained our unity during the Civil War by refusing to recognize the validity of abolitionists or their pro-slavery counterparts. During the civil rights era our church attempted to distance ourselves from those advocating for desegregation by refusing to recognize those engaging in civil disobedience. Our church has always taken the safe way of approving what was done in the past on our behalf rather than support and promoting it at the present time. If we are to be true to our confessional standards, then we must not be quiet any longer. We must address systems of oppression, injustice, and discrimination now. We cannot let another generation pass before we speak to these issues.

CONCLUSION

"God gives the message and ministry of reconciliation to the church. The church corporately and through her individual members, seeks to promote reconciliation, love and justice among all persons, classes, races, and nations." (Section 6.32) This section of our confession reminds us of our mission and our calling to ministry that we have received in Christ as Christ's church. It is an all-encompassing mission founded upon our foundational principles. All people have inherent dignity due to them being a creation of God. All people are under the providential care of this creator God. We, as God's people, are called to uphold these truths in a society that all too quickly forgets this. In the beginning we advocated a gospel of "Whosoever Wills." We still do, but the way that we bear witness to this gospel must change as we are faced with new frontier challenges.

Study Questions

1) Based upon an understanding of all people being created in God's image how do we uphold the dignity of individuals?
2) How do we exercise stewardship in a way that honors the universal nature of God's providential care?
3) Where are areas in society where you can see the unjust treatment of others? How can the church serve as a witness to the dignity of all living persons in these areas?
4) What are ways that we engage in the ministry of reconciliation within our particular churches, presbyteries, and synods?
5) How do our churches maintain our commitment to the "whosoever will" gospel and our belief that there are "no eternal reprobates"?
6) Do we, as a church, still avoid political situation? Is this an appropriate response in light of our confessional directives?

THE REPORT OF THE UNIFICATION TASK FORCE

I. MEETING AND OFFICERS

The Unification Task Force (UTF) of the Cumberland Presbyterian Church in America (CPCA) and the Cumberland Presbyterian Church (CPC) met twice since the last meeting of the General Assemblies: November 12-13, 2015 and April 6-7, 2016 in Nashville, Tennessee. Officers elected are Joy Warren (CPC) and William Robinson (CPCA), co-chairs; Craig White (CPCA) and Jay Earheart-Brown (CPC), secretaries. Other members of the UTF from the CPCA are Leon Cole, Elton Hall, Arthur Haywood, Lynne Herring, Anthony Hollis, and Mitchell Walker. Other members of the UTF from the CPC are Steve Mosely, Perryn Rice, Robert Rush, Gloria Villa-Diaz, and Mike Sharpe.

Joy Warren and Mitchell Walker were elected to serve as representatives of the Task Force to this meeting of the General Assemblies.

II. PROPOSED PLAN OF UNION

The 2014 General Assemblies, in concurrent session at Chattanooga, Tennessee, approved for study a Proposed Plan of Union. That plan has been distributed widely across both denominations, and has generated a great deal of discussion and feedback. For almost two years, the plan has been studied. We are grateful for all the responses the Task Force has received, both positive and negative. The Task Force has carefully studied the responses, from the table discussions at Chattanooga, to the surveys distributed at Presbytery meetings and on-line, to individual letters received by the GA offices and by members of the Task Force. On the basis of all the responses to the proposed plan, and several meetings attended by members of the Task Force, we voted in our November meeting not to ask for a formal vote on the plan at the 2016 meetings of the General Assembly, which would have been the earliest possible date for such a vote.

We have, instead, spent significant time revising the Proposed Plan of Union, and present it to the concurrent meetings of the two General Assemblies this year, with the recommendation that the revised plan be approved for study in the two churches. We are proposing no definite time for taking a vote until it appears that the two churches are ready to move ahead with organic union. Of course, we as members of the Task Force, are committed to this effort and would hope and pray that both churches would be ready to move forward sooner rather than later. However, we know that it would not be helpful to push unification before we have established the trust necessary to make the union fruitful for the work of God's kingdom.

With thanksgiving to God for the relationships we have developed as we have worked together for the past four years, and in hopes that all Cumberland Presbyterians may one day live and work together in one church, the UTF submits the following Proposed Plan of Union.

**Proposed Plan for Union of the
Cumberland Presbyterian Church and the Cumberland Presbyterian Church in America**

"There is one, holy, universal, apostolic church. She is the body of Christ, who is her Head and Lord" (*Confession of Faith* 5.01). "The church is one because her head and Lord is one, Jesus Christ. Her oneness under her Lord is manifested in the one ministry of word and sacrament, not in any uniformity of covenantal expression, organization, or system of doctrine" (5.02). "The church, as the covenant community of believers who are redeemed, includes all people in all ages, past, present, and future, who respond in faith to God's covenant of grace, and all who are unable to respond, for reasons known to God, but who are saved by his grace" (5.06). It is on this belief that the Unification Task Force recommends the union of the Cumberland Presbyterian Church in America (CPCA) and the Cumberland Presbyterian Church (CPC). We are one in Christ by the grace of God and the power of the Holy Spirit! We believe that becoming one will strengthen our witness as Christian believers in the world, and that together we will be able to accomplish more for the glory of God. United together in Christ by faith, we are united to one another in love. In this communion we share the grace of Christ with one another, bear one another's burdens, and reach out to all other persons (*Confession of Faith* 5.10).

1.00 Mission Statement for the New Church

The Cumberland Presbyterian Church United affirms the great commission of Christ: "Go, therefore, and make disciples of all nations, baptizing them in the name of the Father, and of the Son, and of the Holy Spirit, and teaching them to obey everything that I have commanded you. And remember I am with you until the end of the age"(Matthew 28:19-20). We celebrate our oneness in faith. As disciples, we seek through worship, global witness, and service to be the hands and feet of Christ and to live out the love of Jesus Christ to the glory of God.

2.00 The Confession of Faith and Government

The Cumberland Presbyterian Church United will use the *Confession of Faith and Government* of the Cumberland Presbyterian Church and the Cumberland Presbyterian Church in America, approved by both General Assemblies of the former denominations in 1984 as its system of faith and government.

NOTE: It should be noted that in the Constitution (4.6, 5.6p) the CPC allows for a session to request permission from Presbytery for a designated elder to be trained and granted permission to serve communion for a one year period of time. This is an exception, NOT A RULE for general practice, for those presbyteries that have difficulty supplying each church with an ordained minister. The responsibility lies with presbytery for proper training and oversight of the designated elder. Again, is this an EXCEPTION. No presbytery is required to apply this exception.

2.01 The Cumberland Presbyterian Church United will use the *Catechism for Cumberland Presbyterians* (2008) for instruction in the faith and will include it in an updated edition of the *Confession of Faith and Government of the Cumberland Presbyterian Church United.*

2.02 The CP *Digest* (CPC) and Summaries of Actions (for both denominations) will continue to serve as resource tools. A new *Digest* will begin with the formation of the Cumberland Presbyterian Church United.

3.00 The Presbyteries and Synods

3.01 In an effort to make union something more than just an idea on paper, and to engage the grassroots in creating the new church, we recommend a restructure of the synod boundaries to create eight synods for the new church, with the following presbyteries in each –

Synod A*	Synod B*	Synod C	Synod D
Brazos River	Angelina	Covenant	Cleveland, Ohio
Del Christo	Arkansas	Missouri	Cumberland
Red River	Choctaw	New Hopewell	North Central
Hong Kong	East Texas	Purchase	Ohio Valley
Japan	Trinity	West Tennessee	
	Andes		
	Cauca Valley		

Synod E	Synod F	Synod G	Synod H
Columbia	East Tennessee	Florence	Birmingham
Elk River	Hiawassee	Hope	Grace
Murfreesboro	Tennessee-Georgia	Huntsville	South Alabama
Nashville	East Coast Korean	Robert Donnell	Tuscaloosa
		Tennessee Valley	

For relationship building during the first six years, all synods will be encouraged to hold an annual general meeting (*Constitution* 8.2) as opposed to a delegated meeting. Synods may petition General Assembly at any point for a change in boundaries.

* NOTE: There are plans for organizing a new presbytery in Central and/or South America in the near future, as well as dreams for organizing a third presbytery in Asia. As soon as it is practical to do so, whether before or after union, two additional synods should be constituted. Synod I would include Andes, Cauca Valley, and any other presbyteries organized in Latin America. Synod J would include Hong Kong, Japan, and any other presbyteries organized in Asia.

3.02 Presbyteries will remain as they are constituted at the time of union. During the first six years of the new church's life, synods will be encouraged to study the most beneficial presbyterial boundaries within their jurisdictionto fulfill of the mission of the church. Presbyteries may petition their synod at any time for a change in boundaries.

4.00 Commissioners and Youth Advisory Delegates to the General Assembly

4.01 Commissioners to the General Assembly

Each Presbytery will be entitled to send 2 minister commissioners and 2 elder commissioners to the General Assembly.

NOTE: If presbytery boundaries remain as currently constituted at the time of unification, this will allow for a total possible membership in the General Assembly of 152 commissioners. Of these potential commissioners, 60 would come from former presbyteries of the CPCA, and 92 would come from the former CPC.

4.02 Youth Advisory Delegates

Each presbytery will be entitled to send up to two Youth Advisory delegates to the General Assembly.

5.00 Moderator and Vice Moderator of General Assembly

5.01 The moderator/vice moderator will be elected each year during the first six years with the two offices alternating between persons from the two former denominations.

5.02 The moderator and vice moderator of the Cumberland Presbyterian Church United will reflect its diverse nature, to include international representatives. The church expects the moderator and vice moderator to travel within the denomination, sharing and gathering information among its local churches. Expenses and particular duties will be detailed in the Standing Rules of the Cumberland Presbyterian Church United.

6.00 Stated Clerk and Associate Stated Clerk of the General Assembly

6.01 The new church shall employ a Stated Clerk and an Associate Stated Clerk. Both positions will be full-time jobs. During the first six years of the Cumberland Presbyterian Church United, the Stated Clerk will serve six years and the Associate Stated Clerk will serve four years, after which each would be elected for a four-year period. One position will be filled by a former CPCA and the other position filled by a former CPC during their first terms. The subsequent election of each position will allow for continuity during transitions. Particular duties and responsibilities of the Stated Clerk and Associate Stated Clerk will be detailed in the Standing Rules of the Cumberland Presbyterian Church United.

7.00 Boards and Agencies of the General Assembly

7.01 Each church has programs in various stages of planning and implementation that are the result of commitment to ministry through the church. Insofar as possible, these plans and programs will be continued without interruption for a period of three years. The Cumberland Presbyterian Church has covenantal relationships with the Cumberland Presbyterian Children's Home in Denton, Texas and Bethel University in McKenzie, Tennessee. These covenantal relationships will remain in effect as they exist at the time of Unification, to be renewed every four years. The Cumberland Presbyterian Church United will continue ecumenical partnerships, such as with the World Communion of Reformed Churches.

7.02 Institutional Boards

The General Assembly shall have the following institutional boards: Trustees of Memphis Theological Seminary to include the Program of Alternate Studies and School of Continuing Education Committee, and Trustees of the Historical Foundation. Representation on each Board of Trustees will remain as they are constituted at the time of union.

7.03 Administrative Boards

The General Assembly shall have the following administrative Boards: The Board of Stewardship, Foundation and Benefits and The Board of Directors of the General Assembly Corporation. During the transition period, each of these boards will have equal number of members from each of the former denominations.

7.04 Commission
The General Assembly shall have the following commission: Chaplains and Military Personnel. Representation on the commission will be merged as they are constituted at the time of union until natural rotation occurs.

7.05 Standing Committees
The General Assembly shall have the following standing committees: Theology and Social Concerns, Judiciary, Our United Outreach, Nominating, and Multi-Cultural Ministry.

Committee representation on the Theology and Social Concerns Committee will remain as constituted at the time of union until natural rotations occurs.

Judiciary and Nominating committees in both denominations will each be merged at the time of union.

Committee representation for Our United Outreach will be expanded to include two elected representatives from each new synod (one voting representative from each of the former denominations until natural rotation occurs).

The Committee on Multi-Cultural Ministry is a new committee that will reflect the diversity of the Cumberland Presbyterian Church United. This committee will be comprised of eight (8) elected persons that will reflect the celebrative understanding of humanity in the areas of culture, language, heritage, and experience in the Cumberland Presbyterian Church United. Believing that all have been created in God's image, this committee works to answer the question of our sameness in God's image lived out in diverse ways.

7.06 The Cumberland Presbyterian Church United will have a Mission Programming Agency to provide coordination and oversight for those ministries formally planned and implemented by the two former denominations. After the three-year period, the new programming and denominational structure will consist of the following ministries and entities –

Christian Education & Nurture (Youth Convention & National Sunday School Convention
Missions (Evangelism, Missionary Auxiliary, Women's Ministry)
Clergy Care & Development
Communications (Cumberland Flag, Cumberland Presbyterian Magazine, Missionary Messenger, website)

Composition of each ministry entity will include equal number of persons from each of the former denominations in the new church at the time of union. Composition of the new Mission Programming Agency will include one staff person and one elected member from each ministry entity, along with one elected member representing each of the synods. The elected members will be equally representative of the two former denominations for the first six years. A Ministry Coordinator would provide executive leadership for the Mission Programming Agency.

8. Denominational Staff & Personnel
Currently, the CPCA employs two full time staff members; the CPC employs twenty-five staff members.

8.01 The new organizational structure will discontinue the positions of Administrative Director (CPCA) and the Director of Ministries (CPC) and will create the positions of Associate Stated Clerk and Ministry Coordinator. The duties and parameters of each position and corresponding selection processes will be determined during the Implementation Phase and detailed in the Standing Rules.

8.02 Staffing for the Cumberland Presbyterian Church United will reflect the diversity of the new church. As new staff positions become available, equal opportunity employment practices will prevail.

8.03 Denominational Offices –During the first six years, steps are to be taken to assure that regional sites be located in a minimum of three and a maximum of five locations. Thus, neither the Center in Huntsville nor the Center in Memphis will be designated as "the denominational center." By placing regional sites in a variety of locations this will assure that all areas of the church will be served equally. These regional sites can make use of offices in existing churches, or in homes of regional staff persons. Possible regional locations could be Memphis, Huntsville, Louisville, Texas, South America, Asia, etc.

8.04 Global Staff

There will be endorsed missionaries and partner missionaries in the new church. The new church will continue to support current and future missionaries and global work. Current missionaries include – CP Missionaries: Boyce and Beth Wallace (Colombia, South America), Patrick and Jessica Wilkerson (Colombia, South America), Carlos and Luz Dary Rivera (Mexico), Anay Ortega (Guatemala), Fhanor and Socorro Pejendino (Guatemala), Jacob and Lindsey Sims (Brazil), Daniel and Kay Jang (Philippines), John and Joy Park (Philippines), DSL (Cambodia-Laos). CP Missionaries working with non-denominational missions: Kenneth and Delight Hopson (Uganda),TTG (Kyrgyzstan). Global Work, there are CP Churches in: Australia, Brazil, Cambodia, Colombia, Guatemala, Haiti, Hong Kong, Japan, Laos, Mexico, Philippines, South Korea, and the USA.

9.00 Stewardship and Finance

9.01 Legal control of assets of both churches will be transferred to the Cumberland Presbyterian Church United through appropriate legal transaction. The intent of all designated gifts and endowments will be honored.

9.02 The Cumberland Presbyterian Church United will develop an approach to the financing of the programs of the church that reflects the stewardship understanding of the new constituency. Such a unitary approach will be developed as soon as possible after formation and no later than the end of the first six years.

10.00 Recognition of Ordination

All ordinations, both clergy and lay (elders and deacons), of both denominations will be recognized by the Cumberland Presbyterian Church United. All future ordinations will be governed by the conditions specified in the Constitution. Persons who are recognized by their respective presbyteries as candidates and licentiates at the time the new church is formed will fulfill the requirements as specified by presbytery at the time they became probationers.

11.00 The Name of the New Denomination

The name of the denomination shall be the Cumberland Presbyterian Church United.

12.00 The Logo of the New Church

A new logo will be fashioned by the new church.

RECOMMENDATION 1: That the revised Plan for Union of the CPC and CPCA be approved for study in the two churches, and that all ministers, sessions, presbyteries, synods, and members of the two churches be encouraged to study the document and provide feedback to the task force during the upcoming year.

III. MEETINGS OF THE TWO GENERAL ASSEMBLIES

Knowing the value of joint worship and fellowship, and convinced that the work toward unification will be aided by the development of personal relationships between leaders and members of our two churches, the Task Force makes the following:

RECOMMENDATION 2: That the General Assemblies of the Cumberland Presbyterian Church in America and the Cumberland Presbyterian Church commit to meeting concurrently in the same city during the same week for the foreseeable future.

IV. COOPERATIVE WORK

The Task Force continues to be encouraged by cooperative work being done in many areas of our two denominations. At the General Assembly level, both churches cooperate in the work of the Historical Foundation, the Unified Committee on Theology and Social Concerns, the Cumberland Presbyterian Youth Conference and Presbyterian Youth Triennium, and the Presbyterian Council for Chaplains and Military Personnel. At the local and presbyterial levels, we continue to receive good reports from joint programs of camping and youth events, revivals, Vacation Bible Schools, joint worship and community meals. We encourage persons engaged in joint ministries to report those events to the Cumberland Presbyterian magazine, and on the Facebook page of the Unification Task Force.

The UTF will make available at its display table during the week of General Assembly a list of suggested activities that individuals and churches can try in their local areas, along with other materials to help promote the work of unification. All commissioners and visitors to the meeting of GA are encouraged to make use of these resources.

Two presbyteries, one from each church, have begun discussion of organizing as a federated, or union presbytery of the two denominations. We encourage churches and presbyteries to explore these options where feasible.

We also remind both churches that we have in place an agreement that allows ministers from both churches to serve congregations in either denomination. Where this has happened, some ministers have dual membership in both denominations, which can only help to unify our ministry and witness, even before formal unification happens.

V. UNIFICATION SUNDAY

We were notified that the Unified Committee on Theology and Social Concerns is recommending to both General Assemblies that we recognize a Unification Sunday on the official calendars of our churches. We concur in this recommendation, and propose the following recommendation:

Recommendation 3: That the third Sunday in February be recognized in the Cumberland Presbyterian Church and the Cumberland Presbyterian Church in America as Unity Sunday, and that all churches be encouraged to pray for our unity in Jesus Christ, and for discernment as we seek to express our unity more fully in the future.

Respectfully Submitted,
Unification Task Force
William Robinson and Joy Warren, co-chairs

THE REPORT OF BOARD OF TRUSTEES OF BETHEL UNIVERSITY

175 YEARS!

August 2016 to July 2017 marks Bethel Seminary/College/University's 175th Birthday!

Think about it for a minute. John Tyler was our President. Gold was discovered/documented in California. University of Notre Dame, The Citadel, and Bethel were all established in 1842. All 175 years ago.

The vision to establish a Cumberland Presbyterian Seminary in 1842 in McLemoresville, Tennessee, was truly visionary. Bethel initially operated under the care of the West Tennessee Synod of the Cumberland Presbyterian Church. It stayed in McLemoresville until 1872 when it moved to its current location in McKenzie.

Originally the Cumberland Presbyterian Church had ten schools, but in 1906 nine of the schools were closed leaving Bethel to be the Only Cumberland Presbyterian College.

We will have a lot of events celebrating our 175th birthday. Hopefully, you can join us!

Today Bethel University values its covenant relationship with The Cumberland Presbyterian Church. We are committed to this relationship and we look forward to the next 175 years. Our Board of Trustees can have no more than 30 persons, of which the majority must be Cumberland Presbyterians. We currently have 22 trustees.

Our fall enrollment for 2015 was 5606. Our enrollment as of March 1, 2016 was 5258. We serve 13,000 alumni worldwide, of which almost 9,000 live in Tennessee.

The student population of Bethel University for the current school year represents 40 states and 23 foreign countries. This diverse population brings many world traditions and countries together to talk and learn from each other.

Bethel University's students are doing well. We are leaders in The Tennessee Intercollegiate State Legislature. Our Renaissance Program is recognized as one of the top music programs anywhere. Athletic teams compete for National Championships. More importantly, we excel in the classroom. We have the largest M.B.A. program in the state of Tennessee. Our graduating students are in demand. They teach, they are doctors/physician assistants/nurses, they are accountants, they are social workers, they volunteer and the list goes on and on.

Bethel University needs your prayers and help. Every day we see students that need financial help. Every day we see students that need a larger chapel to worship in. Please remember us!

Bethel University asks for your continued prayers and support. We ask that you recommend students to us.

Bethel Forevermore!

THE REPORT OF THE BOARD OF TRUSTEES OF THE CUMBERLAND PRESBYTERIAN CHILDREN'S HOME

Thank you for reviewing our report. It offers information but much more. We intend it to include the Gospel of God's word to a hurting world.

We strive to be good stewards of your gifts and donations to us. Many of you come to our campus to visit and work. Most of you send money to pay for the expensive work of ending the cycle of abuse and neglect by bringing healing and hope to children and families. All of you support our mission with your prayers and your commitment of time and energy to support the work. Thank you and God bless you.

I. OVERVIEW

Our 112th year of ministry at the Children's Home serves children and families in different ways:

- **Children's Residential Care,**
- **Children's Emergency Shelter Care,**
- **Single Parent Family Services, and**
- **Cumberland Family Services Counseling.**

In the 21st Century, we focus our ministry on ending the maltreatment of children. Child abuse and neglect not only injure children, but impact the lives and families of adults who were once abused. We must stop the cycle of harm, a harm that can be measured in many ways. Foremost, I believe we are called to this redemptive ministry by God. God has called us to feed, clothe, teach, and love the little, the last, the lost and the least.

The harm also creates a toll in human tragedy correlated with crime, addiction, unemployment, incarceration, broken relationships, mental and emotional dysfunction, ill health, violence and self destructive actions. The cost to society is numbing.

So Cumberland provides a safe, nurturing and loving residence where children and families can live and grow. It also provides tools for healing and health through counseling and parenting training. And most importantly, the Children's Home enacts Christ's command to serve in His name. Here are some numbers to give you a flavor of the scope of our ministry.

Cumberland helps children and families in residential and non-residential programs. In its residential programs, Cumberland served 109 children and 10 single parents. Over 1,856 additional children and families were served through intake and referral services, counseling sessions, or classes in our non-residential programs. Cumberland held over 2,446 separate counseling sessions. In all, 1,975 lives were touched with healing and hope by the Cumberland Presbyterian Children's Home during 2015.

Mission
*In response to Christ's love and example,
we serve children and families
by providing healing and hope.*

Campus

Cumberland's 17-acre campus in Denton, Texas, includes three residential cottages for children and teens and 8 apartments for single parent families. Other features include the Parr Family Resource Building, which houses the Library and Technology Center, therapy rooms, meeting facilities and staff offices. The campus is also home to the Gilbert-Parr Activities Building, which houses Cumberland's recreational facilities and a chapel, the 250-seat Lela Stricklen Hall.

Corporate entity and governance

Cumberland is a non-profit corporation incorporated under the laws of the state of Texas. Cumberland is tax-exempt under IRS Code section 501(c)(3). Cumberland is governed by a board of 18 Trustees. The Cumberland Board of Trustees hired the President, CEO & General Counsel to manage the agency.

Trustees: There are currently 16 trustees: ten Cumberland Presbyterians and six ecumenical partners *(the Board is currently seeking two Ecumenical Partners)*.

Ecumenical Partners: Patricia Long, Caroline Booth, John O'Carroll, Charles Harris, Knight Miller and Kay Goodman

Cumberland Presbyterians: Mamie Hall, Reverend Melissa Knight, Doctor Robin Henson, Reverend Don Tabor, Richard Dean, Mickey Shell, Reverend Lisa Anderson, Carolyn Harmon, Reverend Alfonso Marquez and Reverend Duane Dougherty

Officers: Chair—Richard Dean; Vice-Chair—Patricia Long; Secretary—Caroline Booth.

Leadership

President, CEO & General Counsel: Reverend Richard A. Brown, Esq., LCCA
Vice President, Programs: Doctor Jennifer Livings, LPC-S
Interim Chaplain: Reverend Katie Klein

Organizational Structure

Because our mission calls us to a ministry of service, we have adopted the following "Pyramid of Care©" as an organizational structure. Rather than organizing from the top down, we wish to follow in Christ's example of servant leadership. We place the people we serve, both in residential care and in non-residential care, at the top of the pyramid.

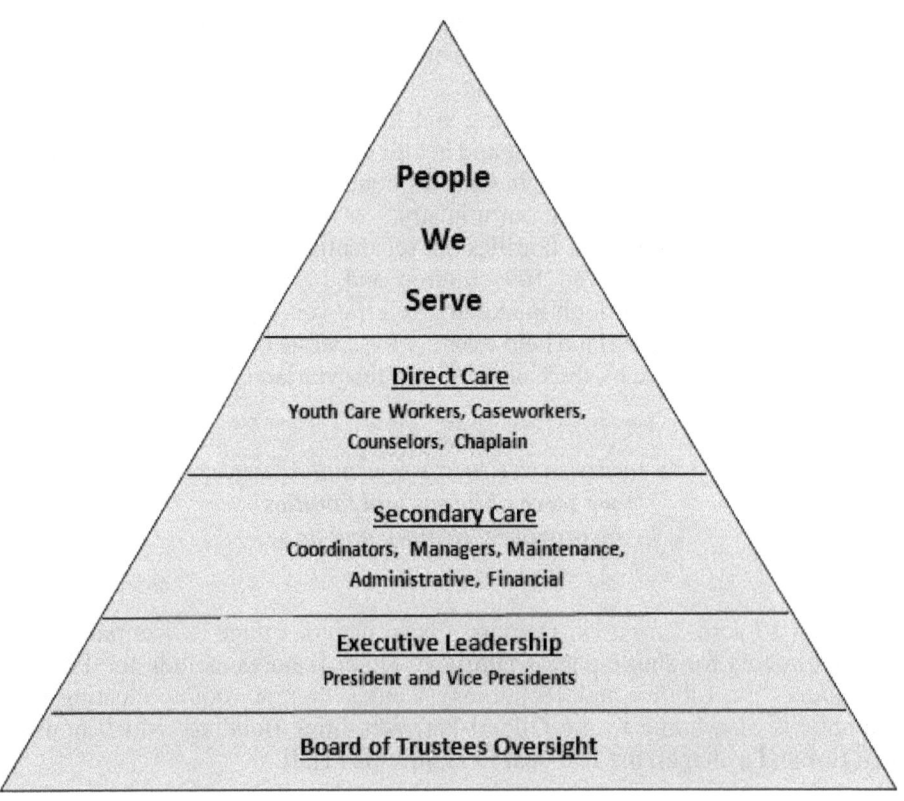

II. OUTCOMES

Memorandum

To: The Board of Trustees
From: Dr. Jennifer Livings, LPC-S
Date: 2-19-2016
Re: VP of Programs Report

In 2015, we had tremendous growth in our communication and teamwork efforts. Our conscious decision to focus on the team approach has not only been collaborative and effective, but our efforts created a solid foundation to support our future growth in areas of goal formation and successful programming. We are passionate about our interworking relationships and have better identified our collective strengths when collaboration is fully operational.

General Residential Operation
We served 92 children in our GRO this past year. We served more children this past year than any other time in our recent history. We have taken great strides in decreasing overtime. We have done well staying within budget. Our GRO team successfully took on all duties associated with the food services program in late 2015. We will be assessing the food needs of the agency and identifying staffing patterns dedicated to providing healthy, economically sound food services. GRO staff are providing volunteer trainings and working collaboratively with volunteers and staff.

Program Highlights
- Creating and incorporating food service responsibilities including budgeting and purchasing.
- GRO staff providing trainings for volunteer preparation.
- Successful management of budget while decreasing overtime.
- Creating music room and music studio for self-expression.
- Cynthia Berrones is our leading LCCA for the GRO.
- Incorporate trauma informed care into program design.

Single Parent Family Program
Our SPF program is in a state of great transition and we are excited about our future changes. Creating program policies and procedures is our top focus for 2016. Our families are receiving excellent support as we have more opportunities to work as a team to provide care. In late 2015, Pastor Katie became the Interim SPF Coordinator. In 2016, we will be working on achieving our long term goal of identifying a program coordinator to develop and implement the SPF program while building a manual, program objectives, and encouraging community involvement. Our main success in SPF has been the use of the Circle of Care interdisciplinary approach to assess the current needs of the program and future program development planning.

Program Highlights
- Served 27 children and families in 2015.
- Pastor Katie accepted the position of Interim SPF Coordinator.
- Preparing for upcoming changes to strengthen program objectives and goals.
- Families experience a Circle of Care approach in planning meetings.

Cumberland Family Services
We are serving more clients and providing more counseling sessions on an annual basis than ever before. CFS is growing visibility in the community as our ability to offer more community counseling services is growing due to our use of interns. Our therapists have full caseloads and all of our children in the GRO receive counseling services after school which is less disruptive to their already busy schedules. Our team is focused on trauma informed care and our children are benefiting from these services.

Program Highlights
- Our Intake Specialist/LPC-Intern has become fully licensed and promoted to Therapist.
- Our student intern has graduated and become an LPC-Intern.
- More Love and Logic class offerings, including four classes offered in Spanish.
- Increase in community clients.
- Adjustment of sliding scale and Love and Logic fees to more appropriately compensate for services rendered while also remaining affordable to the community.
- Continued utilization of agency resources and collaboration with other programs.

III. GIVING

Cumberland Presbyterian Children's Home exists today because of the commitment Cumberland Presbyterian individuals and congregations have made in giving every year and through planned gifts. In her will, Miss Victoria Jackson of Bowling Green, Kentucky, created a home for widows and orphans. Her final act of generosity has allowed thousands of lives to be touched by this ministry. For the past 111 years, many faithful and forward thinking people have blessed the children's home, including the increasingly needed family services, with annually recurring and estate gifts.

We are grateful that more than half of CP churches made direct gifts to the children's home this last year. Through these reliable annual gifts and the endowment built from planned giving, Cumberland Presbyterian Children's Home can keep the church's promise to do more than house, clothe and feed our children. The opportunities for spiritual growth and practical life skills for children and families would not exist without the continued prayers and support from the women and men of Cumberland Presbyterian Churches.

We promise to be good stewards of what you give. When you do your own kitchen table bookkeeping, you know that costs for basic goods increase. We never take the sacrifice you are making for granted. Thank you for helping us keep up with the high cost of providing the one on one relationship building that true change requires, especially when we are focused upon vulnerable and traumatized children and families.

We strive to fulfill the mission to which we believe we have been called. The Cumberland Presbyterian Children's Home does not warehouse residents. We seek to enrich the lives of children, teens and families who have been trapped in the cycle of abuse and neglect like so many children and families in our community and yours. Through your donations, we provide direct care to vulnerable children and families.

We also strive to create a model for care that can be duplicated in homes and campuses anywhere. How can we not take care of the need in front of us? But how can we limit our reach to just the need in front of us? We partner with you to become Christ's tender and caring touch to His traumatized children in whatever place and circumstance. Thank you for your generous giving.

IV. FINANCIAL

Expenses

Based on the unaudited 2015 Financial Statements, Cumberland spent just over $2.5 million bringing healing and hope to children and families. Expenses break down into the following categories:

Residential Childcare	41%
Emergency Shelter Childcare	31%
Cumberland Family Services	9%
Single Parent Family	8%
Administrative	6%
Fundraising	5%

NOTE: 89% of our costs provided care to our residents and clients.

Income

Again based on the unaudited 2015 Financial Statements, Cumberland derived just over $2.4 million in operational income from the following sources:

$1,200,371	Contributions	49.6%
$651,904	Service Compensation	26.9%
$559,048	Endowment Distributions	23.1%
$9,175	Special Events/Other	.4%
$2,420,498	Total	100.0%

NOTE: The fee for service we receive in Service Compensation covers only a fraction of what it takes to enrich the lives of our cottage residents. Your gifts and contributions make it possible for traumatized youth to make a new beginning.

Cumberland Presbyterian Children's Home
Funds Flow Statement
2015 Pro Forma Actual vs. Budget

Sources of Funds	Jan - Dec 15	2015 Budget
Contributions (1)	$ 1,200,371	$ 1,153,000
Cumberland Family Svcs Income	104,882	141,000
Endowment Distributions - Spending P	559,048	559,048
Service Compensation	547,022	530,000
Special Events/Other	9,175	0
Total Pro Forma Sources of Funds	**$ 2,420,499**	**$ 2,383,048**

Expenses	Jan - Dec 15	2015 Budget
Assistance to Individuals & Families	$ 345	$ -
Board Expense	11,719	10,000
Building & Grounds/Maintenance	97,084	85,000
Chaplain	8,822	6,000
Charitable Donations	125	0
Children's Residential Program	175,852	185,000
Computer Expenses	18,042	20,500
Consultation	8,456	12,000
Cumberland Family Services	6,957	9,200
Development	42,580	60,000
Emergency Shelter Program	81,751	93,500
Food and Dining Out-Staff	0	1,000
Furniture & Fixtures	764	6,000
General Assembly	1,020	6,000
Insurance	80,309	71,456
Interest Expense	1,033	1,800
Investment Fees	20,646	0
Licenses & Fees - Professional/Audit	14,882	20,000
Payroll	1,754,571	1,830,000
Operating Permits and Fees	2,823	3,000
Property Taxes	521	500
Single Parent Family Program	4,691	15,000
Staff Recruitment/Retention	3,299	4,000
Staff Training & Development	5,105	1,500
Campus Supplies	29,955	25,000
Travel	1,598	12,000
Utilities	151,144	150,000
Vehicle Expense	12,680	8,000
Total Expenses	**$ 2,536,772**	**$ 2,636,456**
NET PRO FORMA FUNDS FLOW	**$ (116,273)**	**$ (253,408)**

V. STRATEGIC PLAN

With a history of innovation, the Cumberland Board of Trustees has developed a Strategic Vision and a 10-year Strategic Plan. The strategic vision looks to a self-sustaining, fully-staffed ministry in our current location. This vision also sees the replication of our existing programs in other locations, and the vision recognizes the possibility of new programs serving children and families. The 10-year Strategic Plan will work toward fulfilling the vision by improving programs, expanding our outreach and creating sustainability.

Strategic Vision

1. *Self-Sustaining, fully-staffed agency in Denton, Texas*
2. *Replication of our programs*
3. *Work toward complete social service ministry for children and families*

2012-2022 Strategic Objectives

Program Development

· Cumberland will examine, continue to improve on, and strive for excellence in the existing programs as well as add at least one new, self-sustaining program to the agency's continuum of care.
· Cumberland's Denton campus will be a beautiful fully-functioning, synergistic model for other multiple program agencies. Cumberland will replicate one or more of its programs in at least one new geographic location.

Outreach Development

· Cumberland will develop reciprocal professional relationships with institutions such as hospitals, area churches, social service agencies, Bethel University, Memphis Theological Seminary, Texas Woman's University and University of North Texas combining relevant research and mature faith ensuring the long-term sustainability of social service ministry. Cumberland will develop relationships at the highest level with the Texas Department of Family and Protective Services by serving on committees and boards at the state and local level.
· Cumberland will be a significant provider of social services to children and families in Texas and will be the primary social service resource to the Cumberland Presbyterian denomination.

Agency Development

· Cumberland will have a minimum operating budget of $2.5 million with contributions accounting for no more than 20% of the income, be fully staffed for optimum programming outcomes in all locations, and have a total endowment valued at more than $10.2 million.
· Cumberland will become a self-governing agency within a covenant, but not legal relationship, with the General Assembly of the Cumberland Presbyterian Church. The Board of Trustees will meet a minimum of three times per year and become more active in resource development, i.e. recruiting major donors, planned giving, forming relationships with businesses, participating in special events and making gifts of their own that indicate significant support for the agency.

VI. PRESIDENT'S MESSAGE

"Many Hands Makes Light Work"   John Heywood, 16th Century Poet and Playwright

2016 at the Children's Home is about team.

Choose your favorite professional football player. Troy Aikman? Peyton Manning? Lawrence Taylor? Lynn Swann? Rosey Grier? Mean Joe Green? Who is the single greatest professional football player in the history of the game?

With that player in mind, let's have a competition: the best of the best individual player versus the Denton ISD Calhoun Middle School varsity football team. The pro is bigger, faster, smarter and more experienced than any other player who has ever played the game. But who would you bet on in a 60 minute game between Troy Aikman by himself and the 11 thirteen and fourteen year olds on the Calhoun Middle School team?

"Many hands make light work."
In what ways can teamwork provide the path to a secure and productive future?

"Many hands make light work."
<u>What has the Team accomplished since September?</u>

1. Cumberland is engaged in the Foster Care and family service professions

Cynthia Berrones, Melanee Fabbri and I attended the 2015 Child Care Administrators Annual Conference where the themes were "normalcy," "least restrictive placement" and "prudent parent decision making."

The Federal lawsuit handed down in late December 2015 eliminated Group Homes in Texas.

The Children's Right, Inc. movement, funded by The Annie E. Casey Foundation and strongly impacting both state and federal legislators and administrators, set its goal to end all congregate care, such as that provided at CPCH.

Although misguided in many of its actions, The Annie E. Casey Foundation has a mission consistent with our own: "The Annie E. Casey Foundation is limited to initiatives in the United States that have significant potential to demonstrate innovative policy, service delivery and community supports for disadvantaged children and families." I believe the Cumberland Model fits this definition.

The State of Texas continues to place foster kids at CPCH.

Texas Coalition for Homes for Children (TCHC) advocates for group foster care in Austin and Washington, D.C.

I initiated and co-chair a TCHC ad hoc committee developing measureable results for congregate care facilities.

2. CPCH Operations continued to expand its Team effectiveness.

Cynthia Berrones successfully completed her LCCA certification.

Robert Mood and Reverend Katie Klein stepped up when Anna Stokes resigned while Doctor Livings was out on maternity leave.

Jim Lucas has replaced staff so that maintenance requests are timely completed throughout the campus.

The Medical Clinic is set for a grand opening in late Spring or early Summer 2016.

3. Concerted efforts by the Team attacked the annual deficit.

We cut annual administration costs by eliminating two Vice President positions.

The General Residential Operation maintained the quality of service at the same time it has significantly cut overtime.

Donations grew by 5.6% in 2015.

Plans to grow revenue in 2016 focused on the basics: blocking & tackling.

Kay Goodman and Caroline Booth organized the first Advisory Committee meetings in Denton, Texas.

Steps were taken to develop the CPCH greenbelt for commercial production as well as determine the value of CPCH property required for the I-35E highway expansion project.

Social media, traditional print media, speakers and campus facility use increased CPCH's visibility in the community.

Richard Dean, Lisa Anderson and I successfully met with Robert Heflin and Gerber Taylor regarding the risk and return of our endowments managed by the Board of Stewardship in Memphis.

The executive staff added a record number of potential donors during 2015 as shown by the Call Report log.

4. The Team filled the gaps when the system was stressed by loss and reorganization.

When key absences occurred among the executive staff as Jennifer was out on maternity leave and I was involved in a protracted family health crisis, the Team responded with diligence, competence and superlative performance.

When several staff changes occurred, the Team worked together to preserve the quality of care for the children and families.

We have three new Board members and several candidates in the event they are needed. We also suffered the loss to illness of one of our Board members. We continue to remember Barry Smith, his family and caregivers as he seeks health.

<u>Where does the Team go from here?</u>

Executives and Programs develop contingency plans in the event group foster care is ended by the government.

Board members are increasingly engaged in oversight and raising revenue.

Board will discuss and adopt a strategic vision.

<u>Conclusion:</u>

A Team can accomplish what an individual cannot.

Whether we are talking about painting the walls of the Rec and Activity Room in Stricklen, building a labyrinth, playing a game of football against the single greatest football pro of all time or bringing healing and hope to children and families, failing to work together is the greatest impediment to success.

The theological image for this is the body, composed of different parts that work together under the leadership of Christ, the Head. We are called as Christians into God's service to cooperate and collaborate with one another so that in our diversity we become effective to accomplish beyond what we could do by ourselves. I believe each of us here at Cumberland has been called to this mission. Despite the challenges-- despite the temptation to be afraid or paralyzed--God has provided this way to offer vulnerable children and families a chance for a new beginning. It is the way of the body of Christ and of the community of faith. It is the way of the Team.

There is much evidence of teamwork at Cumberland. Let us be servant leaders stirring up even more teamwork.

"Many hands makes light work."

Respectfully Submitted,

Rev. Richard A. Brown, Esq., LCCA
President, CEO & General Counsel

THE REPORT OF THE
JOINT COMMITTEE ON AMENDMENTS

The Joint Committee on Amendments met May 9, 2016 via conference call. Participating were (CPCA): Willie Cowan and Vanessa Bridgett; (CPC): Kimberly Silvus and Wendell Thomas. Also participating was Lynne Herring, Administrative Director (CPCA) and Mike Sharpe, Stated Clerk of General Assembly (CPC).

I. REFERRAL

The committee approved a proposed constitutional amendment to be placed before the 186th General Assembly.

RECOMMENDATION 1: That current Constitution 9.5 be renumbered as 9.6 and the following be inserted as 9.5: : *"The General Assembly, in order to promote the mission work of the Church and the development of new churches outside the United States, may authorize its mission entity, a judicatory, or a commission to act in the place of a presbytery with respect to persons, ministers, and churches lying outside the bounds of the United States and outside the bounds of any existing presbytery. In such a case, the body so designated shall have with respect to the persons, ministers, and churches under its care the same jurisdiction, authority, and responsibilities which are otherwise granted to a presbytery, and the General Assembly rather than a synod shall provide for the oversight and responsibility of the body's ecclesiastical actions."*

Respectfully submitted,
The Joint Committee on Amendments

MEMORIALS / RESOLUTION

I. MEMORIAL FROM MISSOURI PRESBYTERY REGARDING MINISTERS OF OTHER DENOMINATIONS SERVING COMMUNION

WHEREAS, we concur with the permanent committee on Judiciary, in that we affirm that the communion table in any particular Cumberland Presbsyterian Church is the Lord's Table and that not that of our denomination or any local church.

WHEREAS, the committee acknowledged that allowing ministers of other denominations always and only with Presbyterian approval to serve communion in a Cumberland Presbyterian Church, has produced asmany blessings as problems.

WHEREAS, if abuse occurred or some Presbsyteries failed to provide proper oversight, then according to Cumberland Presbyterian Constitution 8.5/b. A Synod has the oversight and responsibility to review the records of the Presbyteries, redress whatever they may have done contrary to order

WHEREAS, we believe that rather than Presbyteries being empowered to provide leadership and care of local congregations just the opposite has occurred.

WHEREAS, we believe in an open table.

WHEREAS, our own Seminary trains candidates from other denominations, who, when ordained, will serve Communion.

WHEREAS, we believe a very high percentage of Cumberland Presbyterians would partake of the Lord's Supper if offered in a non-Cumberland Presbyterian setting administered by a non-Cumberland Presbyterian minister.

THEREFORE, we ask that the 2013 General Assembly ruling rescinding the 1987 ruling be overturned and be replaced with the original ruling. "An ordained minister, although of another church may serve the Lord's Supper in a Cumberland Presbyterian Church, provided this minister has been approved by a judicatory (that is, presbytery) of the church."

Missouri Presbytery at its Spring Meeting of Presbytery on March 19, 2016, passed this memorial to be forwarded to the General Assembly headquarters for consideration at the 2016 General Assembly.

Signed Larry Nottingham, Stated Clerk, Missouri Presbytery

II. MEMORIAL FROM COVENANT PRESBYTERY REGARDING CHURCH WORLD SERVICES

We, the undersigned, do petition the Covenant Presbytery to memorialize the 2016 General Assembly with the following resolution:

WHEREAS, Church World Services has an overall rating by Charity Navigator of 81.75; and

WHEREAS, Church World Services is linked with Presbyterian Church USA, Presbyterian Church of Canada, Reformed Church in America, Evangelical Lutheran Church in America, Evangelical Lutheran Church in Canada, United Church of Christ, Disciples of Christ, Christian Reformed Church, Church of the Brethren, Episcopal Church, Mennonites, Community of Christ, and the Moravian Church and others which accept the homosexual lifestyle as normal, ordain homosexual individuals into the ministry, and/or promote or give acceptance to those who do; and

WHEREAS, Samaritan's Purse which has an overall rating of 96.17 rating by Charity Navigators, and

WHEREAS, Samaritan's Purse is not in league with any of the above organizations and

WHEREAS, it behooves us to use our funds in a prudent, effective and righteous way; and

WHEREAS, Samaritan's Purse has a very evangelical approach to its mission: (see mission statement below)

BE IT RESOLVED, that the 2016 General Assembly dissolve its relationship with Church World Services and join with Samaritan's Purse by the 2017 General Assembly.

Signed: the Elders of Bayou de Chine Cumberland Presbyterian Church
Dr. Kenneth G. Richards, Moderator and Pastor, Jim Crass, Mark Crass, Walter Lawrence, Baker Thompson and Larry Wooten, Treasurer.

Samaritan's Purse is a nondenominational evangelical Christian organization providing spiritual and physical aid to hurting people around the world. Since 1970, Samaritan 1s Purse has helped meet needs of people who are victims of war, poverty, natural disasters, disease, and famine with the purpose of sharing God 1s love through His Son, Jesus Christ. Emergency relief meets desperate needs of victims worldwide. Operation Christmas Child delivers more than 8 million shoebox gifts to poor children in more than 100 countries each year. World Medical Mission sends doctors, equipment, and supplies to underprivileged countries. Community development and vocational programs in impoverished villages and neighborhoods help people break the cycle of poverty and give them hope for a better tomorrow. Vulnerable children are rescued, educated, fed, clothed, and sheltered, letting them know that God loves them, Jesus died and rose again for them, and they are not forgotten.

Covenant Presbytery at its Fall Meeting of Presbytery on October 3, 2015, passed this memorial to be forwarded to the General Assembly headquarters for consideration at the 2016 General Assembly.
Signed Reese Baker, Stated Clerk, Covenant Presbytery

III. MEMORIAL FROM COVENANT PRESBYTERY REGARDING HOMOSEXUALITY

We, the undersigned, do petition the Covenant Presbytery to memorialize the 2016 General Assembly with the following resolution:

WHEREAS, in the beginnjng "God created mankind in his own image, in the image of God he created. them; male and female he created them." (Genesis 1:27) and called it "very good"; and

WHEREAS, "That is why a man- leaves his father and mother and is united to his wife, and they become one flesh." (Genesis 2:24); and

WHEREAS, nowhere in the Bible does it say God ever changed His mind or thought He made a mistake in creating humankind any differently or that marriage should be any different than between a man and a woman; and

WHEREAS, Jesus said, "For this reason a man will leave his father and mother and be united to his wife, and the two will become one flesh." (Matthew 19:5); and

WHEREAS, The Bible is clear that anyone who keeps "practicing" sinful ways in no way conforms to God's plans for humanity -
"We know that the law is good if one uses it properly. We also know that the law is made not for the righteous but for lawbreakers and rebels, the ungodly and sinful, the unholy and irreligious, for those who kill their fathers or mothers, for murderers, for the sexually immoral, for those practicing homosexuality, for slave traders and liars and perjurers-and for whatever else is contrary to the sound doctrine that conforms to the gospel concerning the glory of the blessed God, which he entrusted to me." (1 Timothy 1:8-11); and

WHEREAS, Paul admonishes the faithful - "Because of this, God gave them over to shameful lusts. Even their women exchanged natural sexual relations for unnatural ones. In the same way the men also abandoned natural relations with women and were inflamed with lust for one another. Men committed shameful acts with other men, and received in themselves the due penalty for their error. Furthermore, just as they did not think it worthwhile to retain the knowledge of God, so God gave them over to a depraved mind, so that they do what ought not to be done. They have become filled with every kind of wickedness, evil, greed and depravity. They are full of envy, murder, strife, deceit and malice. They are gossips, slanderers, God-haters, insolent, arrogant and boastful; they invent ways of doing evil; they disobey their parents; they have no understanding, no fidelity, no love, no mercy. Although they know God's righteous decree that those who do such things deserve death, they not only continue to do these very things but also approve of those who practice them." (Romans 1:26-32) and "Do not be yoked together with unbelievers. For what do righteousness and wickedness have in common? Or what fellowship can light have with darkness? What harmony is there between Christ and Belial? Or what does a believer have in common with an unbeliever? What agreement is there between the temple of God and idols? For we are the temple of the living God. "As God has said: 'I will live with them and walk among them, and I will be their God, and they will be my people. Therefore, 'Come out from them and be separate, says the Lord. Touch no unclean thing, and I will receive you.' And, 'I will be a Father to you, and you will be my sons and daughters, says the Lord Almighty.'" (2 Corinthians 6:14-18 and

WHEREAS, the Cumberland Presbyterian Church is currently linked with many other organizations listed below that either accept the homosexual lifestyle as normal, ordain homosexual individuals into the ministry, and/or promote and/or give acceptance to those who do:

BE IT RESOLVED, that the Covenant Presbytery of the Cumberland Presbyterian Church memorialize the 2016 General Assembly to separate itself from the following in all areas by the time of the General Assembly of 2017:

Presbyterian Church USA, Presbyterian Church of Canada, Reformed Church in America, Evangelical Lutheran Church in America, Evangelical Lutheran Church in Canada, United Church of Christ, Disciples of Christ, Christian Reformed Church, Church of the Brethren, Episcopal Church, Mennonites, Community of Christ, and the Moravian Church.

Signed: the Elders of Bayou de Chine Cumberland Presbyterian Church
Dr. Kenneth G. Richards, Moderator and Pastor, Jim Crass, Mark Crass, Walter Lawrence, Baker Thompson and Larry Wooten, Treasurer.

Covenant Presbytery at its Fall Meeting of Presbytery on October 3, 2015, passed this memorial to be forwarded to the General Assembly headquarters for consideration at the 2016 General Assembly.
Signed Reese Baker, Stated Clerk, Covenant Presbytery

GENERAL ASSEMBLY AGENCIES

I. OFFICE OF THE GENERAL ASSEMBLY

A. GENERAL ASSEMBLY OFFICE

	Revised 2016	Proposed 2017
INCOME		
Our United Outreach	$212,836	$211,836
Endowments/Interest	20,000	20,000
Interest on Cash Funds Management	2,500	2,500
Sales of yearbook/digest	2,000	2,000
TOTAL INCOME	**$237,336**	**$236,336**
EXPENSE		
ECUMENICAL RELATIONS		
World Communion of Reformed Churches	$ 6,000	$ 6,000
CANAAC	2,000	2,000
Ecumenical Travel	1,000	1,000
Sub-Total	$ 9,000	$ 9,000
LIAISON WITH CHURCH		
General Assembly Meeting	$ 10,000	$ 10,000
Preliminary Minutes	5,000	5,000
GA Minutes/Mailing	500	500
Yearbook/Mailing	2,500	2,500
Travel/Moderator	8,500	8,500
Travel/Stated Clerk & Staff	8,500	8,500
Sub-Total	$ 35,000	$ 35,000
OFFICE		
Computer Supplies	$ 2,000	$ 2,000
Equipment/Supplies	2,500	2,500
Postage	2,000	2,000
Sub-Total	$ 6,500	$ 6,500
PERSONNEL		
Salaries/Housing	$139,420	$139,420
FICA (Asst to Stated Clerk)	4,300	4,300
Retirement	6,800	6,800
Health Insurance	30,000	30,000
Disability Insurance/Worker's Compensation	800	800
Sub-Total	$181,320	$181,320
STATED CLERK'S CONFERENCE/BOARD EXPENSE		
Legal Fees / Clerk's Conference	$ 1,963	$ 1,963
Corporate Board Expense	2,000	2,000
Sub-Total	$ 3,963	$ 3,963
TOTAL EXPENSE	**$235,783**	**$235,783**
From Reserves	$ 1,553	$ 553

B. GENERAL ASSEMBLY COMMISSIONS AND COMMITTEES

	Revised 2016	Proposed 2017
INCOME		
Contingency	$ 14,000	$ 13,240
Nominating Committee	2,981	2,966
Commission on Chaplains	10,296	10,247
Judiciary Committee	9,710	9,965
Theology and Social Concerns Committee	3,618	3,601
Our United Outreach Committee	92,044	92,044
TOTAL INCOME	**$132,649**	**$132,065**

	Revised 2016	Proposed 2017
EXPENSE		
Contingency	$ 14,000	$ 13,240
Nominating Committee	2,981	2,966
Commission on Chaplains	10,296	10,247
Judiciary Committee	9,710	9,965
Theology and Social Concerns Committee	3,618	3,601
Our United Outreach Committee	92,044	92,044
TOTAL EXPENSE	**$132,649**	**$132,065**

II. MINISTRY COUNCIL

	Revised 2016	Proposed 2017
INCOME		
Endowments		
Grants	$ 21,511	$ 0
ILP Transfers		
MMT Budget Reserve Fund: out ILP	625,727	711,066
DMT Contingency Fund: in Wells Fargo	17,711	10,200
DMT Contingency Fund: in ILP (reimburse)		(23,109)
DMT Leader Development: out ILP		2,902
Contributions/Gifts		
Teacher of the Year	0	0
Patron Membership (DMT)	0	0
Christian Education Season Offering	0	0
DMT - General	6,300	3,600
MC - General	0	0
CMT - General	0	0
Our United Outreach		
OUO Income	1,080,900	985,700*
In lieu of Our United Outreach	6,720	6,720
Birthplace Shrine Chaplaincy	3,750	3,750
Children's Fest	11,000	7,154
Clergy Crisis	6,000	6,000
CP Magazine Subscriptions	30,000	30,000
Cumberland Presbyterians Resources	50,500	65,737
CPWM		
Convention	10,000	10,000
Convention Offering	250	250
General	1,000	1,000
Sales Merchandise	700	700
CPYC	59,039	66,132
Discipleship Blueprints	0	1,700
Encounter	38,012	105,224
Faith Out Loud	9,000	9,000

	Revised 2016	Proposed 2017
Faith in 3D	$ 5,000	$ 5,000
Family Week: Brochure Fees	1,500	1,500
Global Missions Interns and Consultants: out ILP	20,000	20,000
Intersections	6,884	6,280
Ministers Conference	3,600	10,000
Missionary Setup	33,000-	124,000
Missionary Support	258,044	376,484
New Church Development (NCD) Subsidies	198,500	198,500
New Program Initiatives - DMT (Stir)	5,826	5,000
New Exploration Iniative - NCD	71,550	71,550
NPI: Children's CP Curriculum	1,400	600
Presbyterian Youth Triennium	7,000	0
Presbyteries/Councils	116,800	-
Program Planning Calendar - Sales	920	920
The Forum	7,700	9,992
Young Adult Ministry	6,000	2,500
Youth Evangelism Conference	10,000	36,000
Youth Ministry Planning Council	5,000	648
TOTAL INCOME	**$2,598,533**	**$2,872,700**

*GA approved the Ministry Council apportionment that could be as much as $1,080,900. Based on past years actuals (OUO Goal not met) MC budget based on 10% less than apportionment.

EXPENSES
Ministry Council Administration Salaries

Salaries	$ 809,840	$ 807,356
Clergy Housing Allowance	154,208	156,692
Health Insurance	113,400	123,168
Retirement	37,747	37,747
FICA	31,545	31,545
Tax Sheltered Annuity	3,632	3,632
Insurance/Disability	3,172	3,168

Ministry Council Administration General Expenses

Annual Credit Card Fees	$ 3,678	$ 3,678
Computer Equipment	0	0
Computer Software (Wufoo, Adobe, BaseCamp)	10,000	10,000

	Revised 2016	Proposed 2017
CPCA Partnership	0	0
Educational Publications for Distribution	3,000	3,000
Employee Events	2,500	2,500
Employee Recognition	3,450	3,450
Government Fees (annual reports)	40	40
Legal	2,000	2,000
P & C Insurance	19,090	19,090
Staff Resource Materials	1,997	1,997
Subscriptions/Membership	1,250	1,250
Telephone/Internet	624	624
Temporary Help	29,150	29,150
MC/Elected Team Member Recognition	1,040	1,040
Office Supplies	12,000	12,000
Postage	1,800	1,800
Professional Development	0	0
Beth-El Farmworker	$ 40,500	$ 40,500
Birthplace Shrine Chaplaincy: Chaplain's Stipend	3,750	3,750
Children's Fest	11,000	7,154
Church Women United	0	0
Clergy Crisis Support: Distribution	6,000	6,000
Coalition of Applachian Ministry	12,700	12,700
Congregational Expenses	0	3,000
CP Magazine	54,033	54,033
Cumberland Presbyterian Resources	50,500	67,628
CPWM		
General	7,100	7,100
Sales Merchandise	5,300	5,300
Convention	11,950	11,950
Offering	250	250
CPYC	67,650	67,650
Cross-Culture Immigrant Leadership Training	4,000	4,000
Discipleship Blueprints	1,700	2,400
Ecumenical Stewardship Center	3,000	4,500
Ecumenical Youth Ministry Staff Team Partnership	0	500
Encounter	38,012	38,012
Faith in 3D - Partnership	5,000	5,000
Faith Out Loud	9,000	9,000

	Revised 2016	Proposed 2017
Family Week	$ 1,500	$ 1,500
General Assembly	31,400	32,800
General Consultants	9,600	9,600
Global Mission Interns and Consultants	20,000	20,000
Global Social Action	0	0
Intersections	6,884	6,270
Kaleo	0	5,000
Leadership Referral Services	2,100	2,100
Ministers		
Conference	10,225	16,000
Encouragement & Recognition	3,818	3,818
Retreat	1,000	1,000
Missionary Messenger	78,348	78,348
Missionary Setup	33,000	124,000
Missionary Support	258,044	376,484
National Farm Worker	3,500	3,500
National Youth Workers Conference	0	2,000
New Church Development (NCD) Subsidies	205,900	205,900
New Exploraation Initiative	71,550	71,550
New Program Iniatives		
Children's Curriculum	1,400	600
CPWM Girls and Young Women Council	10,200	10,200
CP Learning Circles	12,000	6,000
DMT	0	12,000
PREP Staff Expenses	0	996
Presbyterial Expenses	0	3,000
Presbyterian Youth Triennium	14,000	10,000
Presbyteries/Councils	113,220	113,220
Program Planning Calendar	5,150	5,150
Project Vida	8,500	8,500
Prostestant Church Owned Pub Assoc (DMT)	0	200
Stir	5,826	5,000
Support Ministries	1,000	1,000
The Forum	7,700	8,300
Third Age Ministry	500	500
Travel (includes elected member travel)	83,360	85,210

	Revised 2016	Proposed 2017
Web Development/Maintenance	$ 1,200	$ 1,200
Young Adult Conference	0	18,500
Young Adult Ministry	6,000	2,500
Young Adult Volunteers	0	5,000
Youth Evangelism Conference	10,000	10,000
Youth Ministry Planning Council - UBCD	5,000	2,500
TOTAL EXPENSES	**$2,598,533**	**$ 2,872,700**
Surplus/(Deficit)	$ 0	$ 0

III. BOARD OF STEWARDSHIP

INCOME

Contributions			
	Contributions/Gifts	$ 2,000	$ 3,000
	ILP Contributions	5,000	2,000
	Endowment Contributions	25,000	20,000
	Total Contributions	**32,000**	**25,000**
Our United Outreach		135,000	135,000
Investment Earnings			
	Endowment Earnings	80,000	88,000
	ILP Earnings	17,500	12,000
	Endowment WF Income	16,000	18,000
	Total Investment Earnings	**113,500**	**118,000**
Realized Gain/Loss - Endowment		10,000	17,000
Unrealized Gain/Loss - Endowment		84,488	90,500
	Total Investment Gains/Losses	**94,488**	**107,500**
Service Fees			
	Management Fees - Acct Coordinator	1,600	1,600
	Management Fees	50,000	51,000
	Total Service Fees	**51,600**	**52,600**
TOTAL INCOME		**$426,588**	**$ 438,100**

EXPENSE

Salaries			
	Salaries	$188,660	$ 195,565
	Housing Allowance	21,000	21,000
	Total Salaries	**209,660**	**216,565**
Benefits			
	Health Insurance	67,000	70,000
	Retirement	10,483	10,828
	FICA	9,395	9,790
	Insurance/Disability	800	800
	Total Benefits	**87,678**	**91,418**
Events			
	Conference/Events	500	500
	Tax Guide for Ministers	3,700	3,700
	Total Events	**4,200**	**4,200**
Board Expense			
	Board/Agency Travel	12,500	12,500

	Revised 2016	Proposed 2017
Board/Agency Recognition	$ 600	$ 600
Total Board Expense	**13,100**	**13,100**
Resource Purchases		
Subscriptions	100	100
Total Resources Purchases	**100**	**100**
Contracted Services		
Legal	500	500
Temporary Help	1,000	1,000
Total Contracted Services	**1,500**	**1,500**
Professional Development		
Subscriptions & Membership	1,000	500
Total Professional Development	**1,000**	**500**
Payment/Subsidies		
ESC Stewardship Expense	2,000	2,000
ILP Withdrawal	2,500	2,500
Endowment Distribution	88,000	92,000
Total Payments/Subsidies	**92,500**	**96,500**
Equipment		
Office Equipment	800	800
Computer Equipment	2,000	2,000
Computer Maintenance	150	150
Computer Software	$ 500	$ 500
Total Equipment	**3,450**	**3,450**
Supplies		
Computer Supplies	1,000	500
Office Supplies	2,500	2,500
Total Supplies	**3,500**	**3,000**
Postage/Shipping		
Postage	2,500	2,000
Shipping	300	167
Total Postage/Shipping	**2,800**	**2,167**
Employee Recognition		
Employee Recognition	1,500	1,000
Total Employee Recognition	**1,500**	**1,000**
Travel		
Staff Travel	5,000	4,000
Total Travel	**5,000**	**4,000**
Miscellaneous		
Miscellaneous	500	500
Total Miscellaneous	**500**	**500**
Organization		
Organizational Expense	100	100
Total Organization	**100**	**100**
TOTAL EXPENSE	**$462,588**	**$ 438,100**

IV. HISTORICAL FOUNDATION

INCOME		
Our United Outreach	$ 79,575	$ 79,439
Endowments	48,500	55,000
Gifts	9,000	11,000
ILP Earnings	5,550	6,550
Denomination Day Offering	5,000	5,000
TOTAL INCOME	**$ 147,625**	**$ 156,989**
EXPENSE		
Salaries	$ 85,450	$ 93,141

	Revised 2016	Proposed 2017
FICA / Retirement	13,644	14,053
Insurance	9,199	10,034
Board Travel	5,000	5,000
Legal Fees	200	200
Continuing Education	1,000	1,000
Subscriptions/Memberships	2,000	2,000
Archival Equipment	2,000	2,000
Computer Supplies	500	500
Office Supplies	2,000	2,000
Postage	300	300
Acquisitions	8,000	8,000
Birthplace Shrine	4,000	4,000
Employee Recognition	600	600
Staff Travel	7,000	7,000
Denomination Day Project	5,000	5,000
TOTAL EXPENSE	**$ 145,893**	**$ 154,828**

V. MEMPHIS THEOLOGICAL SEMINARY

	Revised 2016	Proposed 2017
REVENUE		
Student Tuition Fees	$2,926,825	$ 2,591,335
Investment	379,280	306,608
Gifts and Grants	1,326,325	1,671,667
Other Revenues	93,919	129,682
TOTAL REVENUES	**$4,726,349**	**$ 4,699,292**
EXPENSES		
Business Office	$ 337,750	$ 333,191
Dean's Office	145,295	150,325
Chapel	44,487	42,689
Formation For Ministry	117,311	110,840
Financial Leadership Ministry	76,325	82,123
Educational Development Committee	17,250	15,500
Advancement Office	314,617	341,718
Doctor of Ministry	66,920	74,400
Facilities	556,818	568,778
Faculty	916,026	1,063,461
Summer Classes	37,600	37,600
January Classes	11,000	11,000
Financial Aid	64,199	63,616
Information Technology	194,015	156,765
Library	220,958	264,658
President's Office	264,250	263,612
Admissions	155,485	163,224
Student Services	80,161	84,540
Registrar & Institutional Research	130,692	129,347
Public Relations	85,849	0
Communications	38,544	49,588
Student Housing	124,280	97,810
Certificate & Continuing Education	40,390	25,938
Student Government	3,255	2,775
Theology & Arts	23,288	43,216
Scholarships	0	407,972
Program of Alternate Studies	0	130,177
Depreciation	0	214,568
TOTAL EXPENSES		**$5,071,360**
Increase (decrease) in net assets		(372,058)

VI. SHARED SERVICES

	Revised 2016	Proposed 2017
REVENUE		
Our United Outreach	$ 341,066	341,066
TOTAL REVENUES	**$ 341,066**	**$ 341,066**
EXPENSES		
Salaries	$ 49,767	$ 51,011
Health Insurance	25,137	27,651
Retirement	2,488	2,488
FICA	3,807	3,807
Accounting Coordinator	1,600	1,600
Audit	21,000	21,000
Payroll Service	8,500	6,500
Bank Charges	17,500	17,500
Technology System Consultants - EMS	18,000	18,000
Software Maintenance Agreement - Blackbaud	14,500	14,500
Building & Maintenance	49,700	45,845
Pest Control	840	840
Lawn & Ground Maintenance	18,500	18,500
Lawn Treatment	1,500	1,500
Utilities - Building 1	22,806	23,490
Utilities - Building 2	17,579	18,106
Janitorial Service	8,100	8,100
Security System Monitoring	1,100	1,100
Trash Collection	1,850	1,850
Telephone/Internet	8,800	8,800
Heating & AC Maintenance Agreement	10,000	10,000
Insurance/Liability	11,280	11,844
Office Equipment Maintenance	14,000	14,000
Computer Maintenance	500	500
Computer Software	2,500	2,500
Office Supplies	2,500	2,500
Postage	750	750
Employee Events	1,000	1,000
TOTAL EXPENSE	$ 335,605	$ 335,440
Surplus/Deficit	$ 5,461	$ 5,626

The Proceedings of the
ONE HUNDRED EIGHTY-SIXTH GENERAL ASSEMBLY
of the
CUMBERLAND PRESBYTERIAN CHURCH
session held in
NASHVILLE, TENNESSEE
June 20 - 24, 2016

At Nashville, Tennessee and within the facilities of the Sheraton Music City Hotel, there the twentieth day of June in the year of our Lord, Two Thousand Sixteen, at the appointed hour of eight thirty o'clock in the morning, Minister and Elder Commissioners from the various presbyteries, youth advisory delegates and visitors assembled for concurrent meetings of the General Assemblies of the Cumberland Presbyterian Church and the Cumberland Presbyterian Church in America.

FIRST DAY – MONDAY – JUNE 20, 2016

OPENING WORSHIP

In Ballroom A-E of the Sheraton Music City Hotel, the one hundred eighty-sixth General Assembly of the Cumberland Presbyterian Church, the one hundred forty-first General Assembly of the Cumberland Presbyterian Church in America, the Convention of Cumberland Presbyterian Women's Ministry, and visitors gathered for worship at 8:00 a.m. Liturgists for the service were Ms. Yvonne Frierson, National Missionary Society President (CPCA), Elder L. Leon Cole, Jr., Moderator (CPCA), Ms. Athala Jaramillo, Women's Ministry Convention President (CPC). The combined presbyterial choir from Elk River Presbytery (CPCA) and Nashville Presbytery (CPC) was led by Reverend Paula Louder, Nashville Presbytery. The Pianist was Ms. Janice Bane, Nashville Presbytery.

The Reverend Michele Gentry de Correal, Andes Presbytery, retiring Moderator (CPC) presented the sermon, "Called to Serve, Sent to Proclaim," taken from 2 Peter 1:10-11. The Sacrament of Holy Communion was led by Co-Celebrants Reverend Gloria Villa Diaz, Trinity Presbytery (CPC Unification Task Force member), and Reverend Mitchell Walker, Huntsville Presbytery (CPCA Unification Task Force member). Assisting with Communion were: CPCA – Reverend Kay Ward Creer – East Texas, Reverend Tramaine Snodgrass – Huntsville Presbytery, Reverend Nancy Fuqua – Florence Presbytery, Elder Frank Anderson – Birmingham Presbytery, Elder Joy Wallace – Brazos River Presbytery, Reverend Rick E. White– Brazos River Presbytery, Reverend Barbara Clemons – Huntsville Presbytery, Elder Thomas Ward – East Texas Presbytery, Elder Justina Johnson – Ohio Valley Presbytery, Elder Glee Thompson – Tuscaloosa Presbytery; CPC – Reverend Randy Jacob – Choctaw Presbytery, Elder Lola John – Choctaw Presbytery, Reverend Johnny Montano – Cauca Valley Presbytery, Reverend Nobuko Seki – Japan Presbytery, Elder Takeshi Yohena – Japan Presbytery, Reverend Josephina Sanchez – Presbytery of East Tennessee, Reverend Douglas Park –Cumberland East Coast Presbytery, Reverend Seungno Kim - Cumberland East Coast Presbytery, Elder Robin Hughes – Red River Presbytery, Elder Christy Miller – Tennessee-Georgia Presbytery. Ushers were Kay Street, Larry Street, Susie Rolman, Mary Rolman, Jacky Clifton, Raymond Clifton, Rob Truitt, Judi Truitt, Luann Barber, and Nathaniel Matthews.

JOINT EVANGELISM CONFERENCE WORKSHOP

Joint Evangelism Conference Workshops, led by the Reverend T.J. Malinoski, were held at 10:30 a.m. and 2:00 p.m. in Ballroom A-D.

THE ASSEMBLY IS CONSTITUTED

The Moderator, the Reverend Michele Gentry, called the assembly to order at 3:30p.m. Her first order of business was to introduce "Commissioners in Training," the children attending General Assembly. Following the introduction, the Reverend Linda Glenn, West Tennessee Presbytery, presented the Report of the Credentials Committee. There were forty-four (44) ministers, forty (40) elders, for a total of eighty-four (84) commissioners present at 3:30p.m. There were twenty-five (25) Youth Advisory Delegates present. On motion, the report of the Credentials Committee was received, marked Appendix "A" and filed.

Reverend Perryn Rice, Red River Presbytery, prayed the constituting prayer.

ASSEMBLY BUSINESS

On motion, the program was adopted as changed.

Moderator Gentry declared the floor open for nominations for the Office of Moderator of the one hundred eighty-sixth General Assembly. The Reverend Dewayne Tyus, previously endorsed by Nashville Presbytery, was nominated by Elder Carol Warren, Nashville Presbytery. Elder Warren then gave testimony to his qualifications and endorsed Reverend Tyus as Moderator of the one hundred eighty-sixth General Assembly of the Cumberland Presbyterian Church.

There being no further nominations, a motion was made that nominations cease and that the body move to elect by acclamation. Following unanimous vote, Moderator Gentry declared the Reverend Dwayne Tyus, Nashville Presbytery, to be the Moderator of the one hundred eighty-sixth General Assembly of the Cumberland Presbyterian Church.

Elder Warren escorted Moderator Tyus to the podium. Retiring Moderator Reverend Michele Gentry placed the Moderator's cross on Reverend Tyus, and presented him with the gavel.

Retiring Moderator Gentry presented a new Moderator's stole that she commissioned which was made of Guatemalan materials and Mexican workmanship to newly elected Moderator Tyus. This stole, a gift to the General Assembly from Retiring Moderator Gentry, is to replace the current Moderator's stole.

Moderator Tyus opened the floor for nominations for Vice-Moderator. The Reverend Don Wilson, Presbytery del Cristo, nominated the Reverend Nobuko Seki, Japan Presbytery, to serve as Vice-Moderator of the one hundred eighty-sixth General Assembly of the Cumberland Presbyterian Church.

There being no further nominations, a motion was made that nominations cease and the body move to elect. By acclamation, the Reverend Nobuko Seki, Japan Presbytery, was elected as Vice-Moderator of the one hundred eighty-sixth General Assembly of the Cumberland Presbyterian Church.

PRESENTATION BY THE STATED CLERK

The Stated Clerk, Michael Sharpe, invited retiring Moderator, Michele Gentry, to the podium and presented her with replicas of the Moderator's cross and gavel representing the ones used in the one hundred eighty-fifth General Assembly of the Cumberland Presbyterian Church.

GREETINGS FROM THE HOST COMMITTEE

Greetings were expressed by the Reverend Don Tabor, Nashville Presbytery (CPC), on behalf of the Host Committee. The Reverend Rosemary Herron, Elk River Presbytery (CPCA) co-chair of Host Committee, brought greetings to the body. Both told of the sights and amenities of the area.

Reverend Tabor read letters of greeting to the body from Tennessee Governor Bill Haslam and Nashville Mayor Megan Barry.

Reverend Tabor recognized the Planning Committee members by having them stand.

On a personal note, Reverend Tabor asked for prayers for his family on the tragic drive-by shooting of his stepson who has been in critical care for 2 weeks.

COMMUNICATIONS

The Stated Clerk announced that there were no communications.

COMMISSIONER RESOLUTIONS

Reverend Bryon Forester, minister delegate from West Tennessee Presbytery, presented a resolution to the body for consideration. The *Resolution of Repentance, Apology and Resolve* was referred to the Theology & Social Concerns/Unification Task Force Committee.

CORRECTIONS TO THE PRELIMINARY MINUTES

The Stated Clerk reported that a copy of all corrections to the preliminary minutes were handed out to all commissioners during orientation and would be reflected in the final printing of the minutes. There is one Committee change: Commissioner Reverend Josephina Sanchez will serve on the Theology and Social Concerns/Unification Task Force Committee.

COMMITTEE APPOINTMENTS AND REFERRALS

The Stated Clerk reported that all referrals to the committees will be printed in the minutes as presented in the preliminary minutes with the changes handed out during orientation.

REFERRALS TO COMMITTEES

Referrals to the Committee on Chaplains/Historical Foundation

Page **Report**
- 69   The Report of the Board of Trustees of the Historical Foundation
- 92   The Report of the Commission on Military Chaplains and Personnel

Referrals to the Committee on Children's Home/Higher Education

Page **Report**
- 76   The Report of the Board of Trustees of Memphis Theological Seminary
- 116   The Report of the Board of Trustees of Bethel University
- 117   The Report of the Board of Trustees of the Cumberland Presbyterian Children's Home

Referrals to the Committee on Judiciary

Page **Report**
- 46   The Report Two of the Ministry Council, item C
- 94   The Report of the Permanent Committee on Judiciary
- 126   Memorial from Missouri Presbytery Regarding Ministers of Other Denominations serving Communion

Referrals to the Committee on Ministry Council/Communication/Discipleship

Page **Report**
- 38   The Report One of the Ministry Council
        except the shaded areas which are referred to Missions/Ministry and
        item III, which is referred to Board of Stewardship
- 45   The Report Two of the Ministry Council,
        except the shaded areas which are referred to Missions/Ministry and
        item C, which is referred to Judiciary

Referrals to the Committee on Missions/Ministry

Page **Report**
- 39   The Report One of the Ministry Council, the shaded areas only
- 45   The Report Two of the Ministry Council, the shaded areas only

Referrals to the Committee on Stewardship/Elected Officers

Page **Report**
- 31   The Report of the Moderator
- 32   The Report of the Stated Clerk
- 43   The Report One of the Ministry Council, item III
- 58   The Report of the Board of Stewardship, Foundation and Benefits

90 The Report of the Our United Outreach Committee
98 The Report of the Place of Meeting Committee
129 Line Item Budgets Submitted by General Assembly Agencies

Referrals to the Committee on Theology and Social Concerns/Unification Task Force

Page   Report
100 The Report of the Unified Committee on Theology and Social Concerns
110 The Report of the Unification Task Force
126 Memorial from Covenant Presbytery Regarding Church World Services
127 Memorial from Covenant Presbytery Regarding Homosexuality

A booklet provided by the Ministry Council was distributed to commissioners as supplemental information.

INTRODUCTION OF BOARD/AGENCY REPRESENTATIVES

The Stated Clerk introduced the following Board/Agency Representatives:

Bethel University	Robert Truitt
Commission on Chaplains	Mary McCaskey Benedict
Children's Home	Richard Dean
Historical Foundation	Lisa Oliver
Judiciary	Robert Rush
Memphis Theological Seminary	Susan Parker
Ministry Council	Troy Green
Our United Outreach	Ron Gardner
Stewardship	Randy Davidson
Theology & Social Concerns	Sheila O'Mara
Unification Task Force	Joy Warren (CPC)
	Mitchell Walker (CPCA)

A presentation was made by the Our United Outreach Committee by Reverend Cliff Hudson, Development Director. He introduced the Regional OUO Directors: Calotta Edsell – Arkansas and West Tennessee, Carolyn Harmon – Presbytery of East Tennessee, Jeff McMichael – Covenant, Cumberland and North Central Presbyteries, and Susan Parker – Grace and Hope Presbyteries.

A presentation by Troy Green of the Ministry Council introduced new staff members: Nathan Wheeler - Youth & Young Adult Ministry and Chuck Brown –Pastoral Development Ministry Team Leader.

Moderator Tyus introduced his wife, Guin, to the body as well as her brother the Reverend Jesse Freeman, Nashville Presbytery.

RECESS

Moderator Tyus declared the General Assembly of the Cumberland Presbyterian Church in recess at 4:25 p.m. until Thursday at 9:00 a.m.

THE EVENING PROGRAM

A Joint Worship Service led by Young Adults and Youth of the CPCA and CPC was experienced by the Assemblies. With uplifting music and youth led messages, the participants were encouraged to participate at worship stations at the close of worship.

In the lobby of the Sheraton Music City Hotel, the General Assembly of the Cumberland Presbyterian Church, the General Assembly of the Cumberland Presbyterian Church in America and the convention of the Cumberland Presbyterian Women's Ministry and visitors participated in a reception to honor the Reverend Dwayne Tyus, Moderator (CPC) and spouse, Guin; Retiring Moderator Michele Gentry, Elder L. Leon Cole, Jr., Moderator (CPCA), Ms. Yvonne Frierson, National Missionary Society President (CPCA); and Ms. Athala Jaramillo, Women's Ministry Convention President (CPC).

SECOND DAY – TUESDAY – JUNE 21, 2016

The General Assembly began their day with Committees meeting at 8:30 a.m. Each committee held their own devotional in their meeting rooms. The day was devoted to committee work. Attendance for the day: thirty-six (36) Minister Commissioners, thirty-four (34) Elder Commissioners and twenty (20) Youth Advisory Delegates.

At 7:30 p.m., the Discipleship Ministry Team sponsored "Joint Celebration of Generations: Interacting Together." Those who gathered had an enjoyable time of interaction through various activities. At 8:30 p.m., the annual Reception Honoring Women in Ministry was held. Attendees enjoyed rich fellowship as they celebrated Women in Ministry. Many shared that the Ordination Anniversary cards that had been received were so meaningful and uplifting. All agreed that this celebration was a highlight of the Assembly.

THIRD DAY – WEDNESDAY – JUNE 22, 2016

The General Assembly and visitors began the day with a devotional led by Global Community. Participating in the devotional were Reverend Milton Ortiz, Reverend Lynn Thomas, Reverend Johan Daza, Reverend Keishi Ishitsuka, Reverend Johnny Montano and new missionaries to Brazil, Reverend Jacob and Lindsey Sims. Jacob and Lindsey Sims were introduced as new missionaries to Brazil. Jacob spoke about their soon departure to the mission field. Reverends Thomas, Daza and Ishitsuka commissioned the Sims with a Commissioning Prayer. The message was given by Reverend Montano.

The Committees used the remainder of the day in meetings, preparing and reviewing reports and collecting signatures. Attendance for the day: thirty-six (36) Minister Commissioners, thirty-four (34) Elder Commissioners and twenty (20) Youth Advisory Delegates.

At 7:30 p.m., the 186th General Assembly gathered for worship in the Hermitage Ballroom of the Sheraton Music City Hotel. The worship was a celebration of serval new ministries across the denomination. The worship participants were Whitney Brown, Room in the Inn-Memphis; Lisa Anderson, Room in the Inn-Memphis; Joyce Merritt and Justina, Still Waters Ministry; Tommy Clark, Urban Bicycle Food Ministry; Lisa Cook and Jessica, Sacred Sparks Ministry; Barry Anderson and Missy Rose, Iona – A Community of Faith Burrito Ministry; and Gloria Villa Diaz, New Day in Christ Ministry. The participants each told a "Parable" which came out of the ministry that they represented. The Music Leader was Reverend Paula Louder, Nashville Presbytery, with pianist Ms. Janice Bane, Nashville Presbytery. The ushers were Joey Parker, Ettie Parker, Judy Truitt, Rob Truitt, Jared Graham, Jonathan Murphy and Mary Roman.

An offering of $3,585.77 was received to be divided among the ministries participating in the service.

FOURTH DAY – THURSDAY – JUNE 23, 2016

The General Assembly and visitors began the day with joyful singing and a devotional by Youth Advisory Delegate, Shelby Webb, Missouri Presbytery. Her devotional was taken from Hebrews 13:11-16.

CALL TO ORDER

The Moderator, Reverend Dwayne Tyus, called the assembly to order at 9:05 a.m.

There were thirty-seven (37) ministers, thirty-nine (39) elders for a total of seventy-six (76) commissioners, and seventeen (17) youth advisory delegates present as of 9:05 a.m. The opening prayer was given by Reverend Tom Campbell, Arkansas Presbytery.

PARLIMENTARIAN APPOINTED

The Moderator appointed the Reverend Robert Rush as Parliamentarian.

GREETINGS

Greetings were extended from Elder L. Leon Cole, Jr., Moderator (CPCA). Moderator Cole said that it has been a delight to work with members of the CPC at this meeting and throughout the year. This has been a time to learn together and worship together. He enjoyed meeting with the CPC last year in Cali, Colombia as well as working with the last four CPC Moderators. He has also visited with members of

Japan Presbytery for meaningful dialog. Moderator Cole said that he is grateful for the opportunity to do this work for the Lord, and that we are all on the same battlefield with common work to do. We should all keep in mind Who we are working for.

Greetings were extended from Commissioner Reverend Jimmy Peyton, Hope Presbytery, on behalf of the Haiti Council of Churches. Reverend Peyton reported that in April, he along with Reverend Pat Driscoll and two elders, our new work in Haiti was commissioned with 6 provisional churches and 6 candidates. Reverend Peyton led the Assembly in a prayer for the Haiti Council.

PRESENTATIONS

A presentation was made by Reverend Cliff Hudson on behalf of the Our United Outreach Committee. Reverend Hudson reported that the OUO Committee was formed at the 179th General Assembly in 2009. OUO is the primary funding arm of the Cumberland Presbyterian Church. Feeling compelled to pay off the denomination's crippling debt, the OUO Committee, with the dedication of the CPC, was able to eliminate denominational debt in April 2015.

The OUO Committee participants, Calotta Edsel, Ron Gardner, Carolyn Harmon, Cliff Hudson, Jeff McMichael and Susan Parker, led the Assembly in the Denominational Note-Burning Celebration. This celebration also served as a time to honor Elder Ron Gardner for his service to the CPC through the OUO Committee.

Note Burning Celebration

Background: The Our United Outreach Committee was formed by the 179th General Assembly in 2009. Though young, the Committee has worked diligently to fulfill its mission: To educate the Cumberland Presbyterian Church about OUO and to promote it within the church as the primary funding arm of all the agencies, boards, and ministries of the church.

Early on, the original members of the Committee felt a burden to pay off the various components of debt the church owed for various reasons. It was their courage coupled with disciplined action that made possible the consistent pay-down and snowballing of the debt. This resulted in a total elimination of denominational debt in April 2015.

Due to God's grace and blessings, the examples of servant leadership of committee members, and faithful giving to Our United Outreach, over $120,000 per year now goes to ministry rather than debt service.

A Litany Of Grateful Celebration

Leader: Let us give thanks to Almighty God for the blessings we enjoy today.
All: It is right to gratefully acknowledge God's blessings upon us.
Leader: For the knowledge and vision of our leaders, who saw the need and then took action regarding our debt,
All: We give thanks to the Lord.
Leader: For disciplined, inspired perseverance that has produced the desired result,
All: We give thanks to the Lord.
Leader: For those who have been faithful, sharing their dollars and mixing them well in the pot called Our United Outreach to accomplish our purpose,
All: We give thanks to the Lord.
Leader: And to our Lord, our God, who continues to bless the Cumberland Presbyterian Church in new and challenging ways,
All: We lift our hearts and voices in praise and thanksgiving. Thanks be to you, O God!
Prayer Leader: Let us pray. Loving God, we praise you for the generosity and faithfulness of congregations, individuals, presbyteries, and other entities who have joined forces to bring about positive change by retiring our debt. We pray, O God, for continued guidance and provision as we worship and serve you with wisdom and knowledge. We praise you for your Spirit of unity and harmony we enjoy today.

Let the Assembly rise and join voices as our debt is symbolically retired.
Praise God from whom all blessings flow, Praise Him all creatures here below.
Praise Him above ye heavn'ly host. Praise Father, Son, and Holy Ghost!

Participants: Calotta Edsel, Ron Gardner, Carolyn Harmon, Cliff Hudson, Jeff McMichael, and Susan Parker

ANNOUNCEMENTS

The Stated Clerk gave the following announcements and instructions
- The Offering from last evening's worship service was $3,485.77
- Reminded that the YAD's would be invited to vote prior to the Commissioner vote.
- Instructed Commissioners/YAD's wishing to address the Assembly to approach the aisle microphone, introduce themselves by name and the Presbytery they represent.
- Anyone making a motion should write out the motion and give a copy to the Engrossing Clerk before returning to their seat.
- Committees will be seated in the front together during the presentation of the committee's report
- Explained how to use the colored cards to gauge responses to current discussion.

Moderator Tyus shared some of the rules of order to be used during the meeting.

ASSEMBLY BUSINESS

NOMINATING COMMITTEE

The Report of the Nominating Committee was presented by Nancy Bean, Committee Chair, who was given permission to address the body by motion as she is not a member of the body. A Motion was made to place these names in the report into nomination. The Moderator opened the floor for further nominations. Carla Bellis, Great Rivers Synod, Missouri Presbytery was nominated for the Ministry Council in place of Vicky Hoover Ainley. A vote was taken for all nominees except Ainley and Bellis. By vote, all persons nominated, with the exception of Ainley and Bellis were elected. A vote by ballot was taken. The Credentials Committee reported that Carla Bellis, Great Rivers Synod, Missouri Presbytery was elected.

MINISTRY COUNCIL/COMMUNICATION/DISCIPLESHIP COMMITTEE

The Report of the Ministry Council/Communications/Discipleship Committee was presented by YAD Justin Barkley (Grace Presbytery). Jim Buttram, Tennessee Georgia Presbytery made the Motion that the report be concurred in and the recommendations be adopted. Motion passed. The report was marked Appendix "B" and filed.

THE REPORT OF THE COMMITTEE ON CHAPLAINS/HISTORICAL FOUNDATION

The Report of the Committee on Chaplains/Historical Foundation was presented by Reverend Michele Gentry, Andes Presbytery. The report was read by YAD's, Abby Herman (Trinity Presbytery) and Kaylee Liehr (Murfreesboro Presbytery). A Motion was made that the report be concurred in and the recommendations be adopted.

A Substitute Motion was made to make Recommendation 7 read: "That General Assembly encourage each presbytery in the USA to communicate with their congregations to have a special offering on May 28, 2017 for Memorial Day and all subsequent Sundays on or before Memorial Day." The Substitute Motion passed. On vote, the report was concurred in and the recommendations adopted. The report was marked Appendix "C" and filed.

COMMITTEE ON CHILDREN'S/HIGHER EDUCATION

The Report of the Committee on Children's Home/Higher Education was presented by YAD's Sarah Cagle (Presbytery of East Tennessee), Eleanor Forester (West Tennessee Presbytery), James Hood (Hope Presbytery) and Elizabeth Warren (Arkansas Presbytery). A Motion was made by Reverend Kristi Lombard that the report be concurred in and the recommendations be adopted. Motion passed. The report was marked Appendix "D" and filed.

RECESS

The Moderator announced a 20 minute recess at 10:25 a.m.

CALL TO ORDER

Moderator Tyus called the meeting back to order at 10:46 a.m.

THE REPORT OF THE COMMITTEE ON THEOLOGY AND SOCIAL CONCERNS/UNIFICATION TASKFORCE

The Report of the Committee on Theology and Social Concerns/Unification Task Force was presented by Reverend Cardelia Howell-Diamond (Robert Donnell Presbytery). A Motion was made to concur with the report as corrected and adopt its recommendations.

A Motion made to divide the question into three parts: Part III Sec. A-B, Sec. C-E, and Section F. Motion passed.

Part III Sec. A-B including Recommendations 1-8 passed.

Sec. C-E including Recommendations 9-11 passed.

Sec. F including Recommendation 12: A Substitute Motion was made and seconded to approve the *Resolution of Repentance, Apology, and Resolve*.

Resolution of Repentance, Apology and Resolve

Whereas, we Cumberland Presbyterians are considering the call of God to "Go" during this 186th meeting of the General Assembly; and

Whereas, Jesus sent the twelve with these instructions: "As you go, proclaim the good news. The kingdom of heaven has come near. Cure the sick, raise the dead, cleanse the lepers, cast out demons." (Matthew 10:7-8); and

Whereas, we seek the healing of our divisions as Cumberland Presbyterians; and

Whereas, the Cumberland Presbyterian Church was founded in 1810 in Dickson County, Tennessee, USA, and grew rapidly in a nation that endorsed, participated in, and benefited from the practice of enslaving African men, women and children who were brought to this nation through the brutal trans-Atlantic slave trade; and

Whereas, the Cumberland Presbyterian Church was inconsistent in its condemnation of American slavery as an institution -- an institution that condoned the buying and selling of persons made in the image of God; an institution in which African American families were often separated, and individuals were beaten and abused in body and mind; and

Whereas, the Cumberland Presbyterian Church often condoned the segregation of its African American members into separate balconies, congregations, and classes because of the influence of cultural ideas of racial superiority and inferiority; and

Whereas, the Cumberland Presbyterian Church refused to allow its African American members full and equal membership following emancipation and the end of slavery; organizing instead separate congregations, presbyteries, and other judicatories that were denied representation in the General Assembly, and

Whereas, the Cumberland Presbyterian Church encouraged and supported the organization of the Cumberland Presbyterian Church in America (originally the Colored Cumberland Presbyterian Church) in 1874 in order to avoid the difficult work of integration, and to avoid offending its members who continued to hold fast to ideas of racial superiority; and

Whereas, the Cumberland Presbyterian Church was complicit in accepting Jim Crow segregation, lynching as a means of social control, economic oppression of freed slaves, and denial of educational opportunities; and

Whereas, the Cumberland Presbyterian Church and the Cumberland Presbyterian Church in America have both suffered from their separation, a separation that is harmful to the witness of the Church and a denial of our oneness in Christ; and

Whereas, the Cumberland Presbyterian Church laments the loss of friendship, gifts and graces from which our life, worship, witness and service would have been enriched had we not been separated all these years; and

Whereas, the Cumberland Presbyterian Church affirms the providence of God, whose purpose it is "that the whole creation
be set free from its bondage to sin and death, and be renewed in Jesus Christ" (COF, 1.15); and

Whereas, the Cumberland Presbyterian Church acknowledges our ongoing need for repentance, so that "In response to God's initiative to restore relationships, (we) make honest confession of sing against God, (our) brothers and sisters, and all of creation, and amend the past so far as is in (our) power." (COF, 4.07); therefore, be it

Resolved, that the Cumberland Presbyterian Church repent and seek God's forgiveness for the many ways we have benefitted from, participated in, condoned, and been blind to our role in racism, oppression of our African American brothers and sisters, and all forms of brutality; and be it further

Resolved, that the Cumberland Presbyterian Church apologize to our African American brothers and sisters, seek their forgiveness, and work to restore the broken relationships our sin has caused; and be it further

Resolved, that the Cumberland Presbyterian Church commit itself to preach the Word of God without compromise, and that we resolve to "oppose, resist, and seek to change all circumstances of oppression -- political, economic, cultural, racial, by which persons are denied the essential dignity God intends for them in the work of creation (COF, 6.30). We seek to promote reconciliation, love and justice among all persons, classes, races, and nations: (COF, 6.32). (Quoted in the Resolution Marking the 50th year since the end of World War II, by Japan Presbytery of the CPC)

The Substitute Motion passed. Report marked Appendix "E" and filed.

THE REPORT OF THE COMMITTEE ON STEWARDSHIP/ELECTED OFFICIALS

The Report of the Committee on Stewardship/Elected Officials was presented by Reverend Don Wilson, Del Cristo Presbytery. The report was read by YAD's Zeke Lake (Arkansas Presbytery), Charli Uhlrich (North Central Presbytery), Allison Hood (Hope Presbytery) and Cameron Kurtz (Red River Presbytery). A Motion was made that the report be concurred in and the recommendations be adopted.

A Motion was made to divide the question dividing Section D, Recommendations 6, 7, 8 from the rest of the report. Motion passed.

By vote, Sections A, B, and C including Recommendations 1-5, 9, 10 passed.

LUNCH RECESS

Moderator Tyus announced a recess for lunch until 2:00 p.m.

CALL TO ORDER

Moderator Tyus called the meeting back to order at 2:00 p.m.

Moderator Tyus introduced Jamie Berkley who brought greetings from the CPWM Convention. She shared that the Convention took up an offering for their two projects: providing furniture for missionaries and supporting Sacred Sparks, a ministry helping the homeless in Nashville that Reverend Lisa Cook is involved with. The Convention enjoyed field trips to mission projects and had a very successful convention which included joint worship services with the CPCA National Missionary Society.

On motion, the Assembly granted excuses to YAD Elizabeth Warren (Arkansas Presbytery) and Elder Christy Miller (Tennessee-Georgia Presbytery) from the afternoon session.

THE REPORT OF THE COMMITTEE ON STEWARDSHIP/ELECTED OFFICIALS (Continued)

A motion was made to divide Recommendation 6 from the rest of the Recommendations being considered. The Motion passed.

The Body considered Recommendation 6. On vote, Recommendation 6 was adopted.

A Substitute Motion was made to replace Recommendation 8: That the following statement be added to the By-laws of the General Assembly, Article 10.02 Election Tenure: 03. When nominating persons to boards, agencies and teams, priority consideration be given to persons whose individual life and/or church involvement demonstrates a commitment to support OUO. Motion passed with necessary majority.

The report was marked Appendix "F" and filed.

THE REPORT OF THE COMMITTEE ON MISSIONS/MINISTRY

The Report of the Committee on Missions/Ministry was presented by YAD's Shelby Webb (Missouri Presbytery), Daniel Fowler (Grace Presbytery) and Ryan Day (Columbia Presbytery). A Motion was made that the report be concurred in and the recommendations be adopted. Motion passed. The report was marked Appendix "G" and filed.

THE REPORT OF THE COMMITTEE ON JUDICIARY

Moderator Tyus asked Vice Moderator Reverend Nobuko Seki to take the gavel to enable him to participate with the Committee on Judiciary.

The Report of the Committee on Judiciary was presented by Reverend Perryn Rice (Red River Presbytery). The report was read by YAD's Jose Garcia (Choctaw Presbytery), Madeline Stence (North

Central Presbytery and Rande Johnson (West Tennessee Presbytery). A Motion was made that the report be concurred in and the recommendations be adopted.

A Motion was made to divide the question considering Recommendations 2, 3, and 5 in reverse order. Motion passed.

Following discussion of Recommendation 5: Recommendation 5 was denied.

Following discussion of Recommendation 3: Recommendation 3 was denied. Recommendation 2 died when 3 was denied.

A Motion was made to refer Recommendations 2, 3, and 5 back to Judiciary and the Missions Ministry team. Motion passed.

Following discussion of Recommendations 1, 4, 6, 7, by vote, Recommendations 1, 4, 6 and 7 were adopted.

The report was marked Appendix "H" and filed.

The Moderator returned to the podium.

RESOLUTION OF GRATITUDE

A Resolution of Gratitude was presented by the Reverend Anne Hames (West Tennessee Presbytery), expressing gratitude to Nashville Presbytery.

Resolution of Thanks for the 186 General Assembly

Praise God from whom all blessings flow!

We thank the good Lord for calling us to this time and this place to do the work of the Church. We have worshipped, prayed, talked, debated, played and renewed old friendships. Now may we GO!

We thank the King of Kings and the Lord of Lords for Mike and the office of the General Assembly who, worked so tirelessly to pull all the details of this Assembly together. Now may they GO!

We thank our Lord and Savior for Don and all the faith servants of Christ who are part of the Nashville Presbytery for sharing their gifts of hospitality with us. Now may they GO!

We praise God for calling Dwayne to be our Moderator and Nobuko to be our Vice-Moderator. We pray God's blessings on them as they begin this new opportunity in ministry. We appreciate all the work of the retiring moderators Michele and Kip. Now may they GO!

We thank the Holy Spirit for the worship services we have been able to participate in. We praise the Spirit for Edward, Emily, Michele, Paul, Roger, Tiffany and Trey who shared the Good News of the Gospel of Jesus Christ through preaching. Now may they GO!

We thank our Lord and Savior Jesus Christ for Barry, Gloria, Jason, Jessica, Joyce, Justina, Lisa, Missy Rose and Tommy who shared their testimony of the work they do for the glory of God. Now may they continue to GO!

We also give thanks for each commissioner, youth delegate and the beautiful children who have come near and far to do the work of the Church. We pray that we are all refreshed and reinvigorated to return to the work and the worship that the Lord God has called each of us to accomplish for His glory. Now may we, each and every one of us GO!

We thank the everlasting Father for the people who have cooked for us, made our beds, served our meals and worked as the supporting staff to make our stay comfortable and productive. We pray that they may come to know the love Jesus Christ and then GO!

Finally brothers and sisters let us thank the Lord for His Word: the Word written, the Word spoken and the Word made flesh.

Hear the Word again:

*So let's go outside, where Jesus is, where the action is-not trying to be privileged inside us, but taking our share in the abuse of Jesus. This "insider world" is not our home. We have our eyes peeled for the City about to come. Let's take our place outside with Jesus, no longer pouring out the sacrificial blood of animals but **pouring out sacrificial praises from our lips to God in Jesus' name.** (Hebrews 13:13-15, The Message)*

And all of God's children said, "AMEN!"

The Body responded with a hearty "Amen!" On vote, the body accepted the resolution. The Resolution was marked Appendix "I" and filed.

READING OF THE MINUTES

The printed minutes for Monday were distributed with the committee reports, and the minutes for Tuesday, Wednesday and Thursday were read by the Engrossing Clerk. On motion, the minutes were approved as corrected.

RECESS

The Moderator announced a 15 minute recess to prepare for Closing Worship.

CLOSING WORSHIP

The Closing Worship was led by Reverend Perryn Rice, Red River Presbytery. The Music Leader was Reverend Paula Louder, Nashville Presbytery, with Ms. Jackie Clifton, Nashville Presbytery, serving as pianist. Reverend Rice's sermon, "Outside" was based on Hebrews 13: 12-13a.

A Memorial Roll of Ministers and Elders who died during the past year was read during worship. The list included: Reverend R. Brent Turpen (Red River Presbytery- November 27, 2015), Reverend Billy T. Smith (Nashville Presbytery - June 16, 2016), Reverend Larry Moss (Covenant Presbytery -November 26, 2015), Reverend Jaime Ortiz (Andes Presbytery -March 19, 2016), Reverend James Talley (Cumberland Presbytery -March, 2016), Reverend Carlton Hatcher (Cumberland Presbytery – 2016), Elder Clifford Johnson (Robert Donnell - East Point CPC), Elder John Stipes (Robert Donnell – Eidson Chapel CPC), Elder John Outlaw (Robert Donnell – Scottsboro CPC), Elder Cora Drake (Robert Donnell – Big Cove CPC), Elder Bruce Allen (Robert Donnell - Goosepond CPC), Elder Ricky Jordan (Robert Donnell – Goosepond CPC), Elder Gary Moore (Pleasant Grove CPC), Dale Bellis (Orange CPC), Thelma Cravens (wife of Reverend Wilbur Cravens) and Leong Wong Ang (wife of Reverend John Ang).

ADJOURNMENT

A Motion was made to adjourn to meet June 19-23, 2017 at Innisbrook Resort & Conference Center, near Tampa, Florida. Motion passed. The Closing Prayer was given by Reverend Perryn Rice, Red River Presbytery at 4:20 p.m.

AUDITED FINANCIAL STATEMENTS OF

THE AGENCIES OF
THE CUMBERLAND PRESBYTERIAN
CHURCH CENTER

DECEMBER 31, 2015

THE AGENCIES OF
THE CUMBERLAND PRESBYTERIAN CHURCH CENTER

TABLE OF CONTENTS
DECEMBER 31, 2015

	PAGE
Independent Auditor's Report	1
Combined Statement of Financial Position	2
Combined Statement of Activity	3
Combined Statement of Cash Flows	4
Individual Statements of Financial Position	
Our United Outreach	5
General Assembly Corporation	6
Ministry Council	7
Shared Services	8
Historical Foundation	9
Board of Stewardship, Foundation, and Benefits	10
Small Church Loan Program	11
Insurance Program	12
Ministerial Aid	13
Investment Loan Program	14
Retirement Fund	15
Endowment Program	16
Individual Statements of Activity	
Our United Outreach	17
General Assembly Corporation	18
Ministry Council	19
Shared Services	20
Historical Foundation	21
Board of Stewardship, Foundation, and Benefits	22
Small Church Loan Program	23
Insurance Program	24
Ministerial Aid	25
Investment Loan Program	26
Retirement Fund	27
Endowment Program	28
Notes to Financial Statements	29 - 42

To the General Assembly Corporation
The Agencies of The Cumberland Presbyterian Church Center
Memphis, Tennessee

INDEPENDENT AUDITOR'S REPORT

We have audited the accompanying combined financial statements of The Agencies of The Cumberland Presbyterian Church Center, which comprise the combined statement of financial position as of December 31, 2015, and the related combined statements of activities and cash flows for the year then ended, and the related notes to the combined financial statements.

Management's Responsibility for the Financial Statements

Management is responsible for the preparation and fair presentation of these financial statements in accordance with accounting principles generally accepted in the United States of America; this includes the design, implementation, and maintenance of internal control relevant to the preparation and fair presentation of financial statements that are free from material misstatement, whether due to fraud or error.

Auditor's Responsibility

Our responsibility is to express an opinion on these combined financial statements based on our audit. We conducted our audit in accordance with auditing standards generally accepted in the United States of America. Those standards require that we plan and perform the audit to obtain reasonable assurance about whether the financial statements are free from material misstatement.

An audit involves performing procedures to obtain audit evidence about the amounts and disclosures in the combined financial statements. The procedures selected depend on the auditor's judgment, including the assessment of the risks of material misstatement of the combined financial statements, whether due to fraud or error. In making those risk assessments, the auditor considers internal control relevant to the entity's preparation and fair presentation of the combined financial statements in order to design audit procedures that are appropriate in the circumstances, but not for the purpose of expressing an opinion on the effectiveness of the entity's internal control. Accordingly, we express no such opinion. An audit also includes evaluating the appropriateness of accounting policies used and the reasonableness of significant accounting estimates made by management, as well as evaluating the overall presentation of the combined financial statements.

We believe that the audit evidence we have obtained is sufficient and appropriate to provide a basis for our audit opinion.

Opinion

In our opinion, the combined financial statements referred to above present fairly, in all material respects, the financial position of The Agencies of The Cumberland Presbyterian Church Center as of December 31, 2015, and the changes in their net assets and their cash flows for the year then ended in accordance with accounting principles generally accepted in the United States of America.

FOUTS & MORGAN
Certified Public Accountants

Memphis, Tennessee
May 31, 2016

THE AGENCIES OF
THE CUMBERLAND PRESBYTERIAN CHURCH CENTER

COMBINED STATEMENT OF FINANCIAL POSITION
DECEMBER 31, 2015

ASSETS

Cash	$ 533,354
Due from other agencies, boards, and divisions	5,636,964
Accounts receivable	7,404
Interest and dividends receivable, net of allowance for uncollectible interest	87,021
Health insurance tax credit receivable	9,706
Securities and investments	
Cash equivalents	6,379,870
Mortgage backed securities	7,542,127
Equity mutual funds	1,774,184
Real estate investment trusts	5,414,125
Private investment entities	67,163,648
Real estate	90,573
Inventory - at lower of cost or market	686
Prepaid expenses	113,245
Loans receivable, net of allowance for loan losses	9,886,146
Buildings and land	2,760,412
Furniture and equipment	156,745
Less: Accumulated depreciation	(679,061)
Total Assets	$ 106,877,149

LIABILITIES AND NET ASSETS

Liabilities:	
Accounts payable	$ 29,416
Accrued expenses	17
Notes payable to individual investors	1,878,581
Unearned subscriptions	9,702
Due to other agencies, boards, and divisions	5,908,667
Funds held in trust for others	31,346
Depository accounts held for church organizations	9,782,104
Total liabilities	17,639,833
Net Assets:	
Unrestricted	8,340,561
Temporarily restricted	1,315,576
Permanently restricted	56,852,028
Net assets available for benefits, at fair value	22,729,151
Total net assets	89,237,316
Total Liabilities and Net Assets	$ 106,877,149

See accompanying notes.

THE AGENCIES OF
THE CUMBERLAND PRESBYTERIAN CHURCH CENTER

COMBINED STATEMENT OF ACTIVITY
FOR THE YEAR ENDED DECEMBER 31, 2015

	Unrestricted	Temporarily Restricted	Permanently Restricted	Net Assets Available for Benefits	Totals
Revenues, gains, and other support:					
Contributions and gifts	$ 4,848,178	$ 684,481	$ 2,290,068	$ -	$ 7,822,727
Insurance program premium revenue	1,971,952	-	-	-	1,971,952
Endowment earnings	-	-	428,148	-	428,148
Interest and dividend income	148,769	48,498	16,962	106,734	320,963
Management service fees	51,613	-	-	(17,607)	34,006
Registration fees	81,160	-	-	-	81,160
Sales and subscription income	202,596	-	-	-	202,596
Net realized and unrealized gain on investments	(288,507)	-	(483,831)	(310,078)	(1,082,416)
Rental income	1,300	-	-	-	1,300
Other income	195,861	-	-	-	195,861
Participant retirement contributions	-	-	-	663,084	663,084
Net assets released from restriction	1,792,456	(1,247,951)	(544,505)	-	-
Total revenues, gains, and other support	9,005,378	(514,972)	1,706,842	442,133	10,639,381
Recovery of provision for loan losses	27,000	-	-	-	27,000
Net revenues, gains, and other support - after provision for loan losses	9,032,378	(514,972)	1,706,842	442,133	10,666,381
Expenses:					
Our United Outreach	606,819	-	-	-	606,819
General Assembly Corporation	769,744	-	-	-	769,744
Ministry Council	4,337,099	-	-	-	4,337,099
Shared Services	365,914	-	-	-	365,914
Historical Foundation	172,615	-	-	-	172,615
Board of Stewardship, Foundation and Benefits	344,195	-	-	-	344,195
Small Church Loan Program	42,349	-	-	-	42,349
Insurance Program	2,206,879	-	-	-	2,206,879
Ministerial Aid	63,694	-	-	-	63,694
Investment Loan Program	60,756	-	-	-	60,756
Retirement Fund	-	-	-	1,461,432	1,461,432
Endowment Program	-	-	2,236,260	-	2,236,260
Total expenses	8,970,064	-	2,236,260	1,461,432	12,667,756
Change in net assets	62,314	(514,972)	(529,418)	(1,019,299)	(2,001,375)
Net assets at beginning of year	8,278,247	1,830,548	57,381,446	23,748,450	91,238,691
Net assets at end of year	$ 8,340,561	$ 1,315,576	$ 56,852,028	$ 22,729,151	$ 89,237,316

See accompanying notes.

THE AGENCIES OF
THE CUMBERLAND PRESBYTERIAN CHURCH CENTER

COMBINED STATEMENT OF CASH FLOWS
FOR THE YEAR ENDED DECEMBER 31, 2015

Cash flows from operating activities	
Combined change in net assets	$ (2,001,375)
Adjustments to reconcile combined change in net assets to net cash used in operating activities:	
Depreciation	65,290
Net realized/unrealized (gain) loss on investments - Investment Loan Program	274,627
Net realized/unrealized (gain) loss on investments - Retirement Fund	1,405,307
Net realized/unrealized (gain) loss on investments - Endowment Program	2,678,125
Recovery of provision for loan losses	(27,000)
(Increase) decrease in operating assets:	
Due from other agencies, boards, and divisions	422,661
Accounts receivable	2,770
Interest and dividends receivable	4,993
Health insurance tax credit receivable	7,886
Inventory	685
Prepaid assets	(106,541)
Increase (decrease) in operating liabilities:	
Accounts payable	26,159
Accrued expenses	(279)
Unearned subscriptions	(4,306)
Due to other agencies, boards, and divisions	(471,431)
Funds held in trust for others	(1,558)
Notes payable to individual investors	554,770
Depository accounts held for church organizations	390,606
Net cash provided by (used in) operating activities	3,221,389
Cash flows from investing activities	
Proceeds from sale of investments:	
Endowment Program	22,872,247
Retirement Fund	9,628,990
Investment Loan Program	5,641,303
Purchase of investments:	
Endowment Program	(26,398,242)
Retirement Fund	(10,018,239)
Investment Loan Program	(6,589,685)
Loan principal payments received	1,783,496
Loan principal disbursed	(60,000)
Net cash provided by (used in) investing activities	(3,140,130)
Net increase in cash	81,259
Cash at the beginning of the year	452,095
Cash at the end of the year	$ 533,354

See accompanying notes.

THE AGENCIES OF
THE CUMBERLAND PRESBYTERIAN CHURCH CENTER
OUR UNITED OUTREACH
STATEMENT OF FINANCIAL POSITION
DECEMBER 31, 2015

ASSETS

Endowment earnings receivable	$ 30,984
Endowments - held by Endowment Program	2,536,425
Total Assets	$ 2,567,409

LIABILITIES AND NET ASSETS

Liabilities:	
Cash borrowed from other agencies, boards, and divisions	$ 15,012
Due to outside church organizations	34,799
Total liabilities	49,811
Net Assets:	
Unrestricted	(18,829)
Permanently restricted	2,536,427
Total net assets	2,517,598
Total Liabilities and Net Assets	$ 2,567,409

See accompanying notes.

THE AGENCIES OF
THE CUMBERLAND PRESBYTERIAN CHURCH CENTER
GENERAL ASSEMBLY CORPORATION
STATEMENT OF FINANCIAL POSITION
DECEMBER 31, 2015

ASSETS

Endowment earnings receivable	$ 5,737
Health insurance tax credit receivable	1,432
Inventory	686
Due from other agencies, boards, and divisions	275,310
	283,165
Endowments - held by Endowment Program	432,491
Total Assets	$ 715,656

LIABILITIES AND NET ASSETS

Liabilities:	
Accounts payable	$ 449
Cash borrowed from other agencies, boards, and divisions	178,595
Due to other agencies, boards, and divisions	13,337
Funds held in trusts for others	31,346
Total liabilities	223,727
Net Assets:	
Unrestricted	59,441
Permanently restricted	432,488
Total net assets	491,929
Total Liabilities and Net Assets	$ 715,656

See accompanying notes.

THE AGENCIES OF
THE CUMBERLAND PRESBYTERIAN CHURCH CENTER
MINISTRY COUNCIL
STATEMENT OF FINANCIAL POSITION
DECEMBER 31, 2015

ASSETS

Cash	$ 185,720
Accounts receivable	5,041
Endowment earnings receivable	166,168
Health insurance tax credit receivable	879
Due from other agencies, boards, and divisions	1,817,766
Securities and investments	
Real estate	51,818
	2,227,392
Endowments - held by Endowment Program	16,012,138
Total Assets	$ 18,239,530

LIABILITIES AND NET ASSETS

Liabilities:	
Accounts payable	$ 19,371
Accrued expenses	17
Unearned subscriptions	9,702
Total liabilities	29,090
Net Assets:	
Unrestricted	1,080,503
Temporarily restricted	1,117,796
Permanently restricted	16,012,141
Total net assets	18,210,440
Total Liabilities and Net Assets	$ 18,239,530

See accompanying notes.

THE AGENCIES OF
THE CUMBERLAND PRESBYTERIAN CHURCH CENTER
SHARED SERVICES
STATEMENT OF FINANCIAL POSITION
DECEMBER 31, 2015

ASSETS

Cash	$ 115,064
Accounts receivable	977
Buildings and land	2,760,412
Less: Accumulated depreciation	(522,316)
Furniture and equipment	156,745
Less: Accumulated depreciation	(156,745)
Total Assets	$ 2,354,137

LIABILITIES AND NET ASSETS

Liabilities:	
Accounts payable	$ 1,500
Net Assets:	
Unrestricted	2,352,637
Total Liabilities and Net Assets	$ 2,354,137

See accompanying notes.

THE AGENCIES OF
THE CUMBERLAND PRESBYTERIAN CHURCH CENTER
HISTORICAL FOUNDATION
STATEMENT OF FINANCIAL POSITION
DECEMBER 31, 2015

ASSETS

Cash	$	54,828
Endowment earnings receivable		17,601
Health insurance tax credit receivable		1,326
Due from other agencies, boards, and divisions		192,127
Securities and investments		
Real estate		38,755
		304,637
Endowments - held by Endowment Program		1,446,625
Total Assets	$	1,751,262

LIABILITIES AND NET ASSETS

Net Assets:		
Unrestricted	$	67,848
Temporarily restricted		197,780
Permanently restricted		1,485,634
Total net assets		1,751,262
Total Liabilities and Net Assets	$	1,751,262

See accompanying notes.

THE AGENCIES OF
THE CUMBERLAND PRESBYTERIAN CHURCH CENTER
BOARD OF STEWARDSHIP, FOUNDATION, AND BENEFITS
STATEMENT OF FINANCIAL POSITION
DECEMBER 31, 2015

ASSETS

Cash	$	697
Endowment earnings receivable		23,450
Health insurance tax credit receivable		6,069
Due from other agencies, boards, and divisions		440,725
		470,941
Endowments - held by Endowment Program		1,899,572
Total Assets	$	2,370,513

LIABILITIES AND NET ASSETS

Liabilities:		
Cash borrowed from other agencies, boards, and divisions	$	41,957
Net Assets:		
Unrestricted		428,984
Permanently restricted		1,899,572
Total net assets		2,328,556
Total Liabilities and Net Assets	$	2,370,513

See accompanying notes.

THE AGENCIES OF
THE CUMBERLAND PRESBYTERIAN CHURCH CENTER
SMALL CHURCH LOAN PROGRAM
STATEMENT OF FINANCIAL POSITION
DECEMBER 31, 2015

ASSETS

Interest receivable, net of allowance for uncollectible interest	$	1,686
Loans receivable, net of allowance for loan losses		148,417
Due from other agencies, boards, and divisions		284,447
Total Assets	$	434,550

LIABILITIES AND NET ASSETS

Net Assets:		
Permanently restricted	$	434,550
Total Liabilities and Net Assets	$	434,550

See accompanying notes.

THE AGENCIES OF
THE CUMBERLAND PRESBYTERIAN CHURCH CENTER
INSURANCE PROGRAM
STATEMENT OF FINANCIAL POSITION
DECEMBER 31, 2015

ASSETS

Cash	$	17,925
Accounts receivable		1,386
Prepaid expenses		113,245
Due from other agencies, boards, and divisions		2,057,818
Total Assets	$	2,190,374

LIABILITIES AND NET ASSETS

Liabilities:		
Accounts payable	$	1,482
Net Assets:		
Unrestricted		2,188,892
Total Liabilities and Net Assets	$	2,190,374

See accompanying notes.

THE AGENCIES OF
THE CUMBERLAND PRESBYTERIAN CHURCH CENTER
MINISTERIAL AID
STATEMENT OF FINANCIAL POSITION
DECEMBER 31, 2015

ASSETS

Cash	$	63,809
Endowment earnings receivable		9,683
Due from other agencies, boards, and divisions		315,148
		388,640
Endowment Funds - held by Endowment Program		2,969,846
Total Assets	$	3,358,486

LIABILITIES AND NET ASSETS

Net Assets:		
Unrestricted	$	388,640
Permanently restricted		2,969,846
Total net assets		3,358,486
Total Liabilities and Net Assets	$	3,358,486

See accompanying notes.

THE AGENCIES OF
THE CUMBERLAND PRESBYTERIAN CHURCH CENTER
INVESTMENT LOAN PROGRAM
STATEMENT OF FINANCIAL POSITION
DECEMBER 31, 2015

ASSETS

Interest and dividends receivable, net of allowance for uncollectible interest	$ 39,980
Securities and investments	
Cash equivalents	2,099,506
Bonds and mortgage backed securities	7,542,127
Loans receivable, net of allowance for loan losses	7,171,584
Total Assets	$ 16,853,197

LIABILITIES AND NET ASSETS

Liabilities:	
Accounts payable	$ 6,614
Notes payable to individual investors	1,878,581
Due to other agencies, boards, and divisions	3,393,453
Depository accounts held for church organizations	9,782,104
Total liabilities	15,060,752
Net Assets:	
Unrestricted	1,792,445
Total Liabilities and Net Assets	$ 16,853,197

See accompanying notes.

THE AGENCIES OF
THE CUMBERLAND PRESBYTERIAN CHURCH CENTER
RETIREMENT FUND
STATEMENT OF FINANCIAL POSITION
DECEMBER 31, 2015

ASSETS

Interest and dividends receivable, net of allowance for uncollectible interest	$ 12,592
Securities and investments	
Cash equivalents	251,493
Equity mutual funds	589,745
Real estate investment trusts	1,344,907
Private investment entities	20,530,414
Total Assets	$ 22,729,151

LIABILITIES AND NET ASSETS

Net Assets:	
Net assets available for benefits, at fair value	$ 22,729,151
Total Liabilities and Net Assets	$ 22,729,151

See accompanying notes.

THE AGENCIES OF
THE CUMBERLAND PRESBYTERIAN CHURCH CENTER
ENDOWMENT PROGRAM
STATEMENT OF FINANCIAL POSITION
DECEMBER 31, 2015

ASSETS

Cash equivalents	$ 330,875
Interest and dividends receivable, net of allowance for uncollectible interest	32,763
Securities and investments	
Cash equivalents	4,028,871
Equity mutual funds	1,184,439
Real estate investment trusts	4,069,218
Private investment entities	46,633,234
Loans receivable, net of allowance for loan losses	2,566,145
	58,845,545
Less: Net endowment assets of The Agencies of The Cumberland Presbyterian Church Center, as reflected on separate statements of financial position	(25,297,097)
Total Assets	$ 33,548,448

LIABILITIES AND NET ASSETS

Liabilities:	
Due to other agencies, boards, and divisions	$ 2,467,078
Total liabilities	2,467,078
Net Assets:	
Permanently restricted:	
Cumberland Presbyterian Children's Home	6,614,477
Discipleship Ministry Team	2,013,717
Missions Ministry Team	13,626,097
Memphis Theological Seminary	9,911,393
Board of Stewardship, Foundation, and Benefits	1,899,572
Our United Outreach	2,536,425
General Assembly Corporation	432,491
Communications Ministry Team	114,736
Pastoral Development Ministry Team	257,588
The Historical Foundation	1,446,625
Ministerial Aid	2,969,846
Bethel University	2,887,437
Other designated persons and organizations	11,668,063
Total net assets	56,378,467
Less: Net endowment assets of The Agencies of The Cumberland Presbyterian Church Center, as reflected on separate statements of financial position	(25,297,097)
Total Liabilities and Net Assets	$ 33,548,448

See accompanying notes.

THE AGENCIES OF
THE CUMBERLAND PRESBYTERIAN CHURCH CENTER
OUR UNITED OUTREACH
STATEMENT OF ACTIVITY
FOR THE YEAR ENDED DECEMBER 31, 2015

	Unrestricted	Temporarily Restricted	Permanently Restricted	Totals
Revenues, gains, and other support:				
Contributions	$ 2,446,873	$ -	$ 83,736	$ 2,530,609
Endowment earnings	-	-	17,018	17,018
Income from oil royalties	16,293	-	-	16,293
Net realized and unrealized gain on investments	-	-	(19,130)	(19,130)
Net assets released from restriction	127,399	-	(127,399)	-
	2,590,565	-	(45,775)	2,544,790
Expenses:				
Distribution to other agencies, boards, and divisions of The Cumberland Presbyterian Church:				
Bethel University	116,725	-	-	116,725
Board of Stewardship	140,070	-	-	140,070
Commission on Chaplains	8,171	-	-	8,171
Committee on Theology and Social Concern	2,860	-	-	2,860
Committee on Judiciary	7,704	-	-	7,704
Communications Ministry Team	270,335	-	-	270,335
Contingency Fund	2,218	-	-	2,218
Cumberland Presbyterian Children's Home	70,035	-	-	70,035
Discipleship Ministry Team	280,140	-	-	280,140
Evaluation Committee	3,500	-	-	3,500
General Assembly Council	186,760	-	-	186,760
Historical Foundation	70,035	-	-	70,035
Legal Expense	25,000	-	-	25,000
Memphis Theological Seminary	134,001	-	-	134,001
Ministry Council	196,565	-	-	196,565
Missions Ministry Team	312,823	-	-	312,823
Nominating Committee	2,393	-	-	2,393
OGA - Contingency Loan	119,993	-	-	119,993
Pastoral Development Ministry Team	107,387	-	-	107,387
Program of Alternate Studies	29,415	-	-	29,415
Shared Service (Accounting)	67,901	-	-	67,901
Shared Service (Computer Tech)	74,950	-	-	74,950
Shared Service (Maintenance/Operations)	229,400	-	-	229,400
Shared Service (Old Building)	16,213	-	-	16,213
Shared Service (OUO Committee)	87,402	-	-	87,402
Unification Task Force	20,000	-	-	20,000
Property tax	6,384	-	-	6,384
	2,588,380	-	-	2,588,380
Change in net assets	2,185	-	(45,775)	(43,590)
Net assets at beginning of year	(21,014)	-	2,582,202	2,561,188
Net assets at end of year	$ (18,829)	$ -	$ 2,536,427	$ 2,517,598

See accompanying notes.

THE AGENCIES OF
THE CUMBERLAND PRESBYTERIAN CHURCH CENTER
GENERAL ASSEMBLY CORPORATION
STATEMENT OF ACTIVITY
FOR THE YEAR ENDED DECEMBER 31, 2015

	Unrestricted	Temporarily Restricted	Permanently Restricted	Totals
Revenues, gains, and other support:				
Our United Outreach	$ 195,449	$ -	$ -	$ 195,449
Contributions and gifts	399,140	-	-	399,140
Endowment earnings	22,729	-	-	22,729
Interest income	8,778	-	-	8,778
Other income	179,568	-	-	179,568
Net realized and unrealized gain on investments	-	-	(3,190)	(3,190)
Net assets released from restriction	29,461	-	(29,461)	-
	835,125	-	(32,651)	802,474
Expenses:				
Conferences and events	133,956	-	-	133,956
Employee benefits	42,199	-	-	42,199
Equipment maintenance	2,036	-	-	2,036
Grants made	352,449	-	-	352,449
Miscellaneous	78	-	-	78
Payroll taxes	4,416	-	-	4,416
Postage and shipping	980	-	-	980
Printing and publications	2,096	-	-	2,096
Retirement	9,135	-	-	9,135
Salaries	206,208	-	-	206,208
Supplies	1,479	-	-	1,479
Travel	14,712	-	-	14,712
Total expenses	769,744	-	-	769,744
Change in net assets	65,381	-	(32,651)	32,730
Net assets at beginning of year	(5,940)	-	465,139	459,199
Net assets at end of year	$ 59,441	$ -	$ 432,488	$ 491,929

See accompanying notes.

THE AGENCIES OF
THE CUMBERLAND PRESBYTERIAN CHURCH CENTER
MINISTRY COUNCIL
STATEMENT OF ACTIVITY
FOR THE YEAR ENDED DECEMBER 31, 2015

	Unrestricted	Temporarily Restricted	Permanently Restricted	Totals
Revenues, gains, and other support:				
Our United Outreach	$ 1,187,543	$ -	$ -	$ 1,187,543
Contributions	-	651,562	446,339	1,097,901
Endowment earnings	(709,250)	-	109,069	(600,181)
Gifts - designated	1,635,389	-	-	1,635,389
Gifts - undesignated	186,226	-	-	186,226
Interest income	19,520	41,773	-	61,293
Registration fees	81,160	-	-	81,160
Rental income	1,300	-	-	1,300
Sales of materials, literature, etc.	166,267	-	-	166,267
Subscription income	36,128	-	-	36,128
Net realized and unrealized gain on investments	-	-	(121,504)	(121,504)
Net assets released from restrictions	2,045,319	(1,221,250)	(824,069)	-
	4,649,602	(527,915)	(390,165)	3,731,522
Expenses:				
Automobile expenses	4,664	-	-	4,664
Computer expenses	14,213	-	-	14,213
Conferences and events	91,922	-	-	91,922
Consulting fees	32,157	-	-	32,157
Contract labor	29,791	-	-	29,791
Dues and subscriptions	2,749	-	-	2,749
Employee benefits	146,818	-	-	146,818
Equipment maintenance	360	-	-	360
Grants made	2,209,783	-	-	2,209,783
Legal fees	1,830	-	-	1,830
Miscellaneous expense	16,146	-	-	16,146
Missionary support	297,579	-	-	297,579
Office expense	3,920	-	-	3,920
Payroll taxes	35,041	-	-	35,041
Postage and shipping	50,760	-	-	50,760
Printing and publications	158,318	-	-	158,318
Purchases for resale	44,562	-	-	44,562
Relocation expenses	474	-	-	474
Rent expense	510	-	-	510
Retirement	42,409	-	-	42,409
Salaries	962,710	-	-	962,710
Supplies	15,892	-	-	15,892
Telephone	1,648	-	-	1,648
Training expenses	515	-	-	515
Travel expenses	172,328	-	-	172,328
Total expenses	4,337,099	-	-	4,337,099
Change in net assets	312,503	(527,915)	(390,165)	(605,577)
Net assets at beginning of year	768,000	1,645,711	16,402,306	18,816,017
Net assets at end of year	$ 1,080,503	$ 1,117,796	$ 16,012,141	$ 18,210,440

See accompanying notes.

THE AGENCIES OF
THE CUMBERLAND PRESBYTERIAN CHURCH CENTER
SHARED SERVICES
STATEMENT OF ACTIVITY
FOR THE YEAR ENDED DECEMBER 31, 2015

	Unrestricted	Temporarily Restricted	Permanently Restricted	Totals
Revenues, gains, and other support:				
Our United Outreach	$ 388,464	$ -	$ -	$ 388,464
Gifts	48,727	-	-	48,727
	437,191	-	-	437,191
Expenses:				
Accounting fees	20,020	-	-	20,020
Bank fees	16,663	-	-	16,663
Computer expenses	2,084	-	-	2,084
Consulting fees	39,029	-	-	39,029
Depreciation expense	65,289	-	-	65,289
Employee benefits	18,687	-	-	18,687
Equipment maintenance	25,249	-	-	25,249
Insurance expense	40,264	-	-	40,264
Interest expense	323	-	-	323
Legal fees	50	-	-	50
Occupancy expenses	71,834	-	-	71,834
Office expense	110	-	-	110
Payroll taxes	3,718	-	-	3,718
Postage and shipping	601	-	-	601
Retirement	2,430	-	-	2,430
Salaries	48,601	-	-	48,601
Supplies	2,194	-	-	2,194
Telephone	8,768	-	-	8,768
Total expenses	365,914	-	-	365,914
Change in net assets	71,277	-	-	71,277
Net assets at beginning of year	2,281,360	-	-	2,281,360
Net assets at end of year	$ 2,352,637	$ -	$ -	$ 2,352,637

See accompanying notes.

THE AGENCIES OF
THE CUMBERLAND PRESBYTERIAN CHURCH CENTER
HISTORICAL FOUNDATION
STATEMENT OF ACTIVITY
FOR THE YEAR ENDED DECEMBER 31, 2015

	Unrestricted	Temporarily Restricted	Permanently Restricted	Totals
Revenues, gains, and other support:				
Our United Outreach	$ 70,035	$ -	$ -	$ 70,035
Contributions and gifts	13,456	32,919	19,097	65,472
Endowment earnings	-	-	9,855	9,855
Interest income	-	6,725	-	6,725
Sales of materials, literature, etc.	201	-	-	201
Net realized and unrealized gain on investments	-	-	(10,848)	(10,848)
Net assets released from restriction	95,961	(26,701)	(69,260)	-
	179,653	12,943	(51,156)	141,440
Expenses:				
Archival acquisitions	31,098	-	-	31,098
Archival equipment	4,296	-	-	4,296
Birthplace shrine	5,592	-	-	5,592
Computer equipment and supplies	49	-	-	49
Conferences and events	112	-	-	112
Contract labor	5,725	-	-	5,725
Dues and subscriptions	1,869	-	-	1,869
Employee benefits	9,715	-	-	9,715
Insurance expense	1,554	-	-	1,554
Legal fees	244	-	-	244
Miscellaneous expense	78	-	-	78
Payroll taxes	6,022	-	-	6,022
Postage and shipping	324	-	-	324
Printing and publications	54	-	-	54
Purchases for resale	51	-	-	51
Retirement	7,689	-	-	7,689
Salaries	78,720	-	-	78,720
Supplies	740	-	-	740
Training expenses	5,487	-	-	5,487
Travel expenses	13,196	-	-	13,196
Total expenses	172,615	-	-	172,615
Change in net assets	7,038	12,943	(51,156)	(31,175)
Net assets at beginning of year	60,810	184,837	1,536,790	1,782,437
Net assets at end of year	$ 67,848	$ 197,780	$ 1,485,634	$ 1,751,262

See accompanying notes.

THE AGENCIES OF
THE CUMBERLAND PRESBYTERIAN CHURCH CENTER
BOARD OF STEWARDSHIP, FOUNDATION AND BENEFITS
STATEMENT OF ACTIVITY
FOR THE YEAR ENDED DECEMBER 31, 2015

	Unrestricted	Temporarily Restricted	Permanently Restricted	Totals
Revenues, gains, and other support:				
Our United Outreach	$ 140,070	$ -	$ -	$ 140,070
Contributions and gifts	7,099	-	13,454	20,553
Endowment earnings	396	-	12,962	13,358
Interest income	17,039	-	-	17,039
Management service fees	51,613	-	-	51,613
Net realized and unrealized gain on investments	-	-	(14,083)	(14,083)
Net assets released from restriction	91,765	-	(91,765)	-
	307,982	-	(79,432)	228,550
Expenses:				
Computer expenses	612	-	-	612
Contract labor	976	-	-	976
Dues and subscriptions	497	-	-	497
Employee benefits	62,042	-	-	62,042
Grants made	63,299	-	-	63,299
Miscellaneous	2,105	-	-	2,105
Office expense	403	-	-	403
Payroll taxes	7,149	-	-	7,149
Postage and shipping	1,592	-	-	1,592
Retirement	8,909	-	-	8,909
Salaries	178,184	-	-	178,184
Stewardship fees	2,000	-	-	2,000
Stewardship materials and events	95	-	-	95
Supplies	2,054	-	-	2,054
Travel and board meetings	14,278	-	-	14,278
Total expenses	344,195	-	-	344,195
Change in net assets	(36,213)	-	(79,432)	(115,645)
Net assets at beginning of year	465,197	-	1,979,004	2,444,201
Net assets at end of year	$ 428,984	$ -	$ 1,899,572	$ 2,328,556

See accompanying notes.

THE AGENCIES OF
THE CUMBERLAND PRESBYTERIAN CHURCH CENTER
SMALL CHURCH LOAN PROGRAM
STATEMENT OF ACTIVITY
FOR THE YEAR ENDED DECEMBER 31, 2015

	Unrestricted	Temporarily Restricted	Permanently Restricted	Totals
Revenues, gains, and other support:				
Contributions	$ -	$ -	$ 42,349	$ 42,349
Interest income	-	-	16,962	16,962
Net assets released from restriction	42,349	-	(42,349)	-
	42,349	-	16,962	59,311
Expenses:				
Distribution to other agencies, boards, and divisions of The Cumberland Presbyterian Church:				
Investment Loan Program	42,349	-	-	42,349
Change in net assets	-	-	16,962	16,962
Net assets at beginning of year	-	-	417,588	417,588
Net assets at end of year	$ -	$ -	$ 434,550	$ 434,550

See accompanying notes.

THE AGENCIES OF
THE CUMBERLAND PRESBYTERIAN CHURCH CENTER
INSURANCE PROGRAM
STATEMENT OF ACTIVITY
FOR THE YEAR ENDED DECEMBER 31, 2015

	Unrestricted	Temporarily Restricted	Permanently Restricted	Totals
Revenues, gains, and other support:				
Premium revenue	$ 1,971,952	$ -	$ -	$ 1,971,952
Contributions	110,268	-	-	110,268
Interest income	16,105	-	-	16,105
Net realized gain on investments	7,303	-	-	7,303
Net unrealized gain on investments	(21,183)	-	-	(21,183)
	2,084,445	-	-	2,084,445
Expenses:				
Bad debt expense	6,541	-	-	6,541
Dues and subscriptions	763	-	-	763
Employee benefits	163	-	-	163
Insurance premiums	2,171,189	-	-	2,171,189
Payroll taxes	1,876	-	-	1,876
Postage and shipping	601	-	-	601
Retirement	1,226	-	-	1,226
Salaries	24,520	-	-	24,520
Total expenses	2,206,879	-	-	2,206,879
Change in net assets	(122,434)	-	-	(122,434)
Net assets at beginning of year	2,311,326	-	-	2,311,326
Net assets at end of year	$ 2,188,892	$ -	$ -	$ 2,188,892

See accompanying notes.

THE AGENCIES OF
THE CUMBERLAND PRESBYTERIAN CHURCH CENTER
MINISTERIAL AID
STATEMENT OF ACTIVITY
FOR THE YEAR ENDED DECEMBER 31, 2015

	Unrestricted	Temporarily Restricted	Permanently Restricted	Totals
Revenues, gains, and other support:				
Contributions	$ 1,000	$ -	$ 500	$ 1,500
Endowment earnings	9,945	-	19,928	29,873
Interest income	9,722	-	-	9,722
Net realized and unrealized gain on investments	-	-	(22,643)	(22,643)
Net assets released from restriction	36,382	-	(36,382)	-
	57,049	-	(38,597)	18,452
Expenses:				
Ministerial aid	63,694	-	-	63,694
Change in net assets	(6,645)	-	(38,597)	(45,242)
Net assets at beginning of year	395,285	-	3,008,443	3,403,728
Net assets at end of year	$ 388,640	$ -	$ 2,969,846	$ 3,358,486

See accompanying notes.

THE AGENCIES OF
THE CUMBERLAND PRESBYTERIAN CHURCH CENTER
INVESTMENT LOAN PROGRAM
STATEMENT OF ACTIVITY
FOR THE YEAR ENDED DECEMBER 31, 2015

	Unrestricted	Temporarily Restricted	Permanently Restricted	Totals
Revenues, gains, and other support:				
Interest income	$ 595,266	$ -	$ -	$ 595,266
Interest expense	(517,661)	-	-	(517,661)
Net interest income - before provision	77,605	-	-	77,605
Provision for loan losses	27,000	-	-	27,000
Net interest income	104,605	-	-	104,605
Net gain (loss) on investments	(274,627)	-	-	(274,627)
	(170,022)	-	-	(170,022)
Expenses:				
Accounting fees	5,075	-	-	5,075
Legal fees	2,572	-	-	2,572
Management fee	50,000	-	-	50,000
Office expenses	2,078	-	-	2,078
Postage and shipping	700	-	-	700
Supplies	331	-	-	331
Total expenses	60,756	-	-	60,756
Change in net assets	(230,778)	-	-	(230,778)
Net assets at beginning of year	2,023,223	-	-	2,023,223
Net assets at end of year	$ 1,792,445	$ -	$ -	$ 1,792,445

See accompanying notes.

THE AGENCIES OF
THE CUMBERLAND PRESBYTERIAN CHURCH CENTER
RETIREMENT FUND
STATEMENT OF ACTIVITY
FOR THE YEAR ENDED DECEMBER 31, 2015

	Net Assets Available for Benefits
Additions to Net Assets attributed to:	
Investment income:	
Interest and dividend income	$ 106,734
Management service fees	(17,607)
Net realized gain on investments	107,472
Net unrealized gain on investments	(417,550)
Net investment income	(220,951)
Contributions:	
Contributions by participants	663,084
	442,133
Deductions from Net Assets attributed to:	
Disbursements to participants	1,461,432
Change in plan assets available for benefits	(1,019,299)
Net assets available for benefits at beginning of year	23,748,450
Net assets available for benefits at end of year	$ 22,729,151

See accompanying notes.

THE AGENCIES OF
THE CUMBERLAND PRESBYTERIAN CHURCH CENTER
ENDOWMENT PROGRAM
STATEMENT OF ACTIVITY
FOR THE YEAR ENDED DECEMBER 31, 2015

	Unrestricted	Temporarily Restricted	Permanently Restricted	Totals
Changes in Permanently Restricted Net Assets:				
Revenues, gains, and other support:				
Contributions	$ -	$ -	$ 2,290,068	$ 2,290,068
Interest and dividend income	-	-	426,684	426,684
Net realized gain on investments	-	-	210,472	210,472
Net unrealized gain on investments	-	-	(694,303)	(694,303)
	-	-	2,232,921	2,232,921
Expenses:				
Distribution for designated purposes	-	-	843,013	843,013
Distribution of earnings	-	-	1,901,308	1,901,308
Other expenses	-	-	34,985	34,985
	-	-	2,779,306	2,779,306
Change in net assets	-	-	(546,385)	(546,385)
Net assets at beginning of year	-	-	56,924,852	56,924,852
Net assets at end of year	$ -	$ -	$ 56,378,467	$ 56,378,467
Represented by funds held in trust for others:				
Bethel University	$ -	$ -	$ 2,887,437	$ 2,887,437
Cumberland Presbyterian Children's Home	-	-	6,614,477	6,614,477
Memphis Theological Seminary	-	-	9,911,393	9,911,393
Other designated persons and organizations	-	-	11,668,063	11,668,063
	-	-	31,081,370	31,081,370
Represented by funds held for The Agencies of The Cumberland Presbyterian Church Center:				
Discipleship Ministry Team	-	-	2,013,717	2,013,717
Missions Ministry Team	-	-	13,626,097	13,626,097
Board of Stewardship, Foundation, and Benefit	-	-	1,899,572	1,899,572
Our United Outreach	-	-	2,536,425	2,536,425
General Assembly Corporation	-	-	432,491	432,491
Communications Ministry Team	-	-	114,736	114,736
Pastoral Development Ministry Team	-	-	257,588	257,588
The Historical Foundation	-	-	1,446,625	1,446,625
Ministerial Aid	-	-	2,969,846	2,969,846
	-	-	25,297,097	25,297,097
Net assets at end of year	$ -	$ -	$ 56,378,467	$ 56,378,467

See accompanying notes.

THE AGENCIES OF
THE CUMBERLAND PRESBYTERIAN CHURCH CENTER

NOTES TO FINANCIAL STATEMENTS
DECEMBER 31, 2015

Note A - Nature of Activities and Significant Accounting Policies

Nature of Activities - By the covenant of Abraham and his descendants according to faith, God has established the church in the world through His Son Jesus Christ. This household of faith, the universal church, consists of all those persons in every nation and every age who confess Jesus Christ as Lord and Savior and who respond to His call for discipleship. The church in the world never exists for herself alone, but to glorify God and work for reconciliation through Christ. Christ claims the church and gives her the word and sacraments in order to bring God's grace and judgment to persons.

The General Assembly is the highest judicatory of this church and represents in one body all the particular churches thereof. It bears the title of the General Assembly of the Cumberland Presbyterian Church and constitutes the bond of union, peace, correspondence, and mutual confidence among all its churches and judicatories. The Agencies of The Cumberland Presbyterian Church Center have been established by the General Assembly and in 2000 it caused the Cumberland Presbyterian Church General Assembly Corporation to be formed. The Agencies consist of the following entities:

Cumberland Presbyterian Church General Assembly Corporation
Ministry Council of the Cumberland Presbyterian Church, Inc.
Board of Stewardship, Foundation, and Benefits of the Cumberland Presbyterian Church, Inc.
Historical Foundation of the Cumberland Presbyterian Church and the Cumberland Presbyterian Church in America

Contributions - Contributions received are recorded as unrestricted, temporarily restricted, or permanently restricted, depending on the existence and/or nature of any donor restrictions.

Support that is restricted by the donor is reported as an increase in unrestricted net assets if the restriction expires in the reporting period in which the support is recognized. All other donor restricted support is reported as an increase in temporarily or permanently restricted net assets depending on the nature of the restriction. When a restriction expires, temporarily restricted net assets are reclassified to unrestricted net assets.

Donated Equipment and Services - Donated equipment is reflected as contributions in the accompanying financial statements at their estimated values at the date of receipt. No equipment was donated to the Center during the year ended December 31, 2015. No amounts have been reflected in the statements for donated services because they did not meet the criteria for recognition under FASB ASC 958-605-25.

Use of Estimates - The preparation of financial statements in conformity with generally accepted accounting principles requires management to make estimates and assumptions that affect the reported amounts of assets and liabilities and disclosure of contingent assets and liabilities at the date of the financial statements and the reported amounts of revenues and expenses during the reporting period. Actual results could differ from these estimates.

NOTES CONTINUED

Note A - Nature of Activities and Significant Accounting Policies - Continued

The Cumberland Presbyterian Church Investment Loan Program, Inc.'s notes receivable will consist of loans made to congregations, governing bodies, church organizations, and other qualifying related entities. The ability of each borrower to repay its loan generally depends upon the contributions received from its members. The number of members of each congregation and its revenue is likely to fluctuate.

The Program must rely on the borrower's or guarantor's continued financial viability for repayment of loans. If a borrower or guarantor experiences a decrease in contributions or revenues, payments on that loan may be adversely affected. Even though the loans are collateralized by real estate, realization of the appraised value upon default is not assured and is dependent upon the local economic conditions of the borrower. Therefore, the determination of the adequacy of the allowance for notes receivable losses is based on estimates that are particularly susceptible to significant changes in the economic environment and market conditions for the geographic areas where the borrowers are located.

While management uses available information to recognize losses on notes receivable, further reductions in the carrying amounts of notes receivable may be necessary based on changes in the economic conditions for the geographic area of the borrowers. It is therefore reasonably possible that the estimated losses on notes receivable may change materially in the near term. However, the amount of the change that is reasonably possible cannot be estimated.

Promises to Give - Unconditional promises to give are recognized as revenue or gains in the period received and as assets or decreases of liabilities depending on the form of the benefits received. Conditional promises to give are recognized when the conditions on which they depend are substantially met. The Center has no promises to give at December 31, 2015.

Inventory - Inventories are stated at the lower of cost or market. Cost is determined using the average cost method.

Depreciation - In years past, Shared Services has recorded property and equipment as assets and depreciated them. Depreciation of property and equipment was computed using the straight-line method over the estimated useful lives of the assets. Purchases of equipment after 1996 are not capitalized, but expensed when purchased; therefore, no depreciation expense has been recorded for items acquired in 1997 and thereafter. The difference between the cost of fixed assets expensed and depreciation expense that would be recorded is immaterial. In 2008, the Center purchased land and two incomplete office buildings. The cost of these plus the construction costs necessary to complete the new Center were capitalized and are being depreciated over an estimated useful life of 39 years. In 2009, the Shared Services agency purchased a large amount of computer equipment and capitalized these costs. The computer equipment purchased is being depreciated over an estimated useful life of four years.

Property and Equipment - Property and equipment is recorded at historical cost. Donated property and equipment is recorded at fair market value at the date of donation. Such donations are reported as unrestricted support unless the donor has restricted the donated asset to a specific purpose. Assets donated with explicit restrictions regarding their use and contributions of cash that must be used to acquire property and equipment are reported as restricted support. Absent donor stipulations regarding how long those donated assets must be maintained, the Center reports expirations of donor restrictions when the donated or acquired assets are placed in service as instructed by the donor. The Center re-classes temporarily restricted net assets to unrestricted net assets at that time.

NOTES CONTINUED

Note A - Nature of Activities and Significant Accounting Policies - Continued

Investments - Investments are stated at fair value. Investments in private investment entities are valued based on the Center's proportional share of the net asset valuations reported by the general partners of the underlying entities. The reported values of all other investments (with the exception of notes receivable) are measured by quoted prices in active markets. Realized and unrealized gains and losses are reflected in the statement of activities. (See Note L)

The Center's investments include various types of securities in various companies within various markets. Investment securities are exposed to several risks, such as interest rate, market and credit risks. Due to the risks associated with certain investment securities, it is at least reasonably possible that changes in the values of investment securities will occur in the near term and those changes could materially affect the amounts reported in the Center's combined financial statements.

Fair Value Measurements - Fair value under accounting principles generally accepted in the United States of America is defined as the price that would be received to sell an asset or paid to transfer a liability in an orderly transaction between market participants at the measurement date. Generally accepted accounting principles establishes a three-tier fair value hierarchy that prioritizes the inputs used to measure fair value. These tiers include: Level 1, defined as observable inputs such as quoted prices available in active markets for identical assets or liabilities; Level 2, defined as pricing inputs other than quoted prices in active markets that are either directly or indirectly observable; and Level 3, defined as unobservable inputs about which little or no market data exists, therefore requiring an entity to develop its own assessment about the assumptions the market participants would use in pricing an asset or liability.

Income Tax Status - The Center is a not-for-profit organization exempt from federal income taxes under Internal Revenue Code (IRC) Section 501 (c)(3). Thus, no provision for federal income taxes has been made. The Center has a defined contribution retirement plan which is qualified under Internal Revenue Code Section 403 (b); no provision for income taxes has been included in the Plan's financial statements.

Cash and Cash Equivalents - For purposes of the statement of cash flows, all highly liquid investments with a maturity of three months or less are considered to be cash equivalents. However, cash and cash equivalents reported as securities and investments by the Endowment Program, Investment Loan Program and Retirement Fund are considered investments for purposes of the statement of cash flows.

Loans Receivable and Allowance for Losses - Loans receivable are stated at unpaid principal balances, less the allowance for notes receivable losses. Inter-agency loans are shown as due to/from other agencies, boards, and divisions.

The allowance for loans receivable is maintained at a level which, in management's judgment, is adequate to absorb credit losses inherent in the loans receivable portfolio. The amount of the allowance is based on management's evaluation of the collectability of the portfolio, including the nature of the portfolio, credit concentrations, trends in historical loss experience, economic conditions, and other risks inherent in the portfolio. Although management uses available information to recognize losses on notes receivable, because of uncertainties associated with the various local economic conditions of the borrowers and collateral values, it is reasonably possible that a material change could occur in the allowance for notes receivable in the near term. However, the amount of the change that is reasonably possible cannot be estimated. When considered necessary, the allowance is increased by a charge to expense and reduced by actual charge-offs, net of recoveries.

NOTES CONTINUED

Note B - Retirement Plan

General - The Cumberland Presbyterian Church Retirement Plan Number Two is available to certain employees of the Church and its agencies. All agencies, boards, and divisions match each employee's contribution up to five percent of the employee's salary. The total retirement contribution expense for The Agencies of The Cumberland Presbyterian Church Center for 2015 was $70,572.

The Plan obtained its latest determination letter on January 31, 1972, in which the Internal Revenue Service stated that the Plan, as then designed, was in compliance with the applicable requirements of the Internal Revenue Code. The Plan has been amended since receiving the determination letter. However, the Plan administrator and the Plan's tax counsel believe that the plan is currently designed and being operated in compliance with the applicable requirements of the Internal Revenue Code. The Plan is a "church plan" and is, therefore, not subject to ERISA.

Eligibility - Employees who are 18 years of age are immediately eligible to participate in the plan.

Vesting - Participants are immediately 100% vested in their accounts.

Investments - The Plan's investments are held by a bank-administered trust fund. The trust is the funding vehicle for the Plan, and all contributions are made to the trust. The cost and market value of the Plan's investments at December 31, 2015, are as follows:

	Cost	Market Value
Total	$ 18,499,342	$ 22,729,151

Note C - Endowment Program

The Endowment Program includes assets of The Agencies of The Cumberland Presbyterian Church Center and the assets of other agencies, boards, and divisions.

The Program's investments, other than notes receivable, real estate, and certificates of deposit, are held by a bank-administered trust fund. The costs and market value of the Program's investments held in trust at December 31, 2015, are as follows:

	Cost	Market Value
Total	$ 46,692,598	$ 55,943,257

The Center has interpreted the Uniform Prudent Management of Institutional Funds Act ("UPMIFA") requiring a portion of a donor restricted endowment of perpetual duration be classified as permanently restricted assets. The amount of the endowment that must be retained permanently is in accordance with explicit donor stipulations as outlined in their respective trust agreements.

NOTES CONTINUED

Note C - Endowment Program - Continued

The primary objective of these endowments is to provide a balance between capital appreciation, preservation of capital, and current income. This is a long-term goal designed to maximize returns without undue risk. The Board of Stewardship has set distribution rates with certain beneficiaries of the Endowment Program.

Unless otherwise stated in the donor agreement, the Board of Stewardship shall select the investment portfolio where the endowments will be invested as described in the Investment Policy of the Center. The Investment Policy of the Center outlines the asset allocations, permissible investments, and objectives of the portfolios.

Endowment Net Asset Composition by Type of Fund as of December 31, 2015:

	Permanently Restricted	Total
Donor-restricted endowment funds	$ 56,378,467	$ 56,378,467
Total funds	$ 56,378,467	$ 56,378,467

Changes in Endowment Net Assets for the year ended December 31, 2015:

	Permanently Restricted	Total
Endowment net assets, beginning of year	$ 56,924,852	$ 56,924,852
Investment return	(92,132)	(92,132)
Contributions	2,290,068	2,290,068
Appropriation of endowment assets for expenditures	(2,744,321)	(2,744,321)
Endowment net assets, end of year	$ 56,378,467	$ 56,378,467

Description of Amount Classified as Permanently Restricted Net Assets (Endowment Only):

Permanently Restricted Net Assets -

The portion of perpetual endowment funds that is required to be retained permanently either by explicit donor stipulation or by UPMIFA	$ 56,378,467
Total endowment funds classified as permanently restricted net assets	$ 56,378,467

NOTES CONTINUED

Note D - Investment Loan Program

Nature of Activities - On March 19, 1999, the State of Tennessee approved the charter for the Cumberland Presbyterian Church Investment Loan Program, Inc., a subsidiary corporation of the Board of Stewardship, Foundation and Benefits of the Cumberland Presbyterian Church, Inc. The Program is designed to allow participants to help provide the loans needed to finance the growth of Cumberland Presbyterian congregations in the 21st century.

1. It provides building loans secured by first mortgages to congregations, presbyteries, and church agencies.

2. It allows congregations, presbyteries, church agencies, and individual members of the Cumberland Presbyterian Church to invest their funds in interest bearing accounts from which withdrawals can be made "on demand" replacing the function of the Cash Funds Management Program.

3. All participants have the opportunity to invest funds for specific terms (such as three years or five years) in order to receive a higher rate of interest. A prospectus outlines the added investment options offered.

Securities and Investments - The cost and market values of Investment Loan Program investments at December 31, 2015, are as follows:

	Cost	Market Value
Total	$ 10,225,907	$ 9,641,633

Notes Payable to Individual Investors - Notes payable to individual investors are made through a general offering in the states of Kentucky, New Mexico, Tennessee, and Texas to eligible individual investors and must be purchased in minimum face amounts of $500. All notes payable to individual investors shown in these financial statements are Adjustable Rate Ready Access Notes. Adjustable Rate Ready Access Notes are payable on demand and pay an adjustable interest rate that may be adjusted each month. Additions of principal may be made to Adjustable Rate Ready Access Notes at any time. Withdrawals from Adjustable Rate Ready Access Notes may be made at any time and are payable upon written request of the investor; however, the Program reserves the right to require the investor to provide up to thirty (30) days written notice of any intended withdrawal before such withdrawal is made. Both additions to and withdrawals from Adjustable Rate Ready Access Notes must be made in minimum amounts of $250. The Program may review certain factors, such as investment gap analysis, loan demand, cash flow needs, and the current policy of the Federal Reserve, before establishing each month's rate of interest.

The notes are non-negotiable and may be assigned only upon the Program's written consent. The notes are unsecured and of equal priority with all other current indebtedness of the Program.

NOTES CONTINUED

Note D - Investment Loan Program - Continued

Depository Accounts Held for Church Organizations - The Cumberland Presbyterian Church Investment Loan Program, Inc. accepts depository accounts in which church organizations may place funds with the Program, in minimum amounts of $500. All depository accounts shown in these financial statements are Adjustable Rate Ready Access accounts. Like the Program's notes, depository accounts are general obligations of the Program, are unsecured and not insured, and are of equal priority with all other current indebtedness of the Program including notes. The interest rate on the depository accounts is adjusted pursuant to the policies of the Cumberland Presbyterian Church Investment Loan Program, Inc. as they may be adopted from time to time by its Board of Directors. The Cumberland Presbyterian Church Investment Loan Program, Inc. may terminate any depository account upon sixty (60) days written notice to the church organization.

Loans Receivable - Amounts that have been loaned are included on the Statement of Financial Position as loans receivable. There are 23 loans outstanding at December 31, 2015.

Loans receivable are collectible primarily through monthly payments based on up to a twenty-five year amortization period. Interest rates, as determined by the board, are based on the Prime Interest Rate as reported in the Wall Street Journal plus 2.5% per annum. On loans originated for $500,000 or less, the interest rate will be adjusted triennially. On loans originated for more than $500,000, the interest rate will be adjusted annually for the term of the loan.

The composition of loans is as follows:

Loans receivable (secured by real estate)	$	8,180,584
Less: allowance for loan losses		(1,009,000)
	$	7,171,584

A summary of changes in the allowance for loan losses is as follows:

Balance at beginning of year	$	1,036,000
Recovery of provision charged to operations		(27,000)
Balance at end of year	$	1,009,000

Estimated receipts of principal payments for the five years subsequent to 2015 are:

Year ending December 31,		Amount
2016	$	389,236
2017		403,003
2018		422,680
2019		443,161
2020		935,179
Thereafter		4,578,325
	$	7,171,584

NOTES CONTINUED

Note E - Funds Held in Trust

The Discipleship Ministry Team leader of the Ministry Council is responsible for certain funds held in trust for outside groups. Funds invested by the executive director in Investment Loan Program amounted to the following as of December 31, 2015:

P.R.E.M. $ 207,486

The General Assembly Corporation is responsible for funds held in trust for certain committees and commissions. These funds are shown as liabilities in the Statement of Financial Position of the General Assembly Corporation. Activity in these funds for the year ended December 31, 2015, is as follows:

	Nominating Committee	Committee on Judiciary	Non-USA Moderator Travel Fund
Balance January 1, 2015	$ 6,042	$ 2,902	$ 5,847
Our United Outreach	2,379	495	-
Contributions	-	6,226	-
Disbursements	(3,032)	(6,838)	-
Balance December 31, 2015	$ 5,389	$ 2,785	$ 5,847

	Committee on Theology and Social Concerns	Commission on Chaplains
Balance January 1, 2015	$ 14,969	$ 8,993
Our United Outreach	184	525
Contributions	1,592	6,060
Disbursements	(2,637)	(7,000)
Balance December 31, 2015	$ 14,108	$ 8,578

Note F - Insurance Program

The Cumberland Presbyterian Group Health and Life Insurance Program is a fully insured, experience-rated plan with a policy year ending on the last day of February. Any excess of premium over medical claims and other plan expenses is retained by the insurer; excess losses are no longer carried forward as a charge against the experience for subsequent policy years, as in the past, but must be absorbed by the insurer. The plan is the responsibility of the Board of Stewardship, Foundation, and Benefits.

The plan has one Investment Loan Program account and one account in the Endowment Program. Both are used as a stabilization reserve to provide some protection against unexpected medical claims volatility. The balance at December 31, 2015 of the Investment Loan Program account is $85,714. The balance at December 31, 2015 of the Endowment Program account is $1,972,104.

NOTES CONTINUED

Note G - Concentrations of Credit Risk Arising from Cash Deposits in Excess of Insured Limits

The Center maintains its cash balances in a financial institution located in Memphis, Tennessee. The balances are insured by the Federal Deposit Insurance Corporation up to $250,000 as of December 31, 2015. At various times there were balances that exceeded these FDIC limits. Cash and cash equivalents classified as securities and investments are items held in equities backed by the Federal Government. These equities, while backed by the Federal Government, are not insured by the Federal Deposit Insurance Corporation. At December 31, 2015, a total of $253,146 exceeded the FDIC limits.

Note H - Real Estate

Real estate assets of both the Ministry Council and the Historical Foundation are held for investment and are therefore not depreciated. These assets amounted to the following at December 31, 2015:

Property Location	Ministry Council	Historical Foundation	Total
San Francisco, California	$ 51,818	$ -	$ 51,818
Birthplace Shrine Chapel, Dickson County, Tennessee	-	21,500	21,500
McAdow Home, Dickson County, Tennessee	-	17,255	17,255
Total	$ 51,818	$ 38,755	$ 90,573

Note I - Leases

The Ministry Council leases three copiers and two postage machines for use in its offices. Lease payments for the year ended December 31, 2015, totaled $12,715. The minimum lease payments for the next five years ended December 31 are as follows:

2016	$ 12,208
2017	10,288
	$ 22,496

NOTES CONTINUED

Note J - Combined Statement of Activities Expenses

The total expenses of various Agencies are included in the Combined Statement of Activities as follows:

Expense Description	Agencies
Our United Outreach	Our United Outreach
General Assembly Corporation	General Assembly Corporation
Ministry Council	Ministry Council
Shared Services	Shared Services
Historical Foundation	Historical Foundation
Board of Stewardship, Foundation, and Benefits	Board of Stewardship, Foundation, and Benefits
Small Church Loan Program	Small Church Loan Program
Insurance Program	Insurance Program
Ministerial Aid	Ministerial Aid
Investment Loan Program	Investment Loan Program
Retirement Fund	Retirement Fund
Endowment Program	Endowment Program

Costs originating from Shared Services (formerly Central Services - made up of Building and Maintenance, Computer Services Division, and Central Accounting Division) are now funded by Our United Outreach appropriations instead of being charged to the various applicable agencies based on usage.

Inter-agency revenue and expense items for Our United Outreach and endowment earnings have been eliminated on the combined statement of activity.

Note K - Fair Value Measurements

Prices for closed-end bond funds and equity mutual funds are readily available in the active markets in which those securities are traded, and the resulting fair values are categorized as level 1.

Prices for mortgage backed securities, bond mutual funds, and real estate investment trusts are determined on a recurring basis based upon inputs that are readily available in public markets or can be derived from information available in publicly quoted markets and are categorized as level 2.

NOTES CONTINUED

Note K - Fair Value Measurements - Continued

There is limited or no observable data for the prices of private investment entities that are held by the Center and the resulting fair values of these securities are categorized as level 3.

Fair values of assets measured on a recurring basis at December 31, 2015 are as follows:

	Fair Value	Quoted Prices In Active Market for Identical Assets (Level 1)	Significant Other Observable Inputs (Level 2)	Significant Unobservable Inputs (Level 3)
December 31, 2015				
Mortgage backed securities	$ 7,542,127	$ -	$ 7,542,127	$ -
Equity mutual funds	1,774,184	1,774,184	-	-
Real estate investment trusts	5,414,125	-	5,414,125	-
Private investment entities	67,163,648	-	-	67,163,648
Total	$ 81,894,084	$ 1,774,184	$ 12,956,252	$ 67,163,648

Because of the multiple number and complexity of the calculations necessary, management does not believe it is practicable to estimate fair value of loans receivable, net of allowance for loan losses. Therefore, no adjustment has been made to the net carrying value of $9,886,146 listed on the Combined Statement of Financial Position.

NOTES CONTINUED

Note K - Fair Value Measurements - Continued

The following table provides information related to the previously mentioned investments that are valued based primarily on net asset value at December 31, 2015:

	Fair Value	Unfunded Commitments	Redemption Frequency (If Currently Eligible)	Redemption Notice Period
Private Investment Entities				
GT Emerging Markets (QP), L.P.	$ 5,532,457	None	Annual	90 Days
GT Offshore Fund, Ltd. (Class A)	8,089,179	None	Annual	90 Days
GT Offshore Fund, Ltd. (Class B)	10,369,626	None	Annual	90 Days
GT Institutional Fixed Income Fund LP	11,260,156	None	Annual	90 Days
GT ERISA Fund, Ltd. (Class A)	3,480,475	None	Annual	90 Days
GT ERISA Fund, Ltd. (Class B)	4,512,577	None	Annual	90 Days
GT Real Assets, L.P.	1,153,784	None	Annual	90 Days
GT Special Opportunities III, L.P.	1,893,980	None	see note	see note
Palladian Partners VIII L.P.	277,608	None	Annual	90 Days
Midland Intl Equity QP Fund, L.P.	9,047,858	None	Quarterly	60 Days
Midland U.S. QP Fund, L.P.	11,545,946	None	Quarterly	60 Days
	$ 67,163,646			

The GT Special Opportunities III, L.P. provides for an annual redemption upon 90 days notice after an initial lock-up period of eighteen months.

The following table summarizes fair value by fund for investments in private investment entities that are valued based primarily on net asset value at December 31, 2015:

	Retirement Fund	Endowment Program	Total Fair Value
Private Investment Entities			
GT Emerging Markets (QP), L.P.	$ 1,682,228	$ 3,850,229	$ 5,532,457
GT Offshore Fund, Ltd. (Class A)	-	8,089,179	8,089,179
GT Institutional Fixed Income Fund LP	3,646,851	7,613,305	11,260,156
GT Offshore Fund, Ltd. (Class B)	-	10,369,626	10,369,626
GT ERISA Fund, Ltd. (Class A)	3,480,475	-	3,480,475
GT ERISA Fund, Ltd. (Class B)	4,512,577	-	4,512,577
GT Real Assets, L.P.	358,071	795,713	1,153,784
GT Special Opportunities III, L.P.	567,233	1,326,747	1,893,980
Palladian Partners VIII LP	75,711	201,897	277,608
Midland Intl Equity QP Fund, L.P.	2,733,532	6,314,326	9,047,858
Midland U.S. QP Fund, L.P.	3,473,735	8,072,211	11,545,946
	$ 20,530,413	$ 46,633,233	$ 67,163,646

NOTES CONTINUED

Note K - **Fair Value Measurements** - Continued

Assets measured at fair value on a recurring basis using significant unobservable inputs (Level 3):

Fair value at beginning of year	$ 55,611,839
Investments and distributions, net	11,223,627
Realized/unrealized gains (losses)	328,182
Fair value at end of year	$ 67,163,648

Gains and losses (realized and unrealized) for Level 3 assets included in net assets for the year are reported as follows:

On the Combined Statement of Activity, under Revenues, gains, and other support:

Permanently restricted net assets:	
Endowment program	$ 183,025
Net assets available for benefits:	
Retirement fund	145,157
Total net assets	$ 328,182

These investments without readily determinable values comprise approximately 62.84% of total assets at December 31, 2015.

All assets have been valued using a market approach.

A description of the Private Investment Entities and the investment objectives is as follows:

<u>GT Emerging Markets (QP), L.P.</u> - This fund is organized as a "fund of funds" which seek to achieve long-term capital appreciation through investments in limited partnerships, off-shore corporations, open-end mutual funds, closed-end mutual funds, commingled trust funds, and separately managed accounts that invest primarily in "emerging markets." Investments may also be made in industrialized nations such as the United States and Japan.

<u>GT Offshore Fund, Ltd. / GT ERISA Fund, Ltd.</u> - These are open-ended "umbrella" funds, incorporated as exempted companies in the Cayman Islands with multiple classes of Shares. Each class of share is separately valued and pursues its own clearly defined investment objective(s) and strategy(ies). These funds overall investment objectives are as follows:

Class A is broadly diversified among multiple investment managers and multiple investment strategies. The strategies employed may include multi-strategy arbitrage, capital structure arbitrage, distressed debt, long/short equity or niche financing.

Class B seeks to achieve a superior rate of return exceeding that of the MSCI World Index with less volatility while minimizing market risk through a hedged approach. The primary investment strategy will be a long/short equity strategy. This class is broadly diversified among multiple investment managers and multiple long/short equity strategies.

NOTES CONTINUED

Note K - **Fair Value Measurements** - Continued

GT Real Assets, L.P. - This fund is organized as a "fund of funds" investment vehicle that will pool and invest funds, generally through "Managed Investment Vehicles," for the purpose of generating attractive risk-adjusted returns by opportunistically investing in a broad spectrum of resources, real assets, and other investment strategies.

GT Special Opportunities, III, L.P. - This fund is organized as a "fund of funds" investment vehicle that will pool and invest funds, generally through "Managed Investment Vehicles," for the purpose of achieving a superior rate of return. The fund focuses on a very limited number of investment strategies that are considered to be opportunistic based upon prevailing market conditions. At times, the fund may only invest in one strategy and do so in a non-diversified manner, perhaps with only a single manager. The strategies sought by the fund will often be niche-focused. Accordingly, the risk level for the fund is anticipated to be extremely high.

Midland International Equity QP Fund, L.P. - This is an international equity fund which seeks to identify listed companies selling at a discount to intrinsic net worth on liquid stock exchanges of non-U.S. countries. The focus of this fund is long-term capital appreciation. This fund seeks to outperform the MSCI EAFE Index, net of fees and taxes, over a full market cycle.

Midland U.S. QP Fund, L.P. - This fund's objective is to outperform the broad U.S. equity market, defined as the Russell 3000 Index, net of fees and taxes over a full market cycle. The fund seeks to compound capital at attractive rates through direct and indirect long-term ownership of publicly traded businesses domiciled in the United States.

Note L - Securities and Investments

Securities and investments at December 31, 2015 are as follows:

	Ministry Council	Historical Foundation	Investment Loan Program	Retirement Fund	Endowment Program	Total
Cash and cash equivalents	$ -	$ -	$ 2,099,506	$ 251,493	$ 4,028,871	$ 6,379,870
Mortgage backed securities	-	-	7,542,127	-	-	7,542,127
Equity mutual funds	-	-	-	589,745	1,184,439	1,774,184
Real estate investment trusts	-	-	-	1,344,907	4,069,218	5,414,125
Private investment entities	-	-	-	20,530,414	46,633,234	67,163,648
Real estate	51,818	38,755	-	-	-	90,573
	$ 51,818	$ 38,755	$ 9,641,633	$ 22,716,559	$ 55,915,762	$ 88,364,527

Note M - Subsequent Events

Subsequent events were evaluated through May 31, 2016, which is the date the financial statements were available to be issued.

BETHEL UNIVERSITY

FINANCIAL STATEMENTS AND OTHER INFORMATION

JULY 31, 2015 AND 2014

BETHEL UNIVERSITY

Table of Contents

	Page
INDEPENDENT AUDITOR'S REPORT	1 - 3
FINANCIAL STATEMENTS	
Statements of Financial Position	4
Statements of Activities	5 - 6
Statements of Cash Flows	7 - 8
Notes to Financial Statements	9 - 34
SUPPLEMENTARY INFORMATION	
Financial Responsibility Composite Score (unaudited)	35
University Key Financial Ratios (unaudited)	36 - 39
Unrestricted Net Assets Exclusive of Property, Buildings, Equipment, and Related Debt (unaudited)	40
OTHER INFORMATION	
Schedule of Expenditures of Federal Awards	41
Notes to Schedule of Expenditures of Federal Awards	42
INDEPENDENT AUDITOR'S REPORT ON INTERNAL CONTROL OVER FINANCIAL REPORTING AND ON COMPLIANCE AND OTHER MATTERS BASED ON AN AUDIT OF FINANCIAL STATEMENTS PERFORMED IN ACCORDANCE WITH *GOVERNMENT AUDITING STANDARDS*	43 - 44
INDEPENDENT AUDITOR'S REPORT ON COMPLIANCE FOR THE MAJOR PROGRAM AND ON INTERNAL CONTROL OVER COMPLIANCE REQUIRED BY OMB CIRCULAR A-133	45 - 47
SCHEDULE OF FINDINGS AND QUESTIONED COSTS	48 - 50

Independent Auditor's Report

The Board of Trustees
Bethel University
McKenzie, Tennessee

Report on the Financial Statements

We have audited the accompanying financial statements of Bethel University (the "University"), which comprise the statements of financial position as of July 31, 2015 and 2014, and the related statements of activities and cash flows for the years then ended, and the related notes to the financial statements.

Management's Responsibility for the Financial Statements

Management is responsible for the preparation and fair presentation of these financial statements in accordance with accounting principles generally accepted in the United States of America; this includes the design, implementation, and maintenance of internal control relevant to the preparation and fair presentation of financial statements that are free from material misstatement, whether due to fraud or error.

Auditor's Responsibility

Our responsibility is to express an opinion on these financial statements based on our audits. We conducted our audits in accordance with auditing standards generally accepted in the United States of America and the standards applicable to financial audits contained in *Government Auditing Standards*, issued by the Comptroller General of the United States. Those standards require that we plan and perform the audit to obtain reasonable assurance about whether the financial statements are free from material misstatement.

An audit involves performing procedures to obtain audit evidence about the amounts and disclosures in the financial statements. The procedures selected depend on the auditor's judgment, including the assessment of the risks of material misstatement of the financial statements, whether due to fraud or error. In making those risk assessments, the auditor considers internal control relevant to the entity's preparation and fair presentation of the financial statements in order to design audit procedures that are appropriate in the circumstances, but not for the purpose of expressing an opinion on the effectiveness of the entity's internal control. Accordingly, we express no such opinion. An audit also includes evaluating the appropriateness of accounting policies used and the reasonableness of significant accounting estimates made by management, as well as evaluating the overall presentation of the financial statements.

The Board of Trustees
Bethel University

We believe that the audit evidence we have obtained is sufficient and appropriate to provide a basis for our audit opinion.

Opinion

In our opinion, the financial statements referred to above present fairly, in all material respects, the financial position of Bethel University as of July 31, 2015 and 2014, and the changes in its net assets and its cash flows for the years then ended in accordance with accounting principles generally accepted in the United States of America.

Other Matters

Other Information

Our audits were conducted for the purpose of forming an opinion on the financial statements as a whole. The accompanying schedule of expenditures of federal awards, as required by Office of Management and Budget Circular A-133, *Audits of States, Local Governments, and Non-Profit Organizations,* is presented for purposes of additional analysis and is not a required part of the financial statements. Such information is the responsibility of management and was derived from and relates directly to the underlying accounting and other records used to prepare the financial statements. The information has been subjected to the auditing procedures applied in the audit of the financial statements and certain additional procedures, including comparing and reconciling such information directly to the underlying accounting and other records used to prepare the financial statements or to the financial statements themselves, and other additional procedures in accordance with auditing standards generally accepted in the United States of America. In our opinion, the information is fairly stated, in all material respects, in relation to the financial statements as a whole.

Disclaimer of Opinion on Supplementary Information

Our audits were conducted for the purpose of forming an opinion on the financial statements as a whole. The Schedules of Financial Responsibility Composite Score, University Key Financial Ratios, and Unrestricted Net Assets Exclusive of Property, Buildings, Equipment and Related Debt, which are the responsibility of management, are presented for purposes of additional analysis and are not a required part of the financial statements. Such information has not been subjected to the auditing procedures applied in the audit of the financial statements and, accordingly, we do not express an opinion or provide any assurance on it.

The Board of Trustees
Bethel University

Other Reporting Required by Government Auditing Standards

In accordance with *Government Auditing Standards*, we have also issued our report dated October 14, 2015, on our consideration of the University's internal control over financial reporting and on our tests of its compliance with certain provisions of laws, regulations, contracts, and grant agreements and other matters. The purpose of that report is to describe the scope of our testing of internal control over financial reporting and compliance and the results of that testing, and not to provide an opinion on internal control over financial reporting or on compliance. That report is an integral part of an audit performed in accordance with *Government Auditing Standards* in considering the University's internal control over financial reporting and compliance.

Crosslin & Associates, PLLC

Nashville, Tennessee
October 14, 2015

BETHEL UNIVERSITY
STATEMENTS OF FINANCIAL POSITION

ASSETS

	July 31,	
	2015	2014 - Restated
Cash and cash equivalents	$ 1,629,656	$ 1,058,990
Perkins loan cash	121,257	76,644
Receivables:		
Contributions, net (Note B)	3,095,957	2,752,506
Students, net of allowances of $1,642,713, and $1,537,124, respectively	1,894,824	1,372,950
Perkins loans, net of allowances of $227,246 and $233,504, respectively	229,462	270,453
Other	303,045	83,724
Note receivable	7,792,839	7,998,454
Inventories	236,476	273,836
Prepaid expenses and deposits	171,460	153,446
Investments (Note C)	6,415,396	6,418,407
Beneficial interest in assets held by others (Note D)	3,660,425	3,692,558
Property, buildings, and equipment:		
Land	461,570	705,511
Buildings and improvements	64,058,325	63,440,243
Equipment, furniture and automobiles	8,172,402	7,906,415
Library books	1,284,514	1,284,514
Property held under capital leases (Note F)	405,440	5,893,443
Construction in progress	2,249,390	839,591
	76,631,641	80,069,717
Less: Accumulated depreciation	(19,347,823)	(21,924,607)
Total property and equipment, net	57,283,818	58,145,110
Total assets	$ 82,834,615	$ 82,297,078

LIABILITIES AND NET ASSETS

Liabilities:		
Accounts payable and student account deposits	$ 6,689,778	$ 6,483,151
Accrued payroll and benefits	758,835	523,136
Deferred tuition revenue	4,373,119	6,708,638
Debt (Note E)	45,625,243	44,715,695
Obligations under capital leases (Note F)	61,048	464,140
Advances from the federal government	411,781	411,781
Total liabilities	57,919,804	59,306,541
Net Assets:		
Unrestricted	12,074,952	9,182,954
Temporarily restricted (Notes G and H)	2,252,644	3,701,005
Permanently restricted (Notes G and H)	10,587,215	10,106,578
Total net assets	24,914,811	22,990,537
Total liabilities and net assets	$ 82,834,615	$ 82,297,078

See accompanying notes to financial statements.

BETHEL UNIVERSITY
STATEMENTS OF ACTIVITIES

	Year Ended July 31, 2015			
	Unrestricted	Temporarily Restricted	Permanently Restricted	Total
Revenue, gains and other support:				
Regular tuition and fees	$ 54,803,497	$ -	$ -	$ 54,803,497
Degree completion tuition	9,969,474	-	-	9,969,474
Institutional scholarships and grants	(13,489,677)	-	-	(13,489,677)
Net tuition and fees	51,283,294	-	-	51,283,294
Bookstore income	1,603,502	-	-	1,603,502
Private gifts and contracts	2,453,030	336,809	32,990	2,822,829
Investment income	40,153	40,006	-	80,159
Unrealized gain on beneficial interests in assets held by others	-	-	(32,133)	(32,133)
Auxiliary fund revenues	7,012,353	-	-	7,012,353
Government grants	1,143,928			1,143,928
Other income	1,538,379	-	-	1,538,379
Net assets released from restrictions	1,825,176	(1,825,176)	-	-
Reclassification	(479,780)	-	479,780	-
Total revenue, gains and other support	66,420,035	(1,448,361)	480,637	65,452,311
Expenses:				
Education and general:				
Instruction	44,373,389	-	-	44,373,389
Academic support	1,626,696	-	-	1,626,696
Student services	7,191,508	-	-	7,191,508
Institutional support	6,169,543	-	-	6,169,543
Auxiliary enterprises	4,166,901	-	-	4,166,901
Total expenses	63,528,037	-	-	63,528,037
Net increase (decrease) in net assets	2,891,998	(1,448,361)	480,637	1,924,274
Net assets, beginning of year-restated	9,182,954	3,701,005	10,106,578	22,990,537
Net assets, end of year	$ 12,074,952	$ 2,252,644	$ 10,587,215	$ 24,914,811

	Year Ended July 31, 2014 - Restated		
Unrestricted	Temporarily Restricted	Permanently Restricted	Total
$ 56,246,891	$ -	$ -	$ 56,246,891
12,353,628	-	-	12,353,628
(12,958,497)	-	-	(12,958,497)
55,642,022	-	-	55,642,022
1,984,512	-	-	1,984,512
4,089,036	1,049,022	27,294	5,165,352
166,742	157,674	-	324,416
-	-	203,212	203,212
7,225,816	-	-	7,225,816
463,486			463,486
1,133,336	-	-	1,133,336
2,358,695	(2,358,695)	-	-
-	-	-	-
73,063,645	(1,151,999)	230,506	72,142,152
44,303,528	-	-	44,303,528
1,360,448	-	-	1,360,448
7,484,713	-	-	7,484,713
9,842,644	-	-	9,842,644
5,710,108	-	-	5,710,108
68,701,441	-	-	68,701,441
4,362,204	(1,151,999)	230,506	3,440,711
4,820,750	4,853,004	9,876,072	19,549,826
$ 9,182,954	$ 3,701,005	$ 10,106,578	$ 22,990,537

See accompanying notes to financial statements.

BETHEL UNIVERSITY
STATEMENTS OF CASH FLOWS

	Year ended July 31,	
	2015	2014 - Restated
CASH FLOWS FROM OPERATING ACTIVITIES:		
Increase in net assets	$ 1,924,274	$ 3,440,711
Adjustments to reconcile change in net assets to net cash provided by operating activities		
Non-cash:		
Allowance for doubtful student accounts, contributions and Perkins loans receivable	99,331	(958,728)
Disposal of property and equipment	-	445,549
Unrealized gain on investments and beneficial interests in assets held by others	(107,868)	(527,627)
Non-cash contributions	(171,180)	(3,185,000)
Gain on the change in fair value of interest rate swap	(245,586)	(125,533)
Depreciation	2,918,820	4,029,589
(Increase) decrease in:		
Perkins loan cash	(44,613)	36,099
Contributions receivable, net	(343,451)	3,151,628
Student accounts receivable	(627,463)	(309,742)
Perkins loans receivable	47,249	(13,916)
Other receivables	(219,321)	22,776
Inventories	37,360	7,013
Prepaid expenses and deposits	(18,014)	(25,660)
Increase (decrease) in:		
Accounts payable and student account deposits	1,804,845	(504,429)
Accrued payroll and benefits	235,699	(363,857)
Deferred tuition revenue	(2,335,519)	(4,483,598)
Contributions restricted for long-term investments	(32,990)	(27,294)
Total adjustments	997,299	(2,832,730)
Net cash provided by operating activities	2,921,573	607,981
CASH FLOWS FROM INVESTING ACTIVITIES:		
Withdrawal of investments, net	143,012	486,728
Payments received on note receivable	205,615	201,546
Payment of accounts payable for property, buildings and equipment	(1,598,218)	(117,120)
Purchases of property, buildings and equipment	(1,886,348)	(452,780)
Net cash (used in) provided by investing activities	(3,135,939)	118,374
CASH FLOWS FROM FINANCING ACTIVITIES:		
Payments on annuity obligations	-	(707)
Proceeds from notes payable and line-of-credit	11,512,988	4,244,473
Payments on notes payable and line-of-credit	(10,357,854)	(4,360,750)
Repayments of capital lease obligations	(403,092)	(456,942)
Contributions restricted for long-term investments	32,990	27,294
Net cash provided by (used in) investing activities	785,032	(546,632)

See accompanying notes to financial statements.

BETHEL UNIVERSITY
STATEMENTS OF CASH FLOWS - Continued

	Year ended July 31,	
	2015	2014 - Restated
Net increase in cash and cash equivalents	570,666	179,723
Cash and cash equivalents at beginning of year	1,058,990	879,267
Cash and cash equivalents at end of year	$ 1,629,656	$ 1,058,990
Supplemental disclosures of cash flow information:		
Interest paid	$ 2,722,774	$ 3,409,897
Non-cash financing and investing activities:		
Purchases of property and equipment	2,057,628	4,854,527
Amount financed through capital leases, accounts payable, debt, or received through donations	(171,280)	(4,401,747)
Total paid for property and equipment	$ 1,886,348	$ 452,780

See accompanying notes to financial statements.

BETHEL UNIVERSITY
NOTES TO FINANCIAL STATEMENTS
JULY 31, 2015 AND 2014

A. SUMMARY OF SIGNIFICANT ACCOUNTING POLICIES

Organization and Business Purpose

Bethel University (the "University") is a private, residential, coeducational University affiliated with the Cumberland Presbyterian Church, dedicated primarily to educating students in the liberal arts and science while also offering select pre-professional programs, a graduate teacher education program, a master of business administration program, and an online criminal justice program. In addition to its traditional academic programs, the University also offers a degree-completion program. The University is accredited by the Southern Association of Colleges and Schools, Commission on Colleges, and its education emphasizes academic excellence, high achievement, intellectual and personal integrity, and participation in community life. Its Christian heritage finds expression in commitment to the values of personal growth, justice, community, and service.

Accrual Basis and Financial Statement Presentation

The financial statements of the University have been prepared on the accrual basis of accounting.

The University classifies its revenues, expenses, gains, and losses into three classes of net assets based on the existence or absence of donor-imposed restrictions. Net assets of the University and changes therein are classified as follows:

> Unrestricted net assets - Net assets that are not subject to donor-imposed stipulations and net assets where donor-imposed stipulations have been met within the reporting period.
>
> Temporarily restricted net assets - Net assets subject to donor-imposed stipulations that may or will be met by actions of the University.
>
> Permanently restricted net assets - Net assets subject to donor-imposed stipulations that are required to be maintained permanently by the University. Generally, the donors of these assets permit the University to use all or part of the income earned on related investments for general or specific purposes.

The amount for each of these classes of net assets is displayed in the statements of financial position and the amount of change in each class of net assets is displayed in the statements of activities.

BETHEL UNIVERSITY
NOTES TO FINANCIAL STATEMENTS
JULY 31, 2015 AND 2014

A. SUMMARY OF SIGNIFICANT ACCOUNTING POLICES - Continued

Use of Estimates in the Preparation of Financial Statements

The preparation of financial statements in conformity with accounting principles generally accepted in the United States of America requires management to make assumptions that affect the reported amounts of assets and liabilities, disclosure of contingent assets and liabilities at the date of the financial statements and the reported amounts of revenues and expenses during the reporting period. The more significant areas include the recovery period for property and equipment, the allocation of certain operating expenses to functional categories, the collection of contributions receivable and the adequacy of the allowance for doubtful student receivables. Management believes that such estimates have been based on reasonable assumptions and that such estimates are adequate. Actual results could differ from those estimates.

Contributions

The University reports gifts of cash and other assets as restricted support if received with donor-imposed stipulations that limit the use of the donated assets. When a donor-imposed restriction expires, *i.e.,* when the purpose of the restriction is accomplished, temporarily restricted net assets are reclassified to unrestricted net assets and reported in the statement of activities as net assets released from restrictions. The University has elected to report contributions received with donor-imposed restrictions as an increase to unrestricted net assets if the restrictions are met in the same fiscal year that the contributions are received.

The University reports gifts of land, equipment and other assets as unrestricted support unless explicit donor-imposed stipulations specify how the donated assets must be used. Gifts of long-lived assets with explicit restrictions that specify how the assets are to be used and gifts of cash or other assets that must be used to acquire long-lived assets are reported as restricted support. Absent explicit donor-imposed stipulations regarding how long the long-lived assets must be maintained, the University reports expirations of donor-imposed restrictions when the donated or acquired long-lived assets are placed in service.

Contribution of services are recognized if the services received (a) create or enhance non-financial assets or (b) require specialized skills, provided by individuals possessing those skills and would typically need to be purchased if not provided by donation.

In the event a donor makes changes to the nature of a restricted gift which affects its classification among the net asset categories, such amounts are reflected as reclassifications in the statements of activities.

BETHEL UNIVERSITY
NOTES TO FINANCIAL STATEMENTS
JULY 31, 2015 AND 2014

A. SUMMARY OF SIGNIFICANT ACCOUNTING POLICIES - Continued

Perkins Loan - Cash

As required by federal regulations, cash related to the Federal Perkins Loan Program is maintained in a separate bank account.

Student Accounts Receivable

The University records accounts receivable at their estimated net realizable value. An allowance for doubtful accounts is recorded based upon management's estimate of uncollectible accounts determined by analysis of specific student balances and a general reserve based upon agings of outstanding balances. Past due balances and delinquent receivables are charged against the allowance when they are determined to be uncollectible by management.

Notes Receivable - Students

Notes receivable from students at July 31, 2015 and 2014, totaled $229,462 and $270,453, respectively, net of allowances of $227,246 and $233,504, respectively. Student loans are granted by the University under the federally funded Perkins loan program. These funds are disbursed based upon the demonstration of financial need on the Perkins loan, at which time the loan will also begin accruing interest. Perkins loan amounts are then repaid through a third party billing service. Student loans are considered past due when payment has not been received within 30 days. At July 31, 2015 and 2014, student loans represented 0.28% and 0.33%, respectively, of total assets.

The allowance for doubtful accounts is established based on prior collection experience and current economic factors which, in management's judgment, could influence the ability of loan recipients to repay the amounts per the loan terms. Loan balances are written off only when they are deemed to be permanently uncollectible.

Contributions Receivable

Contributions receivable are recorded at their estimated fair value using a discount rate commensurate with the rate on U.S. Government Securities whose maturities correspond to the maturities of the contributions. Contributions receivable are considered to be either conditional or unconditional promises to give. A conditional contribution is one which depends on the occurrence of a specified uncertain future event to become binding on the donor. Conditional contributions are not recorded as revenue until the condition is met, at which time they become unconditional. Unconditional contributions are recorded as revenue at the time verifiable evidence of the promise to give is received.

BETHEL UNIVERSITY
NOTES TO FINANCIAL STATEMENTS
JULY 31, 2015 AND 2014

A. SUMMARY OF SIGNIFICANT ACCOUNTING POLICIES - Continued

Inventories

Inventories consist primarily of books and supplies and are stated at the lower of cost or market. Cost is determined using the average cost method.

Investments

Investments in marketable equity securities with readily determinable fair values and investments in debt securities are stated at their fair values in the statements of financial position. Fair value of investments is determined based on quoted market prices or using Level 2 or 3 inputs as described in Note I. All gains and losses (both realized and unrealized) and other investment income are reported in the statements of activities.

Property and Equipment

Property and equipment are recorded at cost at the date of acquisition or fair value at the date of donation in the case of gifts. Depreciation on property and equipment is calculated on the straight-line method over estimated useful lives of 20 – 40 years for buildings and improvements, 5 – 7 years for equipment and furniture, 5 years for automobiles, and 20 years for other property. Property held under capital leases is being depreciated on the straight-line method based on the shorter of the estimated useful life of the property to the University or the life of the capital lease. Library books and repairs/renovations to buildings and equipment that do not add value or extend the useful life of the assets are expensed as incurred. Depreciation and operation and maintenance charges are allocated to appropriate functional expense categories.

The estimate to complete construction in progress is $1,760,471 as of July 31, 2015.

Deferred Revenue

Deferred revenue consists primarily of charges and cash receipts collected prior to year-end for services rendered after year-end. These receipts pertain to upcoming tuition and fees.

Advances from the Federal Government for Student Loans

The Perkins Loan Program is a campus-based program providing revolving loan funds for financial assistance to eligible postsecondary school students based on financial need. The Department of Education provides funds along with the University, which are used to make loans to eligible students at low interest rates. Refundable government advances for Perkins at both July 31, 2015 and 2014 totaled $411,781.

BETHEL UNIVERSITY
NOTES TO FINANCIAL STATEMENTS
JULY 31, 2015 AND 2014

A. SUMMARY OF SIGNIFICANT ACCOUNTING POLICIES - Continued

Derivative Instruments

The University accounts for its derivative instruments under Financial Accounting Standards Board Accounting Standards Codification (ASC) 815, *Derivatives and Hedging,* which establishes accounting and reporting standards requiring that derivative instruments be recorded in the statements of financial position at estimated fair value. Changes in a derivative's fair value are included in the statements of activities as a component of the change in net assets in the period of change. As described in Note E, the University had interest rate swap agreements, which were considered derivative instruments. The University's interest rate risk management strategy was to stabilize cash flow requirements by maintaining interest rate swap contracts to convert certain variable-rate debt to a fixed rate. On July 30, 2015, the University paid $132,989 to terminate the interest rate swap agreements. As of July 31, 2015 and 2014, the University's liability under the interest rate swap agreements as reflected in the Statements of Financial Position was $0 and $245,586, respectively.

Advertising Costs

Advertising costs are expensed as incurred and totaled approximately $1,373,849 and $1,554,126 for the years ended July 31, 2015 and 2014, respectively.

Tax Status

The University is exempt from Federal income taxes under §501(a) of the Internal Revenue Code ("IRC") as an organization described in IRC §501(c)(3). Accordingly, no provision for income taxes has been made in the accompanying financial statements. The University is not classified as a private foundation.

The University accounts for the effect of any uncertain tax positions based on a more likely than not threshold to the recognition of the tax positions being sustained based on the technical merits of the position under examination by the applicable taxing authority. If a tax position or positions are deemed to result in uncertainties of those positions, the unrecognized tax benefit is estimated based on a cumulative probability assessment that aggregates the estimated tax liability for all uncertain tax positions. Tax positions for the University include, but are not limited to, the tax-exempt status and determination of whether certain income is subject to unrelated business income tax; however, the University has determined that such tax positions do not result in an uncertainty requiring recognition.

BETHEL UNIVERSITY
NOTES TO FINANCIAL STATEMENTS
JULY 31, 2015 AND 2014

A. SUMMARY OF SIGNIFICANT ACCOUNTING POLICIES - Continued

Fair Value Measurements

Assets and liabilities recorded at fair value in the statements of financial position are categorized based on the level of judgment associated with the inputs used to measure their fair value. Related disclosures are included in Note I. Level inputs, as defined by Financial Accounting Standards Board Accounting Standards Codification ("ASC") 820, *Fair Value Measurements and Disclosures,* are as follows:

Level 1 - Values are unadjusted quoted prices for identical assets and liabilities in active markets accessible at the measurement date.

Level 2 - Inputs include quoted prices for similar assets or liabilities in active markets, quoted prices from those willing to trade in markets that are not active, or other inputs that are observable or can be corroborated by market data for the term of the instrument. Such inputs include market interest rates and volatilities, spreads and yield curves.

Level 3 - Certain inputs are unobservable (supported by little or no market activity) and significant to the fair value measurement. Unobservable inputs reflect the University's best estimate of what hypothetical market participants would use to determine a transaction price for the asset or liability at the reporting date.

Classification of Expenses

Expenses are classified functionally as a measure of service efforts and accomplishments. Direct expenses incurred for a single function are allocated entirely to that function. Joint expenses applicable to more than one function are allocated on the basis of objectively summarized information or management estimates.

Reclassifications

Certain reclassifications have been made to the fiscal 2014 financial statements in order for them to conform to the fiscal 2015 presentation.

B. CONTRIBUTIONS RECEIVABLE

Contributions receivable at July 31, 2015 and 2014 consist of the following:

	2015	2014
Contributions receivable (present value)	$ 3,263,547	$ 2,920,096
Less: allowance for doubtful contributions	(167,590)	(167,590)
	$ 3,095,957	$ 2,752,506

BETHEL UNIVERSITY
NOTES TO FINANCIAL STATEMENTS
JULY 31, 2015 AND 2014

B. CONTRIBUTIONS RECEIVABLE - Continued

Expected maturities of contributions receivable at July 31, 2015 are as follows:

Fiscal Year Ending July 31,	Amount
2016	$ 1,257,632
2017	502,969
2018	581,577
2019	325,785
2020	225,577
Thereafter	457,456
Total expected contributions	3,350,996
Less: allowance for net present value using a weighted average discount rate of 1.00%	(87,449)
Present value of contributions receivable	$ 3,263,547

C. INVESTMENTS

The investments of the University are principally administered by the University or by the Board of Stewardship of the Cumberland Presbyterian Church, Inc. (the "Board"). The funds administered by the Board are co-mingled with funds of other agencies of the Church. The University's portion represents approximately 5.3% and 6.0% of the funds administered by the Board at July 31, 2015 and 2014, respectively. The investments of the University, including investment property with a book value of $3,185,000, are invested as follows:

	2015	2014
Administered by the Board:		
Marketable equity and debt securities	$3,039,801	$3,072,565
Administered by the University:		
Marketable equity and debt securities	12,669	4,044
Certificates of deposits (partially pledged in 2013, see Note E)	100,092	99,941
Investment Property and Other	3,262,834	3,241,857
	$6,415,396	$6,418,407

BETHEL UNIVERSITY
NOTES TO FINANCIAL STATEMENTS
JULY 31, 2015 AND 2014

D. BENEFICIAL INTEREST IN ASSETS HELD BY OTHERS

Beneficial interest in assets held by others represents arrangements in which a donor establishes and funds a perpetual trust administered by an individual or organization other than the University. The fair value of perpetually held trusts in which the University had a beneficial interest as of July 31, 2015 and 2014, was $3,660,425 and $3,692,558, respectively. The University records these trusts at estimated fair value. Income distributed to the University from the beneficial interest assets is temporarily restricted for scholarships.

E. DEBT

The University has the following debt obligations at July 31, 2015 and 2014:

	2015	2014
Note payable to Regions Bank, payable in monthly installments of $25,737 including interest of 4.79% through July 17, 2015, with a final payment of $1,396,516 due August 17, 2015; collateralized by certain real property; refinanced July 30, 2015.	$ -	$ 1,627,008
Note payable to Regions Bank, payable in monthly installments of $25,936 including interest of 4.79% through July 17, 2015, with a final payment of $2,636,959 due August 17, 2015; collateralized by certain real property; refinanced July 30, 2015.	-	2,807,181
Note payable to Regions Bank, payable in monthly installments of $10,108 including interest of 4.18% through February 28, 2016; collateralized by certain real property; refinanced July 30, 2015.	-	697,028
Step down revolver credit agreement with Regions Bank, bearing interest of 6.35%. Monthly principal payments of $26,000 plus accrued interest are due through March 15, 2015, at which time all unpaid principal and interest are due; collateralized by substantially all real property; note maturity extended until refinanced July 30, 2015.	-	4,444,146

BETHEL UNIVERSITY
NOTES TO FINANCIAL STATEMENTS
JULY 31, 2015 AND 2014

E. <u>DEBT</u> - Continued

	2015	2014
Note payable to Kubota Credit Corporation, U.S.A., 0% interest, collateralized by specified equipment.	2,411	5,364
Bond bearing interest at the greater of 3.25% or a variable per annum rate based on LIBOR plus certain basis points (6.12% at July 31, 2014), payable in monthly principal payments of $26,389 plus interest through April 4, 2015, with a final payment of $3,203,965 due May 4, 2015; collateralized by certain real property; note maturity extended until refinanced July 30, 2015.	-	3,430,556
Credit loan totaling $2,000,000 with Regions Bank, bearing interest at 6.25%, payable in equal monthly principal and interest payments with a maturity date of August 16, 2016; collateralized by certain real property; refinanced July 30, 2015.	-	914,037
Bond bearing interest at a variable per annum rate based on LIBOR plus certain basis points (5.32% at July 31, 2014), payable in monthly principal and interest payments through July 28, 2016, with a final payment of $1,558,366 due August 30, 2016; collateralized by certain real property; refinanced July 30, 2015.	-	1,830,167
Bond bearing interest at a variable per annum rate based on LIBOR plus certain basis points (4.99% at July 31, 2014), payable in monthly principal and interest payments through July 28, 2016, with a final payment of $1,551,166 due September 16, 2016; collateralized by certain real property; refinanced July 30, 2015.	-	1,830,167

BETHEL UNIVERSITY
NOTES TO FINANCIAL STATEMENTS
JULY 31, 2015 AND 2014

E. DEBT - Continued

	2015	2014
Bond bearing interest at a variable per annum rate based on LIBOR plus certain basis points (3.33% at July 31, 2014), payable in monthly principal and interest payments through July 28, 2016, with a final payment of $1,561,066 due September 1, 2016; collateralized by certain real property; refinanced July 30, 2015.	-	1,830,167
Bond bearing interest at a variable per annum rate based on LIBOR plus certain basis points (5.00% at July 31, 2014), payable in monthly principal and interest payments through July 28, 2016, with a final payment of $1,562,902 due September 15, 2016; collateralized by certain real property; refinanced July 30, 2015.	-	1,830,167
Note payable to Regions Bank, payable in monthly installments of $180,180 including interest of 5.25% through June 20, 2018, with a final payment of $15,593,640 due July 20, 2018; collateralized by substantially all real property.	19,219,554	-
Note payable to Farmers and Merchants Bank, bearing interest at 6% with the full principal payment due on February 28, 2017; collateralized by accounts receivable.	720,450	1,237,711
Note payable to Farmers and Merchants Bank, bearing interest at 6% with the full principal payment due on July 29, 2015; collateralized by accounts receivable; paid in full August 18, 2015.	400,592	-
Note payable to Farmers and Merchants Bank, bearing interest at 6% with the full principal payment due on August 25, 2015; collateralized by accounts receivable; maturity extended to November 25, 2015.	400,590	-

BETHEL UNIVERSITY
NOTES TO FINANCIAL STATEMENTS
JULY 31, 2015 AND 2014

E. <u>DEBT</u> - Continued

	2015	2014
Note payable to City of Paris, bearing interest at 0%, with monthly principal payments of $8,663 due beginning on September 30, 2014, through final maturity on August 31, 2022.	736,313	831,600
Line-of-credit totaling $500,000 with First Bank, bearing interest at 4.5%, maturing on August 1, 2015; collateralized by real property; paid in full on August 24, 2015.	13,610	188,610
Note payable at First Bank, bearing interest at 5%, maturing on August 23, 2015; collateralized by real property; paid in full on August 21, 2015.	400,000	-
Note payable at Carroll County Bank & Trust, bearing interest at 6.4%, with the full principal balance maturing on October 21, 2014; paid in full on August 28, 2014.	-	400,100
Note payable to Carroll County Bank & Trust, bearing interest at 6.4% with the full principal balance paid in August 2014.	-	300,100
Note payable to Carroll Bank & Trust, bearing interest at 5.0%, with the full principal balance maturing June 11, 2016; collateralized by certain real property.	1,965,573	-
Note payable to Carroll Bank & Trust, bearing interest at 5.0%, with the full principal balance maturing October 8, 2015; collateralized by certain real property.	500,150	-

- 19 -

BETHEL UNIVERSITY
NOTES TO FINANCIAL STATEMENTS
JULY 31, 2015 AND 2014

E. **DEBT** - Continued

	2015	2014
Note payable to a related party private company totaling $16,666,000, bearing interest at one year LIBOR plus 7%, payable in monthly installments of interest only. Starting on August 1, 2016, and continuing until August 1, 2018, principal payments due in monthly installments of $126,258, with the remaining balance due at final maturity on August 31, 2018. (See Note P).	16,666,000	16,666,000
Line-of-credit with a related party private company totaling $5,000,000, bearing interest at one year LIBOR plus 9%, payable in monthly installments of interest only starting on August 31, 2013, and continuing until August 31, 2018; at which time the outstanding balance is due.	4,600,000	3,600,000
	45,625,243	44,470,109
Interest rate swap	-	245,586
	$45,625,243	$44,715,695

The anticipated maturities of the University's notes payable are as follows:

Fiscal Year Ending July 31,	Amount
2016	$ 5,094,451
2017	3,458,021
2018	18,412,490
2019	18,339,768
2020	103,950
Thereafter	216,563
	$45,625,243

BETHEL UNIVERSITY
NOTES TO FINANCIAL STATEMENTS
JULY 31, 2015 AND 2014

E. DEBT - Continued

Interest Rate Swap

During fiscal year 2011, the University entered into interest rate swap agreements with Regions Bank having an original notional amount of $6,337,500 to reduce the risk associated with debt interest rate fluctuations on portions of the Special Project bonds payable. During fiscal year 2012, the notional amount was increased to $8,450,000 in line with the related bonds payable. The University did not engage in trading these derivatives. The financial instruments were used to manage interest rate risk. The notional amounts were being amortized over the life of the agreements and at July 31, 2014, the remaining amount totaled $7,320,669. The interest rate swap agreements provided for the University to receive interest at a variable rate of 63.456% of LIBOR plus 321 basis points and to pay a fixed monthly interest rate of 5.32% expiring in August 2016.

Gains or losses on the derivatives are included as a component of the change in unrestricted net assets in the statement of activities. The University's interest rate risk management strategy was to stabilize cash flow requirements by maintaining the interest rate swap contracts to convert certain variable-rate debt to fixed rate. The fair value of the derivative was a liability at July 31, 2014, totaling $245,586.

On July 30, 2015, the University called the Special Project bonds and refinanced the outstanding balance. On this same date, the University paid $132,989 to Regions Bank as a final payment on the interest rate swap agreements. As of July 31, 2015, the University has no further obligations under the interest rate swap agreements.

Interest Expense

For the years ending July 31, 2015 and 2014, Bethel University incurred interest expense of $2,722,774 and $3,409,897, respectively.

Compliance with Covenants

The Regions loan agreement contains a debt service coverage ratio that requires the University to maintain various levels of debt coverage, tested monthly in arrears. Compliance with this covenant does not begin until August 2015. Additionally, the loan agreement contains a debt to net worth ratio, which the University was in compliance at July 31, 2015.

BETHEL UNIVERSITY
NOTES TO FINANCIAL STATEMENTS
JULY 31, 2015 AND 2014

F.   OBLIGATIONS UNDER CAPITAL LEASES

The University has entered into capital lease agreements for certain computer equipment relating to the University's notebook computer program. The agreements expire at various dates through March 2016. Equipment under capital lease at July 31, 2015 and 2014, totaled $405,440 and $516,836, net of accumulated depreciation of $385,204 and $5,376,616, respectively.

Minimum future lease payments under capital leases as of July 31, 2015, are as follows:

Fiscal Year Ending July 31,	Amount
2016	$ 61,804
Less: Amount representing interest	(756)
Present value of net minimum lease payments	$ 61,048

Interest rates on capitalized leases range from 4.26% to 4.37% and are imputed based on the lessor's implicit rate of return.

BETHEL UNIVERSITY
NOTES TO FINANCIAL STATEMENTS
JULY 31, 2015 AND 2014

G. TEMPORARILY AND PERMANENTLY RESTRICTED NET ASSETS

At July 31, 2015 and 2014, temporarily restricted net assets are available for the following purposes:

	2015	2014
Scholarships	$ 108,963	$ -
Contributions and other	2,143,681	3,701,005
	$2,252,644	$3,701,005

At July 31, 2015 and 2014, permanently restricted net assets are as follows:

	2015	2014
Beneficial interest in assets held by others	$ 3,660,425	$ 3,692,558
Student loan fund	-	3,965
Endowments	6,926,790	6,410,055
	$10,587,215	$10,106,578

The endowments represent nonexpendable funds that are subject to restrictions requiring the principal to be invested and only the income used as specified by the donors

Net assets were released from donor restrictions by incurring expenses satisfying the restricted purposes. The following is a summary of the assets released from restrictions for the years ended July 31, 2015 and 2014:

	2015	2014
Institutional support expenditures	$ 443,222	$1,958,645
Scholarship and grant expenditures	353,854	23,218
Other expenditures	1,028,100	376,832
	$1,825,176	$2,358,695

BETHEL UNIVERSITY
NOTES TO FINANCIAL STATEMENTS
JULY 31, 2015 AND 2014

H. **ENDOWMENT**

The University's endowment consists of individual donor-restricted funds established for a variety of purposes. As required by U.S. generally accepted accounting principles, net assets associated with endowment funds are classified and reported based on the existence or absence of donor-imposed restrictions.

Interpretation of Relevant Law

The Board of Trustees of the University has interpreted the applicable state laws as requiring the preservation of the original gift as of the gift date of the donor-restricted endowment funds absent explicit donor stipulations to the contrary. As a result of this interpretation, the University classified as permanently restricted net assets (a) the original value of gifts donated to the permanent endowment, (b) the original value of subsequent gifts to the permanent endowment, and (c) accumulations to the permanent endowment made in accordance with the direction of the applicable donor gift instrument at the time the accumulation is added to the fund. The remaining portion of the donor-restricted endowment fund that is not classified in permanently restricted net assets is classified as temporarily restricted net assets until those amounts are appropriated for expenditure by the University in a manner consistent with the standard of prudence prescribed by applicable state laws. In accordance with applicable state laws, the University, considers the following factors in making a determination to appropriate or accumulate donor-restricted endowment funds:

- The duration and preservation of the fund
- The purposes of the University and the donor-restricted endowment fund
- General economic conditions
- The possible effect of inflation and deflation
- The expected total return from income and the appreciation of investments
- Other resources of the University
- The investment policies of the University

BETHEL UNIVERSITY
NOTES TO FINANCIAL STATEMENTS
JULY 31, 2015 AND 2014

H. ENDOWMENT - Continued

Changes in Endowment Net Assets

	Temporarily Restricted	Permanently Restricted	Total
Endowment net assets, August 1, 2013	$ 84,693	$ 9,876,072	$ 9,960,765
Investment return:			
Investment income	157,674	-	157,674
Net appreciation (realized and unrealized)	-	203,212	203,212
Total investment return	157,674	203,212	360,886
Contributions	-	27,294	27,294
Appropriation of endowment assets for expenditure (scholarships)	(242,367)	-	(242,367)
Endowment net assets, July 31, 2014	-	10,106,578	10,106,578
Reclassification	619,998	479,780	1,099,778
Investment return:			
Investment income	40,006	-	40,006
Net depreciation (realized and unrealized)	-	(32,133)	(32,133)
Total investment return	40,006	(32,133)	7,873
Contributions	-	32,990	32,990
Appropriation of endowment assets for expenditure (scholarships)	-	-	-
Endowment net assets, July 31, 2015	$ 660,004	$10,587,215	$ 11,247,219

Return Objectives and Risk Parameters

The University has adopted investment and spending policies for endowment assets that attempt to provide a predictable stream of funding to programs supported by its endowment while seeking to maintain the purchasing power of the endowment assets. Endowment assets include those assets of donor-restricted funds that the University must hold in perpetuity or for a donor-specified period(s). Under this policy, as approved by the Board of Trustees, the endowment assets are invested with an overall total return objective as established for each time horizon: 1) Short Term, 2) Intermediate, and 3) Long Term according to the funding needs of the University. The returns will be compared with the generally accepted indices, i.e., the S&P 500, certain Bond Indices,

BETHEL UNIVERSITY
NOTES TO FINANCIAL STATEMENTS
JULY 31, 2015 AND 2014

H. ENDOWMENT - Continued

and MSCI EAFE stock indices, and an index of U.S. Treasury Bills depending on the time horizon in place. At July 31, 2015 and 2014, the endowment assets consist of investments in certificates of deposit, marketable debt and equity securities, and beneficial interests in assets held by others.

Strategies Employed for Achieving Objectives

To satisfy its rate-of-return objectives, the University relies on a total return strategy in which investment returns are achieved through both capital appreciation (realized and unrealized) and current yield (interest and dividends). The University targets an investment allocation based on the three time horizons described above and that places emphasis on diversification of assets within prudent risk constraints.

Spending Policy and How the Investment Objectives Relate to Spending Policy

During fiscal year 2009, the University's Board of Trustees adopted a spending policy, which is based on the "Total Return" concept of determining the amount available for distribution. Total Return takes into consideration all of the elements of long-term investment return. The appropriate spending amount is based on the projected long-term Total Return of the funds, less an estimate of future inflation. The goal of the Total Return approach is to provide for a level of current income that protects the future purchasing power of the fund, thereby providing for increasing amounts of future income. The University anticipates that this percentage will be in the range of 3 to 5% of market value based on historical measurements of Total Return and Inflation. The market value of the fund will be noted each year on a specific date and a three-year rolling average market value will be established. The rolling three-year market value will be multiplied by the approved spending percentage which will be set annually.

BETHEL UNIVERSITY
NOTES TO FINANCIAL STATEMENTS
JULY 31, 2015 AND 2014

I. FAIR VALUES OF FINANCIAL INSTRUMENTS

Required disclosures concerning the estimated fair values of financial instruments are presented below. The estimated fair value amounts have been determined based on the University's assessment of available market information and appropriate valuation methodologies. The following table summarizes required fair value disclosures under ASC 825, *Financial Instruments*, and measurements at July 31, 2015 and 2014 for the assets and liabilities measured at fair value on a recurring basis under ASC 820, *Fair Value Measurements and Disclosures*:

	Carrying Amount	Estimated Fair Value	Measured at Fair Value	Fair Value Measurements Using		
				Level 1	Level 2	Level 3
July 31, 2015						
Assets:						
Investments:						
Cash and cash equivalents	$ 251,867	$ 251,867	$ 251,867	$ 251,867	$ -	$ -
Certificates of deposits	100,092	100,092	100,092	100,092	-	-
Equity funds:						
Mutual Funds	102,626	102,626	102,626	102,626	-	-
U.S. Equities	421,017	421,017	421,017	421,017	-	-
Total Equity Funds	523,643	523,643	523,643	523,643	-	-
Venture Capital Investment	2,354,794	2,354,794	2,354,794	-	-	2,354,794
Property	3,185,000	3,185,000	3,185,000	-	-	3,185,000
Total Investments	$ 6,415,396	$ 6,415,396	$6,415,396	$ 875,602	-	$5,539,794
Beneficial interests in trusts	3,660,425	3,660,425	3,660,425	-	3,660,425	-
Liabilities:						
Notes payable and long-term obligation	45,686,291	50,805,043	-	-	-	-

BETHEL UNIVERSITY
NOTES TO FINANCIAL STATEMENTS
JULY 31, 2015 AND 2014

I. FAIR VALUES OF FINANCIAL INSTRUMENTS - Continued

Required disclosures concerning the estimated fair values of financial instruments are presented below. The estimated fair value amounts have been determined based on the University's assessment of available market information and appropriate valuation methodologies. The following table summarizes required fair value disclosures under ASC 825, *Financial Instruments*, and measurements at July 31, 2015 and 2014 for the assets and liabilities measured at fair value on a recurring basis under ASC 820, *Fair Value Measurements and Disclosures*:

	Carrying Amount	Estimated Fair Value	Measured at Fair Value	Fair Value Measurements Using		
				Level 1	Level 2	Level 3
July 31, 2014						
Assets:						
Investments:						
Cash and cash equivalents	$ 155,592	$ 155,592	$ 155,592	$ 155,592	$ -	$ -
Certificates of deposits	99,941	99,941	99,941	99,941	-	-
Bond funds	361,924	361,924	361,924	-	361,924	-
Equity funds:						
Mutual Funds	76,552	76,552	76,552	76,552	-	-
U.S. Equities	13,154	13,154	13,154	13,154	-	-
Total Equity Funds	89,706	89,706	89,706	89,706	-	-
Venture Capital	1,147,582	1,147,582	1,147,582	-	-	1,147,582
Other Limited Partnerships	1,378,662	1,378,662	1,378,662	-	-	1,378,662
Investment Property	3,185,000	3,185,000	3,185,000	-	-	3,185,000
Total Investments	$ 6,418,407	$ 6,418,407	$6,418,407	$345,239	$361,924	$5,711,244
Beneficial interests in trusts	3,692,558	3,692,558	3,692,558	-	3,692,558	-
Liabilities:						
Notes payable and long-term obligation	45,179,835	50,241,843	-	-	-	-

- 28 -

BETHEL UNIVERSITY
NOTES TO FINANCIAL STATEMENTS
JULY 31, 2015 AND 2014

I. FAIR VALUES OF FINANCIAL INSTRUMENTS - Continued

Changes in Level 3 assets are as follows:

	Fair Value Measurements Using Significant Unobservable Inputs (Level 3)	
	2015	2014
Beginning Balance	$5,711,244	$2,015,007
Purchases and sales, net	(171,450)	362,245
Unrealized gain	-	148,992
Contributions	-	3,185,000
Ending Balance	$5,539,794	$5,711,244

The following methods and assumptions were used to estimate the fair value of each class of financial instruments:

<u>Cash equivalents, receivables, accounts payable and accrued payroll and benefits, deferred revenue and advances from the Federal government for student loans</u>

The carrying values of these items approximate their fair values due to the short maturities of these instruments.

<u>Investments</u>

Fair values are based on quoted market prices, where available, and Level 2 and 3 inputs. The carrying amounts and the fair values of the University's investments are presented in Note C.

<u>Notes payable and obligations under capital leases</u>

For fixed rate debt, fair value was estimated using discounted cash flow analyses based on the University's current incremental borrowing rates for similar types of borrowing arrangements.

J. FUND RAISING ACTIVITIES

The University conducts fundraising activities each year. The total cost of these activities for fiscal years 2015 and 2014, was $1,030,307 and $1,032,705, respectively.

BETHEL UNIVERSITY
NOTES TO FINANCIAL STATEMENTS
JULY 31, 2015 AND 2014

K. RETIREMENT PLAN

The University's full-time employees may participate in either a retirement plan administered by the Cumberland Presbyterian Board of Finance or the TIAA/CREF Plan, which is a national pension plan. The University makes payments to the plans by withholding an employee-elected percentage from the employee's salary with the University matching the employee's deduction up to five percent (5%). During 2014, the University did not match contributions. Total matching contributions were made by the University for fiscal years 2015 and 2014, of $454,206 and $-0-, respectively.

L. CONCENTRATION OF RISKS

Concentration of Risk

The University generates revenue predominantly from tuition and fees, investment income, gifts, auxiliary enterprises and contributions. In planning and budgeting during a fiscal year, significant reliance is placed on meeting tuition, gift, auxiliary, investment earnings and contribution goals in order for the University to sustain successful operations. In the event that enrollment or gifts and contributions significantly decrease in any one year, operations could be adversely affected.

Financial instruments that potentially subject the University to concentrations of credit risk and market risk consist principally of cash equivalents, investments, and student receivables.

The University, in connection with its activities, grants credit to students that involves, to varying degrees, elements of credit risk. The maximum accounting loss from credit risk is limited to the amounts that are recognized in the accompanying statements of financial position as student accounts receivable at July 31, 2015 and 2014.

The University also has two bank deposits in excess of those insured under regulatory insurance limits.

BETHEL UNIVERSITY
NOTES TO FINANCIAL STATEMENTS
JULY 31, 2015 AND 2014

M. OPERATING LEASES

The University leases office space for satellite campuses relating to its degree-completion program. These leases expire at various dates through fiscal year 2021. Minimum future rental payments under non-cancelable operating leases as of July 31, 2015 are as follows:

Fiscal Year Ending July 31,	Amount
2016	$ 2,841,877
2017	2,551,578
2018	2,501,670
2019	2,404,055
2020	274,712
Thereafter	212,000
	$10,785,892

Rent expense under the non-cancelable operating leases totaled $2,906,508 and $2,599,490 for the years ended July 31, 2015 and 2014, respectively.

On July 31, 2013, the University entered into a sale-leaseback agreement with a related party for a building in Paris, Tennessee. The purchasor entered into a note receivable with the University for $8,200,000, which approximated the carrying value of the building, and therefore, no gain or loss was recognized. The purchasor will be paying the note receivable over 30 years at an interest rate of 2%. The University will lease the building for six years with monthly payments of $120,275. The note receivable totaled $7,792,839 and $7,998,454 at July 31, 2015 and 2014, respectively.

BETHEL UNIVERSITY
NOTES TO FINANCIAL STATEMENTS
JULY 31, 2015 AND 2014

N. FUNCTIONAL ALLOCATION OF EXPENSES

During the years ended July 31, 2015 and 2014, the University allocated the cost of interest, certain professional fees and the operation and maintenance of physical plant, including depreciation expense of $2,918,920 and $4,029,589 respectively, over the cost of providing instruction, research, academic support, institutional support and auxiliary enterprises as follows:

	2015	2014
Instruction	$6,113,190	$6,382,294
Academic support	224,105	195,984
Student services	990,753	1,078,236
Institutional support	849,960	1,417,915
Auxiliary enterprises	574,061	822,589
Total operation and maintenance of physical plant	$8,752,069	$9,897,018

O. LITIGATION AND CONTINGENCIES

The University is a defendant in legal actions from time to time in the normal course of operations. It is not currently possible to state the ultimate liability, if any, in these matters. In the opinion of management, any resulting liability from these actions will not have a material adverse effect on the financial position of the activities of the University.

P. RELATED PARTY TRANSACTIONS

During fiscal years 2015 and 2014, the University had an agreement with a company owned by a member of the University's faculty. Under the agreement, the company developed and is maintaining the following online programs of study for the University:

Master of Business Administration
Master of Arts in Education
Master of Science in Criminal Justice
Bachelor of Science in Organizational Leadership
Bachelor of Science in Criminal Justice
Bachelor of Science in Emergency Services Management
Associates of Arts
Associates of Science
Dual Enrollment

BETHEL UNIVERSITY
NOTES TO FINANCIAL STATEMENTS
JULY 31, 2015 AND 2014

P. RELATED PARTY TRANSACTIONS - Continued

Specifically, the company is responsible for developing course work, producing lectures and graphic presentations, and maintaining student records. Fees under the agreement range from $149 to $319 per student, per course. The most recent agreement was executed effective April 1, 2015 for twelve (12) months, and automatically renews for an additional term of twelve (12) months unless terminated in accordance with the agreement. Total fees incurred during fiscal years 2015 and 2014 were $7,096,337 and $7,535,299, respectively.

During fiscal year 2015, the University entered into an agreement with a company co-founded by a member of the Board of Trustees. Under the agreement, the company will develop and maintain the Registered Nurse to Bachelor of Science in Nursing (RN to BSN) online program of study for the University. Specifically, the company is responsible for developing course work, producing lectures and graphic presentations, and maintaining student records. Fees under the agreement are the greater of twenty percent (20%) of the credit hour tuition rate or a minimum of $50 per user for licensing rights to the product, including all enhancements, modifications, and new releases or modules. The agreement was executed March 9, 2015 and shall continue for five (5) years, which will automatically extend for an additional two (2) years unless terminated in accordance with the agreement. There were no fees incurred during the fiscal year 2015.

The University entered into a note payable and a line-of-credit with a private company owned by a member of the Board of Trustees. Total outstanding balances during fiscal year 2015 and 2014 were $21,266,000 and $20,266,000 respectively (See Note E).

The University entered into a leasing arrangement with a related party as described in Note M.

Q. CORRECTION OF ERRORS

Accounts Receivable

In fiscal years 2014 and 2013, the University inaccurately valued student accounts receivable. Consequently, the comparative financial statements presented for the year ended July 31, 2014, have been restated to accurately value the amount due. The restatement reflects the impact of reducing the student accounts receivable to the net realizable value. The required adjustments to the various accounts for July 31, 2014 and 2013 are presented below.

BETHEL UNIVERSITY
NOTES TO FINANCIAL STATEMENTS
JULY 31, 2015 AND 2014

Depreciation and Classification of Asset

In fiscal years 2014 and 2013, the University inaccurately over depreciated certain buildings having an estimated useful life of 40 years. Consequently, the comparative financial statements presented for the year ended July 31, 2014 have been restated to accurately value property, buildings, and equipment. The restatement reflects the impact of correctly depreciating buildings as having 40-year lives instead of 20-year lives. Additionally, a building donated during 2014 that has not been placed into service has been reclassified as investment property. The required adjustments to the various accounts as of and for the year ended July 31, 2014, are as follows:

	As Previously Stated	Effects of the Adjustments	Restated Amount
Student Receivables, net of allowances	$ 5,942,697	($ 4,569,747)	$ 1,372,950
Investments	3,233,407	3,185,000	6,418,407
Total property, buildings and equipment, net	58,036,311	108,799	58,145,110
Net Assets: Unrestricted - beginning balance	$ 6,166,553	$ 1,345,803	$ 4,820,750
Increase in unrestricted net assets	4,292,349	69,855	4,362,204
Net Assets: Unrestricted	$10,458,902	$1,275,948	$ 9,182,954

R. SUBSEQUENT EVENTS

The University has evaluated subsequent events through October 14, 2015, the issuance date of the University's financial statements, and has determined that the following subsequent event requires disclosure.

On September 28, 2015, the United States Department of Agriculture approved and obligated to fund a Campus Facility Acquisition of certain Bethel University buildings through a Rural Development Communities Facilities Loan of up to $50,000,000 with NCCD – Bethel Properties, LLC, a separate legal entity independent of Bethel University, at a rate of 3.25% with a repayment term of 40 years. After NCCD-Bethel Properties uses such funds to acquire certain Bethel University buildings, they will be leased to Bethel University in a sale-lease back transaction qualifying as a capital lease. The transaction is expected to be funded on December 1, 2015, at which time Bethel University plans to pay off all long-term debt.

SUPPLEMENTARY INFORMATION

BETHEL UNIVERSITY
FINANCIAL RESPONSIBILITY COMPOSITE SCORE
YEAR ENDED JULY 31, 2015
(Unaudited)

As explained on the United States Department of Education's website (https://studentaid.ed.gov/sa/about/data-center/school/composite-scores),

Section 498(c) of the Higher Education Act of 1965, as amended, requires for-profit and non-profit institutions to annually submit audited financial statements to the Department to demonstrate they are maintaining the standards of financial responsibility necessary to participate in the Title IV programs. One of many standards, which the Department utilizes to gauge the financial responsibility of an institution, is a composite of three ratios derived from an institution's audited financial statements. The three ratios are a primary reserve ratio, an equity ratio, and a net income ratio. These ratios gauge the fundamental elements of the financial health of an institution, not the educational quality of an institution.

The composite score reflects the overall relative financial health of institutions along a scale from negative 1.0 to positive 3.0. A score greater than or equal to 1.5 indicates the institution is considered financially responsible.

Schools with scores of less than 1.5 but greater than or equal to 1.0 are considered financially responsible, but require additional oversight. These schools are subject to cash monitoring and other participation requirements.

For the fiscal years ended July 31, 2013, 2014, and 2015, management calculated the University's financial responsibility composite scores as follows:

Ratios:	2013	2014	2015
Primary Reserve Ratio:	(0.0852)	0.0102	0.0784
Expendable Net Assets	($ 6,222,642)	$ 700,412	$ 4,979,459
Total Expense	$ 73,048,254	$ 68,701,441	$ 63,528,037
Equity Ratio:	0.2333	0.2794	0.3008
Modified Net Assets	$ 19,549,826	$ 22,990,537	$ 24,914,811
Modified Assets	$ 83,808,083	$ 82,297,078	$ 82,834,615
Net Income Ratio:	0.0506	0.0597	0.0435
Change in Unrestricted Net Assets	$ 3,893,177	$ 4,362,204	$ 2,891,998
Total Unrestricted Revenue	$ 76,941,431	$ 73,063,645	$ 66,420,035
Strength Factor Scores:			
Primary Reserve strength factor score	(0.8519)	0.1020	0.7838
Equity strength factor score	1.3996	1.6762	1.8047
Net Income strength factor score	3.0000	3.0000	3.0000
Composite Score:			
Primary Reserve Weighted Score	(0.3407)	0.0408	0.3135
Equity Weighted Score	0.5598	0.6705	0.7219
Net Income Weighted Score	0.6000	0.6000	0.6000
Total Composite Score (Rounded):	0.8	1.3	1.6

BETHEL UNIVERSITY
UNIVERSITY KEY FINANCIAL RATIOS
YEAR ENDED JULY 31, 2015
(Unaudited)

The financial health of the University can be evaluated through the use of ratios. The following ratios are customarily utilized by higher education institutions to measure financial condition. There are four fundamental financial questions addressed by analysis of four core ratios.

- Are resources sufficient and flexible enough to support the mission? – Primary Reserve Ratio
- Do operating results indicate the institution is living within available resources? – Net Operating Revenues Ratio
- Does asset performance and management support the strategic direction? - Return on Net Assets
- Are financial resources, including debt, managed strategically to advance the mission? - Viability Ratio

When combined, these four ratios deliver a single measure of the University's overall financial health, referred to as the Composite Financial Index. The following charts analyze the aforementioned ratios for the fiscal year ended July 31, 2013, 2014, and 2015:

Composite Financial Index

The Composite Financial Index (CFI) is built with the values of its four component ratios: 1) Primary Reserve, 2) Net Operating Revenue, 3) Return on Net Assets, and 4) Viability Ratio. Once each of the four ratios is calculated, further weighting is conducted to measure the relative strength of the score and its importance in the composite score. The CFI combines the four core ratios identified below into a single score. The combination, using a prescribed weighting plan, allows a weakness or strength in one ratio to be offset by another ratio result. The CFI reflects a picture of the financial health of the institution at a point in time.

COMPOSITE FINANCIAL INDEX (CFI)

FY13	FY14	FY15
2.0	2.2	1.3

BETHEL UNIVERSITY
UNIVERSITY KEY FINANCIAL RATIOS
YEAR ENDED JULY 31, 2015
(Unaudited)

Primary Reserve Ratio

The Primary Reserve Ratio is intended to address the question of sufficiency and flexibility for support of the mission. The ratio measures the financial strength of the University by comparing expendable net assets, which includes those assets the University can access and spend quickly to meet obligations, to total expenses at the end of every fiscal year. This ratio identifies the University's financial strength and flexibility by identifying how long the University can function by using reserves without the generation of any new net assets. A primary reserve ratio of .40 or 40% is advisable, implying that the university has the ability to cover over 4 ½ months of expenses. Key items that can impact this ratio include principal payments on debt, using net assets to fund capital construction projects, endowment returns, and total operating expenses. Although not reaching the benchmark, the University's ratio is trending in a positive direction.

PRIMARY RESERVE RATIO   **EXPLANATION**

FY13	FY14	FY15	
$4,820,750	$9,182,954	$12,074,952	+ unrestricted net assets EOY
$4,853,004	$3,701,005	$2,252,644	+ temporarily restricted net assets EOY
$60,950,721	$58,145,110	$57,283,818	-- land, building, and equipment, net of depreciation EOY
$44,125,905	$44,715,695	$45,625,243	+ long-term debt EOY
$73,048,254	$68,701,441	$63,528,037	total expenses
-0.10	-0.01	0.04	ratio
-0.74	-0.06	0.32	strength factor
-0.3	0.0	0.1	weighted value

BETHEL UNIVERSITY
UNIVERSITY KEY FINANCIAL RATIOS
YEAR ENDED JULY 31, 2015
(Unaudited)

Net Operating Revenues Ratio

The Net Operating Revenues Ratio is intended to indicate if the University is living within its available resources. The University needs to generate some level of surplus over long periods of time because operations are one source for reinvestment in future initiatives. Short-term deficits may occur as a result of strategic decisions. It is when deficits are unplanned or unmanaged and occurring as a result of core operations that evaluation of operations is necessitated. A positive ratio indicates the University is in good financial condition. An organization should establish a target percentage, and establishing a benchmark should be in line with operating growth. A ratio of 2 to 4 percent indicates the University operated within its means and should be maintained over time; however, fluctuations from year to year are normal. A large ratio identifies an operating surplus and a stronger financial position. While a negative ratio indicates an operating loss for the year, universities need to be careful about too large of a positive ratio, indicating under spending on mission critical initiatives.

NET OPERATING REVENUES RATIO (%):
Using Change in Unrestricted Net Assets

FY13	FY14	FY15	EXPLANATION
$3,893,177	$4,362,204	$2,891,998	change in unrestricted net assets
$76,941,431	$73,063,645	$66,420,035	total unrestricted revenue
5.1	6.0	4.4	ratio
3.89	4.59	3.35	strength factor
0.4	0.5	0.3	weighted value

Return on Net Assets Ratio

The Return on Net Assets Ratio is intended to assess if the asset performance and management support the strategic direction. The ratio measures whether the University is financially better off than in the previous year by measuring total economic return or the level of change in total net assets. This ratio is the most comprehensive measure of growth or decline in wealth over time. There is not a specific threshold; however, 3 to 4 percent is a generally acceptable real rate of return. An improving trend in this ratio indicates the university is increasing its net assets and is likely to be in a position to set aside financial resources to strengthen its future financial flexibility. Key items that may impact this ratio include changes in the net operating revenue ratio, endowment returns, capital gifts and grants, capital transfers, and endowment gifts. This indicator can be greatly impacted when borrowing money for a capital project and when the capital item is added to Net Assets. Looking at the trend will even out the anomalies.

BETHEL UNIVERSITY
UNIVERSITY KEY FINANCIAL RATIOS
YEAR ENDED JULY 31, 2015
(Unaudited)

Return on Net Assets Ratio - Continued

RETURN ON NET ASSETS RATIO (%) — **EXPLANATION**

FY13	FY14	FY15	
$6,877,462	$3,440,711	$1,924,274	change in net assets
$12,672,364	$19,549,826	$22,990,537	total net assets BOY
54.3	17.6	8.4	ratio
10.00	8.80	4.118	strength factor
2.0	1.8	0.8	weighted value

Viability Ratio

The Viability Ratio is intended to address the question of whether financial resources are being strategically managed to advance the mission of the University. It measures availability of expendable net assets for coverage of debt should the University be required to settle its obligations as of the date on the balance sheet. A 1:1 ratio is desired, indicating adequate net assets to meet obligations. This ratio is one of the most basic determinants of clear financial health and is regarded as governing the University's ability to assume new debt. A ratio of 1.25 or greater indicates a strong creditworthy University with sufficient resources to satisfy debt obligations; however, each university should identify the ratio that is right for its mission specific needs. A viability ratio that falls below 1:1 hinders the university's ability to respond to adverse condition, to secure external capital, and to have flexibility to fund new objectives. Key items that may impact this ratio include principal payments on debt, using net assets for capital construction projects, issuance of new debt, and endowment returns. Although not reaching the benchmark, the University's ratio is trending in a positive direction.

VIABILITY RATIO — **EXPLANATION**

FY13	FY14	FY15	
$4,820,750	$9,182,954	$12,074,952	+ unrestricted net assets EOY
$4,853,004	$3,701,005	$2,252,644	+ temporarily restricted net assets EOY
$60,950,721	$58,145,110	$57,283,818	-- land, building, and equipment, net of depreciation EOY
$44,125,905	$44,715,695	$45,625,243	+ long-term debt EOY
$44,125,905	$44,715,695	$45,625,243	long-term debt EOY
-0.16	-0.01	0.06	ratio
-0.39	-0.03	0.14	strength factor
-0.1	0.0	0.0	weighted value

BETHEL UNIVERSITY
UNIVERSITY KEY FINANCIAL RATIOS
YEAR ENDED JULY 31, 2015
(Unaudited)

Unrestricted Net Assets Exclusive of Property, Buildings, Equipment, and Related Debt

The Southern Association of School and Colleges, Commission on Colleges (SACSCOC), has various core requirements for meeting standards. One such standard is core requirement 2.11.1 requiring, among other things, the University to present a statement of financial position of unrestricted net assets, exclusive of plant assets and plant-related debt, which represents the change in unrestricted net assets attributable to operations. The chart below is provided to meet this SACSCOC requirement. Although the University's net unrestricted assets, excluding plant, property, equipment, and related debt is negative, the trend over the past three fiscal years is positive, indicating the University has taken measures to strengthen its financial stability.

Statements of Financial Position of
Unrestricted Net Assets, Exclusive of Plant
Assets and Plant-Related Debt

	July 31,		
	2015	**2014**	**2013**
Restatement of Net Assets without plant and plant-related debt			
Unrestricted Net Assets	*$ 12,074,952*	*$ 9,182,954*	*$ 4,820,750*
Less: property, plant, and equipment, net	(57,283,818)	(58,145,110)	(60,950,721)
Add: plant-related debt	36,624,268	38,743,588	40,099,587
URNA not including plant and debt	**$ (8,235,271)**	**$(10,218,568)**	**$(16,030,384)**

OTHER INFORMATION

BETHEL UNIVERSITY
SCHEDULE OF EXPENDITURES OF FEDERAL AWARDS
YEAR ENDED JULY 31, 2015

Federal Grantor/Pass-through Grantor/ Program or Cluster Title	Federal CFDA Number	Federal Expenditures
U.S. Department of Education - Direct Awards		
Student Financial Assistance - Cluster: (1)		
Federal Direct Student Loans Program (Note C)	84.268	$58,063,438
Federal Perkins Loan Program (Note B)	84.038	19,898
Federal Work-Study Program (Note D)	84.033	143,136
Federal Supplemental Educational Opportunity Grants Program (Note D)	84.007	333,435
Federal Pell Grant Program	84.063	15,011,028
Teacher Education Assistance for University and Higher Education Grant	84.379	76,464
Total Student Financial Assistance - Cluster		73,647,399
U.S. Department of Education - Pass-through Program from:		
Special Education: Grants to States Tennessee Teachers Assistants Grant	84.027A	32,946
Total U.S. Department of Education		73,680,345
U.S. Department of Homeland Security – Pass-through Program from:		
Tennessee Emergency Management Agency: Hazard Mitigation Grant (1) (Note D)	97.039	1,056,994
Total Expenditures of Federal Awards		$74,737,339

(1) Tested as a major program

See independent auditor's report.

BETHEL UNIVERSITY
NOTES TO SCHEDULE OF EXPENDITURES OF FEDERAL AWARDS
YEAR ENDED JULY 31, 2015

A. BASIS OF PRESENTATION

The accompanying schedule of expenditures of federal awards is presented in accordance with the requirements of OMB Circular A-133, *Audits of States, Local Governments, and Non-Profit Organizations*, on the accrual basis of accounting consistent with the basis of accounting used by the University in the preparation of its financial statements.

B. FEDERAL PERKINS LOAN PROGRAM - CFDA #84.038

The outstanding loan balance for the Federal Perkins Loan Program at July 31, 2015 was $229,462, net of the allowance for uncollectible loans of $227,246. Total loan disbursements for the program for the year ended July 31, 2015, were $19,898. These disbursements include expenditures such as loans to students, repayments of fund capital, and administrative expenditures.

C. FEDERAL DIRECT LOANS PROGRAM - CFDA #84.268

During the fiscal year ending July 31, 2015, the University processed $58,063,438 of new loans under the Federal Direct Loans program (which includes subsidized and unsubsidized Stafford Loans, Parents' for Undergraduate Students, and Supplemental Loans for Students)

D. MATCHING FUNDS

The University provided matching funds of $111,145 for the Federal Supplemental Educational Opportunity Grants program and $47,712 for the Federal Work Study program during the fiscal year ended July 31, 2015.

The University provided matching funds, the majority of which were in-kind, of $176,166 for the Hazard Mitigation Grant, while the State of Tennessee, Department of Military also provided matching funds of $176,166.

Independent Auditor's Report on Internal Control Over
Financial Reporting and on Compliance and Other Matters
Based on an Audit of Financial Statements Performed in
Accordance with *Government Auditing Standards*

The Board of Trustees
Bethel University
McKenzie, Tennessee

We have audited, in accordance with the auditing standards generally accepted in the United States of America and the standards applicable to financial audits contained in *Government Auditing Standards* issued by the Comptroller General of the United States, the financial statements of Bethel University (the "University"), which comprise the statements of financial position as of July 31, 2015, and the related statements of activities and cash flows for the year then ended, and the related notes to the financial statements, and have issued our report thereon dated October 14, 2015.

Internal Control Over Financial Reporting

In planning and performing our audit of the financial statements, we considered the University's internal control over financial reporting (internal control) to determine the audit procedures that are appropriate in the circumstances for the purpose of expressing our opinion on the financial statements, but not for the purpose of expressing an opinion on the effectiveness of the University's internal control. Accordingly, we do not express an opinion on the effectiveness of the University's internal control.

A *deficiency in internal control* exists when the design or operation of a control does not allow management or employees, in the normal course of performing their assigned functions, to prevent, or detect and correct misstatements on a timely basis. A *material weakness* is a deficiency, or a combination of deficiencies, in internal control such that there is a reasonable possibility that a material misstatement of the entity's financial statements will not be prevented, or detected and corrected on a timely basis. A *significant deficiency* is a deficiency, or a combination of deficiencies, in internal control that is less severe than a material weakness, yet important enough to merit attention by those charged with governance.

The Board of Trustees
Bethel University

Our consideration of the internal control was for the limited purpose described in the first paragraph of this section and was not designed to identify all deficiencies in internal control that might be material weaknesses or significant deficiencies. Given these limitations, during our audit we did not identify any deficiencies in internal control that we consider to be material weaknesses. However, material weaknesses may exist that have not been identified.

Compliance and Other Matters

As part of obtaining reasonable assurance about whether the University's financial statements are free from material misstatement, we performed tests of its compliance with certain provisions of laws, regulations, contracts, and grant agreements, noncompliance with which could have a direct and material effect on the determination of financial statement amounts. However, providing an opinion on compliance with those provisions was not an objective of our audit, and accordingly, we do not express such an opinion. The results of our tests disclosed no instances of noncompliance or other matters that are required to be reported under *Government Auditing Standards*.

Purpose of this Report

The purpose of this report is solely to describe the scope of our testing of internal control and compliance and the results of that testing, and not to provide an opinion on the effectiveness of the University's internal control or on compliance. This report is an integral part of an audit performed in accordance with *Government Auditing Standards* in considering the University's internal control and compliance. Accordingly, this communication is not suitable for any other purpose.

Crosslin & Associates, PLLC

Nashville, Tennessee
October 14, 2015

Independent Auditor's Report on Compliance For The Major Program and on Internal Control Over Compliance Required by OMB Circular A-133

The Board of Trustees
Bethel University
McKenzie, Tennessee

Report on Compliance for Each Major Federal Program

We have audited Bethel University's (the "University") compliance with the types of compliance requirements described in the *OMB Circular A-133 Compliance Supplement* that could have a direct and material effect on the University's major federal program for the year ended July 31, 2015. The University's major federal program is identified in the summary of auditor's results section of the accompanying schedule of findings and questioned costs.

Management's Responsibility

Management is responsible for compliance with the requirements of laws, regulations, contracts, and grants applicable to its federal programs.

Auditor's Responsibility

Our responsibility is to express an opinion on compliance for each of the University's major federal programs based on our audit of the types of compliance requirements referred to above. We conducted our audit of compliance in accordance with auditing standards generally accepted in the United States of America; the standards applicable to financial audits contained in *Government Auditing Standards*, issued by the Comptroller General of the United States; and OMB Circular A-133, *Audits of States, Local Governments, and Non-Profit Organizations*. Those standards and OMB Circular A-133 require that we plan and perform the audit to obtain reasonable assurance about whether noncompliance with the types of compliance requirements referred to above that could have a direct and material effect on a major federal program occurred. An audit includes examining, on a test basis, evidence about the University's compliance with those requirements and performing such other procedures as we considered necessary in the circumstances.

We believe that our audit provides a reasonable basis for our opinion on compliance for each major federal program. However, our audit does not provide a legal determination of the University's compliance.

The Board of Trustees
Bethel University

Opinion on Each Major Federal Program

In our opinion, the University complied, in all material respects, with the types of compliance requirements referred to above that could have a direct and material effect on its major federal program for the year ended July 31, 2015.

Report on Internal Control Over Compliance

Management of the University is responsible for establishing and maintaining effective internal control over compliance with the types of compliance requirements referred to above. In planning and performing our audit of compliance, we considered the University's internal control over compliance with the types of requirements that could have a direct and material effect on each major federal program to determine the auditing procedures that are appropriate in the circumstances for the purpose of expressing an opinion on compliance for each major federal program and to test and report on internal control over compliance in accordance with OMB Circular A-133, but not for the purpose of expressing an opinion on the effectiveness of internal control over compliance. Accordingly, we do not express an opinion on the effectiveness of the University's internal control over compliance.

A *deficiency in internal control over compliance* exists when the design or operation of a control over compliance does not allow management or employees, in the normal course of performing their assigned functions, to prevent, or detect and correct, noncompliance with a type of compliance requirement of a federal program on a timely basis. A *material weakness in internal control over compliance* is a deficiency, or combination of deficiencies, in internal control over compliance, such that there is a reasonable possibility that material noncompliance with a type of compliance requirement of a federal program will not be prevented, or detected and corrected, on a timely basis. A *significant deficiency in internal control over compliance* is a deficiency, or a combination of deficiencies, in internal control over compliance with a type of compliance requirement of a federal program that is less severe than a material weakness in internal control over compliance, yet important enough to merit attention by those charged with governance.

Our consideration of internal control over compliance was for the limited purpose described in the first paragraph of this section and was not designed to identify all deficiencies in internal control over compliance that might be material weaknesses or significant deficiencies. We did not identify any deficiencies in internal control over compliance that we consider to be material weaknesses. However, material weaknesses may exist that have not been identified.

The Board of Trustees
Bethel University

The purpose of this report on internal control over compliance is solely to describe the scope of our testing of internal control over compliance and the results of that testing based on the requirements of OMB Circular A-133. Accordingly, this report is not suitable for any other purpose.

Crosslin & Associates, PLLC

Nashville, Tennessee
October 14, 2015

BETHEL UNIVERSITY
SCHEDULE OF FINDINGS AND QUESTIONED COSTS
YEAR ENDED JULY 31, 2015

I. SUMMARY OF INDEPENDENT AUDITOR'S RESULTS

Financial Statements

Type of auditor's report issued: Unmodified

Internal control over financial reporting:

- Material weakness(es) identified? ___Yes _X_ No
- Significant deficiency(ies) identified? ___Yes _X_ None Reported

Noncompliance material to financial statements noted? ___Yes _X_ No

Federal Awards

Internal control over major program:

- Material weakness(es) identified? ___Yes _X_ No
- Significant deficiency(ies) identified? ___Yes _X_ No

Type of auditor's report issued on compliance for major program: Unmodified

Any audit findings disclosed that are required to be reported in accordance with section 510(a) of Circular A-133? ___Yes _X_ No

BETHEL UNIVERSITY
SCHEDULE OF FINDINGS AND QUESTIONED COSTS
YEAR ENDED JULY 31, 2015

I. SUMMARY OF INDEPENDENT AUDITOR'S RESULTS - Continued

Major Program:

CFDA Number	Name of Federal Program	Amount Expended
SFA Cluster:		
84.063	Federal Pell Grant Program	$15,011,028
84.268	Federal Direct Student Loans Program (new loans processed)	58,063,438
84.038	Federal Perkins Loan Program	19,898
84.007	Federal Supplemental Educational Opportunity Grants Program	333,435
84.033	Federal Work Study Program	143,136
84.038	Perkins Loans ($456,708 outstanding balance of loans)	-
84.379	TEACHER Education Assistance for College and Higher Education Grant	76,464
97.639	Hazard Mitigation Grant	1,056,994

Dollar threshold used to distinguish between type A
and type B programs $300,000

Auditee qualified as low-risk auditee   __Yes X No

II. FINANCIAL STATEMENT FINDINGS

None reported.

III. FINDINGS AND QUESTIONED COSTS FOR FEDERAL AWARDS

None reported.

BETHEL UNIVERSITY
SCHEDULE OF FINDINGS AND QUESTIONED COSTS
YEAR ENDED JULY 31, 2015

IV. PRIOR AUDIT FINDINGS AND QUESTIONED COSTS

ITEM #LF 14-1

STUDENT DEPOSITS/CASH MANAGEMENT

Criteria, Condition, Context, Cause and Effect

The balance of student account deposits that related to excess financial aid (those amounts exceeding tuition), exceeded the total balance of student financial aid cash on hand. These funds were being temporarily used for operational purposes. Per the 2013-2014 Federal Student Aid Handbook, as the trustee of these funds, use of these funds outside of the intended purpose is not allowed.

Recommendation and Benefits

While these funds, which represent credit balances on the student accounts, were being properly issued to the student within the 14 day period as required by the Department of Education, the funds are not allowed to be used for any other purpose. Prudent policy would be to maintain these funds in a separate account until these credit refunds are issued to the students. This will allow the University to better monitor its operational cash position and ensure compliance with DOE regulations related to student financial aid.

Status

This is not a finding for the year ended July 31, 2015.

**CUMBERLAND PRESBYTERIAN
CHILDREN'S HOME**

FINANCIAL STATEMENTS
AND
AUDITORS' REPORT

DECEMBER 31, 2015

CUMBERLAND PRESBYTERIAN CHILDREN'S HOME

TABLE OF CONTENTS

	Page
Independent Auditors' Report	1
Statement of Financial Position	3
Statement of Activities	4
Statement of Cash Flows	5
Statement of Functional Expenses	6-7
Notes to the Financial Statements	8-14
Supplemental Information	
Schedule of Board of Stewardship Endowments	16-17

Members:
AMERICAN INSTITUTE OF
CERTIFIED PUBLIC
ACCOUNTANTS
TEXAS SOCIETY OF CERTIFIED
PUBLIC ACCOUNTANTS

HANKINS, EASTUP, DEATON, TONN & SEAY
A PROFESSIONAL CORPORATION
CERTIFIED PUBLIC ACCOUNTANTS

902 NORTH LOCUST
P.O. BOX 977
DENTON, TX 76202-0977

TEL. (940) 387-8563
FAX (940) 383-4746

Independent Auditors' Report

Cumberland Presbyterian Children's Home
Denton, Texas

We have audited the accompanying financial statements of Cumberland Presbyterian Children's Home (a nonprofit organization), which comprise the statement of financial position as of December 31, 2015 and the related statements of activities and cash flows for the year then ended, and the related notes to the financial statements.

Management's Responsibility for the Financial Statements

Management is responsible for the preparation and fair presentation of these financial statements in accordance with accounting principles generally accepted in the United States of America; this includes the design, implementation, and maintenance of internal control relevant to the preparation and fair presentation of financial statements that are free from material misstatement, whether due to fraud or error.

Auditor's Responsibility

Our responsibility is to express an opinion on these financial statements based on our audit. We conducted our audit in accordance with auditing standards generally accepted in the United States of America. Those standards require that we plan and perform the audit to obtain reasonable assurance about whether the financial statements are free of material misstatement.

An audit involves performing procedures to obtain audit evidence about the amounts and disclosures in the financial statements. The procedures selected depend on the auditor's judgment, including the assessment of the risks of material misstatement of the financial statements, whether due to fraud or error. In making those risk assessments, the auditor considers internal control relevant to the entity's preparation and fair presentation of the financial statements in order to design audit procedures that are appropriate in the circumstances, but not for the purpose of expressing an opinion on the effectiveness of the entity's internal control. Accordingly, we express no such opinion. An audit also includes evaluating the appropriateness of accounting policies used and the reasonableness of significant accounting estimates made by management, as well as evaluating the overall presentation of the financial statements. We believe that the audit evidence we have obtained is sufficient and appropriate to provide a basis for our audit opinion.

Opinion

In our opinion, the financial statements referred to above present fairly, in all material respects, the financial position of Cumberland Presbyterian Children's Home as of December 31, 2015, and the changes in its net assets and its cash flows for the year then ended in accordance with accounting principles generally accepted in the United States of America.

Hankins, Eastup, Deaton, Tonn & Seay

Hankins, Eastup, Deaton, Tonn & Seay
Denton, Texas
June 1, 2016

Page left blank intentionally

CUMBERLAND PRESBYTERIAN CHILDREN'S HOME

STATEMENT OF FINANCIAL POSITION
DECEMBER 31, 2015

ASSETS:

Cash and cash equivalents	$ 450,740
Due from Board of Stewardship	83,576
Other receivables	55,272
Prepaid expenses	1,211
Land, buildings and equipment, net	3,845,824
Other long-term investments	9,610,868
TOTAL ASSETS	**$14,047,491**

LIABILITIES AND NET ASSETS:

Liabilities:	
Accounts payable and accrued liabilities	$ 99,904
Total Liabilities	99,904
Net Assets:	
Unrestricted	6,433,575
Temporarily restricted	38,046
Permanently restricted	7,475,966
Total Net Assets	13,947,587
TOTAL LIABILITIES AND NET ASSETS	**$14,047,491**

See Accompanying Notes to the Financial Statements.

CUMBERLAND PRESBYTERIAN CHILDREN'S HOME

STATEMENT OF ACTIVITIES
FOR THE YEAR ENDED DECEMBER 31, 2015

	Unrestricted	Temporarily Restricted	Permanently Restricted	Total
Revenues, Gains and Other Support:				
Contributions and grants	$ 735,138	$ -	$ 413,042	$ 1,148,180
CPS revenue	524,813	-	-	524,813
Other program fees	99,401	-	-	99,401
Denominational support	77,614	-	-	77,614
Income on long-term investments	83,239	-	45,379	128,618
Oil and gas royalties	6,402	-	-	6,402
Special events	9,175	-	-	9,175
Rents	28,451	-	-	28,451
Other	200	-	-	200
Subtotal	1,564,433	-	458,421	2,022,854
Net assets released from Restrictions	352,478	(24,820)	(327,658)	-
Total Revenue, Gains and Other Support	1,916,911	(24,820)	130,763	2,022,854
Expenses and Losses:				
Expenses:				
Program services:				
Children's residential program	1,175,811	-	-	1,175,811
Emergency shelter program	835,681	-	-	835,681
Single parent family program	197,760	-	-	197,760
Cumberland family services	233,467	-	-	233,467
Management and general	187,823	-	-	187,823
Fundraising	165,900	-	-	165,900
Total Expenses	2,796,442	-	-	2,796,442
Losses:				
Unrealized losses on investments	79,379	215	114,864	194,458
Total Expenses and Losses	2,875,821	215	114,864	2,990,900
Change in net assets	(958,910)	(25,035)	15,899	(968,046)
Net assets at beginning of year	7,392,485	63,081	7,460,067	14,915,633
Net assets at end of year	$ 6,433,575	$ 38,046	$ 7,475,966	$13,947,587

See Accompanying Notes to the Financial Statements.

CUMBERLAND PRESBYTERIAN CHILDREN'S HOME

STATEMENT OF CASH FLOWS
FOR THE YEAR ENDED DECEMBER 31, 2015

Cash Flows from Operating Activities:	
Change in net assets	$ (968,046)
Adjustments to reconcile change in net assets to net cash provided by operating activities:	
Depreciation	211,043
(Increase) Decrease in receivables	(5,696)
(Increase) Decrease in prepaid expenses	12,535
Increase (Decrease) in accounts payable/accrued liabilities	(10,694)
Unrealized losses on investments	194,458
Contributions restricted for long-term investment	(413,042)
Net Cash Provided (Used) by Operating Activities	(979,442)
Cash Flows from Investing Activities:	
Purchase of fixed assets	(24,820)
Investment withdrawals	942,124
Net gains (losses) on investments	(194,458)
Net Cash Provided by Investing Activities	722,846
Cash Flows from Financing Activities:	
Proceeds from contributions restricted for investment in endowment	413,042
Net Cash Provided by Financing Activities	413,042
Net Increase in Cash and Cash Equivalents	156,446
Cash and Cash Equivalents at Beginning of Year	294,294
Cash and Cash Equivalents at End of Year	$ 450,740
Supplemental Data:	
Interest paid during the year	$ 1,009

See Accompanying Notes to the Financial Statements.

CUMBERLAND PRESBYTERIAN CHILDREN'S HOME

STATEMENT OF FUNCTIONAL EXPENSES
FOR THE YEAR ENDED DECEMBER 31, 2015

	Program Services			
	Children's Residential Program	Emergency Shelter Program	Single Parent Family Program	Cumberland Family Services
Salaries and Wages	$ 600,159	$ 453,779	$ 117,104	$ 131,742
Employee Benefits	89,280	67,504	17,420	19,599
Payroll Taxes	45,694	34,549	8,916	10,031
Total Salaries and Related Expenses	735,133	555,832	143,440	161,372
Activities and travel	35,631	15,616	1,793	1,199
Clothing and supplies	36,977	19,192	1,063	10,895
Food and dining out	79,924	39,851	1,261	255
Training and education	29,116	9,677	-	1,152
Medical and dental	3,514	2,317	-	-
Other program expenses	-	-	345	1,363
Utilities	61,301	46,350	11,961	13,456
Property, liability insurance	32,927	24,896	6,425	7,227
Repairs and maintenance	40,114	30,330	7,827	8,806
Supplies, postage, printing	12,908	9,760	2,519	2,833
Computer software, maintenance	6,601	4,991	1,288	1,449
Permits and fees	1,157	875	226	1,397
Special events expense	-	-	-	-
Vehicle expenses	5,050	3,819	986	1,109
General assembly	-	-	-	-
Professional fees	8,930	6,752	1,743	1,960
Public relations/communications	-	-	-	-
Investment management fees	-	-	-	-
Board expense	-	-	-	-
Interest	-	-	-	-
Total Expenses Before Depreciation	1,089,283	770,258	180,877	214,473
Depreciation	86,528	65,423	16,883	18,994
TOTAL EXPENSES	$ 1,175,811	$ 835,681	$ 197,760	$ 233,467

The accompanying notes are an integral part of this statement

	Supporting Services			
Total	Fundraising	Administration	Total	Total Expenses
$ 1,302,784	$ 73,190	$ 87,828	$ 161,018	$ 1,463,802
193,803	10,888	13,065	23,953	217,756
99,190	5,572	6,687	12,259	111,449
1,595,777	89,650	107,580	197,230	1,793,007
54,239	1,710	-	1,710	55,949
68,127	-	-	-	68,127
121,291	522	-	522	121,813
39,945	-	8,454	8,454	48,399
5,831	-	-	-	5,831
1,708	-	-	-	1,708
133,068	7,476	8,971	16,447	149,515
71,475	4,015	4,819	8,834	80,309
87,077	4,892	5,871	10,763	97,840
28,020	21,146	1,889	23,035	51,055
14,329	805	966	1,771	16,100
3,655	141	170	311	3,966
-	891	-	891	891
10,964	616	739	1,355	12,319
-	-	1,020	1,020	1,020
19,385	1,090	1,307	2,397	21,782
-	22,394	-	22,394	22,394
-	-	20,646	20,646	20,646
-	-	11,719	11,719	11,719
-	-	1,009	1,009	1,009
2,254,891	155,348	175,160	330,508	2,585,399
187,828	10,552	12,663	23,215	211,043
$ 2,442,719	$ 165,900	$ 187,823	$ 353,723	$ 2,796,442

CUMBERLAND PRESBYTERIAN CHILDREN'S HOME

NOTES TO FINANCIAL STATEMENTS
DECEMBER 31, 2015

NOTE A - SUMMARY OF SIGNIFICANT ACCOUNTING POLICIES

Organization

Cumberland Presbyterian Children's Home (CPCH) is a nonprofit organization originally chartered in Kentucky in 1904 and moved to Denton, Texas in 1932. Its purpose is to provide long-term residential basic child care for children between the ages of 3 and 17. CPCH is licensed to care for up to 40 children. CPCH's primary sources of revenue are income from child care, donations and income from long-term investments.

Basis of Presentation

The accompanying financial statements have been prepared on the accrual basis of accounting in accordance with accounting principles generally accepted in the United States of America. Net assets and revenues, expenses, gains, and losses are classified based on the existence or absence of donor-imposed restrictions. Accordingly, net assets of CPCH and changes therein are classified and reported as follows:

> Unrestricted Net Assets – not subject to donor-imposed restrictions. Unrestricted net assets may be designated for specific purposes by action of the Board of Directors.
>
> Temporarily Restricted Net Assets – subject to donor-imposed stipulations that may be fulfilled by actions of CPCH to meet the stipulations or that become unrestricted at the date specified by the donor.
>
> Permanently Restricted Net Assets – subject to donor-imposed stipulations that they be retained and invested permanently by CPCH to use all or part of the investment return on these net assets for specified or unspecified purposes.

Income Taxes

CPCH is exempt from Federal income taxes under Section 501(c)(3) of the Internal Revenue Code. In addition, CPCH has been determined by the Internal Revenue Service not to be a private foundation within the meaning of Section 509(a)(1) and 170 (b)(1)(A)(vi) of the Code.

Fixed Assets

All acquisitions of property and equipment in excess of $5,000 and all expenditures for repairs, maintenance, or improvements that significantly prolong the useful lives of the assets are capitalized. Prior to 1/1/13 CPCH used an acquisition cost threshold of $1,000 but increased the threshold to $5,000 at that date in order to reduce the administrative costs of recording and tracking items of furniture and equipment. Purchases of property and equipment are recorded at cost. Donations of property and equipment are recorded as support at their estimated fair value at the date of gift. Such donations are reported as unrestricted support unless the donor has restricted the donated asset to a specific purpose. Assets donated with explicit restrictions regarding their use and contributions of cash that must be used to acquire property and equipment are reported as restricted support. Absent donor stipulations regarding how long those donated assets must be maintained, CPCH reports expirations of donor restrictions when the donated or acquired assets are placed in service as instructed by the donor. CPCH reclassifies temporarily restricted net assets to unrestricted net assets at that time. Property and equipment are depreciated using the straight-line method over the estimated useful life of assets.

CUMBERLAND PRESBYTERIAN CHILDREN'S HOME

NOTES TO FINANCIAL STATEMENTS
DECEMBER 31, 2015

The class lives of the more significant items within each property classification are as follows:

Vehicles	5 years
Equipment	5 to 10 years
Furniture and fixtures	5 to 10 years
Buildings	20 to 40 years

Investment Securities

Investments in marketable securities with readily determinable fair values and all investments in debt securities are valued at their fair values in the statement of financial position. Unrealized gains and losses are included in the change in net assets.

Estimates

The preparation of financial statements in conformity with generally accepted accounting principles requires management to make estimates and assumptions that affect the reported amounts of assets and liabilities at the date of the financial statements and the reported amounts of revenues and expenses during the reporting period. Accordingly, actual results could differ from those estimates.

FASB 116 and 117

In accordance with Statement of Financial Accounting Standards ("SFAS") No. 116, *Accounting for Contributions Received and Contributions Made*, contributions received are recorded as unrestricted, temporarily restricted, or permanently restricted support depending on the existence and/or nature of donor restrictions. CPCH reports gifts of cash and other assets as restricted support if they are received with donor stipulations that limit the use of the donated assets. When a donor restriction expires, that is, when a stipulated time restriction ends or purpose restriction is accomplished, temporarily restricted net assets are reclassified to unrestricted net assets and reported in the statement of activities as net assets released from restrictions. Contributions that are restricted by the donor are reported as increases in unrestricted net assets if the restrictions expire in the fiscal year in which the contributions are recognized.

Unconditional promises to give are recorded as revenue when received. Unconditional promises to give that are due within one year are recorded at the face amount of the commitment. Unconditional promises to give that are due beyond one year are not reflected at the face amount of the commitment, but when material are discounted to a present value, or net realizable value, using a 3% discount rate. Unconditional promises to give that are determined to be uncollectible are written off as an expense at that time. At December 31, 2015, CPCH had no outstanding unconditional promises to give.

CPCH reports gifts of land, buildings, and equipment as unrestricted support unless explicit donor stipulations specify how the donated assets must be used. Gifts of long-lived assets with explicit restrictions that specify how the assets are to be used and gifts of cash or other assets that must be used to acquire long-lived assets are reported as restricted support. Absent explicit donor stipulations about how long those long-lived assets must be maintained, CPCH reports expirations of donor restrictions when the donated or acquired long-lived assets are placed in service.

CUMBERLAND PRESBYTERIAN CHILDREN'S HOME

NOTES TO FINANCIAL STATEMENTS
DECEMBER 31, 2015

Contributed Services and Materials

In addition to receiving cash contributions, CPCH occasionally receives in-kind contributions from various donors. It is the policy of CPCH to record the estimated fair market value of certain in-kind donations as an asset or expense in its financial statements, and similarly increase donations by a like amount.

A substantial number of volunteers have donated significant amounts of time to CPCH's programs and supporting services. Contributions of donated services that create or enhance non-financial assets or that require specialized skills, are provided by individuals possessing these skills, and would typically need to be purchased if not provided by donation, are recorded at their fair values in the period received. For the year ended December 31, 2015, there were no amounts recorded for contributed services and materials.

Cash and Cash Equivalents

For purposes of the statement of cash flows, CPCH considers all highly liquid investments with a maturity of three months or less to be cash equivalents.

NOTE B – INVESTMENTS

Investments in equity securities with readily determinable fair values and all investments in debt securities are measured at fair value. All non cash contributions are recorded at fair value at the date of receipt. Stock is recorded at the average of the high and low selling price on the date received. Investments sold are recorded at amount received on the trade date.

Investment income and realized gains and losses are reported as increases in unrestricted net assets unless the donor placed restrictions on the income's use. The change in fair value between years along with realized gains or losses are reflected in the statement of activities in the year of the change.

Some investments are held and managed by the Board of Stewardship, Finance and Benefits of the Cumberland Presbyterian Church, while other investments are held in an investment brokerage account in the name of CPCH, and are managed by investment managers of the brokerage firm. No single investment exceeds five percent of CPCH's net assets.

NOTE C – ENDOWMENTS

CPCH's endowments consist of 88 individual donor-restricted funds established by individual donors for a variety of purposes. Net assets associated with endowments are classified and reported based on the existence or absence of donor-imposed restrictions.

A reconciliation of the beginning and ending balances of endowment funds is as follows:

	Permanently Restricted
Balance, 12/31/14	$6,973,573
Contributions	49,644
Earnings	45,379
Investment losses	(49,468)
Distributions	(327,658)
Balance, 12/31/15	$6,691,470

CUMBERLAND PRESBYTERIAN CHILDREN'S HOME

NOTES TO FINANCIAL STATEMENTS
DECEMBER 31, 2015

Funds with Deficiencies

From time to time, the fair value of assets associated with individual donor restricted endowment funds may fall below the level that the donor requires CPCH to retain as a fund of perpetual duration. CPCH did not have any net deficiencies of this nature as of December 31, 2015.

Return Objectives and Risk Parameters

CPCH has adopted investment and spending policies for endowment assets that attempt to provide a predictable stream of funding to programs supported by its endowment while seeking to maintain the purchasing power of the endowment assets. Under this policy, as approved by the board of trustees, the endowment assets are invested in equity securities, fixed-income securities and short-term reserves with asset allocation within defined acceptable ranges, while assuming a moderate level of investment risk. CPCH expects its endowment funds, over time, to provide an average rate of return sufficient to provide operating funds as needed. Actual returns in any given year may vary from this amount.

Strategies Employed for Achieving Objectives

To satisfy its long-term rate-of-return objectives, CPCH relies on a total return strategy in which investment returns are achieved through both capital appreciation (realized and unrealized) and current yield (interest and dividends). CPCH targets a diversified asset allocation that places a greater emphasis on equity-based investments to achieve its long-term return objectives within prudent risk constraints.

Spending Policy and How the Investment Objectives Relate to Spending Policy

CPCH has no written spending policy that commits it to annual distributions from any of the endowment's fund balances. CPCH normally appropriates for distribution each year sufficient earnings needed to fund its operating budget. Accordingly, over the long term, CPCH expects the current spending policy to allow its endowment to continue to grow. This is consistent with CPCH's objective to maintain the purchasing power of the endowment assets held in perpetuity or for a specified term as well as to provide additional real growth through new gifts and investment return.

NOTE D – FAIR VALUE OF FINANCIAL INSTRUMENTS

CPCH's financial instruments, none of which are held for trading purposes, include cash, securities and receivables. CPCH has estimated fair value of financial instruments in accordance with requirements of SFAS No. 157. The estimated fair value amounts have been determined by CPCH, using available market information and appropriate valuation methodologies. However, considerable judgment is necessarily required in interpreting market data to develop the estimates of fair value. Accordingly, the estimates presented herein are not necessarily indicative of the amounts that CPCH could realize in a current market exchange. The use of different market assumptions and estimation methodologies may have a material effect on the estimated fair value amounts. The carrying amount of cash and cash equivalents, and receivables approximated fair market value at December 31, 2015 because of their relatively short maturity and market terms. The fair value of long term investments at December 31, 2015 is determined based on quoted market values for U.S. government securities, fixed income securities and equity securities.

CUMBERLAND PRESBYTERIAN CHILDREN'S HOME

NOTES TO FINANCIAL STATEMENTS
DECEMBER 31, 2015

NOTE D – FAIR VALUE OF FINANCIAL INSTRUMENTS (CONT'D)

Financial instruments are considered Level 1 when their values are determined using quoted prices in active markets for identical assets that the reporting entity has the ability to access at the measurement date. Level 2 inputs are inputs other than quoted prices included within Level 1, such as quoted prices for similar assets in active or inactive markets, inputs other than quoted prices that are observable for the asset, or inputs that are derived principally from or corroborated by observable market data by correlation or other means.

Financial instruments are considered Level 3 when their values are determined using pricing models, discounted cash flow methodologies or similar techniques and at least one significant model assumption or input is unobservable. Level 3 financial instruments also include those for which the determination of fair value requires significant management judgment or estimation.

In accordance with these definitions, the following table represents CPCH's fair value hierarchy for its investments measured at fair value as of December 31, 2015:

	Quoted Prices for Active Markets for Identical Assets (Level 1)	Significant Other Observable Inputs (Level 2)	Total
Equity securities	$8,463,767	$ -	$8,463,767
Fixed income securities	-	1,147,101	1,147,101
Total	$8,463,767	$1,147,101	$9,610,868

The estimated fair value of investments was determined by CPCH in accordance with its investment policy. Estimated fair value is determined by CPCH based on a number of factors, including: comparable publicly traded securities, the costs of investments to CPCH, as well as the current and projected operating performance. Changes in unrealized appreciation or depreciation of the investments are recognized as unrealized gains and losses in the statement of activities. Because of the inherent uncertainty of these valuations, the estimated values may differ from the actual fair values that may or may not be ultimately realized.

NOTE E - LAND, BUILDINGS AND EQUIPMENT

Land, buildings and equipment at December 31, 2015 consist of the following:

	Cost	Accumulated Depreciation	Book Value
Land	$ 23,477		$ 23,477
Construction in progress	24,820		24,820
Buildings	5,774,167	$2,430,809	3,343,358
Campus infrastructure	583,513	232,383	351,130
Furniture & equipment	346,640	308,382	38,258
Vehicles	171,761	106,980	64,781
Total	$6,924,378	$3,078,554	$3,845,824

CUMBERLAND PRESBYTERIAN CHILDREN'S HOME

NOTES TO FINANCIAL STATEMENTS
DECEMBER 31, 2015

NOTE F - TEMPORARILY RESTRICTED NET ASSETS

Temporarily restricted net assets are available for the following purposes or periods:

Lena Hart Educational Fund	$ 3,525
Humphrey Scholarship Endowment	734
Walker Trimble Scholarship Fund	1,388
David Long Memorial Fund	197
Sybil V. Cockerham College Fund	1,034
Eleanor Sargeant Endowment	359
Medical clinic	11,180
For periods after December 31, 2015 - term endowment to be received in a future year – Naomi Locke Trust	19,629
Total	$ 38,046

NOTE G - OTHER LONG-TERM INVESTMENTS

	Total	Unrestricted	Temporarily Restricted	Permanently Restricted
Endowments held by the Board of Stewardship	$ 6,634,702	$ -	$ -	$6,634,702
Mutual funds held by First National Bank – Virginia Ekiss Trust	354,877	-	-	354,877
Mutual funds held by Regions Bank – Laura Harpole Trust	102,660	-	-	102,660
Mutual funds held by Fairfield Natl. Bank - Naomi Locke Trust	19,629	-	19,629	-
Funds held at J P Morgan:				
Lena Hart Educational Fund	6,025	-	3,525	2,500
Humphrey Scholarship Endowment	4,215	-	734	3,481
Walker Trimble Scholarship Fund	9,668	-	1,388	8,280
David Long Memorial Fund	1,197	-	197	1,000
Sibyl V. Cockerham College Fund	3,034	-	1,034	2,000
Eleanor Sargeant Endowment	2,939	-	359	2,580
Operating Reserve	2,160,122	2,148,942	11,180	-
4,000 shares Exxon-Mobil held by CPCH - Jessie DiCarlo Endowment	311,800	-	-	311,800
Total	$9,610,868	$2,148,942	$ 38,046	$7,423,880

CUMBERLAND PRESBYTERIAN CHILDREN'S HOME

NOTES TO FINANCIAL STATEMENTS
DECEMBER 31, 2015

NOTE H - PERMANENTLY RESTRICTED NET ASSETS

Permanently restricted net assets are restricted as follows:

Investments in perpetuity, the income from which is expendable to support any activities of CPCH	$7,475,966
Total	$7,475,966

NOTE I – SUBSEQUENT EVENTS

Management evaluates subsequent events through the date of the report, which is the date the financial statements were available to be issued.

NOTE J – COMPONENTS OF INVESTMENT RETURN

Investment return for the year ended December 31, 2015, including interest and dividends on investments and interest earned on cash balances is summarized as follows:

Unrestricted investment return:	
Interest and dividend income:	
JP Morgan investments	$ 65,145
Exxon Mobil stock investment	11,520
Other	6,574
Unrealized losses on investments	(79,379)
Total unrestricted investment return	3,860
Restricted investment return:	
Interest income:	
Board of Stewardship investments	45,379
Unrealized losses on investments	(115,079)
Total restricted investment return (loss)	(69,700)
Total Investment Return (Loss)	$ (65,840)

NOTE K – BANK LINE OF CREDIT

From time to time CPCH draws on a $200,000 line of credit established at Northstar Bank of Texas for working capital purposes. A total of $375,000 was borrowed and repaid on the line of credit during 2015, with no balance owed at the end of the year. Total interest paid during 2015 on the line of credit was $1,009.

SUPPLEMENTAL SCHEDULE

CUMBERLAND PRESBYTERIAN CHILDREN'S HOME

SCHEDULE OF BOARD OF STEWARDSHIP ENDOWMENTS
DECEMBER 31, 2015

Donor-established Endowments:

	Balance
Merlyn & Joann Kitterman Alexander	$ 1,395
W.A. and Elizabeth Bearden Trust	15,887
Grace Johnson Beasley Memorial Endowment	36,989
Bethlehem CPC Memorial Endowment	6,046
Bridges Scholarship Fund	41,320
J.T. and Dorothy Britt Trust	11,186
Children's Home Endowment	322,682
Lavenia Campbell Cole Trust 20%	20,347
Lavenia Campbell Cole Annuity Endowment	82,634
Lavenia Cole Testamentary Trust 25%	612,119
Mrs. A.L. Colvin Memorial Fund	1,055
John W. and Eva Cox Trust Fund	30,970
Steve Curry Trust	543,641
Daniel Class, First Cumberland Presbyterian Church	31,984
Donnie Curry Davis Memorial	187,161
Mary Elberta Davis Memorial	19,971
Fred and Mattie Mae Dwiggins Memorial Trust	80,188
J.S. Eustis Memorial Trust Fund	12,660
Clester H. Evans, Sr., Trust	21,136
John M. Friedel Trust	21,863
Joyce C. Frisby Memorial Endowment	28,117
Vaughn and Mary Elizabeth Fults Trust	20,167
Garner-Miller Memorial Trust	12,442
James C. and Freda M. Gilbert Endowment	113,804
Henry and Jayne Glaspy Memorial Fund	8,254
Rev. W.J. Gregory Memorial	103,738
Glenn Griffin Endowment	44,225
Rev. and Mrs. Henry M. Guynn Memorial	4,595
Chad Harper Endowment	11,618
Newsome and Imogene Harvey Endowment	2,537
Clarence & Lula Herring Endowment	6,038
Kenneth and Clara Holsopple Trust	53,454
George and Lottie M. Hutchins Trust	1,136,844
Norma K. Johnson Memorial Library	11,409
P.F. Johnson Memorial Endowment	18,939
Robert and Genevie Johnson Endowment	4,805
Mr. and Mrs. Robert L. Johnson	11,934
Violet Louise Jolly Endowment	1,205
Eulava Joyce Memorial Trust	9,958
Ruth Cypert and Harlie Klugler Memorial Fund	20,053
Blanche R. Lake Endowment	14,452
Wade P. Lane/Maude Dorough Memorial Trust	9,512
Adolphus M. Latta Memorial Trust	51,324
Mr. and Mrs. Robert F. Little Endowment Fund	35,505
Charles E. and Addie Mae Lloyd Endowment Fund	22,607
Tony and Ann Martin Endowment	2,509
Mrs. Lucille (Lucy) Mast Endowment	2,551

CUMBERLAND PRESBYTERIAN CHILDREN'S HOME

SCHEDULE OF BOARD OF STEWARDSHIP ENDOWMENTS (CONT'D)
DECEMBER 31, 2015

Donor-established Endowments:

	Balance
W.B. and Azales McClurkan, Sr. Memorial	$ 19,328
Williams J. McCall Memorial Trust	9,958
McEwen Church Trust	7,650
McKinley and Barnett Families Endowment	821,799
J.C. McKinley Endowment	18,856
Velma McKinley Trust	18,856
Mary McKnight Memorial Trust	10,617
Kenneth and Mae Moore Endowment Fund	7,041
Operational Trust Fund	148,143
Bert and Pat Owen Endowment	1,566
Hamilton & Merion Parks Family Trust #3	16,147
Joe Parr Trust Fund	78,285
Martha Sue Parr Endowment	1,598
Mary M. Poole Endowment Fund	957,754
Jack and Mary Proctor Memorial Trust Fund	63,859
SQ&K Maurine Proctor Trust	5,656
Mary Acena Prewitt Trust Fund	90,277
Rev. and Mrs. Joe Reed Memorial	2,867
Marguerite D. Richards Endowment	25,433
Agnes Durbin Richardson Trust	30,169
Pat N. & Essie H. Roberts Memorial	58,885
Frances Benefield Roberts Trust Fund	2,332
Rev. and Mrs. John A. Russell Memorial	4,554
John Ann and Mary Shimer	14,990
Rev. W.B. and Lydia Snipes Memorial Trust	19,865
Don M. & Nancy Tabor Endowment Trust	34,438
Townsend Trust Fund	38,432
Hattie A. Wheeless Fund	19,770
Whitfield Family Endowment	12,031
Porter and Hattie S. Williamson Memorial Trust	171,481
Helen Wynn Endowment Fund	11,013
Maxie and Will Young Memorial Endowment	20,757
Dixie Campbell Zinn Memorial Trust	6,240
Dr. John P. Austin Endowment	20,225
Total	$ 6,634,702

**Memphis Theological Seminary
of the Cumberland Presbyterian Church
Financial Statements
July 31, 2015 and 2014**

MEMPHIS THEOLOGICAL SEMINARY OF THE CUMBERLAND PRESBYTERIAN CHURCH

Table of Contents *July 31, 2015 and 2014*

Page

Independent Auditor's Report 3

Financial Statements

    Statements of Financial Position 5

    Statement of Activities 6

    Statement of Functional Expenses 7

    Statements of Cash Flows 8

    Notes to the Financial Statements 9

Supplementary Information

    Schedule of Expenditures of Federal Awards 20

Non-Financial Section

    Independent Auditor's Report on Internal Control over Financial Reporting and on Compliance and Other Matters Based on an Audit of Financial Statements Performed in Accordance with *Government Auditing Standards* 22

    Independent Auditor's Report on Compliance for a Major Program and on Internal Control over Compliance Required by OMB Circular A-133 24

    Schedule of Findings and Questioned Costs 26

    Schedule of Prior Year Findings and Questioned Costs 27

INDEPENDENT AUDITOR'S REPORT

To the Board of Trustees
Memphis Theological Seminary of the Cumberland Presbyterian Church
Memphis, Tennessee

Report on the Financial Statements

We have audited the accompanying financial statements of Memphis Theological Seminary of the Cumberland Presbyterian Church (a nonprofit organization), which comprise the statement of financial position as of July 31, 2015, and the related statements of activities, functional expenses, and cash flows for the year then ended, and the related notes to the financial statements.

Management's Responsibility for the Financial Statements

Management is responsible for the preparation and fair presentation of these financial statements in accordance with accounting principles generally accepted in the United States of America; this includes the design, implementation, and maintenance of internal control relevant to the preparation and fair presentation of financial statements that are free from material misstatement, whether due to fraud or error.

Auditor's Responsibility

Our responsibility is to express an opinion on these financial statements based on our audit. We conducted our audit in accordance with auditing standards generally accepted in the United States of America and the standards applicable to financial audits contained in *Government Auditing Standards*, issued by the Comptroller General of the United States. Those standards require that we plan and perform the audit to obtain reasonable assurance about whether the financial statements are free from material misstatement.

An audit involves performing procedures to obtain audit evidence about the amounts and disclosures in the financial statements. The procedures selected depend on the auditor's judgment, including the assessment of the risks of material misstatement of the financial statements, whether due to fraud or error. In making those risk assessments, the auditor considers internal control relevant to the entity's preparation and fair presentation of the financial statements in order to design audit procedures that are appropriate in the circumstances, but not for the purpose of expressing an opinion on the effectiveness of the entity's internal control. Accordingly, we express no such opinion. An audit also includes evaluating the appropriateness of accounting policies used and the reasonableness of significant accounting estimates made by management, as well as evaluating the overall presentation of the financial statements.

We believe that the audit evidence we have obtained is sufficient and appropriate to provide a basis for our audit opinion.

Opinion

In our opinion, the financial statements referred to above present fairly, in all material respects, the financial position of Memphis Theological Seminary of the Cumberland Presbyterian Church as of July 31, 2015, and the changes in its net assets and its cash flows for the year then ended in accordance with accounting principles generally accepted in the United States of America.

CANNON WRIGHT BLOUNT PLLC   756 RIDGE LAKE BLVD   MEMPHIS TN 38120

PHONE 901.685.7500   FAX 901.685.7569   WWW.CANNONWRIGHTBLOUNT.COM

Other Matters

Our audit was conducted for the purpose of forming an opinion on the financial statements as a whole. The accompanying schedule of expenditures of federal awards, as required by Office of Management and Budget Circular A-133, *Audits of States, Local Governments, and Non-Profit Organizations*, is presented for purposes of additional analysis and is not a required part of the financial statements. Such information is the responsibility of management and was derived from and relates directly to the underlying accounting and other records used to prepare the financial statements. The information has been subjected to the auditing procedures applied in the audit of the financial statements and certain additional procedures, including comparing and reconciling such information directly to the underlying accounting and other records used to prepare the financial statements or to the financial statements themselves, and other additional procedures in accordance with auditing standards generally accepted in the United States of America. In our opinion, the information is fairly stated, in all material respects, in relation to the financial statements as a whole.

Other Reporting Required by *Government Auditing Standards*

In accordance with *Government Auditing Standards*, we have also issued our report dated November 20, 2015, on our consideration of Memphis Theological Seminary of the Cumberland Presbyterian Church's internal control over financial reporting and on our tests of its compliance with certain provisions of laws, regulations, contracts, and grant agreements and other matters. The purpose of that report is to describe the scope of our testing of internal control over financial reporting and compliance and the results of that testing, and not to provide an opinion on internal control over financial reporting or on compliance. That report is an integral part of an audit performed in accordance with *Government Auditing Standards* in considering Memphis Theological Seminary of the Cumberland Presbyterian Church's internal control over financial reporting and compliance.

Report on Summarized Comparative Information

We have previously audited the Memphis Theological Seminary of the Cumberland Presbyterian Church's 2014 financial statements, and we expressed an unmodified audit opinion on those audited financial statements in our report dated December 10, 2014. In our opinion, the summarized comparative information presented herein as of and for the year ended July 31, 2014, is consistent, in all material respects, with the audited financial statements from which it has been derived.

Cannon Wright Blount PLLC

Memphis, Tennessee
November 20, 2015

MEMPHIS THEOLOGICAL SEMINARY OF THE CUMBERLAND PRESBYTERIAN CHURCH

Statements of Financial Position — *July 31, 2015 and 2014*

ASSETS

	2015	2014
Cash and cash equivalents	$ 366,270	$ 472,063
Cash and cash equivalents, temporarily restricted (Note 3)	239,082	145,152
Total cash and cash equivalents	605,352	617,215
Investments, at fair value (Notes 3, and 4)		
Unrestricted	1,861,141	1,668,078
Temporarily restricted	2,096,696	2,080,907
Permanently restricted	6,461,705	6,252,462
Total investments	10,419,542	10,001,447
Tuition and fees receivable, net of allowance of $274,323 in 2015 and $249,147 in 2014 (Note 3)	155,851	176,117
Pledges receivable, net of discounts on pledges (Note 7)	800,740	781,776
Other receivables (Note 11)	103,298	8,366
Capital assets, net of accumulated depreciation (Note 5)	3,219,212	3,311,228
Cash value of life insurance	36,972	40,280
Land held for sale (Note 3)	27,448	27,448
Other assets	78,211	31,858
Total assets	$ 15,446,626	$ 14,995,735

LIABILITIES AND NET ASSETS

	2015	2014
Liabilities		
Accounts payable and accrued expenses	$ 286,106	$ 291,254
Prepaid revenue	123,667	129,688
Line of credit (Note 8)	170,000	270,000
Notes payable (Note 9)	1,515,251	1,607,493
Total liabilities	2,095,024	2,298,435
Net Assets		
Unrestricted		
Board designated	79,437	82,263
Other unrestricted	3,391,099	3,322,418
Temporarily restricted (Note 12)	3,419,361	3,040,157
Permanently restricted	6,461,705	6,252,462
Total net assets	13,351,602	12,697,300
Total liabilities and net assets	$ 15,446,626	$ 14,995,735

See independent auditor's report and notes to the financial statements

MEMPHIS THEOLOGICAL SEMINARY OF THE CUMBERLAND PRESBYTERIAN CHURCH

Statement of Activities

For the Year Ended July 31, 2015
(with summarized comparative totals for the year ended July 31, 2014)

	Unrestricted	Temporarily Restricted	Permanently Restricted	2015 Total	2014 Total
Operating Revenues and Support					
Tuition and fees, net of scholarships of $460,331 and $439,462	$ 2,150,542	$ -	$ -	$ 2,150,542	$ 2,167,591
Contributions and grants	1,006,776	1,013,229	197,887	2,217,892	2,116,182
Other revenue and support	208,869	-	-	208,869	219,443
Net assets released from restrictions	793,505	(793,505)	-	-	-
Total operating revenues and support	4,159,692	219,724	197,887	4,577,303	4,503,216
Expenses					
Educational program services					
Instruction	1,752,064	-	-	1,752,064	1,764,092
Library	232,297	-	-	232,297	227,686
Student services	272,384	-	-	272,384	253,633
Financial leadership for ministry	93,390	-	-	93,390	33,128
Program for alternative studies	144,785	-	-	144,785	144,251
Academic support	136,663	-	-	136,663	137,365
Supporting services					
Institutional support	975,553	-	-	975,553	876,234
Development and fundraising	658,437	-	-	658,437	813,256
Total expenses	4,265,573	-	-	4,265,573	4,249,645
Increase (decrease) in net assets from operations	(105,881)	219,724	197,887	311,730	253,571
Non-operating revenues and expenses					
Investment income (loss) (Note 4)	171,736	159,480	11,356	342,572	1,103,211
Change in net assets	65,855	379,204	209,243	654,302	1,356,782
Net assets, beginning of year	3,404,681	3,040,157	6,252,462	12,697,300	11,340,518
Net assets - end of year	$ 3,470,536	$ 3,419,361	$ 6,461,705	$ 13,351,602	$ 12,697,300

See independent auditor's report and notes to the financial statements

MEMPHIS THEOLOGICAL SEMINARY OF THE CUMBERLAND PRESBYTERIAN CHURCH

Statement of Functional Expenses

For the Year Ended July 31, 2015
(with summarized comparative totals for the year ended July 31, 2014)

	Instruction	Library	Educational Program Services - Student Services	Financial Leadership for Ministry	Program for Alternative Studies	Academic Support	Facilities Operations	Security Services	Institutional Support	Development and Fund Raising	2015 Total	2014 Total
Salaries and Wages	$1,115,117	$116,129	$158,564	$56,526	$72,779	$90,140	$145,944	$ -	$504,480	$214,044	$2,473,723	$2,310,208
Benefits	160,551	32,907	31,630	2,322	12,363	14,033	31,163	-	101,354	42,811	429,134	400,991
Professional Development	10,759	-	1,814	95	-	57	485	-	1,463	848	15,521	15,949
Travel/Auto Expense	682	453	3,357	2,389	4,819	894	3,870	-	5,740	1,481	23,685	33,867
Office Supplies and Expense	12,126	42,325	10,870	2,098	1,413	1,575	4,716	-	47,668	25,249	148,040	167,089
Consultants / Professional	6,000	-	-	-	-	-	-	58,436	60,208	3,890	133,188	138,797
Special Events	27,855	-	8,994	4,654	28,579	-	-	-	29,949	37,871	133,248	165,787
Student / Covenant Groups	44,913	-	-	-	-	-	-	-	-	-	44,913	49,263
Repairs and Maintenance	165	1,218	-	-	-	-	73,247	-	75	-	74,705	54,184
Utilities	-	-	-	-	-	-	78,981	-	-	-	78,981	86,816
Insurance Expense	-	-	-	-	-	-	99,954	-	-	-	99,954	95,634
Property Taxes	-	-	-	-	-	-	20,368	-	-	-	20,368	24,518
Other Expense	4,393	785	4,613	6,576	716	95	(1,194)	-	57,452	8,745	82,181	86,739
Interest Expense	-	-	-	-	-	-	71,411	-	-	-	71,411	93,310
Capital Campaign Expense	-	-	-	-	-	-	-	-	-	252,573	252,573	289,482
Depreciation	-	-	-	-	-	-	183,948	-	-	-	183,948	237,011
Allocation of Facilities Operations & Security	369,503	38,480	52,542	18,730	24,116	29,869	(712,893)	(58,436)	167,164	70,925	-	-
	$1,752,064	$232,297	$272,384	$93,390	$144,785	$136,663	$ -	$ -	$975,553	$658,437	$4,265,573	$4,249,645

See independent auditor's report and notes to the financial statements

MEMPHIS THEOLOGICAL SEMINARY OF THE CUMBERLAND PRESBYTERIAN CHURCH

Statements of Cash Flows — *For the Years Ended July 31, 2015 and 2014*

	2015	2014
Cash Flows from Operating Activities		
Change in net assets	$ 654,302	$ 1,356,782
Adjustments to reconcile change in net assets to net cash provided by (used in) operating activities:		
Depreciation	183,948	237,011
Capital (gains) losses on investments	(271,823)	(992,656)
Bad debt expense	25,656	19,648
Discount on pledges	(12,867)	63,224
Changes in operating assets and liabilities:		
(Increase) decrease in assets		
Tuition, fees and other receivables	(100,322)	18,227
Pledges receivable	(6,097)	(785,000)
Other assets	(46,353)	113,445
Increase (decrease) in liabilities		
Accounts payable and accrued expenses	(5,148)	9,602
Prepaid revenue	(6,021)	(75,231)
Net cash provided by (used for) operating activities	415,275	(34,948)
Cash Flows from Investing Activities		
Withdrawals from investments	30,499	170,376
Investments of endowment gifts	(448,989)	(270,594)
Net earnings on investments-(reinvested)/distributed	272,218	240,112
(Increase) decrease in value of land held for sale	-	(838)
Sale of property held for sale	-	55,241
(Increase) decrease in cash surrender value of life insurance	3,308	(1,572)
Sale of property	-	147,323
Purchases of property and equipment	(91,932)	(144,793)
Net cash flows from (used for) investing activities	(234,896)	195,255
Cash Flows from Financing Activities		
Increase (decrease) in line of credit	(100,000)	195,000
Principal payments on long term debt	(92,242)	(791,869)
Net cash flows from (used for) financing activities	(192,242)	(596,869)
Net increase (decrease) in cash and cash equivalents	(11,863)	(436,562)
Cash and cash equivalents, beginning of year	617,215	1,053,777
Cash and cash equivalents, end of year	$ 605,352	$ 617,215
Supplemental Disclosure:		
Interest paid during the year	$ 77,092	$ 104,106

See independent auditor's report and notes to the consolidated financial statements

MEMPHIS THEOLOGICAL SEMINARY OF THE CUMBERLAND PRESBYTERIAN CHURCH
Notes to the Financial Statements *July 31, 2015 and 2014*

Note 1 – Organization and Purpose

The Memphis Theological Seminary of the Cumberland Presbyterian Church (the "Seminary") is an ecumenical Protestant seminary serving the mid-south region from its campus in Memphis, Tennessee. Memphis Theological Seminary of the Cumberland Presbyterian Church provides postgraduate theological education to clergy and church leaders of the parent denomination and qualified students from other denominations. Memphis Theological Seminary of the Cumberland Presbyterian Church is governed by a Board of Trustees elected by the General Assembly of the Cumberland Presbyterian Church.

Note 2 – Significant Accounting Policies

Financial Statement Presentation

Memphis Theological Seminary of the Cumberland Presbyterian Church prepares its financial statements in accordance with accounting principles generally accepted in the United States of America, which involves the application of accrual accounting. Under generally accepted accounting principles, Memphis Theological Seminary of the Cumberland Presbyterian Church reports information regarding its financial position and activities according to three classes of net assets as follows:

> Unrestricted Net Assets — Net assets that are not subject to donor-imposed stipulations. Unrestricted net assets may be designated for specific purposes by action of the Board of Trustees or may otherwise be limited by contractual agreements with outside parties.
>
> Temporarily Restricted Net Assets — Net assets whose use by the Seminary is subject to donor-imposed stipulations that can be fulfilled by actions of the Seminary pursuant to those stipulations or that expire by the passage of time.
>
> Permanently Restricted Net Assets — Net assets subject to donor-imposed stipulations that they be maintained permanently by the Seminary. Generally, the donors of these assets permit the Seminary to use all or part of the investment return on these assets.

Contributions

Contributions received by Memphis Theological Seminary of the Cumberland Presbyterian Church are recorded as unrestricted, temporarily restricted, or permanently restricted support depending on the existence and/or nature of any donor restrictions. Temporarily restricted net assets are reclassified to unrestricted net assets upon satisfaction of the time or purpose restrictions.

Investment Valuation and Income Recognition

Investments are reported at fair value. Fair value is the price that would be received to sell an asset or paid to transfer a liability in an orderly transaction between market participants at the measurement date. See Notes 3 and 4 for discussion and computation of fair value.

Unrealized holding gains and losses are included in current year revenue and support as a component of investment income. Realized gains and losses are computed using the specific identification method.

Capital Assets

All acquisitions of property and equipment and expenditures for repairs and maintenance that prolong the useful lives of assets in excess of $1,000 are capitalized at cost. Expenditures for normal repair and maintenance are expensed to operations as they occur. Depreciation is provided through the straight-line method over the assets' estimated useful lives which range from three to ten years for equipment, fifteen years for library books and twenty-five to forty years for buildings.

MEMPHIS THEOLOGICAL SEMINARY OF THE CUMBERLAND PRESBYTERIAN CHURCH
Notes to the Financial Statements *July 31, 2015 and 2014*

Note 2 – Significant Accounting Policies (continued)

Cash Equivalents

Cash equivalents are defined as short term, highly liquid investments that are both readily convertible to known amounts of cash and are so near maturity that they present insignificant risk of changes in value because of changes in interest rates.

Use of Estimates in the Preparation of Financial Statements

The preparation of financial statements in conformity with generally accepted accounting principles requires management to make estimates and assumptions that affect the amounts reported in the financial statements and accompanying notes. Actual results could differ from those estimates.

Income Taxes

Memphis Theological Seminary of the Cumberland Presbyterian Church is a not-for-profit organization that is exempt from income taxes under Internal Revenue Code Section 501(c)(3) and is also exempt from state income taxes. The Seminary is generally no longer subject to federal and state audit for tax years prior to the year ended July 31, 2012.

Donated Property, Equipment and Services

Donations of property and use of property are recorded as support at their estimated fair value at the date of donation. Such donations are reported as unrestricted support unless the donor has restricted the donated asset to a specific purpose. The value of donated property was $0 in 2015 and 2014.

Donated services are recognized as contributions if the services (a) create or enhance non-financial assets or (b) require specialized skills, are performed by people with those skills, and would otherwise be purchased by the Organization. There were no contributed services recorded for accounting and consulting in 2015 and 2014.

Functional Allocation of Expenses

The cost of providing the various educational programs and supporting services has been summarized on a functional basis in the statement of functional expenses. Accordingly, certain costs have been allocated among the programs and services benefited.

Reclassification of Prior Year Amounts

Certain amounts in the July 31, 2014, financial statements have been reclassified to conform to the July 31, 2015, presentation.

Subsequent Events

Memphis Theological Seminary of the Cumberland Presbyterian Church evaluated all events or transactions that occurred through November 20, 2015, the date Memphis Theological Seminary of the Cumberland Presbyterian Church approved these financial statements for issuance.

MEMPHIS THEOLOGICAL SEMINARY OF THE CUMBERLAND PRESBYTERIAN CHURCH

Notes to the Financial Statements *July 31, 2015 and 2014*

Note 3 – Fair Value Measurement

The FASB ASC Subtopic 820-10 *Fair Value Measurements,* (formerly SFAS No. 157), defines fair value as the exchange price that would be received for an asset or paid to transfer a liability in the principal or most advantageous market for the asset or liability in an orderly transaction between market participants at the measurement date. SFAS No. 157 established a three-level fair value hierarchy that prioritizes the inputs used to measure fair value. This hierarchy requires entities to maximize the use of observable inputs and minimize the use of unobservable inputs.

The three levels of inputs used to measure fair value are as follows:

- Level 1 – Quoted prices in active markets for identical assets or liabilities.
- Level 2 – Observable inputs other than quoted prices included in Level 1, such as quoted prices for similar assets and liabilities in active markets; quoted prices for identical or similar assets or liabilities in markets that are not active; or inputs that are observable or can be corroborated by observable market data.
- Level 3 – Unobservable inputs that are supported by little or no market activity and that are significant to the fair value of the assets or liabilities. This includes certain pricing models, discounted cash flow methodologies and similar techniques that use significant unobservable inputs.

The estimated fair value of Memphis Theological Seminary of the Cumberland Presbyterian Church's financial instruments has been determined by management using available market information. However, considerable judgment is required in interpreting market data to develop the estimates of fair value. Accordingly, the fair values are not necessarily indicative of the amounts that Memphis Theological Seminary of the Cumberland Presbyterian Church could realize in a current market exchange. The use of different market assumptions may have a material effect on the estimated fair value amounts.

The carrying amounts of cash and cash equivalents, net receivables, cash value of life insurance, payables, accrued liabilities, and debt are a reasonable estimate of their fair value, due to their short term nature, method of computation and interest rates for current debt.

All financial assets that are measured at fair value on a recurring basis (at least annually) have been segregated into the most appropriate level within the fair value hierarchy based on the inputs used to determine the fair value at the measurement date.

MEMPHIS THEOLOGICAL SEMINARY OF THE CUMBERLAND PRESBYTERIAN CHURCH

Notes to the Financial Statements   *July 31, 2015 and 2014*

Note 3 – Fair Value Measurement (continued)

Accounts subjected to the fair values measurement process consist of the following at July 31, 2015:

	Total Fair Value	Quoted Prices in Active Markets for Identical Assets (Level 1)	Significant Other Observable Inputs (Level 2)	Unobservable Inputs (Level 3)
Investment securities				
Cash/Cash Equivalents	$ 446,350	$ 446,350	$ -	$ -
Money market funds	4,274	4,274	-	-
Bonds and bond funds	1,449,162	10,971	1,438,191	-
Common and preferred stocks	136,617	136,617	-	-
Real estate investment funds	736,910	-	736,910	-
Mutual funds	409,957	409,957	-	-
Private Investment entities	7,236,272	-	-	7,236,272
Total investments	$ 10,419,542	$ 1,008,169	$ 2,175,101	$ 7,236,272
Land held for sale	$ 27,448	$ -	$ -	$ 27,448

The private investment entities are investments entered into by the Board of Stewardship to achieve greater rates of return. They include funds whose inputs used to determine fair value are considered unobservable and are therefore Level 3 inputs.

The carrying value of the above land held for sale is based on expected recoverability at the time of sale. Memphis Theological Seminary of the Cumberland Presbyterian Church uses appraised values and other information available to determine the carrying value. The inputs used to determine fair value are considered unobservable and are therefore Level 3 inputs.

MEMPHIS THEOLOGICAL SEMINARY OF THE CUMBERLAND PRESBYTERIAN CHURCH
Notes to the Financial Statements *July 31, 2015 and 2014*

Note 3 – Fair Value Measurement (continued)

Transactions in Level 3 assets for the years ended July 31, 2015 and 2014, were as follows:

	2015	2014
Private investment entities		
Beginning balance	$ 6,967,450	$ 4,289,352
Change in allocation of investments	(168,572)	380,821
Reinvestments	37,735	465,003
Realized/unrealized gains (losses)	399,659	1,832,274
Ending balance	$ 7,236,272	$ 6,967,450
Land held for sale		
Beginning balance	$ 27,448	$ 81,851
Improvements to land previously received	-	838
Sale of Thor Road property	-	(55,241)
Ending balance	$ 27,448	$ 27,448

Investments income (loss) was as follows for the years ended July 31, 2015 and 2014:

	2015	2014
Investment income	$ 70,750	$ 110,933
Realized investment gains (losses)	35,462	(378)
Unrealized investment gains (losses)	236,360	992,656
Net investment income (loss)	$ 342,572	$ 1,103,211

Note 4 – Endowments

Nearly all of Memphis Theological Seminary of the Cumberland Presbyterian Church's investments, which contain endowments, are managed by the Board of Stewardship, Foundation and Benefits of the Cumberland Presbyterian Church, Inc., and maintained in pooled investment accounts with other funds. The investments generally originate from gifts and contributions for which separate identifiable investment accounts are created that indicate the source of the funds and/or the purpose for which the funds are to be used. Many of these accounts are designated for monthly distributions to Memphis Theological Seminary of the Cumberland Presbyterian Church based on one-twelfth of 5% of the rolling average value. The Board of Stewardship, Foundation and Benefits, issues an aggregate amount to Memphis Theological Seminary of the Cumberland Presbyterian Church and charges the applicable accounts for their proportionate share. In addition, Memphis Theological Seminary of the Cumberland Presbyterian Church can request on an as needed basis, additional distributions that will be used for the purpose for which the account was created.

MEMPHIS THEOLOGICAL SEMINARY OF THE CUMBERLAND PRESBYTERIAN CHURCH

Notes to the Financial Statements
July 31, 2015 and 2014

Note 4 – Endowments (continued)

The Seminary has interpreted the Uniform Prudent Management of Institutional Funds Act ("UPMIFA") requiring a portion of a donor restricted endowment of perpetual duration be classified as permanently restricted assets. The amount of the endowment that must be retained permanently is in accordance with explicit donor stipulations as outlined in their respective endowment agreements. The Seminary has other endowment funds that are temporarily restricted by the donor as to purpose and are classified as temporarily restricted until they are expended on their respective purposes. Investment income and net appreciation on these permanently and temporarily restricted endowments is classified as temporarily restricted or permanently restricted if so directed by the donor in the respective endowment agreements or as unrestricted in the absence of donor instructions. The Seminary has other donated funds and board designated funds that are included in investments and are not restricted as to use. These funds, as well as investment income and net appreciation on these funds are classified as unrestricted. Expenditures (withdrawals) of the temporarily restricted and unrestricted funds are approved by management. The funds held by the Board of Stewardship, Foundation and Benefits of the Cumberland Presbyterian Church, Inc. are invested with the primary objective of providing a balance between capital appreciation, preservation of capital, and current income. This is a long-term goal designed to maximize returns without undue risk. The Board of Stewardship selects the investment portfolio where the endowments will be invested as described in the Investment Policy of The Cumberland Presbyterian Church Center, which outlines the asset allocations, permissible investments, and objectives of the portfolios.

Changes in the endowment fund by net asset class for the years ended July 31, 2015 and 2014, were as follows:

	Unrestricted Board Designated	Unrestricted Other	Temporarily Restricted	Permanently Restricted	Total
Balance at July 31, 2013	$ -	$ 1,510,028	$ 1,672,184	$ 5,966,473	$ 9,148,685
Investment Return:					
Investment Income	-	40,111	66,179	-	106,290
Change in market value	-	469,546	507,337	15,395	992,278
Total investment return	-	509,657	573,516	15,395	1,098,568
Contributions	-	-	-	270,594	270,594
Appropriation of endowment assets for expenditure	-	(351,607)	(164,793)	-	(516,400)
Reclassifications	82,263	(82,263)	-	-	-
Balance at July 31, 2014	82,263	1,585,815	2,080,907	6,252,462	10,001,447
Investment Return:					
Investment Income	720	28,871	35,842	-	65,433
Change in market value	2,500	134,328	123,638	11,356	271,822
Total investment return	3,220	163,199	159,480	11,356	337,255
Contributions	-	251,102	-	197,887	448,989
Appropriation of endowment assets for expenditure	(6,046)	(213,403)	(148,700)	-	(368,149)
Reclassifications	-	(5,009)	5,009	-	-
Balance at July 31, 2015	$ 79,437	$ 1,781,704	$ 2,096,696	$ 6,461,705	$ 10,419,542

MEMPHIS THEOLOGICAL SEMINARY OF THE CUMBERLAND PRESBYTERIAN CHURCH
Notes to the Financial Statements
July 31, 2015 and 2014

Note 5 – Capital Assets

Capital assets are as follows at July 31, 2015 and 2014:

	2015	2014
Building and improvements	$ 4,292,602	$ 4,255,844
Furniture and equipment	886,529	874,852
Library books	1,809,944	1,769,930
Vehicles	48,514	48,515
	7,037,589	6,949,141
Less accumulated depreciation	4,418,380	4,234,432
	2,619,209	2,714,709
Land	208,650	208,650
Construction in progress	391,353	387,869
Capital assets, net	$ 3,219,212	$ 3,311,228

Depreciation expense for the years ended July 31, 2015 and 2014, was $183,948 and $237,011, respectively.

Note 6 – Concentration of Credit Risk

Memphis Theological Seminary of the Cumberland Presbyterian Church has cash equivalents invested by the Board of Stewardship, Foundation and Benefits. At July 31, 2015, these funds total $239,082 and are not insured by the Federal Deposit Insurance Corporation (FDIC).

In addition, Memphis Theological Seminary of the Cumberland Presbyterian Church maintains cash balances in accounts at a well-established financial institution located in Memphis, Tennessee. These balances are insured by the Federal Deposit Insurance Corporation up to certain limits. At July 31, 2015, Memphis Theological Seminary of the Cumberland Presbyterian Church had uninsured balances of $67,028.

Memphis Theological Seminary of the Cumberland Presbyterian Church's tuition and fees receivable are from students for which the majority receive some form of financial assistance. Management maintains an allowance for uncollectible based on periodic reviews of each individual student's account.

Note 7 - Pledges Receivable

Pledges receivable primarily represent pledges from numerous donors to be used for a capital campaign which was initiated in the prior year with a feasibility study with most donations and pledges beginning in the current year. The campaign has three purposes: 1) To help fund the construction of a new free-standing chapel; 2) To fund construction of a new classroom/office building; and 3) To increase endowments. At July 31, 2015, pledges receivable for the capital campaign totaled $651,097. This total amount is discounted by $39,053 using a discount rate of 3.07% which is based on the published 20-year Treasury rate at July 31, 2015. Pledges receivable also include a pledge to offset the cost of a faculty member over the next four years. At July 31, 2015, the pledge receivable to offset the cost of the faculty member totaled $200,000. This amount is discounted by $11,304 using the same discount rate as used on the capital campaign pledges.

MEMPHIS THEOLOGICAL SEMINARY OF THE CUMBERLAND PRESBYTERIAN CHURCH
Notes to the Financial Statements *July 31, 2015 and 2014*

Note 7 - Pledges Receivable (continued)

The pledges, net of the discount, are due to be received as follows:

Less than one year	$ 145,269
One year to five years	705,828
Gross contributions receivable	851,097
Less: Discount to present value	(50,357)
Contributions receivable, net	$ 800,740

Note 8 – Line of Credit

Memphis Theological Seminary of the Cumberland Presbyterian Church has a $400,000 revolving line of credit agreement with a local bank. Borrowings outstanding under the agreement ($170,000 at July 31, 2015) bear interest at the bank's prime rate (3.25 percent at July 31, 2015). The line is guaranteed by the Board of Stewardship, Foundation and Benefits.

Note 9 – Notes Payable

Notes payable consist of the following at July 31, 2015 and 2014:

	2015	2014
Note payable, due in monthly installments of $5,360 at a variable interest (4.75% at July 31, 2015) through January 2031	$ 718,284	$ 749,849
Note payable, due in monthly installments of $5,058 at a variable interest (4.75% at July 31, 2015) through April 2032	486,441	525,860
Note payable, due in monthly installments of $1,618 at a variable interest (4.75% at July 31, 2015) through April 2033	248,051	255,484
Note payable, due in monthly installments of $1,436 at a variable interest (4.75% at July 31, 2015) through September 2033	62,475	76,300
Total notes payable	$ 1,515,251	$ 1,607,493

The notes payable are collateralized by income earned from permanently restricted investments and are payable to the Board of Stewardship, Foundation and Benefits.

MEMPHIS THEOLOGICAL SEMINARY OF THE CUMBERLAND PRESBYTERIAN CHURCH
Notes to the Financial Statements — July 31, 2015 and 2014

Note 9 – Notes Payable (continued)

Scheduled principal payments required for the years ending July 31 are as follows:

	Amount
2016	$ 75,889
2017	79,573
2018	83,437
2019	87,186
2020	74,190
Thereafter	1,114,976
Total notes payable	$ 1,515,251

Note 10 – Retirement Plan

Memphis Theological Seminary of the Cumberland Presbyterian Church sponsors a qualified defined contribution retirement plan for eligible employees as defined by the plan under IRC Section 403(b). Employees are eligible to participate in the plan immediately upon hire and contributions to the plan are vested immediately. Each participant in the plan may make voluntary contributions to the plan of up to the lesser of twenty percent (20%) of annual compensation received by the participant during the plan year, or the maximum allowed by law. Memphis Theological Seminary of the Cumberland Presbyterian Church matches participant's contributions to a maximum of 3.5%. Contributions to the plan by Memphis Theological Seminary of the Cumberland Presbyterian Church for the years ended July 31, 2015 and 2014, were $55,409 and $40,604, respectively.

Note 11 – Related Party

Memphis Theological Seminary of the Cumberland Presbyterian Church and the Board of Stewardship are separate corporations but both are affiliated with the Cumberland Presbyterian Church in that the governing board of the Church elects the members of the Board of Trustees of Memphis Theological Seminary of the Cumberland Presbyterian Church and the Board of Stewardship. There are no common board members between Memphis Theological Seminary of the Cumberland Presbyterian Church and the Board of Stewardship. Amounts due to and from the Board of Stewardship as of July 31, 2015 and 2014, are as follows:

	2015	2014
Due the Board of Stewardship from the Seminary:		
Notes Payable	$ 1,515,251	$ 1,607,493
Accrued Interest	$ 1,889	$ 7,570
Seminary assets held by the Board of Stewardship:		
Seminary cash held	$ 239,082	$ 145,152
Seminary investments held	$ 10,267,769	$ 9,861,031
Other Receivables	$ 90,290	$ -

MEMPHIS THEOLOGICAL SEMINARY OF THE CUMBERLAND PRESBYTERIAN CHURCH
Notes to the Financial Statements *July 31, 2015 and 2014*

Note 12 – Temporarily Restricted Net Assets

Temporarily restricted net assets consist of the following at July 31, 2015 and 2014:

	2015	2014
Endowment restrictions	$ 2,096,696	$ 2,080,907
Capital campaign restriction	1,009,418	804,097
Faculty salary restriction	188,696	-
Grant restrictions	110,433	138,420
Other restrictions	14,118	16,733
	$ 3,419,361	$ 3,040,157

Supplementary Information

MEMPHIS THEOLOGICAL SEMINARY OF THE CUMBERLAND PRESBYTERIAN CHURCH
Schedule of Expenditures of Federal Awards — For the Year Ended July 31, 2015

CFDA Number	Federal Grantor / Pass-Through Grantor	Total Expended
84.032	U.S. Department of Education Federal Family Education Loan Program	$ 2,568,448

Basis of Presentation

The accompanying schedule of expenditures of federal awards (the "Schedule") includes the federal grant activity of Memphis Theological Seminary of the Cumberland Presbyterian Church under programs of the federal government for the year ended July 31, 2015. The information in this Schedule is presented in accordance with the requirements of the Office of Management and Budget (OMB) Circular A-133, *Audits of States, Local Governments, and Non-Profit Organizations*. Because the Schedule presents only a selected portion of the operations of the Seminary, it is not intended to and does not present the financial position, changes in net assets or cash flows or Memphis Theological Seminary of the Cumberland Presbyterian Church.

Summary of Significant Accounting Policies

Expenditures reported on the Schedule are reported on the accrued basis of accounting. Such expenditures are recognized following the cost principles contained in OMB Circular A-21, Cost Principles for Education Institutions, wherein certain types of expenditures are not allowable or are limited as to reimbursement. Negative amounts shown on the Schedule represent adjustments or credits made in the normal course of business to amounts reported as expenditures in prior years. Pass-through entity identifying numbers are presented where available.

Non-Financial Information

INDEPENDENT AUDITOR'S REPORT ON INTERNAL CONTROL OVER FINANCIAL REPORTING AND ON COMPLIANCE AND OTHER MATTERS BASED ON AN AUDIT OF FINANCIAL STATEMENTS PERFORMED IN ACCORDANCE WITH *GOVERNMENT AUDITING STANDARDS*

Board of Trustees
Memphis Theological Seminary of the Cumberland Presbyterian Church
Memphis, Tennessee

We have audited, in accordance with the auditing standards generally accepted in the United States of America and the standards applicable to financial audits contained in *Government Auditing Standards* issued by the Comptroller General of the United States, the financial statements of Memphis Theological Seminary of the Cumberland Presbyterian Church (a nonprofit organization), which comprise the statement of financial position as of July 31, 2015, and the related statements of activities, functional expenses, and cash flows for the year then ended, and the related notes to the financial statements, and have issued our report thereon dated November 20, 2015.

Internal Control over Financial Reporting

In planning and performihg our audit of the financial statements, we considered Memphis Theological Seminary of the Cumberland Presbyterian Church's internal control over financial reporting (internal control) to determine the audit procedures that are appropriate in the circumstances for the purpose of expressing our opinion on the financial statements, but not for the purpose of expressing an opinion on the effectiveness of Memphis Theological Seminary of the Cumberland Presbyterian Church's internal control. Accordingly, we do not express an opinion on the effectiveness of Memphis Theological Seminary of the Cumberland Presbyterian Church's internal control.

A *deficiency in internal control* exists when the design or operation of a control does not allow management or employees, in the normal course of performing their assigned functions, to prevent, or detect and correct, misstatements on a timely basis. A *material weakness* is a deficiency, or a combination of deficiencies, in internal control, such that there is a reasonable possibility that a material misstatement of the entity's financial statements will not be prevented, or detected and corrected on a timely basis. A *significant deficiency* is a deficiency, or a combination of deficiencies, in internal control that is less severe than a material weakness, yet important enough to merit attention by those charged with governance.

Our consideration of internal control was for the limited purpose described in the first paragraph of this section and was not designed to identify all deficiencies in internal control that might be material weaknesses or significant deficiencies. Given these limitations, during our audit we did not identify any deficiencies in internal control that we consider to be material weaknesses. However, material weaknesses may exist that have not been identified.

Compliance and Other Matters

As part of obtaining reasonable assurance about whether Memphis Theological Seminary of the Cumberland Presbyterian Church's financial statements are free from material misstatement, we performed tests of its compliance with certain provisions of laws, regulations, contracts, and grant agreements, noncompliance with which could have a direct and material effect on the determination of financial statement amounts. However, providing an opinion on compliance with those provisions was not an objective of our audit, and accordingly, we do not express such an opinion. The results of our tests disclosed no instances of noncompliance or other matters that are required to be reported under *Government Auditing Standards*.

Purpose of this Report

The purpose of this report is solely to describe the scope of our testing of internal control and compliance and the results of that testing, and not to provide an opinion on the effectiveness of the organization's internal control or on compliance. This report is an integral part of an audit performed in accordance with *Government Auditing Standards* in considering the organization's internal control and compliance. Accordingly, this communication is not suitable for any other purpose.

Cannon Wright Blount PLLC

Memphis, Tennessee
November 20, 2015

INDEPENDENT AUDITOR'S REPORT ON COMPLIANCE FOR A MAJOR PROGRAM AND ON INTERNAL CONTROL OVER COMPLIANCE REQUIRED BY OMB CIRCULAR A-133

Board of Trustees
Memphis Theological Seminary of the Cumberland Presbyterian Church
Memphis, Tennessee

Report on Compliance for a Major Federal Program

We have audited Memphis Theological Seminary of the Cumberland Presbyterian Church's compliance with the types of compliance requirements described in the *OMB Circular A-133 Compliance Supplement* that could have a direct and material effect on the Memphis Theological Seminary of the Cumberland Presbyterian Church's major federal program for the year ended July 31, 2015. Memphis Theological Seminary of the Cumberland Presbyterian Church's major federal program is identified in the summary of auditor's results section of the accompanying schedule of findings and questioned costs.

Management's Responsibility

Management is responsible for compliance with the requirements of laws, regulations, contracts, and grants applicable to its federal program.

Auditor's Responsibility

Our responsibility is to express an opinion on compliance for Memphis Theological Seminary of the Cumberland Presbyterian Church's major federal program based on our audit of the types of compliance requirements referred to above. We conducted our audit of compliance in accordance with auditing standards generally accepted in the United States of America; the standards applicable to financial audits contained in *Government Auditing Standards*, issued by the Comptroller General of the United States; and OMB Circular A-133, *Audits of States, Local Governments, and Non-Profit Organizations*. Those standards and OMB Circular A-133 require that we plan and perform the audit to obtain reasonable assurance about whether noncompliance with the types of compliance requirements referred to above that could have a direct and material effect on a major federal program occurred. An audit includes examining, on a test basis, evidence about Memphis Theological Seminary of the Cumberland Presbyterian Church's compliance with those requirements and performing such other procedures as we considered necessary in the circumstances.

We believe that our audit provides a reasonable basis for our opinion on compliance for each major federal program. However, our audit does not provide a legal determination of Memphis Theological Seminary of the Cumberland Presbyterian Church's compliance.

Opinion on a Major Federal Program

In our opinion, Memphis Theological Seminary of the Cumberland Presbyterian Church complied, in all material respects, with the types of compliance requirements referred to above that could have a direct and material effect on its major federal program for the year ended July 31, 2015.

Report on Internal Control over Compliance

Management of Memphis Theological Seminary of the Cumberland Presbyterian Church is responsible for establishing and maintaining effective internal control over compliance with the types of compliance requirements referred to above. In planning and performing our audit of compliance, we considered

Memphis Theological Seminary of the Cumberland Presbyterian Church's internal control over compliance with the types of requirements that could have a direct and material effect on a major federal program to determine the auditing procedures that are appropriate in the circumstances for the purpose of expressing an opinion on compliance for a major federal program and to test and report on internal control over compliance in accordance with OMB Circular A-133, but not for the purpose of expressing an opinion on the effectiveness of internal control over compliance. Accordingly, we do not express an opinion on the effectiveness of Memphis Theological Seminary of the Cumberland Presbyterian Church's internal control over compliance.

A *deficiency in internal control over compliance* exists when the design or operation of a control over compliance does not allow management or employees, in the normal course of performing their assigned functions, to prevent, or detect and correct, noncompliance with a type of compliance requirement of a federal program on a timely basis. A *material weakness in internal control over compliance* is a deficiency, or combination of deficiencies, in internal control over compliance, such that there is a reasonable possibility that material noncompliance with a type of compliance requirement of a federal program will not be prevented, or detected and corrected, on a timely basis. A *significant deficiency in internal control over compliance* is a deficiency, or a combination of deficiencies, in internal control over compliance with a type of compliance requirement of a federal program that is less severe than a material weakness in internal control over compliance, yet important enough to merit attention by those charged with governance.

Our consideration of internal control over compliance was for the limited purpose described in the first paragraph of this section and was not designed to identify all deficiencies in internal control over compliance that might be material weaknesses or significant deficiencies. We did not identify any deficiencies in internal control over compliance that we consider to be material weaknesses. However, material weaknesses may exist that have not been identified.

The purpose of this report on internal control over compliance is solely to describe the scope of our testing of internal control over compliance and the results of that testing based on the requirements of OMB Circular A-133. Accordingly, this report is not suitable for any other purpose.

Cannon Wright Blount PLLC

Memphis, Tennessee
November 20, 2015

MEMPHIS THEOLOGICAL SEMINARY OF THE CUMBERLAND PRESBYTERIAN CHURCH

Schedule of Findings and Questioned Costs　　　　　　　　　　　　*For the Year Ended July 31, 2015*

SECTION I - SUMMARY OF AUDITOR'S RESULTS

Financial Statements

Type of auditor's report issued:	Unqualified
Internal control over financial reporting:	
- Material weakness(es) identified?	_____ yes __X__ no
- Significant deficiencies identified that are not considered to be material weaknesses?	_____ yes __X__ none noted
- Noncompliance material to financial statements noted?	_____ yes __X__ no

Federal Awards:

Internal control over major programs:	
- Material weakness(es) identified?	_____ yes __X__ no
- Significant deficiencies identified that are not considered to be material weaknesses?	_____ yes __X__ none noted
Type of auditor's report issued on compliance for major program:	Unqualified
Any audit findings disclosed that are required to be reported in accordance with section 510(a) of OMB Circular A-133?	_____ yes __X__ no

Identification of major programs:

CFDA 84.032	U. S. Department of Education Federal Family Education Loan Program
Threshold for distinguishing type A and B programs:	$300,000
Auditee qualified as low risk auditee:	__X__ yes _____ no

SECTION II - FINANCIAL STATEMENT FINDINGS

There are no financial statement findings for the year ended July 31, 2015.

SECTION III - FEDERAL AWARD FINDINGS AND QUESTIONED COSTS

There are no federal award findings or questioned costs for the year ended July 31, 2015.

MEMPHIS THEOLOGICAL SEMINARY OF THE CUMBERLAND PRESBYTERIAN CHURCH

Schedule of Prior Year Findings and Questioned Costs *For the Year Ended July 31, 2015*

There were no findings or questioned costs for the year ended July 31, 2014.

APPENDICES

REPORT OF THE CREDENTIALS COMMITTEE
(Appendix A)

The Credentials Committee certifies the list of commissioners on pages 5 and 6 of the Preliminary Minutes with the following changes:

On the part of Minister Delegates, Reverend David Fackler, is replacing Reverend April Watson.

On the part of Elder Delegates, Elder Scott Darnell, Covenant Presbytery, will not be in attendance. In his place, Elder Jennifer Potter, Covenant Presbytery will serve on Ministry Council/Communications/Discipleship.

Enrollment as of 3:15 p.m. is certified as forty-four (44) ministers, 40 (forty) elders for a total of eighty-four (84) Commissions with twenty-five (25) Youth Advisory Delegates.

Respectfully submitted,
Reverend Linda Glenn, Chair
Reverend Ray DeVries
Elder Robin Hughes
Youth Advisory Delegate Daniel Fowler

REPORT OF THE COMMITTEE ON MINISTRY COUNCIL/COMMUNICATIONS/DISCIPLESHIP
(Appendix B)

I. REFERRALS

Referrals to this committee are as follows: The Report Number One of the Ministry Council, except shaded sections which are referred to Missions/Ministry and Item III which is referred to Board of Stewardship, and The Report Number Two of the Ministry Council except shaded sections which are referred to Missions/Ministry and item C which is referred to Judiciary.

II. PERSONS OF COUNSEL

Appearing before this committee were: Ms. Edith Old, Director of Ministries; Reverend Troy Green, Representative from Ministry Council; Reverend Elinor Brown, Discipleship Ministry Team; and Mr. Mark Davis, Communications Ministry Team.

III. CONSIDERATION OF REFERRALS

A. REPORT NUMBER ONE OF THE MINISTRY COUNCIL EXCEPT SHADED SECTIONS WHICH ARE REFERRED TO MISSIONS/MINISTRY AND ITEM III WHICH IS REFERRED TO BOARD OF STEWARDSHIP

The Report Number One of the Ministry Council except shaded sections which are referred to Missions/Ministry and item III which is referred to Board of Stewardship was received and the following recommendations were made:

RECOMMENDATION 1: That Recommendation 1 of the Report Number One of the Ministry Council, "that the 186th General Assembly amend the Ministry Council Bylaws, ARTICLE III, BOARD OF DIRECTORS, AUTHORITY, AND MEETINGS, Section E., Meetings "The board of directors shall meet at least three times annually upon the call of the president or secretary..." to "The board of directors shall meet a least twice a year upon the call of the president or secretary..." beginning in 2017. (MC Bylaws online at http://cpcmc.org/mc/ bylaws/)," be adopted.

RECOMMENDATION 2: That Recommendation 2 of the Report Number One of the Ministry Council, "that the 186th General Assembly urge each congregation and presbytery to proactively recruit and encourage qualified leaders to prayerfully consider opportunities to serve as elected board members at the denominational level, to include the Ministry Council and all other denominational entities," be denied.

The General Assembly communicates directives and instructions to the presbyteries which then pass along that information to congregations, therefore:

RECOMMENDATION 3: That the 186th General Assembly urge each presbytery to proactively recruit and encourage qualified leaders to prayerfully consider opportunities to serve as elected board members at the denominational level, to include the Ministry Council and all other denominational entities.

B. REPORT NUMBER TWO OF THE MINISTRY COUNCIL

We commend the Ministry Council on their hard work, continued exceptional stewardship of all their resources, and the creation of a cooperative and empowering environment.

Respectfully submitted:
The Committee on Ministry Council/Communications/Discipleship

REPORT OF THE COMMITTEE ON CHAPLAINS/HISTORICAL FOUNDATION
(Appendix C)

I. REFERRALS

Referrals to this committee are as follows: The Report of the Board of Trustees of the Historical Foundation and the Report of the Commission on Military Chaplains and Personnel.

II. PERSONS OF COUNSEL

Appearing before this committee were: Susan Knight Gore, Archivist, Historical Foundation; Lisa Oliver, representative, Board of the Historical Foundation; Reverend Mary McCaskey-Benedict, representative, Commission on Military Chaplains and Personnel; and Military Chaplain, Glyn Turner.

III. CONSIDERATION OF REFERRALS

A. REPORT OF THE BOARD OF TRUSTEES OF THE HISTORICAL FOUNDATION

As a committee we want to commend the Board of Trustees of the Historical Foundation and Archivist, Ms. Susan Knight Gore for their hard work and dedication.

RECOMMENDATION 1: That Recommendation 1 of the Report of the Board of Trustees of the Historical Foundation, "that the General Assembly make congregations and presbyteries aware of the 1810 Circle and encourage new members to support this endeavor annually," be adopted.

RECOMMENDATION 2: That Recommendation 2 of the Report of the Board of Trustees of the Historical Foundation, "that congregations be encouraged to have a special offering on the Sunday designated as Denomination Day to help support the special project designated for that year," be adopted.

RECOMMENDATION 3: That Recommendation 3 of the Report of the Board of Trustees of the Historical Foundation, "that the General Assembly make presbyteries, congregations, and individuals aware that the Historical Foundation is interested and has funds to publish books on topics concerning the Cumberland Presbyterian Church and Cumberland Presbyterian Church in America," be adopted.

RECOMMENDATION 4: That Recommendation 4 of the Report of the Board of Trustees of the Historical Foundation, "that the General Assembly encourage all congregations to preserve their session records by depositing them in the Historical Foundation," be adopted.

RECOMMENDATION 5: That Recommendation 5 of the Report of the Board of Trustees of the Historical Foundation, "that the General Assembly instruct each synod and presbytery to deposit their minutes in a timely fashion with the Historical Foundation," be adopted.

RECOMMENDATION 6: That Recommendation 6 of the Report of the Board of Trustees of the Historical Foundation, "that the General Assembly instruct presbyteries to locate the session records when closing a church and then deposit them in the Historical Foundation," be adopted.

B. REPORT OF THE COMMISSION ON MILITARY CHAPLAINS AND PERSONNEL

After reading the Report of the Commission on Military Chaplains and Personnel, we concur in the report and make the following recommendation.

RECOMMENDATION 7: That General Assembly encourage each presbytery in the USA to communicate with their congregations to have a special offering on, May 28, 2017 for Memorial Day and all subsequent Sundays on or before Memorial Day.

Respectfully submitted:
The Committee on Chaplains/Historical Foundation

REPORT OF THE COMMITTEE ON
CHILDREN'S HOME/HIGHER EDUCATION
(Appendix D)

I. REFERRALS

Referrals to this committee are as follows: The Report of the Board of Trustees of Memphis Theological Seminary, The Report of the Board of Trustees of Bethel University and the Board of Trustees of the Cumberland Presbyterian Children's Home.

II. PERSONS OF COUNSEL

Appearing before this committee were: Reverend Richard Brown, President, CEO and General Counsel; Dr. Jennifer Livings, Vice President Programs, Ms. Debbie Garrett, Assistant Vice President of Development; Reverend Lisa Anderson and Reverend Duane Dougherty, members of the Board of Trustees of the Cumberland Presbyterian Children's Home; Reverend Jay Earheart-Brown, President Memphis Theological Seminary; Reverend Susan Parker, Member of the Board of Trustees for Memphis Theological Seminary; and Reverend Michael Qualls, Director of Program of Alternate Studies; and Dr. Robert Truitt, member of Board of Trustees of Bethel University.

III. THE REPORT OF THE BOARD OF TRUSTEES OF MEMPHIS THEOLOGICAL SEMINARY

After the approval of the 183rd General Assembly, "Ministry for the Real World," a comprehensive campaign to raise $25 million though 2020 for operations, capital improvements, and endowment was launched in October 2015. To date, $10 million has been raised. The priority capital improvement project is construction of a new chapel. The second is construction of a home for the Methodist House of Studies. A third initiative is to increase the endowment and create the Baird-Buck Chair in Cumberland Presbyterian Studies.

This endowed chair will add to the many that have already been created to offer scholarships and focused teaching at MTS.

Another emphasis of the "Ministry for the Real World" is to equip ordained and lay ministers to model Christ-like behavior everywhere they are and in every contact they make.

The trustees have done an excellent job in shepherding Memphis Theological Seminary.

RECOMMENDATION 1: That Recommendation 1 of the Report of the Board of Trustees of Memphis Theological Seminary, "that the General Assembly express its gratitude to the five trustees named above for their faithful service to Memphis Theological Seminary and the Cumberland Presbyterian Church," be denied.

RECOMMENDATION 2: That the General Assembly express its gratitude to those who continue to serve, but especially the following individuals for their faithful service to Memphis Theological Seminary and the Cumberland Presbyterian Church:

Ms. Pat Meeks (Cumberland Presbyterian, Cordova, Tennessee – went home to Jesus April 2016); Reverend Robert M. Shelton (Cumberland Presbyterian, Dallas Texas); Mr. Dan Hatzenbuehler (Episcopal, Memphis, Tennessee); Mr. Tim Orr (Cumberland Presbyterian, Newbern, Tennessee) and Mrs. K. C. Warren (Presbyterian USA, Memphis, Tennessee)

As a Seminary that teaches and prepares ministers of all denominations for the life of ministry, the committee commends the efforts of the Real World Campaign.

RECOMMENDATION 3: That Recommendation 2 of the Report of the Board of Trustees of Memphis Theological Seminary, "that the General Assembly encourage individuals, churches, and groups across the Cumberland Presbyterian Church to consider investing in the development of future leaders through the "Ministry for the Real World" campaign," be adopted.

PAS has completed the experimental phase for all four Cumberland Presbyterian Studies courses to be offered on-line. When fully implemented, two could be taken on-line and two in a traditional classroom setting.

The PAS advisory council is exploring partnership with the "Sower's Field" in creating a certification program where potential new church development leaders would consult with missional leaders, PAS and seminary students, current pastors and lay leaders to equip them for new church development.

New academic initiatives include a new degree program, the Master of Arts in Christian Ministry (2-year program), designed for persons who are called to ministries other than ordained pastoral ministries.

RECOMMENDATION 4: That Recommendation 3 of the Report of the Board of Trustees of Memphis Theological Seminary, "that the General Assembly urge all probationers to consider Memphis Theological Seminary and the Program of Alternate Studies as their first options for meeting educational requirements for ordained ministry," be adopted.

RECOMMENDATION 5: That Recommendation 4 of the Report of the Board of Trustees of Memphis Theological Seminary, "that the third Sunday in August, (August 21, 2016 and August 20, 2017) be included in the General Assembly Calendar as Seminary/PAS Sunday, and that the General Assembly encourage all churches to share information about MTS and PAS and receive a special offering on that day, or a more convenient day of the session's choosing," be adopted.

IV. THE REPORT OF THE BOARD OF TRUSTEES OF BETHEL UNIVERSITY

August 2016 to July 2017 marks the Bethel Seminary/College/University's 175th Birthday. The full report of the history of Bethel University is included in the preliminary minutes, page 116.

RECOMMENDATION 6: That the General Assembly encourages all Churches and Presbyteries celebrate the accomplishments of Bethel University's 175 years of education and service to the Cumberland Presbyterian Church and the world. Bethel Forevermore!

Bethel University asks for your continued prayers and support, and asks that we recommend students to Bethel.

RECOMMENDATION 7: That the General Assembly encourage all Churches and Presbyteries to continue to support Bethel University through prayer and financial assistance and to encourage those pursuing higher education to seek information about what Bethel University has to offer.

V. THE REPORT OF THE BOARD OF TRUSTEES OF THE CUMBERLAND PRESBYTERIAN CHILDREN'S HOME

Currently endowment distributions constitute 23.1% of the operating income for the Children's Home. The market determines income of the endowment based on investments made by the managing company. There is concern that this practice is unsustainable. The committee recognizes a significant need to increase funding to sustain the operation of the Children's Home.

There are other opportunities to help the Children's Home in addition to giving money. Each congregation should emphasize opportunities to help. For example, Red River Presbytery is sponsoring a youth convocation Labor Day weekend where youth 4th grade through High School will come to the campus to perform interactive ministry and service at the CP Children's Home. This type of project promotes team building, but also provides opportunities for mentoring and role modeling with the clients at the CP Children's Home. The committee endorses efforts of this nature and encourages more interaction with the CP Children's Home.

RECOMMENDATION 8: That the third Sunday in March (March 19, 2017) be included in the General Assembly Calendar as Children's Home Sunday, and that the General Assembly encourage all churches to share information and a video about Cumberland Presbyterian Children's Home and receive a special offering on that day, or a more convenient day of the session's choosing.

The video can be seen and downloaded at the Cumberland Presbyterian Children's Home Facebook page.

Respectfully Submitted,
The Committee on the Children's Home and Higher Education

REPORT OF THE COMMITTEE ON THEOLOGY & SOCIAL CONCERNS/UNIFICATION TASK FORCE
(Appendix E)

I. REFERRALS

Referrals to this committee are as follows: The Report of the Unified Committee on Theology and Social Concerns, The Report of the Unification Task Force, the Memorial from Covenant Presbytery Regarding Church World Services, and the Memorial from Covenant Presbytery Regarding Homosexuality, the Resolution Adopted by Japan Presbytery and the Resolution of Repentance, Apology and Resolve.

II. PERSONS OF COUNSEL

Appearing before this committee were: Reverend Mitchell Walker (CPCA) and Reverend Joy Warren (CPC), representatives of the Unification Task Force; Reverend Shelia O'Mara, representative from the Unified Committee of Theology and Social Concerns; Reverend Michael Qualls, Director of Program of Alternate Studies; Reverend Jay Earhart-Brown, President of Memphis Theological Seminary; Reverend Michael Sharpe, Stated Clerk of the CPC; Reverend Perryn Rice, Pastor of Lake Highlands Presbyterian Church; Reverend Byron Forester, member of the Permanent Committee of the Theology and Social Concerns; Elder L. Leon Cole, Jr., Moderator of the 141st General Assembly of the CPCA; Rex Hayes, Hunter Hughes, Ethan Kohrs, Will Lombard, Micah Warren, Maggie McClung, Hayden Hughes, Max Moore, Gavin Kohrs, Ana Montaño, and Ariana Hudgins, Kids Connect Commissioners in Training.

III. CONSIDERATION OF REFERRALS

A. REPORT OF THE UNIFIED COMMITTEE OF THEOLOGY AND SOCIAL CONCERNS

1. Study Papers

We commend the Unified Committee on Theology and Social Concerns for their faithful work in preparing the study papers entitled Homelessness as a Justice Issue – A Theological Response and A Confessional Approach to Discrimination. We encourage all ministers and presbyteries to study and discuss them among their members.

The committee found two areas in these respective papers that needed amending. First, in the paper Homelessness as a Justice Issue – A Theological Response, the committee amended the final paragraph before the study questions, second sentence to read, "The scriptures of the Bible continually call us out for being complicit with those who possess all the power and wealth and abandoning the marginalized people that God also loves." Secondly, in the paper A Confessional Approach to Discrimination, the committee amended the quotation of the Confession of Faith, section 1.16, to read "God never leaves or forsakes his people. All who trust God find this truth confirmed in awareness of his love, which includes judgment upon sin, and which leads to repentance, not to greater dependence upon divine grace. All who do not trust God are, nevertheless, under the same providence, even when they ignore or reject it. It is designed to lead them also to repentance and to trust in divine grace."

RECOMMENDATION 1: That Recommendation 1 of the Report of the Unified Committee of Theology and Social Concerns, "that the General Assemblies accept the papers, "Homelessness as a Justice Issue-A Theological Response" and "A Confessional Response to Discrimination" as study papers and that they be used to initiate thought and discussion within the Cumberland Presbyterian Church and the Cumberland Presbyterian Church in America," be adopted.

RECOMMENDATION 2: That Recommendation 2 of the Report of the Unified Committee of Theology and Social Concerns, "that the Office of the General Assembly of both denominations make these papers available to churches through the stated clerks of the presbyteries," be adopted.

2. Unification Efforts

The Committee affirms and supports the work of the Unification Task Force and any recommendation it may have for delaying the timeline for unification and the need to revise the proposed plan for unification.

RECOMMENDATION 3: That Recommendation 3 of the Report of the Unified Committee on Theology and Social Conerns, "that a Sunday be set aside as Unification Sunday and that all churches have a service geared toward unification, "be adopted.

3. Church Calendar

The Committee supports the ongoing focus by the Women's Ministry of the Cumberland Presbyterian Church on domestic violence and would like to see an addition to the church calendar to give a denomination-wide focus on the topic. Nationwide, October is National Domestic Violence Awareness Month.

RECOMMENDATION 4: That Recommendation 4 of the Report of the Unified Committee on Theology and Social Concerns, "that National Domestic Violence Awareness Month be added to the church calendar for the month of October," be adopted.

B. REPORT OF THE UNIFICATION TASK FORCE

The Committee heard from Reverend Mitchell Walker (CPCA) and Reverend Joy Warren (CPC) from the Unification Task Force. The Committee wishes to encourage and give great appreciation to the members of the Unification Task Force for their great faithfulness in pursuing the unification of the CPC and CPCA. The amount of work, time, and effort by each member is priceless and for their diligence, we praise Christ Jesus, our Lord and Savior.

RECOMMENDATION 5: That Recommendation 1 of the Report of the Unification Task Force, "that the revised Plan for Union of the CPC and CPCA be approved for study in the two churches, and that all ministers, sessions, presbyteries, synods, and members of the two churches be encouraged to study the document and provide feedback to the task force during the upcoming year," be adopted.

RECOMMENDATION 6: That Recommendation 2 of the Report of the Unification Task Force, "that the General Assemblies of the Cumberland Presbyterian Church in America and the Cumberland Presbyterian Church commit to meeting concurrently in the same city during the same week for the foreseeable future," be adopted.

RECOMMENDATION 7: That Recommendation 3 of the Report of the Unification Task Force, "that the fourth Sunday in December be recognized in the Cumberland Presbyterian Church and the Cumberland Presbyterian Church in America as Unity Sunday, and that all churches be encouraged to pray for our unity in Jesus Christ, and for discernment as we seek to express our unity more fully in the future," be adopted.

RECOMMENDATION 8: That the Unification Task Force meet with representatives of Memphis Theological Seminary, the Program of Alternate Studies, and the School of Continuing Education and Certification to discuss the pathways of education for clergy.

C. MEMORIAL FROM COVENANT PRESBYTERY REGARDING CHURCH WORLD SERVICES

The Committee discussed the memorial from Covenant Presbytery regarding Church World Service, and was unanimous in the following recommendation:

RECOMMENDATION 9: That the Memorial from Covenant presbytery regarding Church World Services which states: "We, the undersigned, do petition the Covenant Presbytery to memorialize the 2016 General Assembly with the following resolution:

WHEREAS, Church World Services has an overall rating by Charity Navigator of 81.75; and
WHEREAS, Church World Services is linked with Presbyterian Church USA, Presbyterian Church of Canada, Reformed Church in America, Evangelical Lutheran Church in America, Evangelical Lutheran Church in Canada, United Church of Christ, Disciples of Christ, Christian Reformed Church, Church of the Brethren, Episcopal Church, Mennonites, Community of Christ, and the Moravian Church and others which accept the homosexual lifestyle as normal, ordain homosexual individuals into the ministry, and/or promote or give acceptance to those who do; and
WHEREAS, Samaritan's Purse which has an overall rating of 96.17 rating by Charity

Navigators, and

WHEREAS, Samaritan's Purse is not in league with any of the above organizations and

WHEREAS, it behooves us to use our funds in a prudent, effective and righteous way; and

WHEREAS, Samaritan's Purse has a very evangelical approach to its mission: (see mission statement below)

BE IT RESOLVED, that the 2016 General Assembly dissolve its relationship with Church World Services and join with Samaritan's Purse by the 2017 General Assembly.

Signed: the Elders of Bayou de Chine Cumberland Presbyterian Church
Dr. Kenneth G. Richards, Moderator and Pastor, Jim Crass, Mark Crass, Walter Lawrence, Baker Thompson and Larry Wooten, Treasurer.

Samaritan's Purse is a nondenominational evangelical Christian organization providing spiritual and physical aid to hurting people around the world. Since 1970, Samaritan's Purse has helped meet needs of people who are victims of war, poverty, natural disasters, disease, and famine with the purpose of sharing God is love through His Son, Jesus Christ. Emergency relief meets desperate needs of victims worldwide. Operation Christmas Child delivers more than 8 million shoebox gifts to poor children in more than 100 countries each year. World Medical Mission sends doctors, equipment, and supplies to underprivileged countries. Community development and vocational programs in impoverished villages and neighborhoods help people break the cycle of poverty and give them hope for a better tomorrow. Vulnerable children are rescued, educated, fed, clothed, and sheltered, letting them know that God loves them, Jesus died and rose again for them, and they are not forgotten.

Covenant Presbytery at its Fall Meeting of Presbytery on October 3, 2015, passed this memorial to be forwarded to the General Assembly headquarters for consideration at the 2016 General Assembly.

Signed Reese Baker, Stated Clerk, Covenant Presbytery," be denied.

D. MEMORIAL FROM COVENANT PRESBYTERY REGARDING HOMOSEXUALITY

A memorial from Covenant Presbytery was referred to this committee:

RECOMMENDATION 10: The Memorial from Covenant Presbytery regarding Homosexuality which states: "We, the undersigned, do petition the Covenant Presbytery to memorialize the 2016 General Assembly with the following resolution:

WHEREAS, in the beginning "God created mankind in his own image, in the image of God he created. them; male and female he created them." (Genesis 1:27) and called it "very good"; and

WHEREAS, "That is why a man- leaves his father and mother and is united to his wife, and they become one flesh."(Genesis 2:24); and

WHEREAS, nowhere in the Bible does it say God ever changed His mind or thought He made a mistake in creating humankind any differently or that marriage should be any different than between a man and a woman; and

WHEREAS, Jesus said, "For this reason a man will leave his father and mother and be united to his wife, and the two will become one flesh." (Matthew 19:5); and

WHEREAS, The Bible is clear that anyone who keeps "practicing" sinful ways in no way conforms to God's plans for humanity - "We know that the law is good if one uses it properly. We also know that the law is made not for the righteous but for lawbreakers and rebels, the ungodly and sinful, the unholy and irreligious, for those who kill their fathers or mothers, for murderers, for the sexually immoral, for those practicing homosexuality, for slave traders and liars and perjurers-and for whatever else is contrary to the sound doctrine that conforms to the gospel concerning the glory of the blessed God, which he entrusted to me." (1 Timothy 1:8-11); and

WHEREAS, Paul admonishes the faithful - "Because of this, God gave them over to shameful lusts. Even their women exchanged natural sexual relations for unnatural ones. In the same way the men also abandoned natural relations with women and were inflamed with lust for one another. Men committed shameful acts with other men, and received in themselves the due penalty for their error. Furthermore, just as they did not think it worthwhile to retain the knowledge of God, so God gave them over to a depraved mind, so that they do what ought not to be done. They have become filled with every kind of wickedness, evil, greed and depravity. They are full of envy, murder, strife, deceit and malice. They are gossips, slanderers, God-haters, insolent, arrogant and boastful; they invent ways of doing evil; they disobey their parents; they have no understanding, no fidelity, no love, no mercy. Although they know God's righteous decree that those who do such things deserve death, they not only continue to do these very things but also approve of those who practice them." (Romans 1:26-32) and "Do not be yoked together with unbelievers. For what do righteousness and wickedness have in common? Or what fellowship can light have with darkness? What harmony is there between Christ and Belial? Or what does a believer have in common with an unbeliever? What agreement is there between the temple of God and idols? For we are the temple of the living God. "As God has said: 'I will live with them and walk among them, and I will be their God, and they will be my people. Therefore, 'Come out from them and be separate, says the Lord. Touch no unclean thing, and I will receive you.' And, 'I will be a Father to you, and you will be my sons and daughters, says the Lord Almighty.'" (2 Corinthians 6:14-18 and

WHEREAS, the Cumberland Presbyterian Church is currently linked with many other organizations listed below that either accept the homosexual lifestyle as normal, ordain homosexual individuals into the ministry, and/or promote and/or give acceptance to those who do:

BE IT RESOLVED, that the Covenant Presbytery of the Cumberland Presbyterian Church memorialize the 2016 General Assembly to separate itself from the following in all areas by the time of the General Assembly of 2017: Presbyterian Church USA, Presbyterian Church of Canada, Reformed Church in America, Evangelical Lutheran Church in America, Evangelical Lutheran Church in Canada, United Church of Christ, Disciples of Christ, Christian Reformed Church, Church of the Brethren, Episcopal Church, Mennonites, Community of Christ, and the Moravian Church.

Signed: the Elders of Bayou de Chine Cumberland Presbyterian Church
Dr. Kenneth G. Richards, Moderator and Pastor, Jim Crass, Mark Crass, Walter Lawrence, Baker Thompson and Larry Wooten, Treasurer.

Covenant Presbytery at its Fall Meeting of Presbytery on October 3, 2015, passed this memorial to be forwarded to the General Assembly headquarters for consideration at the 2016 General Assembly.
Signed Reese Baker, Stated Clerk, Covenant Presbytery," be denied.

We commend to General Assembly the official statement on homosexuality from the 166th General Assembly of the Cumberland Presbyterian Church.

In 1996 The General Assembly adopted the following statement on Homosexuality (GA Minutes, page 313):

Whereas, in our society today, there are many issues which concern the people of God, one such issue being the rise in acceptance of and openness toward homosexual activity, and we, of the Cumberland Presbyterian Church, believe there is a need to state clearly our understanding of the Biblical teaching about homosexual activity, and

Whereas, it is also our desire to set forth our position regarding the appropriate response of Christians and the church to this critical issue, especially in light of the trend in some Christian bodies toward the ordination of practicing homosexuals, and

Whereas we believe the scripture of the Old and New Testaments to be the inspired word of God, the source of authority for faith and practice, and therefore, contemporary sexual attitudes and behavior are to be judged in the light of the Bible rather than the Bible being reinterpreted, modified, or overturned by current cultural trends in thought and behavior.

Be it resolved that the General Assembly of the Cumberland Presbyterian Church go on record affirming that Biblical teaching makes it clear that the practice of homosexuality is a sin, yet with the understanding that while God loves the sinner, He hates the sin, and His grace is available to all "For God did not send His Son into the world to condemn the world, but to save the world through Him" John 3 17

Be it further resolved, that since the practice of homosexuality is incompatible with a Christian life style and since officers of the church must be "examples to the flock." the General Assembly go on record stating that the Cumberland Presbyterian Church does not condone the ordination of practicing homosexuals as Deacons, Elders or Ministers of Word and Sacrament; and

Be it further resolved, that the General Assembly state as its position that we, as Christians who are ourselves sinners redeemed by the grace of God. We must reach out to those persons who are struggling with homosexuality, offering them Christian love, education, friendship, therapy and intercession to the end that they and we may experience true wholeness through the freeing, renewing grace of God in Jesus Christ.

E. RESOLUTION ADOPTED BY JAPAN PRESBYTERY

The Committee discussed the Resolution from Japan Presbytery which states:

Resolution Adopted by Japan Presbytery of the Cumberland Presbyterian Church, Meeting on 23 November 2015

On the occasion of the 70th year after WWII
Praying to be used as peacemakers, an instrument for peace, at the time of
the great crisis that would destroy the peace

On the occasion of the 70th year after WWII, we, Japan Presbytery of the Cumberland Presbyterian Church, confess again our repentance to God for our nation's wartime aggression on the land of Asian neighbors by which we caused calamity through colonial domination and fifteen years of war.[1]

50 years after WWII, we at last expressed our transgressions to God, which were committed by the state and churches in Japan, and we decided to embark on a new step which would bear fruit of repentance. 10 years after our decision, we resolved again to stand as a peace-maker by renewing our mission to be a watchman and taking seriously our responsibility as the church to be the light of the world and the salt of the earth.

However, we admit that our commitment as a watchman was not a sufficient, and we were weak peace-makers. Our state, Japan, has been driving for the past 10 years developments that would enable the nation to engage in war[2]. In 2006, the government corrupted the Fundamental Law of Education[3]. In 2007, the Japan Defense Agency was upgraded to a ministry, and the Law of the National Referendum was established to enable amending the Constitution[4]. In 2012 the Liberal Democratic Party (LDP, the right-wing conservative party) delivered a draft of constitutional amendments which proposed the establishment of the Defense Force and the diminishing of human rights.[5] In 2013, in order to realize the constitutional amendment, the cabinet of the second Abe administration railroaded through the legislature the National Security Council and the Act on the Protection of Specially Designated Secrets (SDS). In addition, Prime Minister Abe visited the Yasukuni Shrine, an act widely seen as supporting the re-militarization of Japan.[6] In 2014, the government of Japan removed the ban of arms exports by eliminating the "Three Principles on Arms Export." Then the Abe cabinet, in spite of the violation of the Constitution, approved "the use of the right to collective self-defense" at the cabinet meeting[7]. In September 2015, both the Upper House and Lower House railroaded through new security-related laws for

---

[1] Fifteen years of war starting with the Manchurian incident in 1931 and ending with the Japanese surrender in 1945.
[2] See Appendix 1.
[3] See Appendix 2.
[4] See Appendix 3.
[5] See Appendix 4.
[6] See Appendix 5.
[7] See Appendix 6.

realizing "the use of the right to collective self-defense." Furthermore, both Houses authorized the establishment of the "Acquisition, Technology & Logistics Agency (ATLA)" in order to promote arms exports.

Following the established trend, the government intensified the interference in education by enforcing the singing of the national anthem and the payment of respect to the national flag with starting.[8] The government also increased the pressure on the media to support these changes. Under the influence of worsening relations with China and Korea, ethnic discrimination and antiforeignism, reflected in a hate-speech movement and the publication of the anti-Chinese and anti-Korean sentiment, grow rampantly in Japan.

As just described, our country Japan stands at a time of crisis in which the Constitution, written in a spirit of peace, has been corrupted, even though the Japanese had vowed not to commit the same transgressions as in the past.

In the midst of this period, we, Christians, who revere the Lord Christ of peace as the head of our church, have decided to rise as a peace-maker in the world. We oppose the politics which create animosity, division, and conflict, and we refuse the road of settling disputes by swords. We firmly protest against engaging in such evils as war which God abhors, as we confess based on the Confession of Faith 7.06[9]. We, Christians who live in reconciliation brought by Christ and who are given the message and ministry of reconciliation, seek to live "for seeking to promote reconciliation, love, and justice among all persons, classes, races, and nations"[10] (The Confession of Faith 6.32). Japan Presbytery of the Cumberland Presbyterian Church, which experienced reconciliation with Hong Kong Presbytery of the CPC when we confessed our repentance and apology for what we had done wrong during WWII, seek to build a further relationships of mutual trust with our neighbors in Asia.

Not only opposing war which brings suffering and destruction of life, but also seeking more positive peace, we bear witness to the gospel of peace, and "oppose, resist, and seek to change all circumstances of oppression--political, economic, cultural, racial--by which persons are denied the essential dignity God intends for them in the work of creation"11 (the Confession of Faith 6.30). Particularly, we work with Okinawan people in a spirit of solidarity because they had been forced to live under discrimination and suppression from the mainland of Japan by, such as, the concentration of the facilities of the U.S. forces in Japan.

---

[8] See Appendix 7.

[9] The Confession of Faith 7.06: "God's judgment is experienced in history in the freedom of persons and nations to choose to engage in such evils as war, civil strife, slavery, oppression, destruction of natural resources, and political and economic exploitation. God abhors all such acts which cause needless suffering and death."

[10] The Confession of Faith 6.32: "God gives the message and ministry of reconciliation to the church. The church, corporately and through her individual members, seeks to promote reconciliation, love, and justice among all persons, classes, races, and nations."

[11] The Confession of faith 6.30: "The covenant community, governed by the Lord Christ, opposes, resists, and seeks to change all circumstances of oppression--political, economic, cultural, racial--by which persons are denied the essential dignity God intends for them in the work of creation."

We, as Christians who respect human lives and fundamental human dignities which God created, defend the Constitution of Japan which values fundamental human rights, professes an arms-denying pacifism and is built on the principle of popular sovereignty, and stand against any movement which undermines constitutionalism and a spirit of the Constitution of Japan.

Based on the resolution we adopted, we pray that the Lord of peace uses us as an instrument for peace.

APPENDIX

1. Building Nation for Enabling Japan to Engage in War

Japan caused tremendous sufferings to the people of Asian countries including its own country by wars of aggression and colonial domination during the decades before 1945. Because of our deep remorse, we decided to walk as a nation which renounced war, and established a Constitution that renounces the threat or use of force as a means of settling disputes and prohibits maintaining force. The majority of Japanese people valued this decision. However, the political administration of the (Liberal Democratic Party) LDP-led coalition has been trying to remove the constitutional constraints which renounce warfare because of the poor reflection of the past state's transgression against our neighbors, particularly in Asia.

2. Transformed the Fundamental Law of Education for the Worse

From the end of nineteenth century to the end of WWII in 1945, an education in Japan had been based on the Imperial Rescript of Education which required loyalty to the state with the emperor at the center. As the emperor centered educational system was regarded as a one of the causes which led Japan into the mistake of imperial warfare, the nation turned to the principle of sovereignty of the people, the establishment of the Constitution, and the Fundamental Law of Education (FLE) with its requirement to respect human rights. However, at the time of the revision of the FLE in 2006, lawmakers transformed the FLE. The revision of the FLE encouraged the people to do what was right for the state, by adding the ethnic Japanese values such as respecting tradition and culture, and patriotism. Thus, the revised FLE had the effect of transferring sovereignty to the state from the people, contrary to the spirit of the original FLE.

3. The Establishment of the National Referendum Law in advance of the Amendment of the Constitution

The long-term regime of the (Liberal Democratic Party) LDP's party line claims to regain the pride of Japan by revising the Constitution because they regard the Constitution as having been imposed by the U.S. at the time of defeat. At the time of the first Abe-Cabinet, the Prime Minister Shinzo Abe, who exhibits intent to revise the Constitution, established the National Referendum Law (NRL) which specifies the constitutional amendment procedure as the first step for constitutional amendment. As the established NRL does not define the minimum turnout of voters, the risk is high that the Constitution could be amended with support from a minority of the people.

4. The Draft of the Revision of the Constitution which contains the Suppression of Fundamental Human Rights

The Draft of the Revision of the Constitution of the LDP stands basically against constitutionalism which is the idea that a constitution binds national power in order to protect the rights of the people. The draft undermines inviolable human dignities and rights inherent in a human being as an individual by deleting the Article 97 which specifies that "the fundamental human rights by the Constitution guaranteed to the people of Japan are fruits of the age-old struggle of man to be free and are to be held for all time inviolate"[12], and by changing the words from "all people are respected as an individual"[13] to "all people are respected as a human" in Article 13.

Furthermore, it would enable the nation to open the way to constrain human rights by changing the words; "the people's human rights are respected to the utmost extent as long as they are not against the public welfare" to "the people's human rights are respected as long as they are not against the public benefits and order."

5. Prime Minister Abe visits the Yasukuni Shrine

Though a number of shrines exist in Japan, the Yasukuni Shrine is positioned as special because it is the shrine where dead soldiers are honored as gods who died for the emperors between the latter half of the nineteenth century and 1945. This means that their deaths deserve praise as a model to be followed by future generations. Therefore the Yasukuni Shrine has played a significant role in the support, justification, and glorification of Japan's history of aggressive warfare. Though the Yasukuni Shrine was relegated to the one of the religious corporations after WWII, the conservative politicians who hallow the Shrine have been visiting it in order to build its national value as the place to honor Japan's war dead. Japan Presbytery has raised its voice against this matter as a violation of the principle of separation of politics and religion and the freedom of religion, and as an act of glorification of war and of the intent to enable the state to engage in war.

6. The Abe-Cabinet authorized the use of the right to collective-defense in spite of the violation of the constitution

After WWII, Japan, based on the Article 9 of the Constitution, declared the renunciation of war and holding military powers. However, after the establishment of the Self-Defense Forces (SDF) under the Constitution, the government has repeatedly claimed that the Constitution did not deny holding the retention of a minimum power necessary for self-defense, and, when subjected to foreign aggression without having any alternatives, a minimum counterattack was approved by the Constitution because it was an exclusive defense. As for collective-defense, it was not approved because it included the right to counterattack for the country when a foreign country having a close relation is struck though the country is not attacked. Therefore, even though there is no alternative but to revise the constitution to allow collective-defense, the Abe-cabinet authorized the right to collective-defense based on a fraudulent interpretation of the Constitution. The Cabinet authorization was a negation of constitutionalism because what the Abe-cabinet established by the cabinet meeting ignored the constitutional amendment procedure.

7. The Japanese government forces people to show loyalty to the flag of Hinomaru, Rising Sun, and sing the Kimigayo, the Reign of Your Majesty

In 1999 the flag of Hinomaru, Rising Sun, became the national flag and the Kimigayo, Reign of Your Majesty, was adopted as the national anthem by law despite strong opposition from many in Japan, including Japan Presbytery. Japan Presbytery opposed the moves because the flag of Hinomaru, Rising Sun, was related with the imperial system as a symbol of colonial domination and wars of aggression, and the Kimigayo, the Reign of Your Majesty, was the song for praising the emperor. The people who intended to build the nation centered on the emperor made this law even though they promised not to obligate citizens to honor the flag and anthem or compel them to participate in honoring them. However, after the law's establishment, the government compelled elementary, junior high, and high schools to hoist the flag of Hinomaru, Rising Sun, and sing the Kimigayo, the Reign of Your Majesty. By doing so, lawmakers threaten freedom of thought, belief, and conscience for Japan's citizens and children.

---

[12] The Constitution of Japan Article 97: "The fundamental human rights by this Constitution guaranteed to the people of Japan are fruits of the age-old struggle of man to be free; they have survived the many exacting tests for durability and are conferred upon this and future generations in trust, to be held for all time inviolate."

[13] The Constitution of Japan Article 13: "All of the people shall be respected as individuals. Their right to life, liberty, and the pursuit of happiness shall, to the extent that it does not interfere with the public welfare, be the supreme consideration in legislation and in other governmental affairs."

RECOMMENDATION 11: That the Resolution from Japan Presbytery be accepted as information and be referred to the Permanent Committee on Theology and Social Concerns for study and clarification.

F. RESOLUTION OF REPENTANCE, APOLOGY, AND RESOLVE

The Committee prayerfully discussed and sought counsel from CPC and CPCA denominational representatives, as well as the sponsor of the resolution, the "Resolution of Repentance, Apology, and Resolve." We strongly support the spirit of the resolution.

Resolution of Repentance, Apology and Resolve

Whereas, we Cumberland Presbyterians are considering the call of God to "Go" during this 186th meeting of the General Assembly; and

Whereas, Jesus sent the twelve with these instructions: "As you go, proclaim the good news. The kingdom of heaven has come near. Cure the sick, raise the dead, cleanse the lepers, cast out demons." (Matthew 10:7-8); and

Whereas, we seek the healing of our divisions as Cumberland Presbyterians; and

Whereas, the Cumberland Presbyterian Church was founded in 1810 in Dickson County, Tennessee, USA, and grew rapidly in a nation that endorsed, participated in, and benefited from the practice of enslaving African men, women and children who were brought to this nation through the brutal trans-Atlantic slave trade; and

Whereas, the Cumberland Presbyterian Church was inconsistent in its condemnation of American slavery as an institution -- an institution that condoned the buying and selling of persons made in the image of God; an institution in which African American families were often separated, and individuals were beaten and abused in body and mind; and

Whereas, the Cumberland Presbyterian Church often condoned the segregation of its African American members into separate balconies, congregations, and classes because of the influence of cultural ideas of racial superiority and inferiority; and

Whereas, the Cumberland Presbyterian Church refused to allow its African American members full and equal membership following emancipation and the end of slavery; organizing instead separate congregations, presbyteries, and other judicatories that were denied representation in the General Assembly, and

Whereas, the Cumberland Presbyterian Church encouraged and supported the organization of the Cumberland Presbyterian Church in America (originally the Colored Cumberland Presbyterian Church) in 1874 in order to avoid the difficult work of integration, and to avoid offending its members who continued to hold fast to ideas of racial superiority; and

Whereas, the Cumberland Presbyterian Church was complicit in accepting Jim Crow segregation, lynching as a means of social control, economic oppression of freed slaves, and denial of educational opportunities; and

Whereas, the Cumberland Presbyterian Church and the Cumberland Presbyterian Church in America have both suffered from their separation, a separation that is harmful to the witness of the Church and a denial of our oneness in Christ; and

Whereas, the Cumberland Presbyterian Church laments the loss of friendship, gifts and graces from which our life, worship, witness and service would have been enriched had we not been separated all these years; and

Whereas, the Cumberland Presbyterian Church affirms the providence of God, whose purpose it is "that the whole creation be set free from its bondage to sin and death, and be renewed in Jesus Christ" (COF, 1.15); and

Whereas, the Cumberland Presbyterian Church acknowledges our ongoing need for repentance, so that "In response to God's initiative to restore relationships, (we) make honest confession of sing against God, (our) brothers and sisters, and all of creation, and amend the past so far as is in (our) power." (COF, 4.07); therefore, be it

Resolved, that the Cumberland Presbyterian Church repent and seek God's forgiveness for the many ways we have benefitted from, participated in, condoned, and been blind to our role in racism, oppression of our African American brothers and sisters, and all forms of brutality; and be it further

Resolved, that the Cumberland Presbyterian Church apologize to our African American brothers and sisters, seek their forgiveness, and work to restore the broken relationships our sin has caused; and be it further

Resolved, that the Cumberland Presbyterian Church commit itself to preach the Word of God without compromise, and that we resolve to "oppose, resist, and seek to change all circumstances of oppression -- political, economic, cultural, racial, by which persons are denied the essential dignity God intends for them in the work of creation (COF, 6.30). We seek to promote reconciliation, love and justice among all persons, classes, races, and nations: (COF, 6.32). (Quoted in the Resolution Marking the 50th year since the end of World War II, by Japan Presbytery of the CPC)

RECOMMENDATION 12: With great respect to the magnitude of this resolution, the Committee, under conviction of the Holy Spirit and after a period of seeking direction from the Holy Spirit in prayer, in order for us as the Cumberland Presbyterian Church to enter into a time of faithful and continual prayer, and for a time for deeper reflection, and to give the Holy Spirit time to work in the hearts of every member of the Cumberland Presbyterian Church, recommend that the Resolution of Repentance, Apology, and Resolve," be adopted.

We humbly urge that all members of the Cumberland Presbyterian Church to read, study, and digest the book One Family Under God: A Story of Cumberland Presbyterians in Black and White by Thomas D. Campbell in order to better understand the history of the relationship of the CPC and CPCA.

Respectfully submitted,
Committee on Theology and Social Concerns/Unification Task Force

REPORT OF THE COMMITTEE ON STEWARDSHIP/ELECTED OFFICERS
(Appendix F)

I. REFERRALS

Referrals to this committee are as follows: The Report of the Moderator, The Report of the Stated Clerk; The Report Number One of the Ministry Council, item III, The Report of the Board of Stewardship, Foundation and Benefits; The Report of the Our United Outreach Committee; The Report of the Place of Meeting Committee; and The Line Item Budgets Submitted by General Assembly Agencies.

II. PERSONS OF COUNSEL

Appearing before this committee were: Reverend Robert Heflin, Mr. Randy Davidson, and Mr. Mark Duck (Board of Stewardship); Reverend Cliff Hudson and Mr. Ron Gardner (Our United Outreach Committee); Reverend Michael Sharpe, Stated Clerk; and Moderator of the 185th General Assembly, Reverend Michele Gentry.

We wish to express our appreciation to the persons of counsel for their presentations.

III. CONSIDERATION OF REFERRALS

A. REPORT OF THE MODERATOR

We commend the Moderator, Reverend Michele Gentry, for her compassionate and insightful leadership. After listening to the Moderator share her encouraging observations as well as points of concern regarding the need for individuals to serve on the Ministry Council, the committee shares the Moderator's positive expression and genuine concerns.

RECOMMENDATION 1: That Suggestion 1 of the Report of the Moderator, "that both presbyteries and local churches actively recruit and encourage qualified leaders to prayerfully consider opportunities to serve as members of the Ministry Council and the Ministry Teams, submitting their information and recommendation forms in a timely manner to the Nominations Committee," be denied.

The General Assembly communicates, directs and instructs the presbyteries which then pass along that information to the congregations, therefore:

RECOMMENDATION 2: That presbyteries actively recruit and encourage qualified leaders to prayerfully consider opportunities to serve as members of the ministry council and the ministry teams, submitting their information and recommendation forms in a timely manner to the nominations committee.

B. REPORT OF THE STATED CLERK

We commend the excellent work of the Stated Clerk, Reverend Michael Sharpe. The Report of the Stated Clerk was received and the following recommendations are made:

RECOMMENDATION 3: That Recommendation 1 of the Report of the Stated Clerk, "that the appointment of the Evaluation Committee be postponed until 2017," be adopted.

RECOMMENDATION 4: That Recommendation 2 of the Report of the Stated Clerk, "that the 186th General Assembly approve the following dates for the 2016-2017 Church Calendar:

July-2016
9 Program of Alternate Studies Graduation
9-23 PAS Summer Extension School, Bethel, McKenzie, TN
19-23 Presbyterian Youth Triennium, Purdue University, Lafayette, IN

August-2016
6 BU Commencement
20 MTS Fall Semester Begins
21 Seminary/PAS Sunday
22 BU Fall Semester Begins
28-Sept 25 Christian Education Season
30 BU Spring Convocation

September-2016
3 MTS Opening convocation 11 Senior Adult Sunday
18 Christian Service Recognition Sunday
18 International Day of Prayer and Action for Human Habitat

October-2016
Clergy Appreciation Month
2 Worldwide Communion Sunday 9 Pastor Appreciation Sunday
23 Native American Sunday

November-2016
National Domestic Violence Month
Any Sunday Loaves and Fishes Program
1 All Saints Day
4 World Community Day (Church Women United)
6 Stewardship Sunday
9-12 The Forum

13 Day of Prayer for People with Aids and Other Life-Threatening Illnesses
13 Bible Sunday
20 Christ the King Sunday
27-Dec 25 Advent in Church and Home

December-2016
Any Sunday Gift to the King Offering
10 BU Commencement
24 Christmas Eve
25 Christmas Day/Unity Sunday

January-2017
6 Epiphany
9 BU Spring Semester Begins
9-10 Stated Clerks' Conference
11 Human Trafficking Awareness Day
13-16 Faith in 3D
15 Deadline for receipt of 2016 Our United Outreach Contributions
18-20 Ministers Conference, St Columba Conference Center, Bartlett, Tennessee

February-2017
Black History Month
1 Annual congregational reports due in General Assembly office
4 Denomination Day
5 Historical Foundation Offering
5 Our United Outreach Sunday
5 Souper Bowl Sunday
12 Youth Sunday
24-25 30-Hour Famine

March-2017
Women's History Month (USA)
1 Ash Wednesday, the beginning of Lent 1–April 16 Lent to Easter
19 Children's Home Sunday
26-April 1 National Farm Workers Awareness Week

April-2017
2-8 Family Week
9 One Great Hour of Sharing
9 Palm/Passion Sunday
13 Maundy Thursday
14 Good Friday
16 Easter
28-29 30-Hour Famine

May-2017
5 Friendship Day (Church Women United)
6 BU Commencement
13 MTS Closing Convocation & Graduation
28 Memorial Day Offering for Military Chaplains & Personnel for USA churches

June-2017
4 Pentecost
4 Stott-Wallace Missionary Fund Offering/World Mission Sunday
19-23 General Assembly
20-22 CPWM Convention
25-30 Cumberland Presbyterian Youth Conference, Bethel University, McKenzie, Tennessee

July-2017
8 Children's Fest
8 Program of Alternate Studies Graduation
8-22 PAS Summer Extension School, Bethel, McKenzie, Tennessee

August-2017
1-Sept 30 Christian Education Season
5 BU Commencement
19 MTS Fall Semester Begins
20 Seminary/PAS Sunday
21 BU Fall Semester Begins 2
9 BU Spring Convocation 3
0 MTS Opening convocation

September-2017
10 Senior Adult Sunday
17 Christian Service Recognition Sunday
17 International Day of Prayer and Action for Human Habitat

October-2017
Clergy Appreciation Month
1 Worldwide Communion Sunday
15 Pastor Appreciation Sunday
22 Native American Sunday

November-2017
National Domestic Violence Month
Any Sunday Loaves and Fishes Program
1 All Saints Day
3 World Community Day (Church Women United)
5 Stewardship Sunday
8-11 The Forum
12 Day of Prayer for People with Aids and Other Life-Threatening Illnesses
12 Bible Sunday
26 Christ the King Sunday

December-2017
Any Sunday Gift to the King Offering
3-25 Advent in Church and Home
9 BU Commencement
24 Christmas Eve
25 Christmas Day/Unity Sunday," be adopted.

C. REPORT OF THE BOARD OF STEWARDSHIP, FOUNDATION AND BENEFITS

We commend the Board of Stewardship, Foundation and Benefits for their diligent work. After a time of discussion between the committee members and the representatives, the committee makes the following recommendation:

RECOMMENDATION 5: That the Report of the Board of Stewardship, Foundation and Benefits be concurred in.

D. REPORT OF THE OUR UNITED OUTREACH COMMITTEE

We commend the Our United Outreach committee for their diligent work. We affirm the new regional representatives program to increase promotion of Our United Outreach across the denomination.

RECOMMENDATION 6: That Recommendation 1 of the Report of the Our United Outreach Committee, "that General Assembly adopt the following Our United Outreach allocations for 2017:

The allocation is to be as follows:	$2,800,000.00	
Development Coordinator		92,044.00
Legal Fees		25,000.00
Unification Task Force		_35,000.00_
	Sub-total	152,044.00
(Amount to be allocated)	$2,647,956.00	
Ministry Council	$1,323,978.00	50%
Bethel University	132,398.00	5%
Children's Home	79,439.00	3%
Stewardship	159,877.00	6%
General Assembly Office	211,836.00	8%
Memphis Theological Seminary/ Program of Alternate Studies	185,357.00	7%
Historical Foundation	79,439.00	3%
Shared Services	436,913.00	16.5%
Contingency	13,240.00	5%

(Next four items total 1%)

Comm. on Chaplains	10,247.00	.387%
Judiciary Committee	9,665.00	.365%
Theology/Social Concerns	3,601.00	.136%
Nominating Committee	2,966.00	.112%
	$2,467,956.00	
Our United Outreach Goal	$2,800,000.00," be adopted.	

RECOMMENDATION 7: That Recommendation 2 of the Report of the Our United Outreach Committee, "that the following statement be added to the By-Laws of the General Assembly, Article 10.02 Election and Tenure: 03. No person shall be elected to any board whose church does not support Our United Outreach; however, an individual may directly give financial support to Our United Outreach and be eligible to serve on boards and agencies and that the remaining numbers under that Article be re-numbered accordingly," be denied.

RECOMMENDATION 8: When nominating persons to boards/agencies/teams priority consideration is given to person's whose individual life and/or church involvement demonstrates a commitment to support OUO.

E. REPORT OF THE PLACE OF MEETING COMMITTEE

We commend the work of the Place of Meeting Committee.

RECOMMENDATION 9: That the Report of the Place of Meeting Committee be concurred in.

F. LINE ITEM BUDGETS SUBMITTED BY GENERAL ASSEMBLY AGENCIES

The committee discussed the line item budgetary items. No action was required of this committee.

G. REPORT ONE OF THE MINISTRY COUNCIL, SECTION III

RECOMMENDATION 10: That Recommendation 11 of the Report One of the Ministry Council, "that as many churches do not consider giving to Our United Outreach as a tithe as it was envisioned, and that a number of churches do not contribute anything to Our United Outreach, that General Assembly prayerfully consider and recommend opportunities to significantly revitalize Our United Outreach. Opportunities might include but not be limited to setting the deadline for Our United Outreach contributions "to be postmarked by December 31"," be adopted.

Respectfully submitted:
The Committee on Stewardship/Elected Officers

REPORT OF THE COMMITTEE ON MISSIONS/MINISTRY
(Appendix G)

I. REFERRALS

Referrals to this committee are as follows: The Report One of the Ministry Council, the shaded areas only; and The Report Two of the Ministry Council, the shaded areas only.

II. PERSONS OF COUNSEL

Appearing before this committee were: Reverend Milton Ortiz, Missions Ministry Team Leader; Reverend T. J. Malinoski, Evangelism and New Church Development; Reverend Johan Daza, Cross Culture Ministry; Reverend Lynn Thomas, Director Global Cross-Culture Missions Program; and Reverend Charles R. Brown, Pastoral Development Ministry Team Leader.

We wish to express our thanks for the information provided by these persons of counsel.

III. CONSIDERATION OF REPORTS

A. THE REPORT ONE OF THE MINISTRY COUNCIL, THE SHADED AREAS ONLY

1. ON GOING MINISTRIES

We commend the Ministry Council for the supplement provided that explains the ongoing ministries in detail. We also commend the Pastoral Development Ministry team and MTS for developing the program for the Certificate in CP Studies and providing a Spanish interpreter for the group of students.

RECOMMENDATION 1: That Recommendation 3 of the Report One of the Ministry Council, "that the 186th General Assembly urge each presbytery to budget funds in both 2017 and 2018 to send one participant to the Certificate in CP Studies program," be adopted.

2. NEW MINISTRIES

We commend the Missions Ministry Team for its commitment to starting new churches and for assisting with 19 NCDs in the United States (9 Cross-Culture) and 3 overseas.

RECOMMENDATION 2: That Recommendation 4 of the Report One of the Ministry Council, "that the 186th General Assembly urge each presbytery to budget funds in 2017 for current and potential new church development leaders to attend a Church Starters Conference hosted by the MMT in fall 2017," be adopted.

RECOMMENDATION 3: That Recommendation 5 of the Report One of the Ministry Council, "that, in an effort to broaden Cumberland Presbyterian ministry within the United States, the 186th General Assembly encourage presbyteries to invite and welcome churches interested in assimilation into the Cumberland Presbyterian Church and to seek guidance from Missions Ministry Team for information and counsel," be adopted.

RECOMMENDATION 4: That Recommendation 6 of the Report One of the Ministry Council, "that the 186th General Assembly recommend that presbyteries encourage local churches within their bounds to invite Missions Ministry Team to hold evangelism training for the local church and groups of churches for the purpose of encouraging and equipping church leaders and members in sharing the good news of Jesus Christ with others and providing empowering methods and means that people can apply in their context," be denied.

We recognize the expertise of the Missions Ministry Team but there may be other resources that the churches want to utilize to help them learn to promote evangelistic development and growth.

RECOMMENDATION 5: That the 186th General Assembly recommend that presbyteries encourage local churches within their bounds to invite the Missions Ministry Team and/or other resources to hold evangelism training for the local church and groups of churches for the purpose of encouraging and equipping church leaders and members in sharing the good news of Jesus Christ with others and providing empowering methods and means that people can apply in their context.

We commend the Missions Ministry Team for recognizing the need to involve young women in Women's Ministry and for developing a retreat format to encourage their participation.

RECOMMENDATION 6: That Recommendation 7 of the Report One of the Ministry Council, "that the 186th General Assembly recommend that each presbytery appoint a young woman to represent their presbytery at one of these events and serve as a point of contact between the Young Women Planning Team and the presbytery," be adopted.

We commend the Missions Ministry Team for realizing the importance of partnering with the Presbyterial Board of Missions and developing new ways to provide training to the Presbyterial Board of Missions to assist them in providing support and guidance to local churches.

RECOMMENDATION 7: That Recommendation 8 of the Report One of the Ministry Council, "that the 186th General Assembly recommend that each presbytery include a line item in their 2017 budget to send two or more representatives from their Board of Missions to the event. Cost per person is approximately $100," be denied.

Presbyteries each have their own unique budgeting process and financial record keeping and it is not appropriate to tell them a line item is needed for this specific request. The cost per person listed does not take into account costs for travel and we are unsure if it provides for any hotel or meal cost.

RECOMMENDATION 8: That the 186th General Assembly recommend that each presbytery budget to send two or more representatives from their Board of Missions to the Listening to the Spirit-Serving with Conviction event.

We appreciate the work of the Office of Evangelism and New Church Development in making renewed efforts to assist Choctaw Presbytery in meeting needs in that Presbytery, recognizing the importance of the ministry that dates back to 1819.

RECOMMENDATION 9: That Recommendation 9 of the Report One of the Ministry Council, "that the 186th General Assembly encourage churches, presbyteries and synods to be in prayer and become actively involved in the mission to and with Choctaw Cumberland Presbyterians to address immediate needs and future planning," be adopted.

We commend the Missions Ministry Team for recognizing and sharing the diverse challenges that are inherent in developing successful cross culture ministry.

RECOMMENDATION 10: That Recommendation 10 of the Report One of the Ministry Council, "that the 186th General Assembly encourage Boards of Mission (or their equivalent) in United States presbyteries to fund intercultural internship opportunities among probationers, ordained ministers or lay persons within those presbyteries who might be interested in participating in one of the cross-culture ministries in the United States," be denied.

Presbyteries may not be able to afford the cost of funding the internship but may provide support in many ways that could include financial support, prayer support, encouragement, etc.

RECOMMENDATION 11: That the 186th General Assembly encourage Boards of Mission (or their equivalent) in United States presbyteries to support intercultural internship opportunities among probationers, ordained ministers or lay persons within those presbyteries who might be interested in participating in one of the cross-culture ministries in the United States.

B. THE REPORT TWO OF THE MINISTRY COUNCIL, THE SHADED AREAS ONLY

1. LEADERSHIP REFERRAL SERVICES

We commend the Missions Ministry Team on the work of assisting ministers and congregations, as they navigate the search and hiring process.

RECOMMENDATION 12: That Recommendation 1 of the Report Two of the Ministry Council, "that the 186th General Assembly approve shifting primary responsibility for the Leadership Referral Services (LRS) from the Missions Ministry Team to the Pastoral Development Ministry Team effective August 1, 2016," be adopted.

2. GUIDELINES FOR CONGREGATIONS CONSIDERING MERGER

We thank the Office of Evangelism and New Church Development for recognizing the challenges that occur when there is a need or desire to merge congregations.

RECOMMENDATION 13: That Recommendation 2 of the Report Two of the Ministry Council, "that the 186th General Assembly adopt the manual entitled Guidelines for Congregations Considering Merger to assist churches and presbyteries interested in merging Cumberland Presbyterian churches to strengthen their worship, study and witness to the gospel," be adopted.

Respectfully submitted,
Committee on Missions and Ministry

REPORT OF THE COMMITTEE ON JUDICIARY

(Appendix H)

I. REFERRALS

Referrals to this committee are as follows: The Report Number Two of the Ministry Council, item C; The Report of the Permanent Committee on Judiciary; and The Memorial from Missouri Presbytery Regarding Ministers of Other Denominations Serving Communion.

II. PERSONS OF COUNSEL

Elder Mary Lyn Hunter, Missouri Presbytery; Reverend Robert Rush, Permanent Judiciary Committee; Reverend Milton Ortiz, Missions Ministry Team Leader; Reverend Lynn Thomas, Missions Ministry Team; Troy Green, Ministry Council; Johan Daza, Missions Ministry Team; and Stated Clerk Mike Sharpe appeared before the committee to broaden understanding of referred items. Jamie Jordan, legal advisor for the denomination, consulted by way of email.

III. CONSIDERATION OF REFERRALS

A. REPORT TWO OF THE MINISTRY COUNCIL, ITEM C

The committee rejoices in the ministry and mission being done outside of the United States and encourages reports and displays regarding the valuable leadership and resources provided by schools and institutions in South America and Asia. The Ministry Council is absolutely correct in the need to be ever mindful of the global nature of the work of the Cumberland Presbyterian Church. However, also keeping in mind that laws are not the same everywhere, it is legally inappropriate to act as a body upon such reports.

RECOMMENDATION 1: That Recommendation 3 of the Report Two of the Ministry Council, "that the 186th General Assembly give institutions that have a direct relationship (legal and/or expected to report) to a presbytery outside the USA the privilege of sending reports and/or representatives to General Assembly and that these institution's reports and/or representatives be assigned to a Committee of General Assembly," be denied.

B. REPORT OF THE PERMANENT COMMITTEE ON JUDICIARY

1. REFERRAL

The committee wishes to confirm that any Cumberland Presbyterian congregation or presbytery can always establish mission points anywhere God so leads. The committee also wishes to affirm that working with the Missions Ministry Team can highly enhance any mission effort, especially outside the bounds of the United States where laws are different.

In light of Recommendation 4, the committee makes the following recommendation:

RECOMMENDATION 2: That Recommendation 1 of the Report of the Permanent Committee on Judiciary," that contingent upon ratification of the proposed constitutional amendment, the General Assembly designate the Missions Ministry Team as the mission entity authorized to function as a presbytery in accordance with the proposed constitutional amendment," be denied.

The strength of the Presbyterian form of government is its connectional nature and its layers of accountability. Although the argument could be made that it would be appropriate to attach the Missions Ministry Team to a synod when it functions as a presbytery in ordaining ministers and other ecclesiastical decisions, the committee agrees with the Permanent Committee on Judiciary that, with synods meeting less frequently than the Permanent Judiciary Committee and with the fact that the Permanent Judiciary Committee already reviews all synod records, it is logical to assign oversight and review of a body acting in the place of a presbytery with respect to mission work and mission fields. Therefore, the committee makes the following recommendation:

RECOMMENDATION 3: That Recommendation 2 of the Report of the Permanent Committee on Judiciary, "that the General Assembly Bylaw 11.05, which refers to the Judiciary Committee, be amended by inserting "11.05 The committee shall have oversight of and responsibility for ecclesiastical decisions made by a body acting in the place of a presbytery with respect to mission work and mission fields. The oversight and responsibility exercised by the committee shall be the same as that exercised by a synod with respect to a presbytery under its care. The committee shall have oversight of and responsibility for ecclesiastical decisions made by a body acting in the place of a presbytery with respect to mission work and mission fields. The oversight and responsibility exercised by the committee shall be the same as that exercised by a synod with respect to a presbytery under its care. When the committee is performing this role, the Stated Clerk may appoint up to two temporary members from the applicable mission field to serve for the limited purpose of oversight and review. The current 11.05 will then become 11.06," be denied.

2. SAFE SANCTUARY

RECOMMENDATION 4: That Recommendation 3 of the Report of the Permanent Committee on Judiciary, "that the stated clerk's office of each presbytery, rather than the Office of the General Assembly, be designated as the repository for the Safe Sanctuary plans for churches within that presbytery," be adopted.

C. REPORT OF THE JOINT COMMITTEE ON AMENDMENTS

The committee spoke at length with members of the Missions Ministry Team, Ministry Council, the Permanent Judiciary Committee, and the Stated Clerk. Sadly, there seemed to be a lack of sufficient communication between these parties and no meaningful communication between the Missions Ministry Team and the Joint Committee on Amendments. Thus, it seemed to the committee some disagreement and misunderstanding could have been avoided.

For the past three General Assembly meetings, attempts have been made to address the role of the Missions Ministry Team as it establishes churches and leadership beyond the bounds of any existing presbytery or synod. The 185th General Assembly directed the development of this amendment to address this concern. The broad language of this proposal was somewhat worrisome; however, the language was designed to include the various agencies of both the Cumberland Presbyterian Church and the Cumberland Presbyterian Church in America. The broad language is also an effort to account for future changes and possible reorganizations of both denominations.

Because this is a proposed amendment to the Constitution of the Cumberland Presbyterian Church and the Cumberland Presbyterian Church in America, no words may be changed. The only available actions to this committee are to accept, refer, or deny.

RECOMMENDATION 5: That Recommendation 1 of the Report of the Joint Committee on Amendments, "that current Constitution 9.5 be renumbered as 9.6 and the following be inserted as 9.5: "The General Assembly, in order to promote the mission work of the Church and the development of new churches outside the United States, may authorize its mission entity, a judicatory, or a commission to act in the place of a presbytery with respect to persons, ministers, and churches lying outside the bounds of the United States and outside the bounds of any existing presbytery. In such a case, the body so designated shall have with respect to the persons, ministers, and churches under its care the same jurisdiction, authority, and responsibilities which are otherwise granted to a presbytery, and the General Assembly rather than a synod shall provide for the oversight and responsibility of the body's ecclesiastical actions." be denied.

D. THE MEMORIAL FROM MISSOURI PRESBYTERY REGARDING MINISTERS OF OTHER DENOMINATIONS SERVING COMMUNION

The committee agrees with the sentiment of the memorial; however, the committee felt the need for strengthening and clarification.

RECOMMENDATION 6: That the Memorial from Missouri Presbytery regarding Ministers of other denominations serving communion, that states:

"WHEREAS, we concur with the permanent committee on Judiciary, in that we affirm that the communion table in any particular Cumberland Presbyterian Church is the Lord's Table and that not that of our denomination or any local church.
WHEREAS, the committee acknowledged that allowing ministers of other denominations always and only with Presbyterian approval to serve communion in a Cumberland Presbyterian Church, has produced as many blessings as problems.
WHEREAS, if abuse occurred or some Presbyteries failed to provide proper oversight, then according to Cumberland Presbyterian Constitution 8.5/b. A Synod has the oversight and responsibility to review the records of the Presbyteries, redress whatever they may have done contrary to order

WHEREAS, we believe that rather than Presbyteries being empowered to provide leadership and care of local congregations just the opposite has occurred.

WHEREAS, we believe in an open table.

WHEREAS, our own Seminary trains candidates from other denominations, who, when ordained, will serve Communion.

WHEREAS, we believe a very high percentage of Cumberland Presbyterians would partake of the Lord's Supper if offered in a non-Cumberland Presbyterian setting administered by a non-Cumberland Presbyterian minister.

THEREFORE, we ask that the 2013 General Assembly ruling rescinding the 1987 ruling be overturned and be replaced with the original ruling. "An ordained minister, although of another church may serve the Lord's Supper in a Cumberland Presbyterian Church, provided this minister has been approved by a judicatory (that is, presbytery) of the church."

Missouri Presbytery at its Spring Meeting of Presbytery on March 19, 2016, passed this memorial to be forwarded to the General Assembly headquarters for consideration at the 2016 General Assembly. Signed Larry Nottingham, Stated Clerk, Missouri Presbytery," be denied.

The committee affirms the Memorial's rationale as compelling, in addition to the fact that, even though errors do occur, not trusting presbyteries to carry out their responsibilities is contrary to Cumberland Presbyterian government. Also, ordained Cumberland Presbyterian ministers are often invited in non-Cumberland Presbyterian churches to officiate over the Sacrament of Holy Communion, so we recommend the following:

RECOMMENDATION 7: An ordained minister, although of another denomination, may serve the Lord's Supper in a Cumberland Presbyterian church, PROVIDED this minister has submitted to the appropriate training in Cumberland Presbyterian theology and conducting of the Sacrament, AS WELL AS having been approved by presbytery and PROVIDED the presbytery continues oversight of this non-Cumberland Presbyterian minister serving one of its churches.

Respectfully submitted,
The Committee on Judiciary

CHURCH CALENDAR 2016-2017

JULY 2016

9	Program of Alternate Studies Graduation
9-23	PAS Summer Extension School, Bethel University, McKenzie, TN
19-23	Presbyterian Youth Triennium Purdue University, Lafayette, IN

AUGUST 2016

6	BU Commencement
20	MTS Fall Semester begins
21	Seminary/PAS Sunday
22	BU Fall Semester begins
28-Sept 25	Christian Education Season
30	BU Spring Convocation

SEPTEMBER 2016

3	MTS Opening Convocation
11	Senior Adult Sunday
18	Christian Service Recognition Sunday
18	International Day of Prayer and Action for Human Habitat

OCTOBER 2016

1-31	Clergy Appreciation Month
2	Worldwide Communion Day
9	Pastor Appreciation Sunday
23	Native American Sunday

NOVEMBER 2016

Any Sunday in November Loaves and Fishes Program

1	All Saints Day
4	World Community Day (Church Women United)
6	Stewardship Sunday
9-12	The Forum
13	Day of Prayer for People with AIDS and Other Life-Threatening Illnesses
13	Bible Sunday
20	Christ the King Sunday
27-Dec 25	Advent in Church and Home

DECEMBER 2016

Any Sunday in December Gift to the King Offering

10	BU Commencement
24	Christmas Eve
25	Christmas Day/Unity Sunday

JANUARY 2017

6	Epiphany
9	BU Spring Semester begins
9-10	Stated Clerk's Conference
11	Human Trafficking Awareness Day
13-16	Faith in 3D
15	Deadline for receipt of 2016 Our United Outreach contributions
18-20	Ministers Conference St. Columba Conference Center, Bartlett, TN

FEBRUARY 2017

1-28	Black History Month
1	Annual congregational reports due in GA office
4	Denomination Day
5	Historical Foundation Offering
5	Our United Outreach Sunday
5	Souper Bowl Sunday
12	Youth Sunday
24-25	30-Hour Famine

MARCH 2017

1-31	Women's History Month (USA)
1	Ash Wednesday, the beginning of Lent
1-April 16	Lent to Easter
19	Children's Home Sunday
26-April 1	National Farm Workers Awareness Week

APRIL 2017

2-8	Family Week
9	Palm/Passion Sunday
9	One Great Hour of Sharing
13	Maundy Thursday
14	Good Friday
16	Easter
28-29	30-Hour Famine

MAY 2017

5	Friendship Day (Church Women United)
6	BU Commencement
13	MTS Closing Convocation & Graduation
28	Memorial Day Offering for Military Chaplains & Personnel for USA churches

JUNE 2017

4	Pentecost
4	Stott-Wallace Missionary Fund Offering/ World Mission Sunday
19-23	General Assembly, near Tampa, FL
20-22	CPWM Convention, near Tampa, FL
25-30	CPYC, Bethel University, McKenzie, TN

www.ingramcontent.com/pod-product-compliance
Lightning Source LLC
Chambersburg PA
CBHW081830170426
43199CB00017B/2691